The Complete Internet Handbook

for Lawyers

by JERRY LAWSON

Defending Liberty
Pursuing Justice

Law Practice Management Section
American Bar Association

YAHOO! and the YAHOO! logo are trademarks of YAHOO!, Inc.

Screen Shots reprinted with permission.

Earlier sections of this book have been published in *The Internet Lawyer, Legal.online, The Internet Legal Practice Newsletter, The Journal of Public Inquiry,* and *The Monitor,* and as course manuals used by the University of Kentucky College of Law and the Michigan Institute of Continuing Legal Education and Virginia CLE.

Cover design by Gail Patejunas.

Library of Congress Catalog Number 98–74962

ISBN 1–57073–640–5

03 02 01 00 99   5 4 3 2

Discounts are available for books ordered in bulk. Special consideration is given to state bars, CLE programs, and other bar-related organizations. Inquire at Book Publishing, American Bar Association, 750 North Lake Shore Drive, Chicago, Illinois 60611.

Dedication

To the teachers:

Frieda Riley, James B. Shrewsbury, and Robert G. Lawson, who gave me my first clues as to what computers, writing, and law are about.

Larry McGoldrick, whose contagious enthusiasm one winter evening at CPCUG gave me an inkling of the World Wide Web's potential.

Larry Froehlich, who taught by deed. I thought the Internet was just a toy until Larry showed me it is a tool.

Contents

Part One:
Getting Started

**Part Two:
Researching**

Part Three:
Marketing

Part Four:
Ethics and Security Issues

Part Five:
Putting It All Together

Chapter 18: Collaborative Tools   263

Chapter 19: Thinking About the Net   279

Part Six:
Other Voices

Other Voices   **317**

About the Author

Jerry Lawson is a lawyer and founder of Netlawtools, Inc., an Internet consulting and Web site design firm in northern Virginia.

A 1979 graduate of the University of Kentucky College of Law, Mr. Lawson was lead articles editor of the law review. He has worked as a lawyer for a U.S. district court judge, for the U.S. Army (where his assignments included a detail to the Department of Defense Office of General Counsel, two details to the Department of Justice as a Special Assistant United States Attorney, and a tour near the Demilitarized Zone in Korea), for the Department of the Treasury, and for the National Archives and Records Administration.

As an undergraduate, he studied English and computer programming, and he has been writing about practical uses of computer telecommunications since 1987. His articles about lawyer use of the Internet have appeared in many journals, and he has been quoted as an expert on the Internet in publications ranging from *Trial* magazine to the *ABA/BNA Lawyers' Manual on Professional Conduct* to the *Washington Post*.

Mr. Lawson has designed many World Wide Web sites, including law firm sites as well as the popular Internet Tools for Attorneys, at http://www.netlawtools.com.

He welcomes your comments and suggestions at lawson@netlawtools.com.

Acknowledgments

This book had its genesis in the sense of possibility created by visionary Internet pioneers like Burgess Allison, Greg Siskind, Erik Heels, Peter Martin, and Lew Rose.

I appreciate the encouragement provided by those who have given me opportunities to speak and write about the Internet, particularly Herb Cihak, David Shipley, Lee Hickok, Lynn Chard, Susan Swope, Mike Curreri, David Bilinsky, Gayle O'Connor, Josh Blackman, Bob Ambrogi, Sabrina Pacifici, Cindy Chick, Mike De La Rosa, Helen Hinshaw, and Macon Shibut.

I welcome the examples, insights, and inspiration provided by Internet leaders like Sean Flynn, Susan Ross, Wendy Liebowitz, Ken Johnson, Barbara Folensbee-Moore, Kathy Clark, Billie Jo Brooks, Evan Farr, Ross Kodner, Mary Ellen LeBlanc, Mark Pruner, Peter Ozolin, Greg Miller, Errol Weiss, Duncan Kinder, Jill Farmer, Kevin Manson, Rick Klau, Susan Fall, Debbie Steele, and Roger Mahach.

The contributions of Peter Krakaur, Bob Cumbow, Richard Granat, Sam Lewis, Genie Tyburski, Mark Obbie, and Lee Glickenhaus proved particularly valuable, owing to their ability and willingness to provide excellent analysis and advice on short notice.

I am very grateful for the generosity and expertise of the contributors to the "Other Voices" section, my favorite section of this book.

Special thanks to Jeff Flax, Beverly Loder, Tim Johnson, and others at the ABA for helping make this book a reality.

Special, special thanks to my wife, whose insights, editing skills, and support in so many ways improved this book, and my life, immeasurably.

Introduction

Lawyers don't deal in produce, sneakers, or steel. Our stock in trade is information and communication—the very stuff of the Internet. The Internet is going to change our society, including the legal profession, like the Industrial Revolution changed a previous society—only faster.

This book is intended to help lawyers and other legal professionals make the most of their opportunities in the coming revolution by providing the following:

- A general orientation to the Internet
- A source of nuts-and-bolts advice on how the Internet works, with warnings of traps to avoid
- A reference manual of technical information
- A source of ideas on how legal professionals can get the maximum benefit from this fantastic new resource

A key objective of this book is to help you learn enough about the way the Internet works to enable you to obtain your Internet information from the Internet itself. It contains more timely and useful information than any paper book, or for that matter, any paper library.

Currency

When I began this project, Burgess Allison gave me the following advice:

> I think the biggest challenge you'll face is how to counterbalance the conflicting interests of currency vs. longevity. Anything you put in the book that changes frequently will be likely to make the book go "out of

date" very quickly. That will give it a short shelf life and will require rapid updates. But if the only things you cover are things that don't change frequently—especially in this subject matter—then you're probably leaving out the most important stuff. The trick is to balance the two interests. (And it's not easy.)

I've approached the challenge Mr. Allison outlined in two ways:

- By emphasizing fundamental principles and techniques that should change less rapidly, if at all.
- By enlisting the help of the most powerful ally I could find: the Internet itself.

This book will work in tandem with frequently updated material at an accompanying Web site on the ABA's server:

http://www.abanet.org/lpm/netbook

The book you hold in your hands is designed to work hand in hand with the Web site. Neither is complete without the other.

The Web site includes textual explanations of important current developments as well as "clickable" versions of all the hypertext links in the book, plus newer ones. It also includes forms and checklists that can be downloaded into word processors for customization by readers.

User Level

One reason for the phenomenal success of Burgess Allison's *The Lawyer's Guide to the Internet* is that it challenges its audience. He stretches his readers.

I have tried to use the same successful strategy in this book. While this book includes basic tutorial material, I have also tried to include a fair amount of more advanced ideas. I hope that this will make the book more attractive to those who already have some Internet experience and will extend the book's useful life.

For example, the material on advanced uses of discussion groups may not seem very relevant to someone whose immediate objective is to add a signature block to his or her outgoing e-mail. Explanations of sophisticated law firm promotional techniques like push channels may not be of immediate interest to a lawyer who is trying to set up a simple Web site.

These sections, and others, may have significantly more meaning to the same people who reread the book after they have mastered e-mail basics or, having gotten a taste of the benefits of a modest Web site, are wondering how to make it even more valuable.

A Challenge

If you are not already using the Internet, there is no better time than now to jump in. If you are already using the Internet in your law practice, ask yourself how you can get more benefit from it.

Jerry Lawson
Burke, Virginia
lawson@netlawtools.com

PART **ONE**

Getting Started

CHAPTER **ONE**

Why the Internet Matters to Lawyers

And, most important, let's make education our highest priority so that every eight year old will be able to read, every twelve year old can log on to the Internet, every eighteen year old can go to college.

—President Bill Clinton

The Information Highway will transform our culture as dramatically as Gutenberg's press did the Middle Ages.

—Bill Gates

IS BEING ABLE to use the Internet really as significant as being able to read? Is it as revolutionary as the printing press?

Lawyers tend to be skeptical, and a statement like the one just quoted from Bill Gates, the multibillionaire computer mogul, will strike many lawyers as hyperbole. When we hear statements like his, our internal hype detectors tend to sound an alarm. Yet the fascinating thing about the Internet is that as you learn more about it, such statements sound less like hyperbole and more like thoughtful, realistic assessments.

News coverage of the Internet has been intense but shallow. Too many lawyers still have only a hazy notion of what the Internet is and how they can use it to their benefit. A tsunami of media attention has made them suspect that something significant is happening, but they are not sure exactly what it is or how it fits into the practice of law.

Something significant *is* happening. The Internet is not a fad, and in the long run, it and its more technically sophisticated successors will cause profound changes in our society, including the way we practice law.

Increasing Operating Efficiencies

The same powerful Internet communications and research tools that businesses are finding so attractive can be used by lawyers to enhance their practices through

- Vastly improved communications with clients, other lawyers, and courts, a few of which are already allowing or requiring pleadings to be filed electronically;
- Powerful and inexpensive new tools for conducting factual and legal research; and
- Large reductions in overhead, including administrative expenses, communications costs, library expenses, online research fees, and more

Remaining Competitive

A 1997 American Bar Association study found that 64 percent of small firm lawyer respondents reported using the Internet (up from 38 percent the previous year). Of the lawyers who were not already using the Internet, 59 percent reported that they planned to use it in the coming year. Large firms are not being left behind. More than half reported having World Wide Web sites (home pages), and most of the ones who did not have Web sites planned to add one in the coming year.

We look for [law] firms with electronic communications capabilities, especially in litigation matters.

—John Kuelbs, Vice President & General Counsel, Hughes Aircraft (Annual Corporate Revenue: $6 Billion)

Law firms that understand the Internet are more attractive to some clients. Sophisticated clients, especially corporations or other institutions that have discovered the Internet's benefits, are already beginning to refuse to hire law firms that do not know how to use the Internet, especially e-mail. Why is this such a big deal with an increasing number of clients?

Consider a hypothetical law firm whose partners refuse to use word processing technology. They prefer to use only manual typists and hire the best available. This hypothetical firm guarantees that it will meet or exceed the document turnaround times and quality of any competitor that uses word processors. If you were a prospective client, would you retain such a firm, all other factors being equal? Most potential clients would have two reactions:

1. Skepticism that the firm could live up to its quality guarantee
2. Suspicion that the firm's inefficiency would cause its clients to pay higher fees in the long run

If your law firm does not use the Internet, in the future you will run into exactly the same reactions from clients who have learned to use the Internet. Just as clients who use word processing take it and its benefits for granted, clients who use the Internet regularly take it and its benefits for granted. They will have little patience for those who do not know how to use it, and they will not be happy when you bill them for

- Long-distance voice or fax calls that could have been handled via the Internet at no cost;
- Couriers for information that could have been sent via the Internet at no cost (and more securely as well, if encryption were used); and
- Time-consuming paper library or online research in expensive computerized databases, when, with increasing frequency, the same material could be found faster on the Internet at no charge.

Understanding the Internet as a Practice Area

Because so much business activity is moving into Internet-related activities, it will inevitably become a major practice area for law firms. Where there is that much money, there will be contracts to draft and lawsuits to file. Firms that do not have at least a general understanding of how the Internet works will stand little chance of getting much of this business, or of handling it well if they do get it.

Lawyers who do get Internet-related cases will need an understanding of how the Internet works so they can handle the cases properly. You might, for example, think that transactional lawyers would not have much need to understand the Internet. You would be wrong. Consider the following:

- The Securities and Exchange Commission (SEC) allows distribution of disclosure documents on the Internet. In the treatise *Securities Regulation in Cyberspace* (Brown & Co., 1997), Howard Friedman recommends that companies put their proxy statements, annual reports and Form 10-Ks on the part of the Internet known as the World Wide Web in portable document format (PDF) or HyperText Markup Language (HTML) format. A lawyer cannot competently advise clients on related issues without some understanding of how PDF, HTML, and the Web operate.
- Stanford Law School's Securities Class Action Clearinghouse, http://securities.stanford.edu, is an exemplary source of up-to-date, detailed information about securities class actions, including the full text of federal and state complaints, briefs, pleadings, opinions and orders, settlement notices, and the like. Lawyers practicing in this area who know how to use this resource have an advantage over those who do not.
- Since January 1, 1998, the SEC has required electronic filing of many public disclosure statements. Unless you do the extra work to obtain a hardship exemption as explained in Rules 201 or 202 of Regulation S-T, paper filings will not be accepted or processed. Paper filings received by courier are returned by the courier, and paper filings sent by mail are returned by mail.
- Changes in SEC rules have made the World Wide Web a prime venue for takeover fights and proxy battles. The Web's power makes it cheap and easy for investors to organize and to communicate with management. Are the organizations that so use Web pages considered "groups" under Rule 13(d)? If a securities lawyer does not have a basic understanding of the Internet, he or she may not even be able to ask the right questions to protect clients' interests competently.

Rote reliance on traditional legal approaches can lead to disaster when lawyers don't understand the Internet environment. Most lawyers instinctively include choice-of-law clauses when drafting contracts. Where the Internet is concerned, this habit can help subject a client to personal jurisdiction in remote jurisdictions, as explained in Appendix G, "Cyber Issues."

The best lawyers have traditionally added value to their services by going beyond technical legal advice and giving their clients the benefit of their judgment on related business issues. As business analysts Larry Downes and Chunka Mui convincingly demonstrate in *Unleashing the Killer App: Digital Strategies for Market Dominance* (Harvard Business

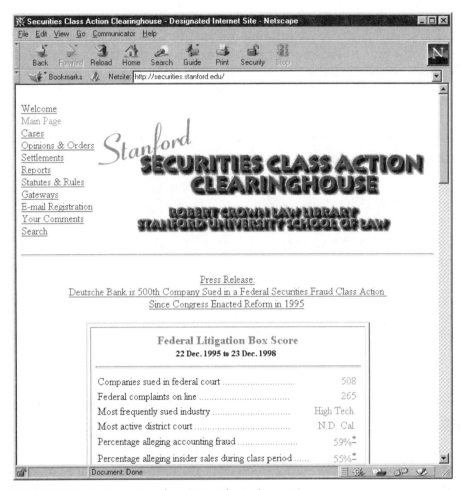

FIGURE 1-1. The Securities Class Action Clearinghouse Site

School Press, 1998), new technologies, especially the Internet, have already revolutionized businesses we don't ordinarily think of as being on the leading edge of technology (e.g., package delivery). We have only seen the first wave of such changes.

We are already living in a world where the *Wall Street Journal* can make more money charging $49 a year for its Internet edition than by charging $150 for the paper version, which lacks many features available to the readers of the online version. The Internet-based bookseller Amazon.com, which was not in existence five years ago, is worth billions, while decades-old companies like Barnes and Noble are struggling to remain competitive.

Both new businesses like Amazon.com and traditional businesses like the *Wall Street Journal* that adapt successfully to the digital world will want lawyers who understand their business environment. Lawyers will need to have a basic understanding of the Internet to attract clients and practice law effectively, even in areas of practice that are not considered high-tech fields.

New Marketing Tools

The Internet offers a means of law firm marketing that is more dignified, less expensive, and in some cases, more effective than conventional advertising. Thousands of law firms have already opened sites on the World Wide Web, the section of the Internet with the most allure to consumers.

Exposing a law firm to prospective clients is an obvious attraction of having an Internet presence. Some firms, however, find that the Internet benefits them more by letting them provide better services to clients at lower cost.

The Internet Will Be Everywhere

Internet use is on the way to becoming so pervasive in American society that it will be difficult to function as a lawyer in nearly any field of law without understanding the basics of how it operates.

For infrastructure and technical reasons, most people did not consider computer telecommunications a primary computer use until a few years ago. Perceptions have changed. Now, a majority of those purchasing computers for home use say that Internet access is their primary motivation. Powerful forces will cause the number of Internet users to continue to grow at a rapid rate over the coming decade.

The Internet is becoming, and in some cases has already become, an essential tool for lawyers, as illustrated by the following examples:

- ◆ The Internet is a preferred method of communicating in class action lawsuits. Plaintiffs have already begun using it to organize class actions. (See, e.g., http://www.classaction.com). Class action defendants will also use the Internet. It provides an easy way of reducing their exposure to lawsuits by overlooked plaintiffs who attack the adequacy of efforts to notify class members, as in *Silber v. Mabon,* 18 F.3d 1449 (9th Cir. 1994).

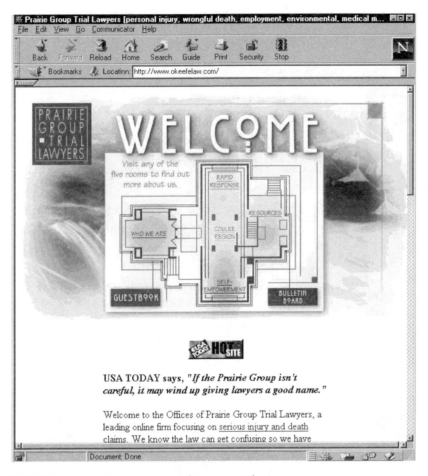

FIGURE 1-2. The Prairie Group Trial Lawyers Web Site

- Organizations with similar interests will use the Internet to manage litigation more efficiently. (See, e.g., **http://www.trialnet.com**).
- Courts will allow or require electronic filing of pleadings. At least four U.S. district courts are experimenting with electronic filing.
- Courts will use the Internet to help manage lawsuits, as the U.S. Court of Appeals did in *Iowa Utilities Board v. FCC,* a case so large that merely listing all the lawyers took four single-spaced pages.
- The Internet will be used to provide legal notices. The Florida attorney general's office, for example, used a Web site to try to publicize its settlement of an action against Toyota dealers regarding automobile leasing.

In many cases, it's not enough to say "If an Internet issue comes up, I'll research it or ask for help," because the Internet is becoming so intertwined with the business and legal worlds that it can pop up

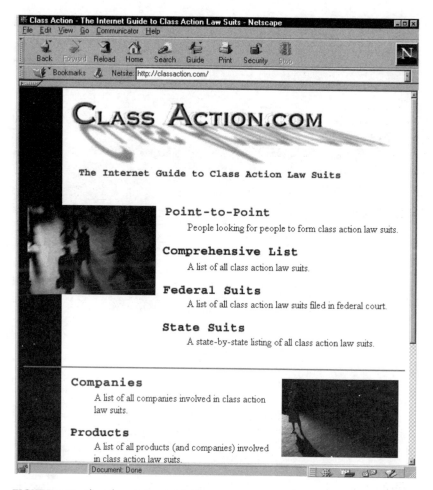

FIGURE 1-3. The Class Action Web Site

unexpectedly at any time, as it did in a recent well-publicized Maryland murder trial. During the trial the issue of whether an expert witness could rely on information obtained from the Internet arose. When judges won't grant recesses, lawyers must work from their existing store of knowledge. Lawyers who have no idea how Internet discussion groups work, for example, might not be able to represent their clients effectively.

Next year, or even next week, for that matter, you may be at a deposition in a commercial case, when an opposing lawyer starts asking your client about a relevant PGP-encrypted document that your client sent by Internet e-mail. If you don't have a clue about what PGP is or how Internet e-mail works, your client may question your competence. These are no longer subjects familiar only to techno nerds. It would be as if the

FIGURE 1-4. The Courts.net Web Site Tracks Electronic Filing Projects

questioning turned to fax machines, and you acted as if you had no idea what they were or how they worked.

Crawling, Walking, Running

In one of my favorite Internet-based discussion groups, ABA LAWTECH, I observed that it was imperative for lawyers in nearly all areas of practice to learn to use the Internet. When another participant expressed her opinion that it was more important for transactional lawyers to learn to use other computer applications like word processing, spreadsheets, and automated accounting systems before moving onto the Internet, I replied as follows:

> It's certainly true that you have to crawl before you can walk and walk before you can run.
>
> I tend to take it as a given that nearly all quasicompetent law firms today have a basic level of computer skills, but I realize you are correct that many firms do not meet this prerequisite, and I welcome your reminder.
>
> My point is: Law firms that do not have the basic computer skills you describe are "crawling." Those that do are "walking."
>
> The Internet is going to allow those firms that learn how to use it to run, leaving the walkers behind in almost as bad a position as the crawlers.
>
> The productivity gains in going from stand-alone personal computers or isolated local area networks to the Internet may eventually be greater than the improvement from moving to personal computers.
>
> We've only begun to see the dim outlines of how the Internet will eventually affect the practice of law.

Conclusion

All lawyers need to understand at least the basics of the Internet for several important reasons:

- It can provide operating efficiencies in business operations, including improved communications, better research tools, and lower overhead.
- It will be necessary to use the Internet to remain competitive when most clients and other law firms are using it.
- It will be a major practice area.
- It is an effective new way to market law firms.
- It will become as pervasive in American life as the telephone, making it difficult to operate as a lawyer in any field of law without a basic understanding of how the Internet works.

Resources

Online

Peter Martin's seminal 1994 address to the New York City Bar, "Five Reasons for Lawyers and Law Firms to Be on the Internet," at:

http://www.law.cornell.edu/papers/5reasons.html. Elaborates on the following
motivations: (1) clients and potential clients are there; (2) other law
firms, as well as non-lawyer purveyors of competing services, are establishing themselves on the Net; (3) conversation among lawyers and
maybe clients about legal issues is already taking place on the Net; (4) it
provides cost-effective access to information; and (5) it provides cost-
effective global communication of data of all sorts.

Ethan Kutash's "Digital Lawyers: Orienting the Legal Profession to Cyberspace," at: http://www-unix.oit.umass.edu/~eleclaw/lawyer.html. Also at *55 Pittsburgh Law Review* 1141 (1994).

In Paper

The Lawyer's Guide to the Internet, by G. Burgess Allison (American Bar
Association: Law Practice Management Section, 1995, 368 pages). A path-
breaking book, insightful and well written. Particularly good at giving
nontechnical types a perspective on the Internet phenomenon.

Unleashing the Killer App: Digital Strategies for Market Dominance, by Larry
Downes and Chunka Mui (Harvard Business School Press, 1998).
Demonstrates through convincing analysis, backed up by many practical
examples, why most businesses will need to understand new technologies, especially the Internet, to thrive or even survive in tomorrow's
world. (Possible economic effects on the legal profession of some of the
trends described are explored in Chapter 20 of this book, "The Future of
the Internet.")

CHAPTER **TWO**

What Is the Internet?

T HE INTERNET is a global computer network. On a technical level, one could say it is a "network of networks." One working definition is: The total of all computers in the world connected to the largest system that allows them to communicate with each other using a system called TCP/IP (for Transfer Control Protocol/Internet Protocol).

Rather than get lost in the sea of jargon, however, it's smarter for lawyers to stay focused on a fundamental but often overlooked fact: The Internet is just a set of sophisticated methods of communication. The two most important ways of communicating for lawyers are e-mail and the World Wide Web. These and some other key features are summarized in the chart at the end of this chapter.

The U.S. Supreme Court's Definition

Here is the Supreme Court's explanation of the Internet in the Communications Decency Act case, *Reno v. American Civil Liberties Union,* 117 S. Ct. 2329 (1997), also available at the Cornell University Law School Web site, http://supct.law.cornell.edu/supct/html/96-511.ZS.html:

> The Internet is an international network of interconnected computers. It is the outgrowth of what began in 1969 as a military program called "ARPANET," which was designed to enable computers operated by the military, defense contractors, and universities conducting defense related research to communicate with one another by redundant channels even if some portions of the network were damaged in a war. While the ARPANET no longer exists, it provided an example for the

development of a number of civilian networks that, eventually linking with each other, now enable tens of millions of people to communicate with one another and to access vast amounts of information from around the world. The Internet is "a unique and wholly new medium of worldwide human communication."

The Internet has experienced "extraordinary growth." The number of "host" computers—those that store information and relay communications—increased from about 300 in 1981 to approximately 9,400,000 by the time of the trial in 1996. Roughly 60% of these hosts are located in the United States. About 40 million people used the Internet at the time of trial, a number that is expected to mushroom to 200 million by 1999.

Individuals can obtain access to the Internet from many different sources, generally hosts themselves or entities with a host affiliation. Most colleges and universities provide access for their students and faculty; many corporations provide their employees with access through an office network; many communities and local libraries provide free access; and an increasing number of storefront "computer coffee shops" provide access for a small hourly fee. Several major national "online services" such as America Online, CompuServe, the Microsoft Network, and Prodigy offer access to their own extensive proprietary networks as well as a link to the much larger resources of the Internet. These commercial online services had almost 12 million individual subscribers at the time of trial.

Anyone with access to the Internet may take advantage of a wide variety of communication and information retrieval methods. These methods are constantly evolving and difficult to categorize precisely. But, as presently constituted, those most relevant to this case are electronic mail ("e-mail"), automatic mailing list services ("mail exploders," sometimes referred to as "listservs"), "newsgroups," "chat rooms," and the "World Wide Web." All of these methods can be used to transmit text; most can transmit sound, pictures, and moving video images. Taken together, these tools constitute a unique medium—known to its users as "cyberspace"—located in no particular geographical location but available to anyone, anywhere in the world, with access to the Internet.

E-mail enables an individual to send an electronic message—generally akin to a note or letter—to another individual or to a group of addressees. The message is generally stored electronically, sometimes waiting for the recipient to check her "mailbox" and sometimes making its receipt known through some type of prompt. A mail exploder is a sort of e-mail group. Subscribers can send messages to a common e-mail address, which then forwards the message to the group's other subscribers. Newsgroups also serve groups of regular participants, but these postings may be read by others as well. There are thousands of such groups, each serving to foster an exchange of information or opinion on a particular topic running the gamut from, say, the music of Wagner to Balkan politics to AIDS prevention to the Chicago Bulls. About 100,000 new messages are posted every day. In most newsgroups, postings are automatically purged at regular intervals. In addition to posting a message that can be read later, two or more individuals wishing to communicate more immediately can enter a chat room to engage in real time dialogue—in other words, by typing messages to one another that appear almost immediately on the others' computer screens. The District Court found that at any given time "tens of thousands of users are engaging in conversations on a huge range of subjects." It is "no exaggeration to conclude that the content on the Internet is as diverse as human thought."

The best known category of communication over the Internet is the World Wide Web, which allows users to search for and retrieve information stored in remote computers, as well as, in some cases, to communicate back to designated sites. In concrete terms, the Web consists of a vast number of documents stored in different computers all over the world. Some of these documents are simply files containing information. However, more elaborate documents, commonly known as Web "pages," are also prevalent. Each has its own address—"rather like a telephone number." Web pages frequently contain information and sometimes allow the viewer to communicate with the page's (or "site's") author. They generally also contain "links" to other documents created by that site's author or to other (generally) related sites. Typically, the links are either blue or underlined text—sometimes images.

Navigating the Web is relatively straightforward. A user may either type the address of a known page or enter one or more keywords into a commercial "search engine" in an effort to locate sites on a subject of interest. A particular Web page may contain the information sought by the "surfer," or, through its links, it may be an avenue to other documents located anywhere on the Internet. Users generally explore a given Web page, or move to another, by clicking a computer "mouse" on one of the page's icons or links. Access to most Web pages is freely available, but some allow access only to those who have purchased the right from a commercial provider. The Web is thus comparable, from the readers' viewpoint, to both a vast library including millions of readily available and indexed publications and a sprawling mall offering goods and services.

From the publishers' point of view, it constitutes a vast platform from which to address and hear from a worldwide audience of millions of readers, viewers, researchers, and buyers. Any person or organization with a computer connected to the Internet can "publish" information. Publishers include government agencies, educational institutions, commercial entities, advocacy groups, and individuals. Publishers may either make their material available to the entire pool of Internet users, or confine access to a selected group, such as those willing to pay for the privilege. "No single organization controls any membership in the Web, nor is there any centralized point from which individual Web sites or services can be blocked from the Web."

(Footnotes omitted.)

How Does the Internet Work?

The core of the Internet is a few thousand large computers, mostly owned by universities, large businesses, and governmental entities. These large machines and networks are connected to each other by special high-capacity phone lines, called *backbones*. The backbones are not part of the regular voice telephone system. The lines are typically leased, and the lessors pay a flat rate, regardless of how much data is transmitted over the lines. The federal government previously subsidized part of this infrastructure, but most of the costs were and still are borne by phone and networking companies, like Sprint and UUNET, and the entities who own the key large computers.

Once your data gets onto the Internet, it travels over this existing "information highway," but you don't have to pay extra for the use of these large leased phone lines. Therefore, once you are on the Internet, you can connect with a computer in Peru or Tokyo for hours at a time, without worrying about getting a mammoth transcontinental phone bill. You only pay for your connection to a *service provider* (usually a local business or one you call using an 800 number) that has a direct connection to the Net. For a fee, you basically piggyback on the service provider's connection. Commercial online services like America Online, CompuServe, and Prodigy are not really "on the Internet," but they have gateways to allow their users access to selected areas of it. So, when you pay for an Internet account, you are renting the right to piggyback on the Internet connection of some large organization that has the technical and financial resources to establish a direct connection to the Internet.

There is a "food chain" effect in Internet access. Most organizations rely on some larger entity for their Internet access. The larger entities often rely in turn on some still larger entity. A few law firms that have established their own high-capacity Internet connections have used them as profit centers by becoming Internet service providers for others.

It's important to keep the Internet in historical perspective. While some form of the Net has been around since the 1960s, the key features that have made it attractive for popular use have only been available for a short time. The Internet is still a toddler by comparison with other forms of communication with comparable impact.

Telegraph	*Telephone*	*Coast-to-Coast Television*	*World Wide Web*
1844	1876	1946	1991

The Changing Face of the Net—And Why It Is Growing Like Topsy

Figure 2-1 shows how the opening section of an Internet site looks using a UNIX shell account. This was what accessing the Internet looked like before the development of graphical user interfaces (also known as GUIs), starting around 1993. Users navigate in the shell environment primarily by typing in various commands. Before GUIs came to the Internet, it was

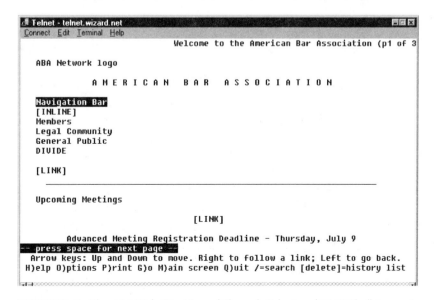

FIGURE 2-1. The ABA Web Site, Viewed Through Telnet and UNIX Shell Account

primarily the province of a relatively small number of technically oriented users. Some people, especially those who are excellent touch typists, still prefer to work in this type of environment, but they are outnumbered by those who prefer GUIs.

Key to the Internet's remarkable growth in recent years has been the wide availability of easy-to-use software and graphical interfaces. Previously, to use the Internet you had to be able to work at the command line of a computer running the difficult UNIX operating system with a text-based system or something comparably difficult.

Things have changed significantly. You can now access the Internet with simple "point and click" software. Figure 2-2 shows the same site viewed through a graphical *browser* program, which is used to access the World Wide Web. Little training time is required to use a browser. The

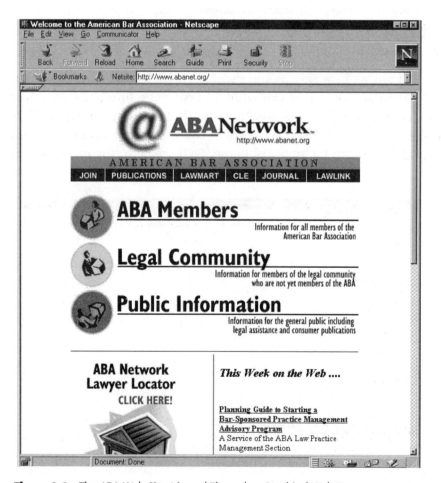

Figure 2-2. The ABA Web Site, Viewed Through a Graphical Web Browser

user does not have to memorize esoteric commands but instead navigates by clicking on highlighted text or graphics options.

The Joy of Hypertext

Hypertext is one of the key features that make graphical Internet software so powerful and easy to use. It is a defining feature of the World Wide Web. Together, graphical user interfaces and hypertext are significantly easier to use than text-based systems. Today's World Wide Web access software, the Web browser, is also much more visually appealing. The user merely selects highlighted words or images that appear on screen, using a mouse or other pointing device. The highlighted word or image is called a *hypertext link*. When the user clicks on a hypertext link, some action will take place. This could be transferring the user to another document on the same computer or to a document on a computer located in New York, San Francisco, London, or Tokyo for that matter. The user does not need to memorize or type in any complicated commands.

In addition to text and graphics, Web sites can contain sound files, video files, and interactivity with computer programs running on distant machines. Using sound, video, and other specialized file types on the Internet may require configuring your browser program with viewer programs known as *helper applications* or *plug-ins*. The latter are more sophisticated and work more seamlessly with the browser. Most helper applications and plug-ins are free. The best modern browsers contain capable built-in e-mail programs, and they are downwardly compatible with older technology like *file transfer protocol* (ftp) and *gopher,* thus providing a uniform Internet user interface.

The trend toward *intranets* demonstrates the ease and effectiveness of hypertext use. Intranets are systems that use Internet technology, especially hypertext, solely for the purpose of distributing information inside an organization. They are like small private Internets. Intranets are spreading like wildfire largely because the hypertext interface is easy to use and reduces training time. Managers noticed that hypertext made it easier for them to find information through the public Internet on a computer belonging to another company thousands of miles away than it was for them to locate information inside their own company's computer system. Intranets and their cousins, *extranets,* are discussed in more detail in Chapter 18, "Collaborative Tools."

Who Owns and Who Runs the Internet?

The computers on the Net all have owners, as do the various backbones. However, no one really owns the Internet as a whole. Nobody really runs it, either. As a result, the Internet often looks chaotic to new users, who approach it in many different ways, with varying levels of success.

The Internet operates on the basis of a sort of benign anarchy. There is a voluntary group called the Internet Society that tries nudging the whole chaotic-looking system in desirable directions. There are committees that set technical standards (often disseminated through documents called RFCs, for Requests for Comment). If you want to establish a new *domain name* (an organizational address on the Internet), there is an organization that decides whether your proposed name is acceptable, but its main function is merely administering the addressing system. None of these organizations, or any other, really "manages" the Internet in the conventional sense.

There is no central authority with the power to discipline Internet abusers. That does not mean there are no safeguards. Considering its size and complexity, the Internet functions amazingly well as a democratic self-regulating organism. As you will learn when you get into the system, there are informal but surprisingly effective mechanisms by which Internet users collectively control the behavior of individuals who would abuse the system, not the least of which is *flaming,* or sending harsh e-mail messages—sometimes in great volume—directly to abusers, or those who are in a position to exercise authority over a particular abuser.

Netiquette

Certain core principles of Internet behavior called *netiquette* are enforced by the community. The term is a little too cute, but the underlying idea is quite serious. Absent a general understanding of and adherence to such principles, the Internet would not work properly, if it worked at all. One such principle is "Don't waste bandwidth." Bandwidth means information carrying capacity. For example, when you have a choice of sites to use, select the one closest to you. The popular Le Web Louvre site, which originated in Paris, is now "mirrored" around the world at other locations, so users can view it without connecting to Paris. This reduces the load on the transatlantic Internet links.

Here are URLs for two popular netiquette guides:

http://www.fau.edu/netiquette/net/
http://www.albion.com/netiquette

Resources

Online
The Scout Report's Toolkit provides a good list of resources for neophytes, at: http://wwwscout.cs.wisc.edu/scout/toolkit

The Internet Help Desk is a good place to look for assistance, at: http://w3.one.net/~alward

Squareone provides good tutorials for beginners, at: http://www.squareonetech.com

Massachusetts lawyer Bob Ambrogi's Web site has an excellent collection of articles about Internet use at: http://www.legaline.com/article.htm

In Paper

The Whole Internet User's Guide, 2nd Edition, by Ed Krol (O'Reilly & Associates, Inc., 1994). A classic general introduction to Internet use. A 1995 version focuses on accessing the Internet under Windows 95.

Net Law: How Lawyers Use the Internet, by Paul Jacobsen (Songline/O'Reilly, 1997, 232 pages). Written by a practicing lawyer in Minnesota, this book is not a tutorial or Internet address catalog, but a lively overview of how real attorneys are benefiting from using the Internet. A strength of the book is the large number of specific examples from lawyers in a variety of areas of practice. Plenty of emphasis on small firms and solo practitioners.

The Internet Guide for Michigan Lawyers, 4th Edition, Mary Ellen LeBlanc, editor. (Michigan Institute of Continuing Legal Education,

See G. Burgess Allison's Law-on-the-Internet Book List at the ABA Web site for a frequently updated bibliography of books about lawyers and the Internet: http://www.abanet.org/lpm/magazine/booklist.html

1998). Under Lyn Chard's leadership, the Michigan Institute of Continuing Legal Education has established a national reputation for excellence, and this outstanding anthology is more evidence that the reputation is well deserved. Localized versions are available for other states, including Illinois, Pennsylvania, Tennessee, and Massachusetts.

Key Internet Features Summarized for Lawyers

Feature	*Purpose*	*Drawbacks*	*Comments*
World Wide Web	Hypertext, graphics, sound, and even video make for an attractive interface.	Operates slowly if graphics feature is used. Difficult to locate the minority of useful sites amid the great mass of worthless ones.	Sometimes called the "Swiss Army Knife of the Internet" because it can be used to access not just the World Wide Web but also ftp, telnet, gopher, e-mail, etc. Easiest to use, most spectacular, and fastest growing Internet feature.
E-mail	Users can send and receive electronic messages.	Easy to become flooded by information you don't want.	Most valuable Internet feature for most lawyers. Can send and receive e-mail to and from other networks (CompuServe, etc.).
Mailing List	This is a system under which e-mail sent to a central location is "echoed" to subscribers.	Can be difficult to learn about relevant ones. Some have low "signal-to-noise" ratio (i.e., there's a lot of chaff).	Extremely useful for keeping in touch with others who are interested in the same topics. May be public or private, moderated or unmoderated.
Newsgroup	This is a collection of publicly accessible messages, divided by subject (more than 40,000 topics at last count).	Most have low signal-to-noise ratio. So many interesting topics, it's easy to get distracted.	Excellent way to get free technical support, do research, or get in contact with experts on specialized subjects.

Key Internet Features Summarized for Lawyers (continued)

Feature	*Purpose*	*Drawbacks*	*Comments*
FTP (File Transfer Protocol)	This is used to transfer files to and from distant computers.	Can be difficult to use unless you have good interface software. Often hard to learn about good files.	Can download wide variety of free files, such as software updates and bug fixes, copies of Supreme Court decisions on the day of issue, etc.
Gopher	Precursor to the World Wide Web, this finding aid added user-friendly menus to help find Internet resources.	Can only use data that someone has linked to a gopher site.	Related search tools are known as Archie & Veronica. Has lost popularity and market share to the World Wide Web, which can do the same things and much more.
Telnet	Users can use this to log on to a remote computer and operate it as if they were at a terminal directly connected to that computer.	Use of UNIX or often unfamiliar systems required for most of the destination computers that allow telnet access.	Can be difficult to navigate after logged on to the remote computer.

CHAPTER **THREE**

E-mail: The Internet
Tool Lawyers Use Most

*When shopping for law firms, I ask how easy it will be to communicate with
us. About 80 percent of the outside firms we hire use e-mail.*

—Christian Liipfert, Staff Attorney, Amoco

MR. LIIPFERT'S DUTIES include helping select outside counsel for a corporation with annual revenues of $31 billion. What's going on here? Is this fondness for e-mail merely an idiosyncrasy of Mr. Liipfert and his employer? No, not at all. Amoco and Mr. Liipfert are just in the vanguard of an increasing number of law firm clients that are learning that Internet e-mail is a fantastically powerful and cost-effective communications tool.

Although the World Wide Web is more glamorous, e-mail is still the most valuable Internet feature for most lawyers. E-mail is the Internet's most stable and reliable service, and its lowest common denominator. If someone has Internet access, they almost certainly have e-mail. At little or no cost, you can rapidly send and receive messages to and from anyone in the world who has an e-mail account. As online services like America Online help millions of ordinary Americans discover the power of Internet e-mail, many clients are beginning to expect, and in a few cases even demand, that their lawyers be accessible through this convenient new medium.

In a year or two, if your business card doesn't have an e-mail address, you will start getting the same type of funny looks and inquiries that you get today if you don't have a fax number. In a few more years, people may react as quizzically to the lack of an e-mail address as they would today to the absence of a telephone number.

> ▼ ▼ ▼ ▼ ▼
>
> *[Many clients and potential clients] use e-mail routinely as part of their everyday business routine, and a law firm is either routinely accessible or it isn't. This has everything to do with being proactive, client-oriented, and accessible.*
>
> —Burgess Allison, Author of *The Lawyer's Guide to the Internet.*

Gaining a Communications Advantage

If you have reasonably easy-to-use e-mail software, don't be surprised if you, like many of your clients, find that you prefer using e-mail to writing paper letters, sending faxes, or calling people on the phone. While e-mail is not right for every situation, it is often more efficient than other methods. It's much faster and you don't have to worry about telephone tag, navigating frustrating voice mail systems, or being put on hold.

For important phone calls, most lawyers like to make a written note of what has been said. With e-mail communications, this is not necessary. You can have a complete record of the communication by sending a copy to your printer. It's even easier if you have a good e-mail program that lets you do fast, easy message storage and filing on your computer. This lets you manage old correspondence with sophisticated automated tools, so there's no more rummaging through file cabinets and stacks of paper for your notes from that phone call last year.

E-mail also has the advantage of being less intrusive. The recipient selects a convenient time to read and reply to e-mail. E-mail doesn't disrupt the recipient's concentration at the wrong time.

In addition, e-mail allows you to be terse without seeming rude. In telephone conversations, most people feel obligated to engage in some social amenities. If someone left a message on your phone answering machine, it would be considered rude to return the call and say, "This is Tom Jones, and the answer is no," and then to hang up. If you do the equivalent by e-mail, you will be considered efficient and even considerate for not wasting the questioner's time. You can be more expansive if you wish, but no idle chitchat is necessary. E-mail gives you a choice you don't have with the telephone.

E-mail sometimes has major advantages over fax machines. E-mail attachments let you send the word processing or spreadsheet or database file that contains the information underlying the main communication. If the recipient has a compatible software program, in addition to printing a clear copy of the original, he or she can also revise the original file without reentering the data, which, of course, would be necessary if you only sent a fax.

In today's increasingly globalized business environment, e-mail makes particularly good sense. How much would it cost to fax a two-hundred-page document from Washington to Tokyo? With Internet e-mail, you can send the same document in an easier-to-read format that is readily revisable by the recipient, at no charge.

You can also take advantage of discussion and networking groups. There are thousands of such mailing lists, on a wide variety of topics, and hundreds designed specifically for lawyers. (See Chapter 7, "Internet Discussion Groups.") Some law firms are using existing Internet mailing lists to market their firms. Others are creating their own lists for distributing firm newsletters, or establishing two-way interaction with clients and prospective clients. (See Chapter 13, "Marketing via Discussion Groups.")

Phone companies in some areas have begun including e-mail addresses in the White Pages. Phone company spokespeople say that they are reacting to customer demand. "It's definitely the direction in which customers are going," according to a Nynex representative.

Exactly how does e-mail work, anyway? Let's take a careful look at the components of an e-mail message.

Analyzing an E-mail Message

Figure 3-1 shows what a typical e-mail message looks like to the recipient. If you are not a good touch typist, the prospect of typing this much material may be intimidating. However, not to worry. Most of it, including the header and the signature block, is generated automatically by decent e-mail programs. As computers become more powerful, voice dictation software is finally becoming practical, so typing skills may not be as important in the future, anyway.

This sample message is from a hypothetical e-mail discussion group named *bizlaw,* a group for lawyers interested in business law. This type of list is frequently used for networking and sharing information. It is analogous to a meeting of a professional society or bar association special interest group, except that instead of having periodic meetings, the members—called *subscribers*—can interact with the rest of the group at their convenience.

FIGURE 3-1. Sample e-mail Message

```
Date: Tue, 11 Jan 2000 08:15:06 -0600

Comment: Business Attorney Mailing List

Originator: bizlaw@hypothetical.com

Errors-To: listkeeper.bizlaw-L@hypothetical.com

Reply-To: bizlaw@hypothetical.com

Sender: bizlaw@hypothetical.com

From: "Eve Barrister, Attorney at Law" ⟨ebarrister@barristers.com⟩

Organization: Barrister & Barrister, P.C.

To: Tom Solicitor ⟨tomsol39@aol.com⟩

Subject: Digital Signatures Act (Was "Re: Do-nothing Legislature")
```

H E A D E R

```
⟩⟩If they don't stop playing around, this legislature will
⟩⟩go home with fewer worthwhile bills passed than any in
⟩⟩the past 30 years, IMHO.


⟩Has anyone heard anything about the status of the Digital
⟩Signature bill, S. 329?
```

Q U O T A T I O N

```
Tom,


The last I heard, it was expected to pass both housees
before the Labor Day recess. That is, unless Johnson tries
to break the Senate filibuster record on the tax bill. :-)

BTW, I have a copy of the Banking Committee's version of
the bill in WordPerfect 5.1 format. They adopted the Utah
"Digital Notary" concept, with some modifications.

I am not "attaching" a copy of this file to this message
because I know many subscribers have difficulty handling
zipped or uuencoded files. I will be glad to send a copy to
anyone who would like. If you want a copy, remember not to
send your request to this mailing list, but contact me
privately, at ebarrister@barristers.com.


Eve Barrister
```

B O D Y

```
****************************************************    S
                                                       I
BARRISTER & BARRISTER                                  G

*** 202/555-5638 (Voice) * 202/555-5609 (Fax) ***
                                                       B
E-mail: ebarrister@barristers.com                      L
                                                       O
WWW: http://www.webland.com/~barristers/               C
                                                       K

PGP public key available upon request or at our WWW site.


DISCLAIMER: Absent a signed retainer agreement, this
message is not intended to establish an attorney-client
relationship. Any reliance on information contained herein
is taken at your own risk.
```

Formattting

The font used here to display this sample message is Courier, a fixed-pitch, or typewriter-style, font. In a fixed-pitch font all the characters are allocated an equal width on the page. The space allowed for the letter "m," for example, is not wider than the space for the letter "l." Most e-mail programs let you select the font to be used to display the messages you receive. The fixed-pitch type is probably the best choice for e-mail programs, because proportional fonts will distort tables or artwork that have been prepared for fixed-pitch display, as is customary.

While changing the display font on your system is easy, it is a mistake to specify fonts, or use italics, bold, etc., on most messages you send, especially to discussion groups. Unless the recipient is using compatible software, your message will look weird.

Check out the length of the lines in the sample, which are relatively narrow. Internet e-mail is *device independent,* and the people reading your messages may be using any of a very wide variety of computer systems. If you set your margins too wide, on some of these systems the text will wrap to the next line and make your message text look strange, as in the following:

```
DISCLAIMER: Absent a signed retainer agreement,
this
message is not intended to establish an attorney-
client
relationship. Any reliance on information
contained
herein is taken at your own risk.
```

You can frequently prevent this unprofessional appearance by setting your default margin to a conservative width, around sixty-five characters.

Headers

Along with other information, the header in Figure 3-1 includes the address of the mailing list generally and the address of the party to contact with complaints about errors, in this case:

listkeeper-bizlaw-L@hypothetical.com.

Many e-mail programs allow you to adjust the amount of header information that is visible. The recipient of the sample message has adjusted his e-mail program so that by default it doesn't display infrequently used technical information. Some e-mail systems don't display any header information. This makes it a good idea to include your e-mail address in the text of your message, preferably in an automatically generated *signature block.*

From the header you can tell that the sample message was distributed by an Internet mailing list. On many mailing lists, if you select the Reply option to a message that you receive from the list, your answer will go to every other subscriber to the list. *Be careful not to embarrass yourself or annoy the other subscribers by sending to the whole list a message that you intended only for one other person.* The sender of the sample message included a reminder of this in the body text for inexperienced readers who might want a copy of the file she offered. In real life, you won't usually get such thoughtful reminders.

Subject lines are particularly important. Some busy people just scan the list of senders and subjects and select the few messages they want to read. Some never get around to reading all their messages. A few e-mail programs, like Eudora, let you specify the urgency of a message you are sending, but this feature will not work unless the recipient has a compatible e-mail program. Subject lines are frequently used to organize and make it easier to find related messages in e-mail archives.

Avoid using subject lines like "Check this Out" that might be mistaken for advertising.

A group of related e-mail messages is called a *thread*. As the thread develops, the subject tends to wander away from that indicated in the original subject line. When this happens, it is a good idea to put in a new subject line, but also to indicate the name of the old one. This is what happened in the Figure 3-1 message. The original subject line was "Do-nothing legislature," but Ms. Barrister changed it when the subject shifted to the Digital Signatures Act.

Quotations

If you are replying to something said in a previous message, it's a good idea to quote the relevant sections of the original. The sample message indicates the most commonly used convention for indicating quotations, the angled bracket marks in the left margin. The double brackets mean that you are quoting someone who was quoting someone else. Other conventions are used. Some e-mail programs just start a new message with the quoted material at the bottom and a header to indicate that it is quoted text.

You should quote the relevant sections, and only the relevant sections, when replying to a discussion group message. One of the most common mistakes made by Internet newcomers is quoting the entire message to which they are replying. This is not a big deal if you are replying to just one person, but the unnecessary repetition will justifiably annoy people if you do it on messages to mailing lists.

The sender of the sample message displayed good judgment in not sending to the mailing list a copy of the WordPerfect file she mentioned. In this way she avoided cluttering up the other subscribers' mailboxes with an unnecessarily long message, in a format that many can't decode, and that many would not be interested in even if they could decode it. (Handling zipped and uuencoded files is explained in a later section.)

Auto-responders

An alternative to replying manually to requests for a file is to set up an *auto-responder*. Some organizations use auto-responders to send out information on a large scale. These are sometimes called *infobots* or *mailbots*. For example, the University of Oregon maintains a large free library of books in ASCII text format compiled by Project Gutenberg. If you send a message to the address almanac@oes.orst.edu with the phrase *send guten alice,* their infobot will send you a complete copy of the text of *Alice in Wonderland* by e-mail. The same technique can be used to distribute electronic marketing brochures about your law firm. This technique gives you the e-mail address of the potential client, information you don't automatically receive after a Web site visit. Some vendors will set up infobots to operate on a twenty-four-hour-a-day basis. A few e-mail programs allow you to specify a reply that will be sent automatically to a message that meets criteria you specify, a do-it-yourself infobot.

Auto-responders are an inexpensive, convenient, and time-saving way to distribute information. In the hypothetical example, Eve Barrister could set up an auto-responder to send a copy of the Digital Signature file to any message with "Get Digital Signature File" in the Subject Block.

Signature Blocks

All good e-mail software gives you the option of automatically attaching a typed description of you and your firm, along with contact information, at the bottom of your outgoing e-mail. Your signature block, sometimes called a sig block, is a time-saver that serves the same function as law firm letterhead in paper mail. Your signature block is a discreet form of marketing—it lets potential clients (and those who might refer potential clients to you) know who you are, what you do, and how to get in touch with you.

While there is no fixed limit, it is commonly stated that signature blocks should not be longer than four or five lines. As long as a signature block is businesslike, without any wasted information, it is unlikely that people will complain if it is a little longer.

Some Internet users put short clever sayings or jokes called *taglines* in their signature blocks. It's probably best for lawyers to avoid this practice, since most jokes will offend someone out there. Even if the joke amuses readers the first time, it will seem pretty old after they've read it in ten of your messages.

The section of the signature block reading "PGP public key available on request or at our web site" is included to give others the option of replying to the sender via secure private e-mail. A signature block is not the same as a *digital signature*. The latter is a technique that allows others to verify that a message in fact came from you and was not forged.

Note that some states have bar rules regulating what you can say on your paper letterhead and business cards. If you are admitted to practice in such a jurisdiction, you would be well-advised to adhere to the same restrictions in your e-mail signature block.

E-mail Netiquette

Four more elements in the sample message illustrate characteristics of Internet e-mail:

1. The typo "housees"
2. The strange smiley face on its side :-)
3. The special acronyms BTW and IMHO
4. The sender's attitude

In regards to the first element, e-mail is supposed to be fast and easy. Most e-mail is seldom proofread by anyone except the sender, and many e-mail programs do not presently have spelling checkers. For these reasons, typos and misspellings are not taken as seriously as they would be in paper correspondence. Despite this, you should exercise care in messages to, for example, potential clients.

The second and third points relate to the dynamics of e-mail, which are very different from face-to-face communication. The absence of non-verbal clues such as facial expression, tone of voice, and the instantaneous inability to correct an inadvertent misunderstanding frequently result in *flame wars,* which are irrational disputes over trivial matters.

Emoticons are typographical symbols used in an effort to reduce the likelihood of misunderstandings. They are meant to indicate the sender's emotional state or intention. The smiley face on its side, like so: :-), in the Figure 3-1 message is one example. It's probably not necessary for lawyers to resort to these aids, but it *is* essential to realize that misunderstanding is a significant danger. Be much more careful in e-mail, especially with people you don't know well, than you would be if speaking to someone in person.

In addition, like CB radio, the e-mail culture has its own insider jargon, and acronyms figure heavily. These include BTW for "by the way" and IMHO for "in my humble opinion" used in the sample message. These acronyms do save a little typing time. Here are a few others you may come across:

FTF	(Face to face—i.e., in-person contact instead of Internet communication)
YMMV	(Your mileage may vary)
JK	(Just kidding)
LOL	(Laughing out loud—i.e., the sender is amused)
ROFL	(Rolling on floor, laughing—i.e., the sender is even more amused)
NHOH	(Never heard of him or her)

NP   (No problem)

RTFM   (Read the [expletive deleted] manual—i.e., "Don't ask such dumb questions")

FWIW   (For what it's worth)

TIA   (Thanks in advance)

And here's one that baffled me the first time I saw it: **TTFN** (meaning Ta-ta for now).

The final instructive point in the sample e-mail message is the sender's attitude. She has volunteered to distribute copies of the bill she found. She's willing to go out of her way to be helpful to other users, even when there is no obvious immediate benefit to her.

Her attitude is *not* an aberration but is typical of the Internet culture. In large part it's a carryover from the days when the Net was a small community dominated by researchers and academics. The Internet's low transaction costs play a role as well. It allows people who want to help others to do so more easily and to have more impact. For example, it will be faster and cheaper for Eve Barrister to reply to e-mail requests than it would be for her to send the material by regular mail or fax.

The prevalence of this type of attitude is probably also explainable as a manifestation of the same type of cooperative spirit that caused pioneers in the American West to help each other. The Internet can be a rough and wild frontier for newcomers, and this type of environment brings out the best in many people. Although there are groups in which rude behavior prevails, most lawyer-specific groups exhibit the professionalism and collegiality that are often described as missing from the modern legal profession.

Despite the flood of new and often unsophisticated users onto the Internet, the cooperative spirit is not dead. It is one of the most appealing aspects of the Internet experience. Its persistence makes mailing lists one of the most useful Internet features for lawyers.

Finding E-mail Addresses

There is no centralized, complete, and accurate directory of Internet users. The most frequently recommended method for finding people's e-mail addresses is a low-tech one: Call them on the telephone and ask them.

If you can't get an address by calling, try some of the many directories. Three of the better ones are located at the following sites:

http://www.whowhere.com

http://www.four11.com

http://www.iaf.net

Dealing with Attached Files

Attached files, known as enclosures, frequently confuse new e-mail users. Ordinary Internet e-mail is designed for plain text only. This roughly corresponds to the characters you could type at a typewritter keyboard.

However, many computer files, like computer programs themselves, or the output of most word processor programs, use unusual characters that can't be transmitted by a regular e-mail message. These are called *binary files*. Binary files can only be sent by e-mail if they are first converted to text format by various methods and treated as an *attachment*. The three such methods commonly used are MIME, UUENCODE, and BinHex. These stand for "Multipurpose Internet Mail Extentions," "Unix to Unix Encoding," and "Binary to Hexidecimal."

You typically don't need to understand any of this to send an attached document. Most modern e-mail programs make it easy. Select the menu choice "Attach," or an attach icon (paper clips are popular), then tell the computer which files to attach.

It's converting attachments that sometimes causes problems. Good e-mail software recognizes attachments and converts between the three attachment formats automatically, without extra work on your part. Yet even if you have such software, you still need to understand this issue because many people to whom you need to send documents may *not* have a good e-mail program. If a recipient of one of your messages is having problems, ask what type or types of encoding he or she can handle, and send it to that person only in that format. Many casual Internet users do not know what types of encoding their software uses or can handle.

Capable e-mail programs let you select the type of encoding to be used. If your message's recipient is having trouble, first try sending the file in MIME (the most common with newer software), then UUENCODED. Try BinHex first with people who are using Macintosh computers.

Never send enclosures to mailing lists. Almost inevitably, some users will not be able to decode them, and some may consider sending the enclosures rude.

Lastly, some e-mail programs give users the option of attaching a separate small file with contact information. These *virtual business cards* are similar to a signature file but are attachments to messages instead of part of the main text body. The point of these files is that they can be easily imported into the recipient's electronic address book. This is a great concept. The drawback is that, as of this writing, there is no universally adopted standard for virtual business cards, so many recipients will not be able to use them.

Opening Zipped Files

Zipped files are another source of confusion for Internet novices. Fortunately, such files are easy to handle if you generally understand what they are and have good software.

Files being transmitted via computer are sometimes compressed, or zipped. There are two reasons for this:

1. To make the files smaller for faster transmission
2. To combine many files into one for easier handling

Compressed files, which frequently have the extension .zip, are not usable until they have been expanded back to their normal size.

The leading compression and decompression programs are PKZIP (http://www.pkware.com) and Winzip (http://www.winzip.com). Some utility programs, like the newer versions of Norton Navigator, have built-in compression and decompression programs.

A few compressed files have the extension .exe, which means they are *self-extracting*. You don't need a utility program to expand them. Instead, just enter the file name at a DOS prompt or, if you use Windows, click twice on the file name in File Manager or Explorer. If the file is not self-extracting, you will need a utility program to expand it.

Selecting E-mail Software

Because you will probably spend more time working with your e-mail software than with any other Internet application, you want to get a powerful and easy-to-use program *and* learn how to use it. The time savings and productivity increase will make it worthwhile. Here are a few questions to ask when choosing an e-mail program:

- How easily does it allow you to sort, organize, store, and retrieve old messages? Some lawyers find themselves using their e-mail programs as a primary storage system for information of all sorts. When they want to store something, they send it to themselves in an e-mail message.
- How easy is it to use the address book? For example, can it import an address automatically, without you retyping it? Does it have shortcuts to allow you to select addressees rapidly?
- Does it have an automatic signature block feature? How many different signature blocks are available? Look for at least two, one for personal use and one for business use.
- Does it have automatic coding and decoding for all types of enclosures (MIME, UUENCODE, and BinHex)?
- Does it have a built-in spelling checker?
- Will it automatically sort incoming messages and categorize them according to criteria you specify? If so, you could, for example, have all messages from a certain mailing list automatically sorted into a particular directory, so you could read them at your leisure. It is also useful to be able to set up automatic replies to messages having certain characteristics.
- Will it allow you to compose and read e-mail messages while you are not connected to the Internet?
- Does it have built-in encryption, or a labor-saving interface with a strong encryption program?

Eudora Pro (different from the Eudora Lite free version, with both available at http://www.eudora.com) and Pegasus Mail (free at http://www.pegasus.usa.com) are good e-mail software choices. Both have a reasonably good mixture of powerful features and relative ease of use. In addition, MS Outlook and MS Outlook Express, the latter bundled with the MS Internet Explorer Web browser, and Netscape Messenger, bundled with the Communicator Suite, have many fans. Because it is intended for the lowest common denominator, the default software included with commercial on-line services like America Online tends to lack useful features common in good stand-alone products.

Basic Tips on Using E-mail

Once you've loaded your e-mail software and are ready to send messages, here are some things to keep in mind:

- Keep your messages short.
- Keep individual paragraphs shorter than you normally would in paper correspondence. The readability of computer monitors is different from paper.
- Be humble. For some reason, something said in e-mail frequently comes across worse than the same comment delivered orally. Some lawyers cultivate the habit of appending "Just my two cents worth" or other disclaimers to the end of all but the most innocuous discussion group postings to reduce the chance that they will come off as overbearing and to lessen the possibility of triggering flame wars.
- You can communicate at low cost with people who don't use e-mail by sending your message via the Internet to a free fax server in their local calling area that translates your e-mail into a fax and transmits it for you. (http://www.savetz.com/fax-faq.html)
- If you don't own your own custom domain name, consider getting an e-mail alias that you won't change if you change Internet service providers. Companies like P.O. Box (http://www.pobox.com) give you a permanent address and forward your mail to any address you specify. ABA members can get a free lifetime forwarding address through the ABA in the format *yourname@abanet.org*. See http://www.abanet.org for details.

When Not to Use E-mail

E-mail is not always appropriate. Because you have no control over when recipients decide to read their e-mail, it is not a good choice when you need a rapid answer. In addition, it is not a good choice when you need confirmation that a message was received.

Sometimes there is no substitute for hearing the other person's voice, or for seeing him or her. Some clients need more hand-holding than others. Smart lawyers know their clients well enough to judge whether to use e-mail or a more personal approach.

Realizing E-mail Dangers—And How to Avoid Them

E-mail presents a number of concerns, some germane for all users and some of particular importance to lawyers.

Security

Unless you encrypt your e-mail messages, they are not totally secure. It is fairly easy for systems administrators near the source or destination of a message to intercept e-mail. If others who know what they are doing invest enough time and money, they can probably get at your e-mail as well. The ability to automate the snooping process for e-mail means that e-mail interception may be a greater risk than alternatives, such as phone wiretapping. Despite the fact that e-mail tampering is a felony under the federal wiretapping statute, it is a threat, especially for lawyers known to handle cases involving large amounts of money.

Fortunately, if you encrypt your e-mail messages with a strong encryption program and handle them properly, they will be much safer than phone calls, faxes, or the U.S. Postal Service. (See Chapter 15, "E-mail Privacy.")

Increased Client Expectations

Because it is such an efficient and rapid means of communication, clients who are used to using e-mail may expect rapid responses. Consider the following rough rules of thumb as outlined in the table below:

Method of Communication	*Clients' Probable Response Time Expectation*
Postal mail	Week
Phone call or fax	Day
E-mail	Hours

Lapses in Judgment

By its nature, e-mail invites informal use. This can be a danger because you may be more likely to write something you regret in an e-mail message than in a letter.

Two factors increase the danger:

- Unlike some intraoffice e-mail systems, Internet e-mail has no "take back" feature that lets you retrieve a message if you have second thoughts after it has been transmitted. When it's gone, it's gone. You can't retrieve it.
- Most e-mail software has a "forward" feature that in an instant allows the recipient of a message to forward copies to any number of people, who may in turn forward copies to any number of other people. Even if your original message was not cause for embarrassment if read only by the original recipient, you have no control over what that person may do with it. Technically, such forwarding of your message may be a violation of copyright law (the author owns the copyright on a letter, not the recipient), but your legal remedy may be inadequate.

At least one law firm that has access to Internet e-mail reportedly allows its associates to receive e-mail but not to send e-mail without the approval of a partner. The danger is real, but few firms will find it necessary to go to this extreme.

Unwanted Permanence

E-mail leaves an electronic paper trail that you may not always want to leave. This was illustrated by an exchange of messages reported by the *Washington Post*. The first message went:

> "Hi David. Please destroy the evidence on the [case] you and I talked about today. Thx, Laura."

The reply was entitled "Evidence Destroyed." The body said:

> "Hi Laura. Ack yr msg. And taken care of. Aloha David"

The *Post* was able to report on this exchange because it had been discovered during litigation. It could be legitimate and ethical under some circumstances to destroy something that could later be considered "evidence." Unfortunately for Laura and David, however, they did not leave an impression of propriety in their casual e-mail messages, which came back to haunt them. The danger is heightened by the fact that owing to the way that automated backups are made on e-mail servers and local area networks, it is sometimes difficult to know where all copies of an e-mail message may wind up.

Alan Brill, of Kroll Associates in New York, suggests the following language for discovery requests:

> Produce any and all files from any personal computer, notebook, or lap-
> top computer, file server, minicomputer, mainframe computer, or other
> storage device, including but not limited to hard disk drives or backup
> or archival tapes (whether stored on-site or at an off-site storage facility)
> containing information relating to [the issue in your case]. This request
> encompasses all forms and manifestations of electronically stored
> and/or retrieved electronic information, including but not limited to
> e-mail. All relevant files that are still on the storage media, but that are
> identified as "erased but recoverable," are to be included.

The "erased but recoverable" language refers to a phenomenon that
was widely publicized during the Iran-Contra prosecutions. Computer
novices are often surprised to learn that erasing a file from a hard disk
does not necessarily eliminate all traces of it. Oliver North discovered this
to his embarrassment during the Iran-Contra investigation. It's easy to recover some "deleted" files with over-the-counter programs like Norton
Utilities. The FBI and some commercial vendors use more sophisticated
techniques that can sometimes recover data that has been erased, or written over multiple times, by detecting residual magnetism. An Internet
reprint of a January 26, 1998, *New York Law Journal* article by Joan E. Feld-
man and Roger I. Kohn, titled "Collecting Computer-Based Evidence,"
gives a good overview, at http://www.nylj.com/tech/012698t6.html.

A good way to avoid potential embarrassment is to make certain that
all personnel in your firm (and your clients) understand that they should
never put anything in any e-mail message, whether intrafirm or on the
Internet, that they would not put in a written memo.

Message Forgery

Forging an e-mail message is sometimes called *spoofing* a message. If the
forger is not very sophisticated, you might be able to detect the forgery
by looking closely at the message header information or having someone
familiar with network routing examine it, but this is not always possible.
Therefore, treat significant or suspicious messages with skepticism.

In situations where it's important that someone be able to verify that
a message came from you and was not altered in transit, you can help
them do so by using a digital signature.

Addressing Mistakes

Compared with other concerns discussed in this section, sending messages to the wrong e-mail address may present the most potential for
embarrassment.

My most memorable personal example was when I read a competitor's discussion group message announcing his upcoming speech. I considered my supervisor at the time to be overly shy about similar public exposure, so to encourage her, I forwarded the competitor's announcement to her, along with a comment that if a speaker as mediocre as our competitor was out there getting speaking invitations, my supervisor should hit the lecture circuit more often. At least I *thought* I forwarded the message to my supervisor. Instead, I inadvertently sent my comment to the competitor who had made the announcement. This was bad enough, but it could have been worse. Imagine if I had misaddressed a similarly embarrassing message to a client, or even worse, a mailing list read by many potential clients.

The lesson: Get in the habit of checking the To, CC, and BCC blocks before you hit the Send button.

Unsolicited Commercial E-mail

Unwanted advertisements, known as *spam,* create annoying e-mail in-box clutter. Equally annoying, senders of junk e-mail frequently use forged headers to deflect complaints. It's difficult to eliminate spam completely, but, until effective legislation is passed to control it (just as junk faxes have been outlawed), there are some ways to reduce it.

- Do not use your real e-mail address on publicly accessible discussion groups. Spammers use automated software called *harvesters* to collect the addresses of posters. To foil such software, some posters use return addresses such as jones32@STOPSPAMaol.com. Human beings can figure out the real address, but this foils those computer programs.
- Use filtering features in your e-mail software to detect and delete e-mail from known offenders automatically.
- Contact on-line directories and ask that your e-mail address be removed. You can find a list of major directories at http://www.search.com.
- Be careful about using "free" Internet services, such as Web site publicizers, that require you to disclose your e-mail address.

In addition, be careful about responding to spammers. Some collect the e-mail addresses of anyone who replies to a message—even those who complain—and they sell the lists as "verified" addresses.

Further information about how to fight back against spammers is available at:

http://www.junkbusters.com/ht/en/junkemail.html

http://www.stopspam.org/email/email.html

Unanswered E-mail

Failing to monitor and answer your e-mail can cause the same problems as failing to monitor and answer your paper letters or phone calls. Despite this, many lawyers fail to manage their e-mail messages.

In a national forum, a senior in-house counsel at Federal Express complained about having difficulty communicating by e-mail with prospective outside counsel he had located on the Internet and was considering hiring. He said that they had held themselves out as using e-mail but failed to respond to his inquiries. Other in-house counsel echoed his complaint. Were their complaints justified?

The American Lawyer magazine conducted a test. They sent e-mail to seventy-six lawyers in thirty-two law firms and corporations that advertised e-mail addresses. After one week, 37 percent had failed to reply:

> Telephone calls to those that did not respond revealed that some lawyers whose Internet addresses are publicly advertised don't even have personal computers, and some don't know what e-mail is. Moreover, big firms had the worst record. The firms with the best response rates were small and mid-size.

What conclusions would you draw about the judgment and competence of a law firm that installed a voice mail system and then neglected to listen to or return the phone calls it received?

Adapting to Technology: Eisenhower's Secret

Some lawyers could benefit by emulating someone who knew how to make technology work for him. As a U.S. Army general, Columbia University president, and president of the United States, Dwight Eisenhower never had to dial the telephone. Like many who occupy such positions, he merely told his clerk or secretary whom he wanted to talk to, then picked up the phone when he was told that the other party was on the line. Because of this, the story is told that when Eisenhower retired from the presidency in 1961, he was confused the first time he picked up a telephone and heard a dial tone.

Some people tell this story to ridicule Eisenhower. My moral is different. Eisenhower was an exceptional manager who understood a fundamental truth: Any corporal could look up a number and dial a telephone. Only Dwight Eisenhower could plan the invasion of Normandy.

Many lawyers believe that they are too busy to sit down at a keyboard and learn how to use the Internet at the hands-on level. They think it's more profitable for them to spend their time on other endeavors, and this may be a rational decision for some. However, such lawyers who don't have someone reliable in their firm to access the Internet for them are going to be just as handicapped as General Eisenhower would have been if he could not have communicated with Omar Bradley, and they'll be just as handicapped as President Eisenhower would have been if he could not have spoken on the phone with Sam Rayburn.

Most lawyers find that it's more efficient to handle their own e-mail, but if this is not for you, take the Eisenhower approach—have a secretary or paralegal regularly download your mail and print it out on paper for you. Dictate outgoing messages like you do your paper letters, and make sure you have a secretary or paralegal who knows how to transmit messages via the Internet.

Some Internet service providers will automatically forward all your e-mail to you via fax for a fee. While it's not the cheapest or most efficient method, this approach may be okay for the cyber-challenged with low-volume e-mail accounts. New voice recognition software may be the answer for some lawyers.

To learn more about the intricacies and benefits of e-mail use, read Kenneth E. Johnson's book, *The Lawyer's Quick Guide to E-mail* (American Bar Association: Law Practice Management Section, 1998).

It's definitely not necessary for every lawyer to be able to operate a computer personally. However, any lawyer who is not plugged in to the new global communications network in one way or another will be at a serious competitive disadvantage over the next decade.

The Medium Is the Message

Marshall McLuhan's famous statement, "The Medium *is* the Message," has become such a cliche that we seldom think about its meaning. McLuhan's point was that by its very nature, television inevitably transformed the substance of any information communicated by that method. The same idea applies to communications via the Internet.

So many people want to learn more about the Internet that knowledgeable speakers tend to be in demand. The speakers I know tend to be more favorably disposed toward invitations received by e-mail than those received by telephone or paper mail (often referred to as *snail mail* by those who have come to understand e-mail's benefits).

The sender's choice of medium communicates some unarticulated but very powerful messages. When a person sends an invitation by e-mail, he or she essentially says, in a very convincing fashion:

- If you work with us, you won't have to waste time on telephone tag and annoying voice mail systems.
- If you work with us, you won't have to waste money on long-distance phone calls, faxes, or overnight couriers.
- I understand how to use modern communications for our mutual benefit.

As the practice of law becomes ever-more competitive, aren't these the types of unspoken messages we all want to send to our clients and potential clients?

PART **TWO**

Researching

CHAPTER **FOUR**

The Internet Research Environment

Everything you need to know is on the Internet. You just can't find it.

—Attributed to an exasperated researcher

IF YOU'VE DONE MUCH research on the Internet, you understand the frustration that inspired this observation. While there is an enormous amount of material available on the Internet, doing research there is difficult:

- ◆ It is hard to find what you want among the masses of data.
- ◆ The available information varies widely in quality.
- ◆ In many cases depth of information is lacking. There is seldom anything approaching the coverage of historical cases that you get in a law library, and coverage of state law cases generally is spotty.
- ◆ Most sites provide little if any technical support.
- ◆ There are so many interesting side trails that it can be difficult for all but the most disciplined researcher to avoid wasting time.
- ◆ There is little uniformity in site organization and presentation. Each site tends to be put together in a unique, and sometimes haphazard, fashion.

As Burgess Allison explains in *The Lawyer's Quick Guide to Netscape Navigator* (American Bar Association: Law Practice Management Section, 1997):

> [E]ach individual who builds his or her own web site becomes a mini-librarian, organizing information and Web pages (and links to other Web pages) into what he or she thinks are "common sense" categories and custom one-of-a-kind organizational schemes. The result is a library-science disaster of Babel-esque proportions.

Despite the difficulty of researching on the Internet, it would be a mistake to assume that law firms do not need access to Internet research tools:

- The Internet is already the best source for a great deal of useful information. It has an exceptional variety of research tools and databases, some of which have no equivalents in expensive commercial databases like LEXIS/NEXIS, Westlaw, or Dialog or the paper-based libraries you are likely to use.
- Almost all the information on the Internet is free.
- The extent and quality of the best resources on the Internet are rapidly increasing. Government agencies, universities, businesses, and law firms are all adding to the store of useful information available on the Net. The future of legal research is the Internet.

Net Research Road Map

The first step in a successful Internet search is deciding which Internet resources to use. Too many researchers omit this step. They learn one research tool, possibly a directory like Yahoo or a search engine like AltaVista, and then turn to it automatically for every research problem.To them, their favorite research tool (often the only tool they know) is synonymous with "Internet research." This approach brings to mind the maxim "If the only tool you have is a hammer, every problem looks like a nail." Good researchers match the tool to the job.

The chart on page 53 illustrates the steps involved in deciding which Internet research tools to apply to a particular legal research project.

To Net or Not to Net

The first step in the decision-making process is deciding whether to use the Internet or conventional research techniques. Notwithstanding the most ardent Internet partisans' view, there are occasions when books, CD-ROMs, or services like LEXIS and Westlaw should be the researcher's first choice.

For the reasons explained previously, it's more difficult to become a skilled researcher on the Internet than it is on commercial services like Westlaw, LEXIS/NEXIS, and Dialog. The Internet is frequently a good

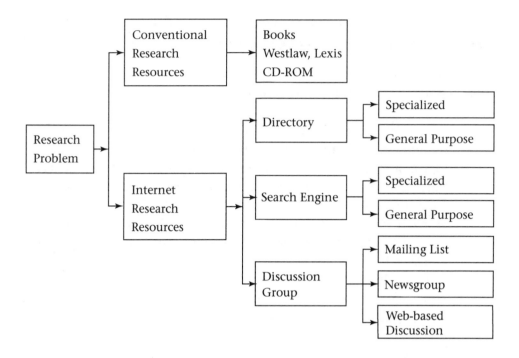

starting point when the issue to be researched involves one or more of the following:

- Federal laws or regulations
- Articles written by top practicing lawyers on topical subjects
- Information about hot factual topics
- Some specialty areas, like intellectual property and high-tech law
- Factual research, like finding statistics, business or product information, locating people or experts, and much more.
- Amenability to interactive research techniques that have no counterpart off the Internet (see Chapter 7, "Internet Discussion Groups")

Don't be penny-wise and pound-foolish when deciding between conventional research sources and the Internet. For example, even though you can get all recent U.S. Court of Appeals decisions free on the Internet, if you need the page number citations for a brief, getting them from LEXIS or Westlaw may actually be more efficient. Factor in the value of your time.

Lastly, remember that the Westlaw and LEXIS commercial databases are now available on the Wide World Web, at:

http://www.westlaw.com

http://www.lexis.com

Three Branches of Internet Research

Assume that you have decided to use the Internet as your primary search tool on a project. There are three general approaches:

1. *Directories* (sometimes known as *subject trees*) are sites assembled by humans that attempt to organize links to Internet sites in a logical manner. Yahoo (http://www.yahoo.com) is the leading general purpose directory. FindLaw (http://www.findlaw.com) concentrates on legal sites. (See Chapter 6, "Directories.")
2. *Search engines* are databases of Internet sites that are searchable by keyword. AltaVista (http://www.altavista.digital.com) is a leading general search engine. Lawcrawler (http://www.lawcrawler.com) concentrates on legal sites. (See Chapter 5, "Search Engines.")
3. *Discussion groups* are used to find a human being who can answer your question or help you find the answer. Many Internet legal discussion groups are available through Legalminds (http://www.legalminds.com) and Counsel Connect (http://www.counsel.com). (See Chapter 7, "Internet Discussion Groups.")

The Washburn University School of Law's site, http://washlaw.edu, shown in Figures 4-1 and 4-2, provides a practical illustration of how all three approaches can be linked from a single Web site.

1. The words in alphabetical order on the left side of the screen are a hypertext *directory*. If you select the phrase "CourtRules," for example, you will be connected to a subpage of the Washburn site with links to information about court rules across the nation.
2. The home page (Figure 4-1) contains not one but two *search engine* links. Each will send a request to a specialized search engine that indexes the Washburn Web site only. For extensive sites like Washburn's, this type of specialized, "one-site-only" search engine is a major convenience.
3. Selecting the choice "DiscussionGroups" leads to a subpage (Figure 4-2) with a selection of *discussion groups*. Washburn has been a national leader in hosting legal discussion groups.

Deciding whether to start a particular research project in a directory, a search engine, or a discussion group is partly a matter of personal

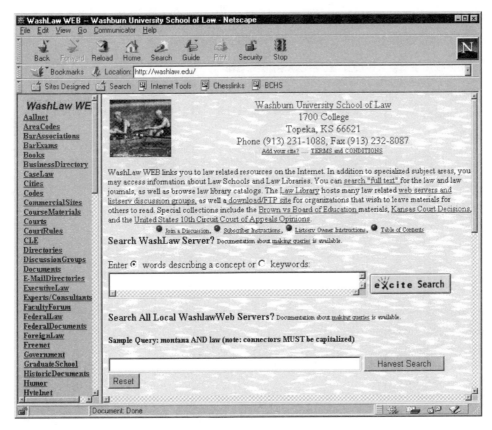

FIGURE 4-1. Washburn Site with Directory, Two Search Engines, and Discussion Group Links at the Same Site

preference, partly a matter of experience, and partly a matter of the nature of the research project. Here are some guidelines:

Directory Indicators

- Are you looking for an overview instead of something very specific?
- Are you unsure about exactly what you're seeking?
- Are you aware of a particular directory that will link to the information you need? This is where a well-organized *bookmark* list comes in handy.
- Are you looking for information that is not indexed by search engines? For example, search engines do not index password-protected sites like those of the *Wall Street Journal* or the *New York Times*. In addition, search engines don't index the contents of files in non-HTML formats, like Portable Document Format (PDF), frequently used at government sites. A directory may be the best way to find such information.

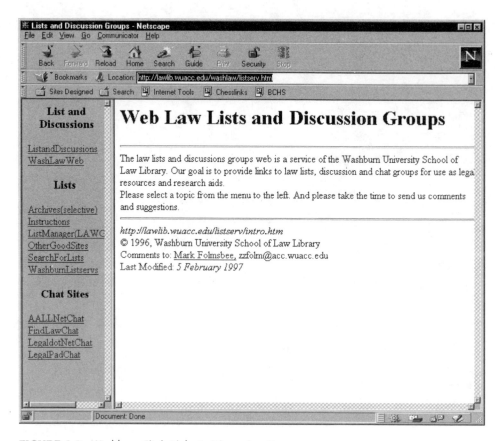

FIGURE 4-2. Washburn Site's Links to Discussion Groups

Search Engine Indicators

- Does the research problem readily lend itself to finding some keywords that will probably be in the documents you're seeking? For example, if you have the name of an individual or a business, a search engine will often be your best bet. The more specific the terms, the better. "Habeas corpus" is a better candidate for search engine treatment than "due process."
- Are you looking for very new information? Some search engines index news sources automatically, while directories, which are compiled by human beings, frequently tend to lag.

Discussion Group Indicators

- Is your question more amenable to human judgment and intelligence than the other methods? For example, do you already know the black letter law but want to learn how experienced lawyers handle the matter in practice?

◆ Do you already know a forum where you are likely to be able to find the answer? For example, if your question deals with the law of a particular state, is there a lawyer mailing list for that state? If the question is about a particular area of law, try the discussion groups at, for example, Counsel Connect (http://www.counsel.com). Use specialized search engines to find legal mailing lists and discussion groups. See the Internet Tools for Attorneys Web site (http://www.netlawtools.com) for links to legal discussion forums.

Interactive research may be the least understood and most under-appreciated research technique. Experienced librarians and other researchers have long used interactive research off the Internet. What gives the Internet version of this technique its special power is the Internet's broad reach and low transaction costs. You can frequently obtain advice from your colleagues or top experts through the Internet at no cost but your time. The Internet's extraordinary networking power lets you extend your reach immeasurably—if you know how to use it.

Portals: Blurring the Lines

To expand their versatility, some directory sites have added search engines. Sites that started as search engines have added directories. This is part of a business trend to make Web sites *portals* that contain so many useful features that many Internet users will want to use them as their regular starting point. Some even allow users to design their own customized starting pages, selecting from among many features those of most interest to them. High popularity allows a portal owner to charge more for advertising and gain other marketing advantages.

Don't let the trend toward portals confuse you. Directories and search engines require different techniques, so it's important to keep them conceptually distinct. If you are typing information into a box on the screen and the computer returns a list of related sites, you are using a search engine. If you are navigating by selecting from a multilayered list of topics on a screen, you are using a directory.

The Lycos Web site, http://www.lycos.com, illustrates these trends. It started out as a search engine. To use the search engine, you type your search request in the box near the top of the page and press the Enter key. Lycos then added a directory. To use the directory, you select one of the logically arranged hypertext links in that section. Lycos has now

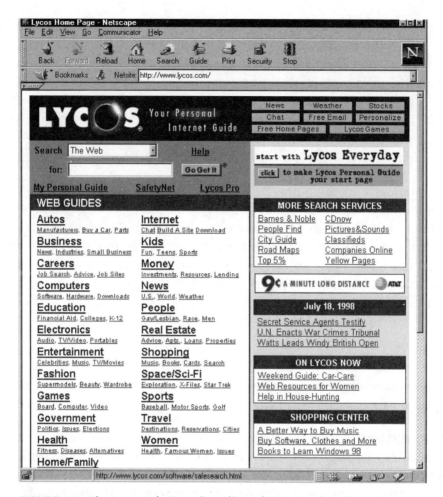

FIGURE 4-3. The Lycos Web Site, a "Portal" Combining Search Engine, Directory, and More

added many other features, including free e-mail, weather reports, stock price reports, and more.

Combinations of Techniques

A skilled researcher will frequently use more than one technique on the same research problem. You might use conventional research techniques to supplement your Internet research, or vice versa.

Even with an Internet-only search, you will frequently use more than one type of Net research tool. The best researchers combine techniques fluidly, shifting from one to the other as needed. You might, for example post a question on an estate planning mailing list. The answer could refer you to a directory at a law firm's Web site. That directory might lead you to a specialized search engine. On another occasion, you might start out using Yahoo's directory structure. After you find a particularly good site through it, you might look for others using a search engine to find similar sites.

Learn to use all the available tools if you want to make the transition from "surfer" to "researcher."

Browser Tips for Web Searchers: Know Your Tools

Performing searches on the World Wide Web is much easier if you understand the key tool, your Web browser.

Creating Bookmarks

When you find a good Web site, you want to be able to return later. All modern browser software keeps a list of preferred sites. These lists are called *bookmarks, hotlists,* or *favorite places,* but the idea is the same. To add a site to your list in Netscape Navigator, for example, you select the menu choice Bookmark, then select Add Bookmark. In MS Internet Explorer, select Favorites, then Add Favorite. When you later want to return to the site, you select the menu choice Bookmark or Favorites and review the list of saved navigational aids.

Newer browser programs will let you move and rename bookmarks as well as create folders or dividers to help organize them. Renaming a bookmark is often a good idea because many Web site designers assign meaningless names to Web pages.

If the built-in bookmark management features are not enough, you can buy separate programs to help you organize and edit your bookmarks.

You can have more than one bookmark collection and switch between them as needed. If, for example, you have bookmarks for hundreds of environmental law sites, you might put them into a separate collection to share with other lawyers who share your interests. Newer browsers will revisit selected bookmarker sites at intervals you specify and then notify you when any have changed. You might, for example, use this feature to monitor new announcements at your state bar association's home page, your favorite CLE group, and a government agency that frequently issues regulations of interest to your clients.

Searching Inside a Web Page

Once you've found a Web page that looks like it might have the information you want, but the page is long, you can use the browser's internal search feature to find the phrase you're seeking. Press Ctrl+F and enter the phrase. This "find" feature works like similar features in word processors. The browser will jump to the first occurrence of the phrase in the current document.

Saving Your Results

Saving files in electronic format is an alternative to printing them on paper. If you save it as Source or HTML, the Web page will retain its original formatting codes, which will make it difficult to read or import into a word processor. To get the information as an ASCII text-only file (i.e., without formatting), save it as text, or cut and paste the part you want into a word processor document, or e-mail the Web page to yourself. Even with these three methods, you may have to do some clean up with your word processor to make the imported text look the way you want.

Using Multiple Browser Windows

Is it taking a long time to complete a download or search? You can always press the Stop button, but there is another option. Newer browsers let you open more than one browser window at the same time. This is usually done by a command under the File menu. While one window is tied up with a slow download, you can use others to visit other sites. Though the performance of one browser window may be slowed by another, this can be a way of getting more done in less time.

Learning Your Favorite Browser's Shortcuts

Become familiar with your browser's time-saving tools. For example, some browsers don't require you to type in a complete address. With later versions of Netscape Navigator, you can automatically file a bookmark when creating it by selecting the File option. With later versions of Internet Explorer, you don't need to visit a search engine before entering a search request: just enter "find" or "go" in front of your search terms and the software will automatically select a search engine for you. Saving a few seconds here and there through similar techniques will add up.

Browser Add-ons: Plug-ins and Helpers

Plug-ins and helper programs are used to extend a Web browser's capacity. Of the two, plug-ins work more seamlessly within a browser.

Adobe Acrobat Reader is a plug-in likely to be needed by Internet researchers. It is used to view documents in Portable Document Format (PDF), which are recognizable because they end in the extension **.pdf.** PDF makes it easy to publish documents on the Internet so they look exactly like their paper counterparts. It is frequently used by government agencies, including the IRS, which uses it to publish tax forms.

You can download Acrobat Reader from the Adobe Web site, at http://www.adobe.com/prodindex/acrobat/readstep.html. Adobe distributes this viewer program at no charge to create demand for its PDF file creation programs.

Other Software Help

Aside from plug-ins and helper programs, there are stand-alone programs that can make Internet research easier. Here is a summary of the major types:

Program Type	Purpose	Comments
Search Assistants	Send request to multiple search engines and process results.	Helpful to reduce time spent visiting multiple search engines and analyzing results.
Off-line Browsers	Visit specified sites during off-peak hours and download them to disk for faster usage.	Good if you repeatedly visit the same sites.
Bookmark Managers	Optimize markers left to help you find sites you have visited.	Useful for serious researchers with large bookmark collections.
Research Organizers	Help manage information you have located on the Internet and stored locally.	Useful if you do extensive Internet research.

Some are free, others are shareware (i.e., can be sampled at no cost), and some are regular commercial software. In addition, newer Web browsers incorporate some off-line browser and bookmark manager features. To find the most recent versions of programs in each category, visit the Web site associated with this book, at http://www.abanet.org/lpm/netbook.

Information Reliability

Anyone can publish information on the Internet—it doesn't take the resources of Random House or NBC. This means, however, that many Web sources lack "gatekeepers" who screen information and stand behind the accuracy of the information they publish. Judging the reliability of information found on the Internet is a constant challenge for the serious Internet researcher.

Genie Tyburski, research librarian with Ballard Spahr Andrews & Ingersoll LLP in Philadelphia, and editor of The Virtual Chase, at http://www.virtualchase.com, provided the following "Checklist for Authenticating Information on the Internet" for this book:

- **Determine the objectivity of a source**.
  Locate and review a site's purpose statement.
  Beware of advertisements or other means of persuasion.
- **Read any site documentation.**
  This generally applies to sites offering primary and secondary legal documents or information.
  Determine (1) the data source, (2) the extent, if any, of editorial enhancements, (3) the updating schedule and method, and (4) the names of the individuals responsible for the site.
- **Ascertain the credentials of the author or publisher**.
  This generally applies to sites providing commentary.
  Look for verifiable evidence of the writer's or publisher's expertise.
- **Identify citation data.**
  Discover the author, title, publisher, and uniform resource locator (URL).
  Ascertain the information's *creation* and *revision* dates. If revised, learn the particulars of the modification.
- **Examine the presentation or appearance of the document.**
  This applies only when required by evidence rules or when necessary to authenticate a source.

Consider whether the document resembles the print version of the same publication or whether it bears familiar official markings.
- **Verify all information.**
Good research practice encompasses substantiating all information regardless of the quality of the source.
When seeking the best of the Web, follow Thomas Jefferson's rule: "We must resort to information which, from the best of men, acting disinterestedly and with the purest motives, is sometimes incorrect."

Is There a Place for Surfing?

While the Internet makes it possible to access an extraordinary range of information, it can be difficult to tell the difference between wasting time and surveying potentially valuable resources. For example, was Abingdon, Virginia lawyer Jackson S. White, Jr., wasting time by reading the *Times of London*? It turns out no, as a matter of fact, as he explained in an e-mail to me:

> Among other things, I'm an Anglophile and read the *Times of London* online almost daily. A British law opinion that I read on the Times' site involved [a legal principle at issue in one of my cases] misleading an opponent, then trying to capitalize on that action. The British court came down hard on the side of fairness with some memorable quotes. Our brief not only cited and quoted from the British opinion but we attached a complete copy for the court. (That opinion was not available online and we had to order it from the British court.) Of course this British opinion is not binding authority here, but we wanted to show that the principle our client advocates is so universal that it not only is followed by U.S. courts but also by our British cousins.

University of Virginia professor and Internet expert Bryan Pfaffenberger is wary of wasting too much time on aimless searches but counsels in his book *Web Search Strategies* (MIS Press, 1996):

> Don't dismiss surfing entirely, though. It's like browsing the stacks in a good library. You may come across a jewel of a site quite by accident. In addition, it's a great idea to surf away from a page that's loaded with relevant links.

A little Web surfing can be beneficial, but most law firms will want to have formal policies in place to prevent abuse. Appendix F contains a sample Internet use policy for law firms.

Assigning Designated Surfers

With a little training, even the rawest beginner will usually learn enough to have some productive results in a short time. However, it currently takes a long time to become an expert Internet researcher. The overall mass of material available on the Internet is vast, and there is a variety of searching tools, with no standard interface.

Still, the Internet's research resources are too important to ignore. All lawyers and law librarians with even minimal aptitude for using computers should probably be trained in the basics of Internet research. Today's legal professional needs a basic understanding of how Internet research works, a general idea of the resources available, and an appreciation of how the Internet differs from other research tools. Yet because it takes a significant investment of time and training to become an expert, it may be most efficient for law firms to assign the bulk of Internet research work to certain lawyers or law librarians as designated Internet research specialists. The "designated surfer" approach lets law firms take advantage of Internet resources while minimizing unproductive training time.

Some people think that the widespread availability of free computer databases will mean the death of the library profession. The future may be bleak for librarians with solely paper-based skills. However, information professionals, whether they call themselves librarians or something else, are going to become much more important in the foreseeable future. The volume of useful electronic information is growing more rapidly than the development of easy-to-use tools to manage it all.

Push Technology

Instead of seeking out new information every day, wouldn't it be easier to find a good distributor of information and let that party send relevant new information to you? That is the idea behind *push* technology. Rather than providing content only as requested, push technologies send it to subscribers without a specific request.

E-mail discussion groups are a primitive yet still effective form of push technology, but push technology that uses Web browsers, or Web browser-type displays, has generated a great deal of interest. Pointcast was one of the earliest successful implementations of more-advanced push techniques. Newer iterations are bundled with the newer browser programs. You can subscribe to various *channels,* and the program will automatically download information from those channels to your hard drive so it is available when you want to see it.

For example, you could use the CNN Financial Network (http://www.cnnfn.com) to keep track of takeover candidates you want to monitor. Lawyers with business interests in Japan will find Nikkei Net (http://satellite.nikkei.co.jp/enews) a wonderful resource.

The word "channel" was not chosen by accident. Push is an attempt to introduce a broadcasting model to the Internet. The similarity to the television paradigm is probably why push has been the subject of so much hype. It's more familiar and comforting to advertisers. If you can hook someone on a push channel like you can on a television program, you can have more assurance that they will see your message regularly.

Push has great potential as a time-saver. The initial hurdle is finding a channel that broadcasts information you want and is not merely a new form of junk mail. At the present time, there are not that many high-quality channels specifically of interest to lawyers, but that could change rapidly.

For some tips on subscribing to channels, go to CNET at http://www.cnet.com/Content/Features/Howto/Push/index.html.

Conclusion

The Internet's value as a research resource increases every month. More data, better search engines, and more useful finding aids are constantly being added. Despite this, the previously discussed problems with researching on the Internet have prevented many law firms from taking advantage of this resource.

If your firm doesn't have access to the Internet, and your competitors have such access *and* know how to use it, you will be at a disadvantage. This will become even more true as even more valuable information makes its way onto the Net and available search tools and indices are refined.

Resources

Online

Law Library Resource Xchange, at: http://www.llrx.com. Cindy Chick and Sabrina Pacific Produce one of the best legal sites.

Genie Tyburski's The Virtual Chase, at: http://www.virtualchase.com. A top choice in the Net-lawyers discussion group's listings of "Best Internet Law Tool."

In Paper

The Lawyer's Quick Guide to Netscape Navigator (American Bar Association Law Practice Management Section 1997) and *The Lawyer's Quick Guide to Microsoft Internet Explorer* (American Bar Association Law Practice Management Section 1997), both by G. Burgess Allison. These books, which focus on browser usage, are not marketed as "legal research" books, but nonexperts may find them more useful as Internet research aids than any of the other books listed here. No books are better at teaching Net navigation to lawyers than these slim volumes (about 150 pages each).

NetResearch: Finding Information Online, by Daniel Barrett (O'Reilly, 1997). A simple overview of the subject. Part of the respected publisher's Songline series of introductory books, which includes *Net Law: How Lawyers Use the Internet,* by Paul Jacobson, which provides many practical examples of lawyers using the Internet for research.

Secrets of the Super Net Searchers: The Reflections, Revelations, and Hard-Won Wisdom of 35 of the World's Top Internet Researchers, by Reva Basch (Online, 1996). Consists solely of interviews with experienced Internet researchers. Some great ideas, but this book is primarily of interest to serious students of the subject.

Web Search Strategies, by Bryan Pfaffenberger (MIS Press, 1996). Bryan Pfaffenberger must be a candidate for the most prolific computer book author around. This book does a good job of covering the basics of searching on the Internet.

World Wide Web Searching for Dummies, 2nd Edition, by Brad Hill (IDG Books Worldwide, 1997). Like most of the *Dummies* series, a better book than you would expect from the insulting title. Even the not-so-dumb will get some good ideas.

CHAPTER **FIVE**

Search Engines

SEARCH ENGINES employ a "random access" approach to information that is similar in function to a book index. Internet search engines index information, including Web sites, and provide programs for searching through the indices. Search engines have three components:

1. A database
2. A method for populating the database
3. An engine for retrieving information from the database

Because search engines have different features and use different rules, it is a good idea to download and study the Help files of search engines you use frequently. To assist readers in further understanding how Internet search engines work, this chapter includes some research examples.

Research Example 5.1: Using a Search Engine

Situation

You are a solo practitioner in a Rocky Mountain state. Your best client relates the following:

> I have more than $5,000 worth of inventory missing, and I'm sure it was stolen. One of my employees who had access to the material has a drinking problem, and I think he might have been the one who took it. I called the police but they did not conduct a serious investigation. My friend told me when he had a similar situation a few years ago, he hired

a retired FBI agent who came in and gave some lie detector tests. They showed that one employee was lying, and the employee then confessed when the examiner told him he had failed. Can I do the same thing?

Issue

Can employees suspected of theft be asked to take polygraph exams?

An Approach

With this type of question, when you can figure out specific words or phrases that will probably be included in the documents you want—such as "polygraph" and "employee"—it is better to use a search engine than a directory.

Suppose that you use the popular AltaVista search engine. You enter its Uniform Resource Locator (URL), or Internet address, http://www.altavista.com, into your browser and press Enter. After a few seconds you see the screen shown in Figure 5-1.

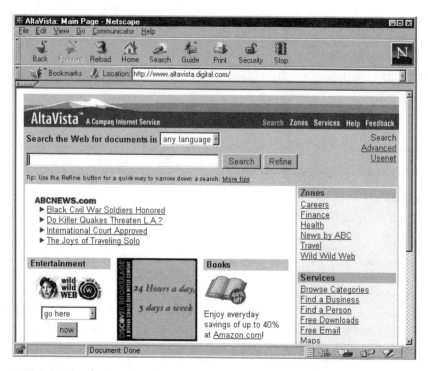

FIGURE 5-1. AltaVista Search Engine

Note that with this particular search engine, to indicate that a word must be included in the documents sought, you use the plus sign (+). So you enter the search request "polygraph +employee" and press the search button. The information shown in Figure 5-2 rapidly appears on screen.

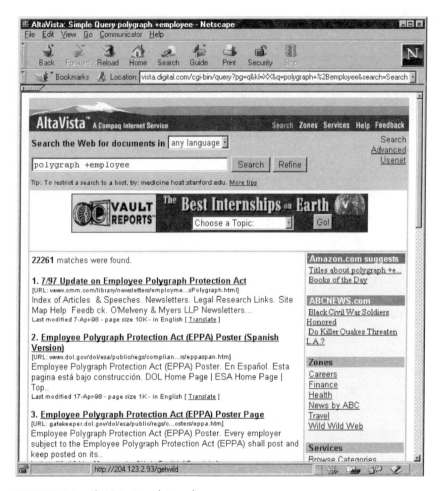

FIGURE 5-2. AltaVista Search Results

There are thousands of documents that match your search request. Fortunately, the search engine uses sophisticated mathematical formulas to rank the found documents (*the drop*) according to its best estimate of relevance to what you are seeking. The search engine returns the results ten documents at a time. AltaVista also provides a brief quotation from the beginning of each returned document, which is a useful feature not shared by all search engines.

Several of the documents look relevant. To read them, you click on the related highlighted phrases to connect to the computer where the documents are located. After looking through a few pages of search results, you select one named "Part 801—Application of the Employee Polygraph Protection Act of 1988." After a few seconds you see the screen shown in Figure 5-3.

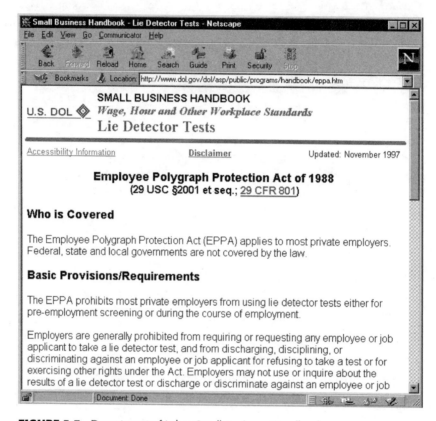

FIGURE 5-3. Department of Labor Small Business Handbook

From the URL block near the top of the browser screen, you can see that it is a Department of Labor document. The letters **dol.gov** in the URL make it fairly easy to tell where you are. (More information about interpreting URLs is contained in Appendix B, "Internet Addressing Outline.")

Results

Links from this page have the information you are seeking. While polygraph tests are generally barred, there is an exception that appears to allow testing in situations like the one concerning your client.

In addition to this Labor Department document (only the top of which is visible in Figure 5-3), your search also found related Labor Department documents, a copy of the statute involved, memoranda on the topic written by lawyers who posted them at their firms' Web sites, a background paper from the American Civil Liberties Union that would be useful if you had to write a brief on this subject, information on how to get more-detailed information free from the ACLU, and even a resume from a woman who was a key congressional staffer involved in the drafting and enactment of the bill. And these materials were merely among the first of the many thousands of documents located. If you looked at more of them, you would probably find still more useful information—all of this with one search that took only a couple of minutes!

You will also need to check the state law to see whether it bars polygraph testing in such situations. Whether it will be faster to do this on the Internet or through conventional legal research depends largely on how much legal information for your state is available on the Internet.

Comments

Is there any way one could find so much relevant information so rapidly without using the Internet? Much, maybe most, of the useful information found in this particular search is probably not duplicated in Westlaw, LEXIS, or other commercial databases. Internet searches will not always be this easy, but this example is not totally atypical either. It is a good illustration of how an Internet search will often be the fastest as well as the cheapest way to get a particular piece of information.

The preceding example and those that follow are merely intended to give novices a feeling for how searches work. Remember these factors:

- The Internet is particularly strong in federal law areas.
- Search engines are most efficient when you can isolate some unusual keywords that will appear in the documents you are searching for, and in few others.
- The Internet is dynamic. By the time you read these research examples, you may not be able to duplicate some of the searches precisely on your computer. The idea is to illustrate principles that can be adapted to other searches.
- The Internet is so enormous and disorganized that there is usually more than one reasonable way in which to approach a problem.

Search engines are not fungible. They have different objectives, indexing philosophies, and search philosophies. Each search engine indexes the Web, updates its database, conducts searches, and ranks search results differently.

Search engines that try to index the World Wide Web look through databases of files compiled by programs called *spiders* or *bots* that travel from site to site and automatically index the results. When you visit the search engine and type in a search request, the engine searches through its database and finds sites that match the criteria you specify.

Listing the results of a search request in random order would usually be useless, since it is common for tens or hundreds of thousands of documents to be found in response to a request. Good search engines try to add value by engaging in sophisticated analysis of the found documents. They use complicated mathematical formulas to rank the found documents according to how closely they match the criteria specified in your search request.

Confidence Scores

Different search engines rank *hits,* or documents matching your search request, by assigning different weights to various factors. The result of this process is a *confidence score,* sometimes expressed as a percentage, that describes how closely the search engine calculates that a particular Web site matches the criteria in your request.

These are some factors that can affect a page's confidence score:

- The number of times a search word appears in a document;
- Whether the search word appears near the top of a document;
- Whether the search word appears in the title, the text body, or both;
- Whether the search word is in a heading, and how high the heading is (The HTML used to format documents on the World Wide Web allows six heading levels, with H1 the most significant and H6 the least significant.);
- How popular the page is (i.e., how many other sites link to it); and
- Whether the search word appears in a *META tag.*

META tags include page information that will be invisible to casual visitors but will help search engines index it correctly. Some Web site owners engage in *index spamming,* which means using an excessive number of possible search terms in META tags in hopes of causing their sites to gain artificially high rankings. Therefore, some search engines now ignore META tags.

Differences in the formulas used can cause a site that gains a high confidence score on one search engine to rank low on another. One search engine might rank a site number 1 in response to a particular search request, while another ranks it number 34,946 in response to the same request.

One of the more subtle criteria that some search engines use is how many times a search word appears as a percentage of the total words in a document. In other words, a short document in which a search word appears only a few times may score higher than a long document in which the word appears many times.

More information about search engine ranking criteria is included in Chapter 12, "Publicizing a Law Firm Web Site." For legal researchers, the key points to remember are these:

- Each search engine indexes the Web differently and ranks search results differently.
- No search engine indexes more than a fraction of the World Wide Web.

For these reasons, if you need a thorough search, *use more than one search engine* because the results frequently differ. The lack of standardization is one of the biggest challenges of Internet research.

After you have experimented with many search engines, you will probably want to select a few and study their search options in detail. For maximum proficiency, learn how your favorites handle the following:

- Boolean searching (X and Y but not Z)
- Proximity searching (X within ten words of Y)
- Case sensitivity
- Exact matching versus truncation (e.g., if you enter a search request for Goldman, some search engines also return gold mine, Goldstein, etc.)

The Web search engine business is competitive because high user numbers translate into higher advertising rates. Be wary of hype in selecting which search engine to use. For example, having the largest database sounds good, but for most searches the database quality and relevancy-ranking algorithm are more important than database size. The problem on the Internet is usually sifting through a mountain of junk to find the few gems for which you are looking.

Some search engines (including AltaVista) can search databases other than ones indexing the World Wide Web. Usenet newsgroup postings and gopher sites are popular alternatives. The default search is often Web sites only, and you need to make a specific choice if you want to look at an alternative database.

Some search engines allow you to restrict your searches to particular fields, such as titles, images, URLs, dates, and so on. Hotbot and AltaVista are particularly strong in this area. Such restrictions can be extremely helpful in sorting the wheat from the chaff.

Some Major Search Engines

As a consumer convenience, some browsers are equipped with links to a selection of search engines. For example, if you are using Netscape Navigator, select the Net Search button. You can use the Netscape list even if you don't use its Navigator program. Just visit the URL http://home.netscape.com/escapes/search/. A good alternative is at http://www.search.com. Here are brief introductions to a few of the general purpose search engines.

- **AltaVista,** http://www.altavista.com—A popular choice that claims to have the largest database, AltaVista gives a high level of control over search request construction. The Refine feature eases the process of sorting out only the most relevant sites.
- **HotBot,** http://www.hotbot.com—Affiliated with *Wired* magazine, this search engine is a favorite of reviewers. It allows structuring of a search request by graphically selecting search operators instead of typing them in at a command line. HotBot is presently strongest at finding material not in a conventional text format, such as pictures, sound files, video files, or PDF files. Use the Media Type option.
- **Infoseek,** http://www.infoseek.com—Infoseek supplements its computerized data gathering with human review of the results to give it a database that is smaller than some of its competitors but better than average in quality. Search results tend to be more precise (i.e., fewer *false drops,* or irrelevant results) but also to have fewer overall relevant documents returned. Database professionals call this combination "high precision, low recall."
- **Excite,** http://www.excite.com—Excite tries to distinguish itself from its competitors by emphasizing "concept searching," which uses sophisticated analysis of indexed documents to help the search engine return documents that have the idea being searched for, even

though they may not contain the identical words used in the search request. This may produce better results for people who have little online searching experience or are searching in an unfamiliar area where they don't know the buzzwords that experts writing on the subject would use. If you are more interested in finding a few high-quality sites than finding every site containing your keywords, use the Web Guide option, which limits the search to Excite's collection of 140,000 prescreened quality sites.

♦ **Northern Light,** http://www.northernlight.com—Northern Light benefits from two innovations: (1) the use of customized folders to organize search results and (2) optional parallel searching of its "Special Collection," a proprietary database of thousands of journals, books, magazines, databases, and news wires not available on any other search engine. There is a charge of one to four dollars for each document retrieved from the collection. Northern Light's biggest weakness is poor accuracy. In one test, half of the pages returned were irrelevant, with many duplicate links and dead links found.

Meta Search Engines

Meta search engines, sometimes called unified search interfaces, are sites that allow you to submit one search request that is then relayed to one or more search engines simultaneously. Some popular examples are Dogpile, at http://www.dogpile.com, and Metacrawler, at http://www.metacrawler.com.

Meta search engines (which have no relationship to the META tags discussed earlier) have their place, but if you are doing a serious search, you will usually be better off going directly to a particular search engine. Meta search engines typically aim at the lowest common denominator of search engines. They normally do not allow use of the more sophisticated features of each particular search engine. Instead of saving time, they can be slower on balance. The exception to this is if the meta search engine has sophisticated features built in to refine the results you receive. Read the online Help file for the meta search engine to learn exactly what it does, and then experiment.

If you can't find a meta search engine that does what you want, you may be able to purchase some software that will help. There are many programs like WebCompass and Web FastFind that will, with varying degrees of success, help conduct Internet searches and organize the results.

Specialized Search Engines

In addition to the general search engines, there are tens of thousands of specialized search engines that cover narrower databases. If you are aware of a specialized search engine that indexes the type of information you want, it will usually be preferable to using a general search engine. You can find links to many specialized search engines at Internet Sleuth, http://www.isleuth.com.

WhoWhere?, operated by Lycos (http://www.whowhere.lycos.com), is one of many search engines dedicated to helping locate people.

Search engines operated by West Group and Martindale-Hubbell are even more specialized. They search only those companies' proprietary lawyer directories. Go to http://www.wld.com and http://www.martindale.com. (In partnership with Martindale-Hubbell, the ABA offers an enhanced version of that database, the ABA Network Lawyer Locator, at http://www.abanet.org/martindale.html.)

It is a good idea to run your own name through these sites and make sure they are not using inaccurate information. In fact, it is smart to run your name periodically through general purpose search engines as well.

For technical and business reasons, it is common for general search engines to be unable to index the databases served by specialized search engines. The lawyer directory sites are examples of this. Biographical or contact information for a lawyer is often available from these specialized search engines when nothing can be found on the AltaVista-type general purpose powerhouse sites that index millions of Web pages.

There are many specialized search engines of value to lawyers. For example, the Securities and Exchange Commission operates EDGAR, a search engine that indexes a large database of corporate information, including annual 10-K filings, at http://www.sec.gov.

Lawcrawler, http://www.lawcrawler.com, is one of the best specialized search engines for lawyers. Using the popular AltaVista software, it searches a database consisting only of legally oriented Web sites. This reduces the percentage of irrelevant results returned.

Other search engines have an even narrower focus. For example, Findlaw, http://www.findlaw.com, has a search engine that searches only a database of U.S. Supreme Court cases.

The following are two useful sites for lawyers that contain direct links to many specialized search engines:

Meta-Index for U.S. Legal Research, at http://gsulaw.gsu.edu/metaindex/
Lawguru.com, at http://www.lawguru.com/search/lawsearch.html

Lastly, some law firms add search engines to their Web sites. These can index the publicly available sections of the Web site or a specialized database. Adding a search engine to a Web site is not exceptionally difficult, and search engines consistently rate highly in surveys of Web site visitors.

Research Example 5.2: Using a Specialized Search Engine

Specialized search engines can save time. If you were looking for information about the advertising laws related to sweepstakes, for example, using a general purpose search engine like HotBot would result in a mass of mostly irrelevant hits. An experienced researcher might go first to the Lawguru site, http://www.lawguru.com/search/lawsearch.html.

Figures 5-4 and 5-5 show the same site, first as it appears when you arrive and next with the pull-down menu selected. The pull-down menu has links to many different specialized search engines, and one of the choices is Advertising Law. Selecting this takes you to The Advertising Law Web Page, designed by Lew Rose, of Arent, Fox, Kitner, Plotkin & Kahn at http://www.webcom.com/~lewrose/search_form.html, shown in Figure 5.6.

FIGURE 5-4. Lawguru Directory of Specialized Search Engines

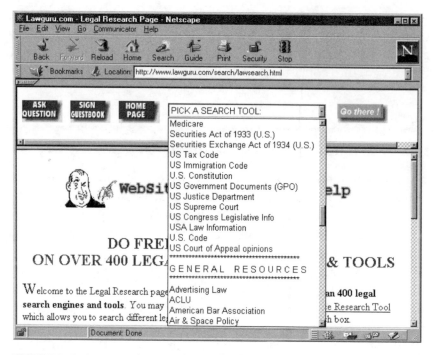

FIGURE 5-5. Lawguru Directory of Specialized Search Engines with Pull-down Menu, selected

Mr. Rose's Web site has plenty of up-to-date information about sweepstakes. As a bonus, if you don't find the answer to your query there, you can navigate to the home page of the site and find the associated Web-based interactive discussion group at http://www.webcom.com/ lewrose/hypernew.html.

Chapter 7 has more information on using discussion groups as research tools.

Tips on Phrasing Search Requests

When phrasing your search request, try to come up with a unique word or phrase that will appear in the documents you want, and no others. For example, if you're looking for information about the drug Stadol, use the name of that drug. If you have a phrase in mind, on most search engines it should be included in quotation marks, like "Wall Street Journal."

In addition, avoid using plurals. Some search engines automatical' look for plurals, while others use truncation—chopping off the end the search term—so they look for plurals automatically. You shoul

CHAPTER **SIX**

Directories

INSTEAD OF searching for particular words or phrases, like search engines do, directories try to organize sites by logic. They arrange hypertext links in a tree-like manner, with broad headings at the top subdivided into narrower categories. The basic idea behind using directories is straightforward. Find the right directory, look for the broad category that is closest to what you want, and then select that link. Repeating the process, keep "drilling down" until you find the material you want. The most difficult part is usually finding the right directory.

There are three general types of directories:

1. *Subject trees* try to be to the Internet what a table of contents is to an encyclopedia. Yahoo (http://www.yahoo.com), Snap (http://www.snap.com), and Looksmart (http://www.looksmart.com) are examples.
2. *Megapages* try to include "pointers" to all significant Internet sites with information on a particular topic. FindLaw (http://www.findlaw.com) is an example of a megapage devoted to law.
3. *Trailblazer pages* are more-focused guides on limited topics. Law firms can create trailblazer pages to demonstrate expertise or attract visitors to the firm's web site. An example is Mark Welch's Probate Law site: (http://www.ca-probate.com.)

Guide, index, subject guide, metapage, and subject index are other terms used to refer to directories.

Research Example 6.1: Using a Directory

Issue

Is the drug known as Phen-Fen considered defective for purposes of product liability?

An Approach

You use Yahoo, http://www.yahoo.com, the most popular Internet directory.

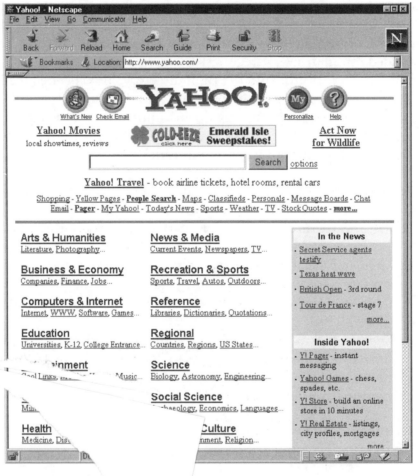

FIGURE 6-1. Yahoo

Under the menu choice "Health," you select "Drugs." You then see the screen as shown in Figure 6-2. You then select "Specific Drugs and Medications."

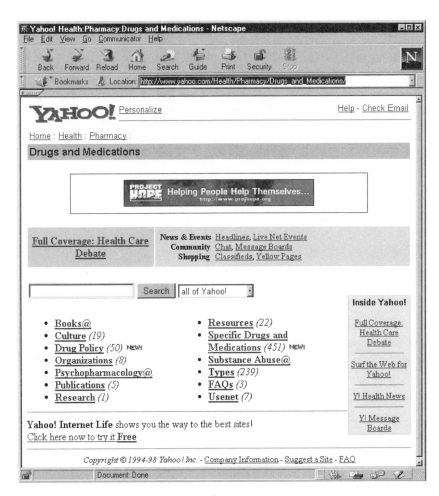

FIGURE 6-2. Yahoo's Section on Specific Drugs

One of the resulting choices to appear on the next screen is Phen-Fen. From there, you can choose from a variety of Web sites devoted to the topic, including at least one plaintiff-oriented law firm site (http://www.dietlaw.com) that provides information about the drug's side effects.

Using Directories vs. Search Engines

Here's a summary of some key differences between directories and search engines:

Directories	*Search Engines*
Like a book's table of contents	Like a book's index
Concepts	Words
Logically ordered	Random access
Assembled by humans	Assembled by computers (i.e., spiders, bots)

Which type of finding aid is better? It depends on various things, including the following:

- The nature of the issue being researched
- Whether you already have a relevant directory bookmarked
- Your personal preferences

In general, directories are good if you have a broad subject area in mind to start your search. If you have an unusual word or phrase that will probably appear in the documents you want and only those documents, a search engine will probably be better.

Search engines demonstrate computers' key strengths: speed and accuracy. They also highlight a major computer disadvantage: blind obedience. Computers cannot think. Though some search engines, like Excite, try to simulate human-type judgment, they still can't do a good job of telling whether a site is logically relevant to the idea you had in mind.

Directories, on the other hand, are compiled by human beings, with the advantages and disadvantages that entails. No human can survey the entire World Wide Web, but humans can exercise judgment, including the best sites and excluding those of marginal value.

When you can consistently make a good decision on whether it is best to use a directory or a search engine for your research projects, you will be on the way to becoming an expert Internet researcher.

Finding Directories

You can find directories through search engines, links from other directories, or books and magazines. Some browser programs provide their users with preconfigured access to a representative sample of directories.

Following are a few of the better general purpose directories:

- **Yahoo** (http://www.yahoo.com)—Yahoo is so important it is discussed in detail in the next section.
- **Magellan** (http://www.mckinley.com)—Magellan adds value through use of a four-star rating system. It also has a fairly good search engine, which takes the place of submenu pages, in an unusual hybrid system. If you can't find what you're looking for among the tens of thousands of rated sites, you can search through hundreds of thousands of unrated sites. You can optionally restrict the search to one of Magellan's top-level directory headings.
- **Argus Clearinghouse** (http://www.clearinghouse.net)—Formerly the University of Michigan Clearinghouse of Subject Matter Index, the Argus directory's great strength is that it is an excellent guide to trailblazer pages.

Lastly, these are two of the newer directories:

Snap (http://www.snap.com)

Looksmart (http://www.looksmart.com)

A Closer Look at Yahoo

Yahoo is probably the most popular Internet research starting point. It includes a search feature as well as its crown jewel: an alphabetically organized hierarchical subject directory. Unlike most Internet directories, Yahoo employs professional librarians to catalog Web sites. It also highlights trailblazer pages (which it calls indices) to make them easier to find.

One of Yahoo's characteristics is both a strength and a weakness: it indexes fewer sites than most of its competitors. Because its human librarians could never keep up with every site being added to the World Wide Web, Yahoo does not aggressively seek out new sites. Whereas search engines like AltaVista employ computer programs to find new Web sites and index every word in them, Yahoo relies mainly on the owners of new Web sites to report those sites and suggest a category in which to place them. Moreover, Yahoo does not catalog every submitted site.

Yahoo's selectiveness is a weakness because it means that the site you are looking for might not be indexed there. It is a strength because search results are easier to manage. There seems to be a higher ratio of substantive sites to worthless ones among those cataloged by Yahoo.

Many wonder about the origin of the name Yahoo. It is an in-joke, standing for "Yet Another Hierarchical Officious Oracle." Yahoo was created by David Filo and Jerry Yang, two Stanford graduate students, for their own use. They decided to post the fruit of their labors publicly on the Internet, and this decision soon led to their becoming multimillionaires.

Yahoo has added a search engine with a special feature. You can narrow the field of topics by using Yahoo's directory and then use the search engine to search *only* the sites within that section of the directory. This reduces the clutter of irrelevant sites typically returned by general purpose search engines.

Yahoo started as just a research tool, but over the years it has worked at becoming a "portal," adding other features such as free e-mail and a versatile geographic map service. The designers of FindLaw used Yahoo's elegant style to create one of the very best legal research starting points, http://www.findlaw.com.

Conventions used by Yahoo are outlined in Figure 6-3.

FIGURE 6-3. Yahoo conventions

Sunglasses icon	Marks the sites that Yahoo considers best.
Bold type	Indicates that the link leads not to an individual Web site but to a submenu with multiple web sites behind it.
A number in parentheses (e.g.: Law Firms (2107))	Shows how many resources are listed behind that hypertext link.
@	Indicates that this heading appears more than once in the directory. Selecting this link takes you to the main appearance of the heading.
New!	Marks a site that has been added within the past three days.
[Xtra!]	Links to Reuters news relevant to that section.

Creating Your Own Directory

It is easy to customize a directory to meet the needs of a law practice. You can translate a bookmark file into HTML format (used for designing World Wide Web pages), so it can more easily be shared by others in your office or even made into the default opening page for your browser. You might have one such default page for your trusts and estates section, for example, and another for your environmental law section. This is a tremendous way to save training time and increase productivity.

There are many HTML editing and conversion programs on the market that make it easy to create HTML pages. Kenneth E. Johnson's book, *The Lawyer's Guide to Creating Web Pages* (American Bar Association: Law Practice Management Section, 1997), is a concise handbook on HTML basics.

HTML is normally thought of as something used to prepare documents for public distribution on the World Wide Web, but it is also a handy tool for sharing information inside an organization by sharing files on disk or, more conveniently, on an intranet, as discussed in Chapter 18, "Collaborative Tools."

CHAPTER **SEVEN**

Internet Discussion Groups

[Internet] search tools take time and experience to master, and skilled researchers often depend more on human "wetware"—intuition and practiced hunches—before proceeding to use software search tools.

—Josh Blackman, with David Jank, *The Internet Fact Finder for Lawyers: How to Find Anything on the Net*

POWERFUL THOUGH they may be, computers are a long way from matching everything that humans know or can do. Internet discussion groups offer a way to tap into the global "wetware" network—the brains of millions of other Internet users.

A New Research Paradigm?

The best use of a new technology is not always obvious. When telephones first came into widespread use, some educated people believed that distributing music would be a major use for them. Kansas farmers, Nevada miners, and Oregon lumberjacks would all be able to hear live symphony orchestras via the telephone.

Television was originally used merely as a kind of radio with a rather static picture added. The standard programming was the classic talking head: an announcer reading a script in a studio. The simple introduction of more visual interest was enough to turn a comedian named Berle into the famed "Uncle Miltie."

Are we making the same type of mistake with the Internet that our predecessors made in the early days of the telephone and television?

Some Internet research and communications techniques are just analogs of conventional methods, but others are not. The new technology makes possible some research techniques that don't have any counterpart off the Internet.

Imagine that you live in a city that continually hosts thousands of year-round international conferences of people interested in particular fields, many of them related to law. Many of the attendees are world-class experts, while others are first-time visitors. Imagine further that this city is set in a science-fiction type universe that lets anyone, anywhere in the world attend these conventions, with no admission fee and no transportation expenses. Just by stepping out their front door, anyone can participate in any of these conventions.

No, there's nothing like this off the Internet!

As Burgess Allison explains in his ground-breaking book, *The Lawyer's Guide to the Internet:*

> For many solos and small firm practitioners, in particular, the art of networking . . . is an important part of practicing in a specific field of law. Meeting people and making the right connections—it's all part of learning who to know and knowing who to ask. As it turns out, one of the key *strengths* of the Net is exactly this type of networking—using net-based discussion groups that cover a broad range of legal specialties and interest groups.

There are three basic types of Internet discussion groups:

1. Mailing lists
2. Newsgroups
3. Web-based discussion groups

Following are examples of legal interest mailing lists:

◆ On Cornell University's LAWSRC-L list, a criminal defense lawyer asks a question about "porcelain chips." He receives a blizzard of responses, including discussions of legal and illegal uses for them, such as how they can be used as a burglar tool, references to statutes outlawing them, and litigation involving them. Much of the useful information provided is not readily retrievable through commercial online services or other conventional legal research sources.

◆ On the ABA's NETWORK2D-L list, a query about the discoverability of information that has been erased from a computer hard disk but is recoverable through the use of various utilities provokes a discussion that covers the legal and technical issues involved in detail.

- On the NET-LAWYERS list, a question about a source for information on the ratings of construction sureties (bonding companies) produces rapid answers from a lawyer with a Washington firm specializing in the area and a law school professor.
- On the Virginia Attorneys Network list, a Virginia attorney living in London obtains information about events back in Richmond that he could not easily get any other way.
- On several lists for law librarians, including PRIVATELAWLIB-L, legal research "stumper" questions are asked and answered on a daily basis.

These examples only touch the surface. Thousands of lawyers and law librarians are already benefiting from the informal marketplace of information that has developed on the hundreds of existing Internet discussion groups designed for the legal profession. And this is only the legal network. When it comes to forums for factual research, the possibilities are even more exciting, since the relevant discussion groups number in the tens of thousands instead of in the hundreds.

The best news is that this research technique will only become more useful as more lawyers learn how to participate and the number of available specialized forums increases.

Why It Works

As a method of research, discussion groups at first seem a little odd to most people who are not familiar with the Internet. It sounds suspicious, right? This would not usually be an efficient research method *off* the Internet. Assuming that you can find the expert you need, why is he or she going to talk to you for free?

The Internet information marketplace is alien to our experience. Why can Net-based discussion groups work so well? One key is the Internet's ability to reduce transaction costs.

For a great many questions that lawyers need to research, there is probably at least one person in the world who

(a) knows the answer, and

(b) would be glad to tell you the answer at no charge, as long as there is little or no inconvenience or expense.

Before the Internet, there was no consistent, inexpensive way for information seekers to find parties with the needed knowledge, and vice versa. The transaction cost of finding someone who had the information you needed and was willing to give it to you would usually be higher than the cost of researching it yourself.

The Internet radically changes this equation. It provides an inexpensive way for the seekers and those with knowledge to get together. On some questions, you may be the seeker. On others, you may be the one who knows the answer. In either case, the Internet allows the easy transfer of information.

Getting Good Results

This method of research is not yet perfect. *It's easy to waste time and even offend people if you do not know what you are doing.* It presently requires sophistication and judgment to use this technique effectively. However, the Internet is still evolving and the information marketplace will improve over time. (This is a prime target area for the deployment of intelligent software agents; sophisticated software that can perform complex tasks.) There will probably be technical improvements in the way Internet discussion groups are operated, including more specialization, better filtering tools, and improved archiving. With such enhanced usefulness, it's conceivable that interactive Internet research could become a dominant research technique in a few decades.

You don't, however, need to wait that long to benefit from Internet discussion groups. They already can be useful if you know what you are doing, and they can produce remarkable results in some cases. When confronted with a difficult research problem, instead of going to the library or searching through Internet databases, try to use the Internet to find someone who knows the answer to your question and just have him or her explain it to you. You might do a little library research first, but only enough to help you phrase your question intelligently.

While this method will not work for every question, after mastering the basics most users will get some good results. In the hands of a skilled researcher, it can produce extraordinary results. You might need to visit a paper library after obtaining an answer, if you think you need to verify it, but this will often be unnecessary.

The key to success is finding the right place to post your question. Some specialized areas are covered much better than others. Among the tens of thousands of newsgroups alone, there is one devoted to nearly every conceivable computer-related and pop culture topic. There are many fewer for areas like automotive or medical discussions. Fortunately, this mix is gradually changing as more and more people discover that you don't have to be a computer geek or a teenage rock music fan to use the Internet.

The Virtual Hallway

Many solo and small law firm practitioners complain that they lack mentors, or others whom they can bounce ideas off. Discussion groups can go a long way toward solving this problem. Now solo lawyers don't have to attend bar meetings to get friendly advice. Geographically isolated lawyers can readily find help. Legal specialists can share views with their peers, located literally anywhere in the world.

The need for peer interaction is probably why the ABA's SOLOSEZ mailing list for sole practitioners is one of the busiest around. You can get subscription information and check the archives at this URL: http://www.abanet.org/discussions/open.html.

Discussion groups are often a good way to get information, such as the following, that is not readily available through conventional research techniques, on or off the Internet:

- ◆ What approaches do expert lawyers take to particular problems?
- ◆ What are the practical risks and consequences of various legal alternatives?
- ◆ What are the most recent significant developments in a field of law?

Good discussion groups excel at tough, real-world questions like these. In many cases you can get free insights from recognized experts in these forums. Some groups number world-class experts and authors of leading treatises among their subscribers.

Mailing Lists

Mailing lists are discussion groups distributed by e-mail. There are thousands of Internet mailing lists. Hundreds are designed specifically for or have strong appeal to lawyers. You can read them to monitor developments and public discussions of an area of law in which you have a strong interest, or you can use them to seek advice when you have a specific question.

Research Example 7.1: Using a Mailing List

Issue

Is there any evidentiary or ethical bar to calling a witness in a civil case who is expected to invoke the privilege against self-incrimination?

An Approach

Two possibile discussion groups come to mind: the Web-based legal ethics forum at Counsel Connect (http://www.counsel.com), or the Legal Ethics mailing list sponsored by Washburn University, LEGALETHICS-L. Suppose that you try the latter. If you are already a subscriber, you can ask your question by simply posting an e-mail message addressed to legalethics-l@lawlib.wuacc.edu.

If you are not already a subscriber, you can become one by sending a message to the address mailing list@lawlib.wuacc.edu with only the message: *subscribe legalethics-l*. You will receive a message explaining how the list commands work. Print and save this message. Note that each list may have some subtle differences in its working mechanisms.

Results

When someone asked this very question on this mailing list, it provoked seventeen replies over the course of three days. Participants in the discussion included leading practitioners and state bar ethics officials as well as teachers at some of the country's finest law schools. Cases, statutes, and ethics rules were cited, and the policy considerations involved were explored in some detail.

In addition to being a time-saver, this "interactive" research method produced results that likely would never have been obtained through conventional research. One of the mailing list subscribers, a law school professor who was drafting an as-yet-unpublished official ethics opinion on the subject, shared the opinion. Mailing list subscribers not only learned the existing law, they learned what the law *would* be.

How Mailing Lists Work

All except the smallest mailing lists are operated by programs called *mail reflectors* or, more colorfully, *mail exploders*. These programs take messages sent to them and forward a copy to everyone on the list of subscribers.

The term *listserv* is frequently used to describe any Internet mailing list. However, just as Coca Cola is only one brand of cola beverage, Listserv is just one of several brands of commercial software used to manage mailing lists. (See http://www.lsoft.com.) Listproc and Majordomo are two other programs frequently used to operate large mailing lists.

To subscribe to a mailing list, typically you need only send an e-mail message in a specified format to the appropriate address. For example, to subscribe to a list about bankruptcy law named BANKRLAW (some mailing list software restricts list names to eight letters, resulting in occasional odd-looking spelling and acronyms), operated by the University of Indiana Law School, you would send an e-mail message to this address: listproc@polecat.law.indiana.edu.

The body of the message should say only: *subscribe bankrlaw Your Name*

Leave the subject line blank. If you deviate from the prescribed format, you will likely receive an automated error message, usually with enough information to let you figure out what you did wrong (e.g., having a signature file or other extraneous text in the body of your message).

If your message was successful, you will usually receive an introductory message with information about the list. *Save this message.* It may come in handy six months later when you are trying to stop your subscription or trying to remember the command you need to track down a message you saw posted to the list a month ago.

Mailing lists may be moderated or unmoderated, public or private. A moderated list has a human being in control. Moderation styles vary, with some moderators screening all messages before they are distributed to the list. Other moderators merely try to guide the discussion, staying in the background as much as possible. In general, moderated lists are more likely to be valuable, since a good moderator will help reduce the number of irrelevant messages. This is called "improving the signal-to-noise ratio."

Knowledgeable, patient lawyers willing to devote their time to moderating discussion groups are not in overly abundant supply. If you locate a group with such a moderator, consider it a real find.

Some lists are open to anyone who wants to subscribe, while others require a moderator's approval or membership in a particular organization.

The best resource to keep up with legally oriented lists is a free directory called Lawlists maintained by a University of Chicago professor named Lyonette Louis-Jacques. It is available through http://www.lib.uchicago.edu/~llou/lawlists/info.html or by sending an e-mail to llou@midway.uchicago.edu.

Potential Problems and How to Avoid Them

Mailing list software distinguishes between two different types of messages. Some messages are intended for distribution to all subscribers. Others are commands intended for administrative use only: for example, a request to be removed from the list, or to "unsubscribe." In the previously used example, this would be phrased *unsubscribe bankrlaw Your Name.*

More sophisticated commands are frequently available. For example, the command syntax used with Listproc brand software to get information about other subscribers would be *recipients bankrlaw.*

Other useful commands will let you get information about the list. You can view available commands (*help bankrlaw*), review old messages (*index bankrlaw*), omit your name from the publicly accessible list of subscribers (*set bankrlaw conceal yes*), and so on. All these examples include the name of the particular list (here, *bankrlaw*) because the same software is frequently used to run many different lists, and it is necessary to specify the one to which the command applies.

A chart listing commands for the most commonly used types of mailing lists is available at http://www.netlawtools.com.

It is critical that you send your messages to *the right address.* There are usually two different mailing list addresses, one for administrative messages and one for messages intended for distribution to the other subscribers. For the BANKRLAW list, the mailing list address is bankrlaw@polecat.law.indiana.edu. The administrative address is listproc@polecat.law.indiana.edu. Hundreds, or even thousands of other subscribers, will consider you thoughtless if you misdirect your administrative messages (like an "unsubscribe" request) into their mailboxes.

Another common problem is using the e-mail software Reply option to make a private reply. Suppose that you want to reply privately to a posting from "Tom." With most e-mail software, using the Reply option in response to Tom's list posting will cause your reply to be distributed to every list subscriber, not just Tom. This could be embarrassing. If you want your reply to be private, get Tom's e-mail address from his message and start a new message to him, instead of using the Reply button.

Yet another problem is the "on vacation" loop mistake. Some e-mail software gives you the option of sending an automatic reply to any e-mail that you receive. Some people use this feature when they are going to be out of their office for a time. Using automatic replies like this can have disastrous results if you are subscribing to an automated mailing list, because any time the mailing list sends you a message, your software replies with an "on vacation" message that goes out to all mailing list subscribers. An out-of-control loop can easily generate hundreds of messages in a short time, to the great annoyance of the other subscribers. (See the sidebar on this page for advice on handling such a problem.)

You need to be careful about what you say in any posting, since you have no control over it after it leaves your computer. You can't cancel or recall a message you have posted to a mailing list, and you have no idea where it may be reposted. Don't post anything on a mailing list that would cause embarrassment if it were read by your mother—or your most important client.

Another danger to watch for on mailing lists is inadvertently being drawn into *flame wars*. There is something about the psychology of electronic communications that makes many otherwise sensible people act irrationally. Maintain your dignity. Refuse to let yourself fall into exchanges of demeaning messages. Fortunately, flame wars and contentious arguments are less common on mailing lists than on newsgroups. Some newsgroups at times sound like conversations during happy hour at a bar where 10 percent of the customers have just escaped from a psychiatric hospital. Mailing lists, especially those frequented largely by lawyers, tend to sound more like gatherings of scholars or professionals.

▼ ▼ ▼ ▼ ▼

Stopping an Out-of-Control Loop.
Mailing list loops can become major problems if not stopped promptly. Most lists automatically send you a copy of any message you post to the list. If you set up an auto-responder, when it receives any message, it automatically sends out another "on vacation" message, and so on. In short order, this type of loop can generate enough messages to fill a LAN's hard drive, crashing an entire network, and greatly annoying the other list subscribers.

If you subscribe to a mailing list where such a problem is occurring, do *not* post a reply to the mailing list. This will merely create a new loop and worsen the problem. Instead, send an e-mail message to the address of postmaster@domain.com, where *domain.com* is the domain name of the place where the loop started. *Postmaster* is the title to the person responsible for running an organization's e-mail.

Newsgroups: Another Interactive Forum

Newsgroups are discussion groups in which messages are distributed differently from regular e-mail. Most are distributed via *Usenet*. Like mailing lists, they are a way of bringing together people with special interests. They are collections of publicly available messages on various topics.

Each message is called an *article*. No continuing subscription is necessary to read the messages or post them on the list.

There are more than 20,000 categories, ranging from the serious (e.g., misc.int-property, for intellectual property discussion) to the technical (e.g., comp.dcom.modems, for discussion of technical modem issues) to the frivolous (e.g., alt.barney.die.die.die, for people who don't like purple TV dinosaurs). More newsgroups are being added all the time.

Newsgroup names are arranged in a hierarchical format, with the general category identifier on the left. Figure 7-1 shows some major top-level newsgroup categories.

FIGURE 7-1. Top-level Newsgroup Categories

Identifier	*Category*	*Example*
biz	Business	biz.jobs.offered
comp	Computers	comp.ibm.software.microsoft.word
news	General news	news.announce.newusers
rec	Recreational	rec.games.chess
soc	Social	soc.rights.human
talk	Debate/Discussion	talk.environment
misc	Miscellaneous	misc.legal.computing
alt	Alternative	alt.business.import.export

The *alt* category has a high percentage of pop culture and sexually oriented groups. This is because starting an alt group does not require compliance with the same formalities that are necessary to start a new group with any other identifier.

A few newsgroups deal with legal topics, including:

♦ misc.legal
♦ misc.legal.moderated
♦ misc.legal.computing
♦ can.legal (Canadian law)

The most useful newsgroups for lawyers are probably *not* those dealing with legal topics. The law-related newsgroups generally have what is called a low signal-to-noise ratio. In other words, too many of the messages are from people who want to talk about the contemporary equivalent of the O.J. Simpson trial, to get free legal advice, or to discuss the low ethical standards of the legal profession, especially the slimy specimen who represented the poster's wife during his divorce.

On the other hand, nonlegal newsgroups can be an exceptional source of technical information. For example, they are a great place to find expert witnesses or get advice on a computer problem.

Just like mailing lists, newsgroups can be moderated or unmoderated. The open nature of newsgroups means that there tend to be a higher percentage of frivolous postings on the average newsgroup than there are on a good mailing list. On the other hand, newsgroups messages are not distributed automatically to all subscribers. You decide when you want to visit a newsgroup, and no message is sent to your computer if you did not request it. You can survey the list of messages and download only the messages or threads that look promising.

▼ ▼ ▼ ▼ ▼

The difference between mailing lists and newsgroups is the difference between inviting a group of friends over for wine on a Sunday evening and putting a billboard that says "Free Booze Here!!!" in your front yard.

—*"Lazlo Nibble," in* Wired

Here are some resources that can be used to search or keep track of Usenet newsgroups:

- **DejaNews** (http://www.dejanews.com)—specializes in newsgroup searching.
- **HotBot** (http://www.hotbot.com/usenet)—has a newsgroup searching feature.
- **Reference.com** (http://www.reference.com)—searches Usenet as well as selected mailing lists and Web-hosted discussion forums.

Newsgroups are distributed by a technically different mechanism than regular e-mail, but many of the same principles apply for users (i.e., don't waste bandwidth, use a signature block, read the group's policies before asking questions, etc.).

Newsgroups are more convenient than mailing lists in that you don't have to make an ongoing commitment to them in the same way you do to a mailing list. You tune in to a newsgroup only when you want to, so there is no mailbox clutter.

A good newsgroup reading program makes it easy to sort through a large volume of messages and find the ones you want. You can do light newsgroup reading with a Web browser like Netscape Navigator, but for serious use, you are better off with a specialized newsreader program. Check a software distribution site like http://www.tucows.com for current recommendations. A program called Gravity has many options and is my current favorite.

Web-Based Discussion Groups

Web-based discussion groups are interactive discussions hosted by Web sites. They are an alternative to mailing lists and newsgroups. The Legalethics.com Web site, at http://www.legalethics.com/webethics.htm, hosts the WebEthics discussion group for ethics issues posed by lawyer Internet use. Figure 7-2 illustrates the site's screen.

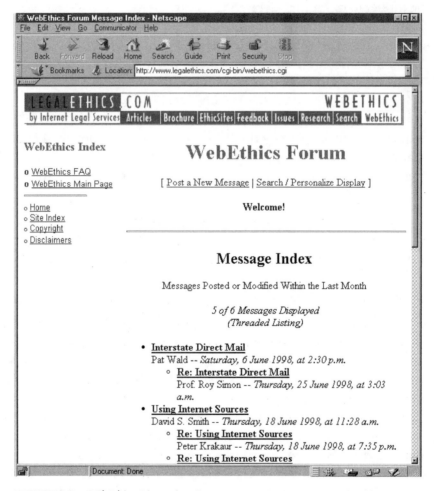

FIGURE 7-2. WebEthics Discussion Group

The usefulness of Web-based discussion groups depends largely on the number and knowledge level of the users. A critical mass of users and message volume are needed. Some Web sites offer the option of having copies of posted messages sent to users by e-mail, which can be particularly worthwhile at useful but low-volume Web-based discussion groups.

Counsel Connect stands out among Web-based discussion group providers as of this writing. It is a popular, relatively inexpensive Web-based service for lawyers that offers approximately fifty high-quality discussion groups in addition to its other features. The URL is http://www.counsel.com.

Because Counsel Connect restricts its user base to lawyers and law-related professionals, the quality of its Web-based discussion groups tends to be far superior to most newsgroups—and on a par with the very best e-mail-based discussion groups.

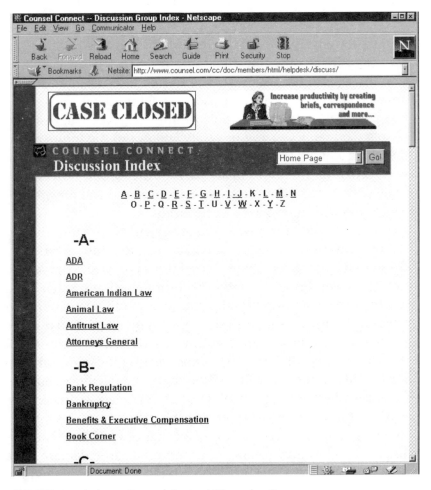

FIGURE 7-3. Index to Counsel Connect Discussion Groups

Asking Questions

Once you have found an appropriate discussion group for posting a question, you can increase your chances of success in several ways. The first is by phrasing the subject line of your question so it will attract the attention of someone knowledgeable. This is important because busy Internet users who are confronted by more information than they have time to read often decide which queries to read based solely on the sender and the subject line. Don't use a subject line that says only "Please Help," as many people do.

You should also do enough preliminary research so that you can phrase an intelligent question. Knowledgeable experts tend to ignore poorly phrased or elementary questions.

In addition, consider the overall efficiency of the process and take measures to improve it, including the following:

◆ Don't ask trivial questions that you should be able to find the answer to easily by other means.

◆ Don't cross-post (i.e., ask your question in more than one forum) unless you have a particular reason for doing so.

◆ If you ask a question that is only of interest to you, suggest that people send replies to you privately and not to the forum at large.

◆ If you ask a question that you expect will result in multiple answers and is of interest to many users of the forum, save everyone time by suggesting that those who answer send you private replies, which you will summarize for the group.

◆ If necessary, verify the advice you are given. Maybe the advice you received was from someone who has an ax to grind, or who doesn't know as much about the subject as he or she thinks. Sometimes you won't need to verify the information. It is often enough just to have something explained to you. In other situations, when a significant issue or amount of money is involved, you may want to do some further work to confirm that an answer is accurate, but this will usually still be easier than answering the question from scratch. Many answers will include suggested reference sources.

◆ Consider whether the particular question you are asking or the particular forum in which you are asking it makes it desirable not to flaunt your identity as a lawyer, or that of your firm. For example, if you wanted to find an expert on a particular rare disease to serve as a witness in a medical malpractice case, you might get better results in a medical professional-oriented mailing list if your signature block did not identify you as an lawyer. Having a tagline in your signature block that reads "Aggressive Pursuit of Claims Against Negligent Doctors Our Speciality" would not be wise.

Accounts with Web-based e-mail services like Hotmail (http://www.hotmail.com) or Yahoo Mail (http://www.yahoo.com) are an alternative for those who want to maintain some privacy. Commercial online services like AOL, Prodigy, and CompuServe are another possibility.

Free *anonymous remailers* will take e-mail messages, strip the identifying information from the headers, and then forward the messages to their ultimate destination. Some anonymous remailers can accept replies and forward them, using a secret database matching pseudonyms and real users. The advantage of this is that a recipient can answer even though he or she does not know who sent the message or where the response is going. The disadvantage is that the anonymous users must trust the integrity of the remailer service provider to keep the database private.

You can find Web sites with up-to-date information about remailers by going to http://www.yahoo.com and looking around for anonymous remailer addresses. Some discussion groups will not allow anonymous postings, and even in those that do, you may find some reluctance by other subscribers to reply to anonymous subscribers.

Why Answer?

When someone posts a question you can answer well, *do so*. This applies particularly in a forum on which you frequently rely for answers from others. I find that in forums where I frequently help other subscribers, I get a better response than most other subscribers when I post my own questions.

In addition to increasing the "yield" you get when you post a question yourself, in some forums developing a reputation as an expert willing to share your expertise can boost your networking or marketing efforts, as discussed in Chapter 13, "Marketing via Discussion Groups."

More Interactive Research Tips

The biggest disadvantage of this form of research is that you can waste a lot of time if you are not careful. You may find the volume you receive from several active mailing lists, or even one very active mailing list, overwhelming. One mailing list alone can easily have forty or more messages a day. Here are some techniques to help you handle a high volume of messages:

- Make sure that you have easy to use and powerful e-mail software (as explained in Chapter 3).
- Once you have good software, learn to use its power. For example, you can create a separate folder for each mailing list, then set up a filter that sorts your mailing list messages automatically into the right folder. That way, you don't have to deal with the clutter until it is convenient to do so.
- Save time by setting up filters that automatically delete messages meeting criteria you specify, either on a topic you are not interested in (a *kill file*) or from a person whose opinions you don't care to read (a *bozo filter*).
- Be cautious in using the Digest option provided by some busy lists. The idea sounds good, but in general, this makes it harder to save individual messages that can be useful.
- Be selective in your subscriptions and reevaluate them periodically. Lists change over time. The subscriber base, level of activity, and utility can change radically. If a list is no longer helping you, cancel it and reduce the mailbox clutter.

Yield Management

If you participate in discussion groups, regularly compare the benefit you receive from a particular group against the time you invest in monitoring it. If this "yield ratio" is poor, drop the group. There's no way to calculate the yield ratio with mathematical precision, but you should be making rough estimates and monitoring the yield ratio continuously. Why continue subscribing to a paper journal that no longer helps you? The same logic applies to discussion group membership.

You may find that there is a discussion group that you enjoy reading but it does not give you any practical benefit. Perhaps the discussions in alt.society.civil-liberty or alt.fan.rush.limbaugh have little to do with your legal practice, but you like participating. However, be sure that you are making a conscious decision to take that time out of your work day for recreation. Don't pretend that it's work and then wonder why you're spending so much time doing Internet legal research.

One way to avoid wasting time in discussion groups is having a reliable assistant screen the message traffic and draw only the most interesting to your attention. Another approach is to divide the responsibility for monitoring the discussion groups relevant to your practice among several lawyers in your firm.

Some mailing lists are used as electronic newsletters, one-way conduits of information, not two-way discussions. For example, the Environmental Protection Agency uses EPA-PRESS to distribute its press releases and the EPAFR-CONTENTS mailing list as an inexpensive way to distribute the table of contents of the entire *Federal Register,* not just the EPA sections. (Subscribe by sending the message *subscribe epa-press Your Name* to listserver@unixmail.rtpnc.epa.gov. If your interests are more specialized, you can use the same format to subscribe to the following other lists operated on the same server: EPA-AIR, EPA-GENERAL, EPA-IMPACT, EPA-MEETINGS, EPA-PEST, EPA-SAB, EPA-SPECIES, EPA-TAX, EPA-TRI, EPA-WASTE, and EPA-WATER).

The free immigration law e-mail newsletter put out by the firm of Siskind, Susser, Haas & Devine is another example. It originated as a marketing tool, but founder Greg Siskind reports that practicing lawyers and even government officials with responsibilities in immigration law are among the tens of thousands of subscribers. For subscription information, see http://www.visalaw.com.

Private Discussion Groups

Private discussion groups have been the most productive single Internet feature in my own legal practice. Most discussion groups are open to anyone. Private groups restrict membership to those meeting specified criteria. Some are by invitation only. When I was lucky enough to be invited to participate in a private discussion group restricted to lawyers whose clients shared interests similar to my clients, my legal research workload dropped by at least 50 percent.

Furthermore, I found that I tended to get more enjoyment from the research that I did perform. Owing to my experience as a law clerk in a court with a heavy criminal docket, and later as a prosecutor, the criminal law and evidence questions that confused some other lawyers in the group were often simple for me. Even when I did not know the answer, I could usually find it quickly. I could frequently provide not just substantive law but practical advice (e.g., on the timing and phrasing of objections or the predilections of particular judges). Many things a lawyer needs to know are not in any law book or computer database.

On the other hand, before I was invited to join the private discussion group, I had great difficulty in dealing with questions on labor law. I had little experience in that area and usually had no idea where to even begin looking for the answer. My situation improved dramatically after I was invited to participate in the private discussion group. I began to post to the list the questions that were difficult for me. I was seldom disappointed in the quality or timeliness of the answers. At one of the periodic face-to-face meetings of the organization sponsoring the discussion group, two other subscribers expressed sentiments similar to mine:

- ◆ "When I send a question out there, I'm amazed at the quality of answers I get in a half hour or hour."
- ◆ "It's the first thing I check in the morning and the last thing I check every evening."

By pooling our knowledge through the Internet, we improved the quality of legal services we provided, while making our lives easier at the same time.

While public discussion groups can be valuable, good private discussion groups tend to be more useful because a sense of community develops. Other users know that I always try to provide good answers to criminal law and evidence questions, so when they see I am again struggling with what is to me an obscure question, the experts in that area go out of their way to help me.

Groups whose members share similar interests are the most likely to be useful. While a certain critical mass is necessary, private groups may dilute their sense of community if they grow too large.

The ABA hosts many private discussion groups. For information, check out http://www.abanet.org/discussions/closed.html.

Becoming an Internet Leader

Suppose that, from among the thousands already in existence, you can't find a mailing list that matches your practice needs. Consider starting your own mailing list, either public or private. Think about other lawyers with interests similar to yours. The Internet makes it easy to construct a "virtual community" of lawyers united not by geography but by mutual interests or shared expertise.

For example, if I represented the plaintiffs in a couple of breast implant cases, I would consider starting a closed mailing list to share information with other plaintiffs' lawyers. As another example, if I were a California lawyer who frequently represented defendants in drunk driving cases, I would start a closed mailing list for defense attorneys if I did not think the existing national DWI defense list was specific enough.

How much does it cost to run a list? You can operate a small list with a regular e-mail account and good e-mail software. Some Internet service providers will handle the technical details of larger multiple lists run by the same list owner for about twenty-five dollars a month. Some universities operate lists as a public service, as does the ABA. You could save a few dollars this way, but many people who are interested in starting a list would prefer to retain sole control of it. (If your list becomes very popular, you may even be able to sell the right to put advertising banners at the bottom of each message, since some lists have demographics highly attractive to advertisers.)

A moderated list will probably be better received by subscribers, as long as you avoid actions that could be interpreted as censorship. A good secretary or paralegal should be able to handle most of the day-to-day work of running a mailing list. Caution: Don't underestimate the time commitment required to monitor a list. Many law firms tend to discount the unbillable time spent by support staff. If you're going to operate a list, devote the time and attention necessary to do it right. Being the owner or moderator of a mailing list has many benefits:

- It can help you develop a valuable network of contacts.
- It can help you stay on top of timely developments in an area of great interest to you.
- It can help you develop or enhance a reputation as a regional or national leader in a particular area of law.
- It can give you the satisfaction of providing a service to other lawyers and improving the legal profession.

Conclusion

Smart lawyers will learn to use the new forms of human interactivity that Internet technology makes possible.

Don't fall into the trap of thinking of the Internet as just a "free Westlaw" or "the world's largest public library, automated." It partially (and only partially) fits both of those descriptions. However, the Internet also offers possibilities that have no counterpart off-line. This new frontier of interactive Internet research is already more valuable in some ways than any of the conventional research tools we now use, and it will only become more useful.

CHAPTER **EIGHT**

Legal Research

SOME LEGAL RESEARCHERS new to the Internet think that it will replace their paper libraries, compact discs, and Westlaw and LEXIS subscriptions. This may happen eventually, but it is not a realistic short-term expectation.

Just as paper libraries have not been eliminated more than twenty years after LEXIS online research became available, the Internet will not soon replace traditional alternatives. For the next few years, the Internet will supplement, not supplant older resources.

Various legal resource materials are now available on the Internet:

- Statutes, including current and proposed, federal, and many states'
- Legislative documents, primarily federal
- Regulations, including the Code of Federal Regulations, *the Federal Register,* and some state materials
- Cases, including U.S. Supreme Court cases for most of the twentieth century, all recent cases from all U.S. courts of appeals, and some state cases, but few trial court opinions
- Legal news, with online versions of publications like *Law Journal Extra, Lawyers Weekly USA,* and many others
- Secondary sources, including many memoranda from practicing lawyers and some law reviews
- Legal research aids, including searchable databases, hypertext indices to particular areas of law, and hundreds of discussion groups focusing on various areas of law
- Archived articles, with many legal organizations, such as the American Trial Lawyers Association, providing current issues and archived articles for their publications

FIGURE 8-1. FindLaw, A Favorite Legal Research Starting Point

The Internet as a Legal Research Environment

The Internet's strengths as a legal research tool are currently in the following areas:

- Federal law and regulations
- Monographs on legal subjects written by practicing lawyers
- Current developments too new to be conveniently available elsewhere
- Some specialty areas like intellectual property and high-tech law

- Some obscure material that is hard to find elsewhere
- Interactive research techniques that have no counterpart off the Internet

An impressive number of legal research tools are available on the Net, and the number of high-quality research sources is increasing rapidly. Coverage, however, is still spotty. It's weak when dealing with case law, especially state case law and cases that are more than a few years old. The organizations that have begun putting free case law on the Internet are starting with the most recent cases. Few of them have begun to work backwards.

There is no free Internet equivalent of a service like Shepard's, and it's unlikely that such a service will be developed in the foreseeable future. This is just too big a project for any one law school to undertake at this time.

One of the most pleasant aspects of Internet legal research is that nearly all the databases are free. The better universities around the country are racing to improve their reputations and provide a public service by putting legal material on the Internet. The relatively low cost of placing material on the Net makes it easy for anyone to become a "publisher." As you might imagine, conventional legal publishers are not entirely enthusiastic about this development.

Still, many of the legal research sources that lawyers use are not yet available, and material on the Internet is generally less well organized. On the other hand, the Internet has some valuable legal resources that are not available through its commercial competitors. In addition, for certain types of research, the Internet is easier to use or more efficient than the paper and commercial service alternatives. It is not that the Internet is better or worse than a paper library, compact discs, Westlaw, or LEXIS. It is simply *different.* Figure 8-2 on page 116 compares the key factors.

Proprietary Legal Databases on the Net

Both Westlaw and LEXIS can be accessed via the Internet at their normal rates. There are also commercial competitors with smaller databases, but significantly lower rates, including:

- Versuslaw, or V., from Versuslaw, Inc., http://www.versuslaw.com
- LOIS Law Library, from Law Office Information Systems, Inc., http://www.pita.com

FIGURE 8-2. Online Commercial Research Services vs. the Net

Proprietary Online Databases (Westlaw, LEXIS, Dialog, etc.)	*The Internet*
High hourly or monthly charges are involved.	Most services are free.
Nearly all the most commonly used case law is readily available.	Case law coverage is spotty, with very few older cases (i.e., pre-1990) available.
Publishers consistently take measures to ensure information quality and timeliness.	Publishers have inconsistent standards for quality and timeliness.
Many law reviews and some other secondary sources are included, but few memoranda from practicing lawyers.	Some recent law review issues are on the Net, and a few are available nowhere else, with many memoranda from practicing lawyers available.
Primarily legal and business information is covered.	Legal and business information is a minority in the total mix.
Shepard's and similar cite-checking is available.	There is no real equivalent to Shepard's.
Centralized "help desk" is accessible by phone.	A few sites have help features, but users who need assistance usually have to rely on ad hoc support networks like discussion groups.
Each service uses only one search interface.	There are many different search engine interfaces.
Some have added value through keynotes, digests, etc.	Similar value-added features are rare.

Citation Issues

When you find a case on the Internet, you are usually dealing with the equivalent of a slip opinion. There is as yet no standardized numbering system that most courts are willing to accept.

The citation dilemma, though, is improving. Efforts are underway to develop a standardized public domain citation system. When court opinions can be published almost instantaneously over the Internet, reliance on book volume and page numbers becomes archaic. Instead of using arbitrarily assigned reporter names and volume and page numbers to designate cases, the system would use more logical and universal information, such as the name of the court, the year an opinion was issued, the sequence number under that year's cases, and the paragraph number. These are sometimes called *vendor neutral* systems.

For example, under the current ABA proposal, a citation to the eighth paragraph of the tenth decision issued in 1998 by the U.S. District Court for the Eastern District of Virginia would read as follows: 1998 EDVA 10, 8. The ABA's Official Citation Resolutions are at http://www.abanet.org/citation/home.html.

Widespread adoption of a uniform system of vendor neutral citation would be a major advance for legal researchers nationwide. Courts across the country have begun to adopt vendor neutral citation systems, but unfortunately they are not uniform.

West Publishing Company admits that citing to the volume number and first page number of the cases in their system of reporters is a "fair use" under the copyright law. However, they assert that the other elements of their reporter system, particularly the page numbers, except for the page number on which a case begins, are protected by copyright. LEXIS is allowed to use these numbers under a license granted by West after some litigation a few years ago.

The sixteenth edition of *A Uniform System of Citation,* familiarly known as "The Blue Book," provides the following advice at Rule 17.3.3, under "Internet Sources":

> Because of the transient nature of many Internet sources, citation to Internet sources is discouraged unless the materials are unavailable in printed form or are difficult to obtain in their original form. When citing to materials found on the Internet, provide the name of the author (if any), the title or top-level heading of the material being cited, and the Uniform Resource Locator (URL). The Uniform Resource Locator is the electronic address of the information and should be given in angled brackets. For electronic journals and publications, the actual date of publication should be given. Otherwise, provide the most recent modification date of the source preceded by the term "last modified" or the date of access preceded by the term "visited" if the modification date is unavailable:

> Mark Israel, *The alt.usage.english FAQ File* (last modified Nov. 17, 1995) ⟨ftp:rtfm.mit.edu/pub/usenet/alt.usage/english/alt.usage.english_FAQ⟩.

Citations to journals that appear only on the Internet should include the volume number, the title of the journal, and the sequential article number. Pinpoint citations should refer to the paragraph number, if available:

> Dan L. Burk, *Trademarks Along the Infobahn: A First Look at the Emerging Law of Cybermarks,* 1 RICH. J.L. & TECH. 1, ¶ 12 (Apr. 10, 1995) ⟨http://www.urich.edu/~jolt/vlil/burk.html⟩.

Here are other sources of guidance on citing to Internet sources:

- ◆ Coalition of E-Journals suggestions for citing to electronic journals: http://www.urich.edu/~jolt/e-journals/citation_proposal.html
- ◆ Emory University's "Citation Formats": http://www.cc.emory.edu/WHSCL/citation.formats.html
- ◆ Andrew Harnac and Gene Kleppinger's "Beyond the MLA Handbook: Documenting Electronic Sources on the Internet": http://falcon.eku.edu/honors/beyond-mla

Verdict and Settlement Research

There are many Web sites with verdict databases, including these two free sites:

- ◆ Law Journal EXTRA!, http://www.ljextra.com/cgi-bin/vds
- ◆ MoreLaw, http://www.morelaw.com

Some firms are beginning to post their own databases on their Web sites. For example, see the following:

- ◆ Law Offices of Thomas E. Miller (construction defects), http://www.constructiondefects.com
- ◆ Kussman & Whitehill (personal injury, medical malpractice, products liability, and insurance bad faith), http://www.lawinfo.com/forum/kussman

A few sites go beyond simple database access and help you find meaning from the mass of numbers. The best example is Cornell University's Judicial Statistical Inquiry Form, http://teddy.law.cornell.edu:8090/questata.htm, a *legal.online* magazine Five Star site. It includes key data from 3.7 million federal cases and 30,000 state court cases. For example, you might want to look for all jury verdicts in toxic tort cases in the Ninth Circuit terminated in 1993. Here you can perform your own analysis of statistics compiled from seventeen years of federal civil cases and some 30,000 state civil cases.

A branch of the U.S. Department of Justice, the Bureau of Justice Statistics collects similar information, emphasizing criminal cases. Go to http://www.ojp.usdoj.gov/bjs. In addition, the *legal.online* magazine Web site has articles that cite and analyze many related sources:

> http://www.legalonline.com/august97/jury.htm
>
> http://www.legalonline.com/august97/juryside.htm

Legal Forms

Many Internet sites, including the following, feature legal forms:

- ◆ FindLaw, http://www.findlaw.com/16forms (a huge collection of links)
- ◆ Legaldocs, http://www.legaldocs.com

Selected Starting Points for Legal Research

Is it possible to compile a comprehensive list of legal research sites in any paper publication? Probably not, though many people have tried to do so. New Internet legal research sites are coming online constantly. Further, even if it were possible, compiling such a list might be of questionable usefulness for two key reasons:

1. Mammoth lists can be overwhelming, especially for inexperienced users.
2. Typing in complicated URLs is wasted effort when it is so much easier to point and click.

To make this book as useful as possible, I have persuaded two respected law librarians, Barbara Folensbee-Moore and Kathy Clarke, to compile a selective list of the "best of the best" links. You should be able to easily access just about any useful legal research site on the Web with just a few links from one of the sites on their list.

An up-to-date hypertext version of the list appears at:
http://www.abanet.org/lpm/netbook.

If you are new to Internet legal research, this list from two experienced law librarians should give you a big head start on developing your own high-quality personal hotlist.

Web Legal Research Sites for Lawyers

Starting Points for Research

These are general sites where information useful to practicing lawyers has been collected and arranged.

FindLaw—Directory of resources organized by category.
http://www.findlaw.com

Yahoo/Law—Directory of resources from a familiar source.
http://www.yahoo.com/Law

Catalaw—Meta-index of legal references, useful as a finding tool to locate specific sources. http://www.catalaw.com

Specific Legal Resources

Grouped by practice specialties, these sites cover information in specific areas. Often the sites will have links to similar information.

Corporate/Securities
Securities Law Home Page. http://www.seclaw.com

IPO Intelligence Online. http://www.ipo-fund.com

Hoover's IPO Central. http://www.ipocentral.com

Hoover's—Short profiles of more than 10,000 public companies.
http://www.hoovers.com

SEC Home Page—Use the Edgar database to find public company filings.
http://www.sec.gov

PR Newswire. http://www.prnewswire.com

Wall Street Research Net—Creates charts on company activities and has useful links for company information. http://www.wsrn.com

NASD Home Page. http://www.nasd.com

Stock Quotes—Has standard fifteen-minute delay. http://www.secapl.com/cgi-bin/qs

Litigation/Intellectual Property
Expert Witnesses—List of sites collected by the Northern California Law Librarians group. http://www.nocall.org/experts.html

American Medical Association—Locate doctors, their specialties, and their credentials. http://www.ama-assn.org

CPSC Home Page—Contains product liability resources. http://www.cpsc.gov

Patent/Trademark Office—Official U.S. patent site. http://www.uspto.gov

IBM Patent Site—Contains decades of patent information. http://patent.womplex.ibm.com

Hieros Gamos Guide to Intellectual Property—Has many links to U.S. and foreign sites of interest. http://www.hg.org/intell.html

Copyright Information from Library of Congress. http://lcweb.loc.gov/copyright

Tax/Trusts/Estates
IRS Home Page—Includes tax forms, instructions, publications, and many administrative materials. http://www.irs.ustreas.gov/cover.html

TaxSites—Has a general collection of tax materials. http://shell5.ba.best.com/~ftmexpat/html/taxsites

ABA Trust and Estates Section—Contains an index of tax sites. http://www.abanet.org/tax/sites.html

Courts (Federal and State)

Villanova Federal Court Locator. http://www.law.vill.edu/Fed-Ct

Federal Court Finder—The Emory University Web site of court information. http://www.law.emory.edu/fedcts

FindLaw/Laws: Cases and Codes. http://www.findlaw.com/casecode

Cornell Law School. http://www.law.cornell.edu

Legal Forms

Legal Docs—Contains sample legal forms, some free and some for a small fee. http://legaldocs.com

FindLaw/Legal Practice Information—Lists links to sites with sample forms. http://www.findlaw.com/16forms

Government (State, Federal, and International)

Piper Resources—Has an index organized by state agencies. http://www.piperinfo.com/state/states.html

Municipal Codes—Includes available codes from localities in all fifty states, especially Florida. http://www.municode.com

National Conference of State Legislatures—Contains a collection of available sites for all fifty states. http://www.ncsl.org/public/sitesleg.htm

GPO Access—Has the *Federal Register, Congressional Record,* and more. http://www.access.gpo.gov/su_docs/

Thomas (Congressional Web site)—Search for bills, bill status, and legislative histories. http://thomas.loc.gov

U.S. House of Representatives Internet Law Library—Contains U.S. and international law and foreign sources. http://law.house.gov

GPO Publications—Contains Government Printing Office catalogs and online information. http://www.access.gpo.gov

The Whitehouse—Has presidential documents, press releases, and more. http://www.whitehouse.gov

U.S. House of Representatives Home Page—Contains general information about the House, committees, and members. http://www.house.gov

U.S. Senate Home Page—Contains general information about the Senate, committees, and members. http://www.senate.gov

Fedworld—Central site for a wealth of federal agency information sources. http://www.fedworld.gov

Federal Statistics—Has information from more than seventy federal agencies. http://www.fedstats.gov

General Resources Useful for Lawyers

Finding Lawyers
Martindale-Hubbell. http://www.martindale.com

West Legal Directory. http://www.wld.com

Hieros Gamos International Law Directory. http://www.hg.org

Legal Newspapers
Lawyer's Weekly—Has access to all state Lawyer's Weekly publications, including searchable archives. http://www.lweekly.com

Law Journal Extra—Home for the *National Law Journal*. http://www.nlj.com

Barbara Folensbee-Moore is head librarian with Pepper Hamilton & Scheetz, in Washington, D.C. Kathy Clarke is head librarian at Mezzullo & McCandlish in Richmond, Virginia.

Resources

A word about paper catalogs of law-related Internet links:
Judging by the large number of books with this theme, this type of catalog is very popular. When dealing with something as dynamic as the Internet, however, some may question the utility of paper catalogs. Given

that an online link collection is potentially fresher as well as easier to use (i.e., no typing of lengthy URLs), is any paper book with this format worth buying? The answer is a qualified yes. Many entries in link catalogs will not change immediately, so not everything is outdated before they make their way into print.

The biggest value of such books may be getting you "in the game." When you find one Internet site that is close to what you are looking for, it will usually be easy to find others, often more up-to-date ones, because they tend to link to each other. (This is why part of the Internet was named the World Wide Web: the intricate pattern of links between sites is like a spider's web linking information literally all around the world). For many new users, the toughest part is finding those initial links, and books and newsletters can be useful in this regard. Even experienced Internet users may occasionally use paper resources like these as a starting point.

Guide to Finding Legal and Regulatory Information on the Internet, by Yvonne G. Chandler (Neal-Schuman, 1998). So far the thickest and most expensive of this genre of books. It includes brief descriptions of almost all sites listed, as well as screen captures of a good number, but almost no other exposition or assistance to the user aside from the catalog of sites. It contains only a few links to law firm Web sites, which in some cases (e.g., Lew Rose's advertising site, http://www.webcom.com/~lewrose, or the Perkins-Coie electronic commerce site, http://www.perkinscoie.com/resource/ecomm/ecomm.htm) are among the most valuable resources available to practical researchers.

How to Access the Federal Government on the Internet, 1998, by Bruce Maxwell (Congressional Quarterly, 1997). Like the other bibliographic books listed here, except more narrow in scope, as indicated in the title.

How to Use the Internet for Legal Research, by Josh Blackman (Legal Research of New York, 1996). One of the better books in this genre. It's not as detailed as some, but the balance between exposition and collected links is a plus.

The Internet Guide for the Legal Researcher, 2nd Edition, by Don MacLeod (Infosources Publishing, 1997). Greatly improved over the first edition, but still basically just a list of sources of legally related information about the Internet. The "how to do it" section in the front has been expanded. In an interesting touch, this edition contains many screen captures of sites discussed.

Law on the Net, 2nd Edition, by James Evans (Nolo Press, 1997). Another bibliography, this one put together by a non-lawyer. It includes legal resources on bulletin board systems and services like CompuServe, America Online, and so forth. Despite Evans's non-attorney status, this book compares favorably with some of its competitors, probably owing to Nolo Press's experience with legal books.

The Legal List: Research on the Internet, 1998, by Diana Botluk (West, 1998). A revision of Erik Heels's groundbreaking book. One innovation: "Suggested Exercises" at the end of chapters. It also has a fair amount of information on legal discussion groups, which is a plus because of their great potential value. There's an excellent accompanying Web site at http://www.lcp.com/The-Legal-List.

A word about legal newsletters: Legal newsletters tend to be pricey, and ones with an Internet theme are no exception. However, each of the ones listed here contains valuable information that should repay their cost over the course of a year if you are an Internet user and take advantage of the tips they contain. Prices shown are for an annual subscription. Inquire about discounts and special offers. Each publisher will be glad to send you a free sample upon request so you can evaluate the newsletter for yourself.

Internet Law Researcher, (201) 890–0008; legalwks@aol.com. Subscription rate: $200. Focuses more specifically on legal research than the other newsletters listed here.

legal.online, (508) 546–7898; subs@legalcom.com. Subscription rate: $99. Good balance of how-to material and bibliographic listings, edited by Bob Ambrogi. There's a related Web site at http://www.legalonline.com.

The Internet Lawyer, (352) 371–3191; aadkins@internetlawyer.com. Subscription rate: $149. Edited by Josh Blackman. Mixes short how-to articles with bibliographic material. There's a related Web site at http://www.internetlawyer.com.

The Internet Newsletter: Legal and Business Aspects, (800) 888–8300, ext. 6170; netnews@ljextra.com. Subscription rate: $129. Many short, punchy items in each issue, and big on practical advice and problem solving. There's a related Web site at http://www.ljextra.com/netnews.

CHAPTER NINE

Factual Research

MY TIME IN THE COURTROOM convinced me that more lawsuits are won or lost on the basis of good or bad factual investigation than of good or bad legal research. The cleverest legal theory fails unless facts can be found to support it. In most of the cases I tried, the applicable law was usually easy to determine. Finding the facts was generally more difficult.

Factual research is a major Internet strength. Numerous though Internet legal resources are, they pale by comparison with the mind-boggling number of places to do factual research. *The Internet Fact Finder for Lawyers,* by Joshua D. Blackman with David Jank (American Bar Association: Law Practice Management Section, 1998), is by far the most useful reference on the subject. There is an associated Web site at http://www.internetlawyer.com/facts.

Instead of trying to duplicate that fine book, the focus here is on how law firms can benefit from Internet factual research in three specific areas:

1. Marketing research
2. Technical support
3. Job placement resources

Marketing Research

The simplest way that factual research can support legal marketing is by making it quick and inexpensive to conduct research on potential clients. If you'd like to be retained by a particular company, give yourself an edge by investing the few minutes that it takes to visit the company's Web site or to run its name through newspaper archives and general-purpose search engines before talking to company officials. A good overview of this approach is Genie Tyburski's essay "To Catch a Client, Or the Competition," at http://www.llrx.com/columns/catch.htm.

Some lawyers use a proactive approach to generate new billings from existing clients. They monitor the Internet for trademark infringements, libel, commercial disparagement, or similar problems for which a lawyer's services may be of use.

In addition, factual research itself can be a profit center. The firm of Brobeck, Phleger & Harrison lets clients submit research requests directly to the firm's librarians through its Web site, http://www.brobeck.com/Library, which is shown in Figure 9-1.

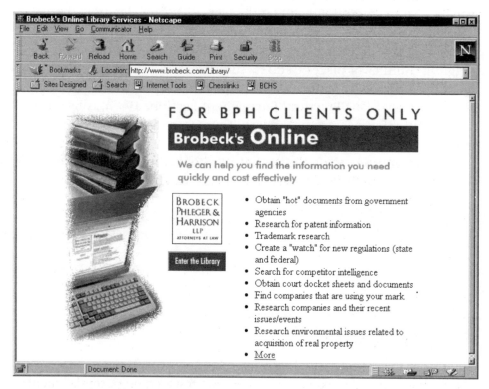

FIGURE 9-1. The Brobeck Library Intake Page

For decades, many businesses have thrived by obtaining free information from government agencies (e.g., court opinions), adding value in some way, and then reselling it. Some law firms do the same thing by monitoring state environmental regulations, for example, and selling their findings through subscription newsletters. The Internet can make it easier for those who have the necessary know-how both to gather this information and to distribute it.

The Internet is also a great source of information and advice on conventional law firm marketing techniques. These are two of the best examples:

- Mike Goldblatt's Lawyer Marketing site, a treasure trove of resources, can be found at http://www.lawyermarketing.com.
- The LawMarketing E-mail discussion group can be joined by sending a blank message to subscribe-lawmarketing@lists.inherent.com.

The latter is a very busy list that discusses all aspects of law firm marketing. Most of the subscribers are marketing specialists at medium to large law firms, with a sprinkling of lawyers and consultants in the mix. (Incidentally, Friday is the list's designated "joke day," when members share humor.) More information about the list is at http://members.aol.com/LawMktng.

Technical Support

The Internet is a wonderful place to find advice on technology questions. This is particularly useful for solos and small law firms that can't afford to have a technical staff at their beck and call.

Many vendor Web sites contain lists of frequently asked questions, along with the answers, which are known as *FAQ* (Frequently Asked Questions) files. The sites also typically provide product alerts, free bug fixes, and more. Yahoo's logical directory structure is a good place to find vendor URLs. Go to http://www. yahoo.com.

Among other resources, *Law Office Computing* magazine emphasizes objective, thorough reviews of products of interest to lawyers, including all manner of Internet-related products. Its Web site is at http://www. lawofficecomputing.com.

Each month *PC Computing*'s "A-List" feature selects the best product in a variety of categories. *PC World* provides monthly "Top Ten" lists, and *PC Magazine* lists "Editors' Choices." Check out the magazines' respective sites:

http://www.pccomputing.com

http://www.pcworld.com

http://www.pcmag.com

In addition, the C|Net Web site— http://www.cnet.com—is a comprehensive source of technical news and reviews.

G. Burgess Allison's deservedly popular "Technology Update" column in the ABA's *Law Practice Management* magazine is an excellent source of objective advice from a top expert. This column is posted at the ABA Web site: http://www.abanet.org/lpm/magazine/tu_intro.html.

The lawyer-oriented technical discussion groups are the ultimate weapon when it comes to technology support. A good group will feature quick answers from knowledgeable subscribers and opportunities to keep up with the latest trends. This is where Roger Kluck, a solo practitioner from Seattle, got help with the following typical questions:

```
I'm a solo in a shared office situation. I'm the techno geek
of the bunch. No one else is even doing backups of their
stuff now. I'm looking for an external backup device that we
can all share. This means parallel ports as the others prob-
ably won't upgrade for SCSI devices. I was pricing Zip and
Jazz drives and storage cartridges/disks. I noticed, how-
ever, that CD-ROM writeable discs are now very cheap. Much
cheaper than Zip or Jazz media. That and with gigabyte
drives, they seem far less hassle without the need for mul-
tiple volumes. They would also seem more reliable and less
prone to failure. (Tapes have failed all too often for me.)
With CD-W drives now at around $400 and disks at around a
dollar a piece, it seems CDs are the long-term cost saver.

So my questions:

1. Other thoughts on the above observations?
2. Is anyone aware of external CD Write units?
3. Can a CD Write work on a parallel port or does it need
   the SCSI for bandwidth?
```

The ABA LAWTECH mailing list is one of the best places to go with questions like these. Subscription information and the constantly updated list archives are available at http://www.abanet.org/discussions/open.html.

Following are other law office technology resource sites:

- Law Product Technology News has all sorts of product reviews at http://www.ljextra.com/ltpn.
- Techweb hosts a database of computer information at: http://www.techweb.com
- Law Journal Extra has a searchable vendor directory at http://www.ljextra.com/public/home/marketplace/new_vendor_dir.html.
- The Macintosh Resource List, as compiled by Randy Singer, is at http://www.mother.com/~randy.

- The ever-helpful FindLaw has two relevant sections—publishers, vendors, and legal directories at http://www.findlaw.com/04publications and links to legal software and technology sites at http://www.findlaw.com/17softtech.

Job Placement Resources

At one time or another, virtually all legal professionals engage in factual research related to employment: they're either trying to find a job or trying to find a suitable employee. The Internet can assist in both of these fact-finding missions.

Researching Job Opportunities

The continuing surplus of new lawyers means that the legal job market is tight and will remain tight. It has been estimated that fewer than 60 percent of the nation's 35,000 law school graduates find full-time employment as practicing lawyers. In this environment, most job seekers welcome any assistance. The Internet's advanced communications features can help in several ways.

Finding Announced Vacancies

Announced vacancies can be located through free or paid services. The biggest question with these sites is their ability to attract a critical mass of employers and employees that will make the site worthwhile. Some of them maintain active databases and will send registrants e-mail when a job meeting their specifications is posted. Sites catering to the legal job placement market include the following:

- Law Employment Center (part of Law Journal Extra): http://www.lawjobs.com
- Seamless Web Site: http://www.seamless.com/jobs
- Heiros Gamos: http://www.hg.org/employment.html
- Emplawyernet: http://www.emplawyernet.com (fee-based; will include a link to the home page of the job hunter or employer)
- Fedworld: http://www.fedworld.gov (not a complete list of federal job openings; a search on the federal job classification number for general attorney, 955, pulls up most of the attorney vacancies)
- Department of Justice: http://www.usdoj.gov/careers/oapm (includes lawyer and non-lawyer positions)

The following are among the more general employment sites:

- E Span: http://www.espan.com
- Career Mosaic: http://www.careermosaic.com
- Online Career Center: http://www.occ.com

The Web sites of newspapers in the city where you would like to work are another avenue. Careerpath has listing from many newspapers at http://www.careerpath.com.

In addition, there are at least two listservs devoted to legal placement. One is Law Jobs. Send a message to listserv@lawlib.wuacc.edu with the text *subscribe lawjobs-l Your Name*. The second is Legal Internships. Send a message to listproc@sunbird.usd.edu with the text *subscribe legalint-l Your name*.

Researching Potential Employers

It is a job placement truism that most of the best jobs are never formally announced. In some cases, employers may not be thinking about hiring anyone—until you show them why they need someone with your talents. Internet factual research can give you an edge in finding a niche that could be turned into your ideal job. Research can also pay off in an additional way. Employers favor those who understand the employer's organization and specialty. The Internet makes it easier to find background information that will help you stand out in an interview.

Distributing Your Resume and Supporting Materials

The Internet can be used to distribute resume information as well as supporting materials such as writing samples—or anything else that you think will demonstrate how you can help prospective employers. The primary distribution means are e-mail and an individual Web site.

Never send mass e-mails to law firms. If a firm indicates that it is willing to receive job applicant materials by e-mail, follow its instructions. In addition, be careful about sending files as e-mail attachments, especially if they are formatted with a particular word processor. You will only annoy those recipients who either don't know how to use them or find them inconvenient.

Web sites are a wonderful way to support a job search. A Web site alone is unlikely to get a job for you, but it will complement your other job search efforts. For example, you can provide your Web site's URL to give potential employers an easy, fast way to access more information about you than a resume can contain. Having a Web site helps you with potential employers who see your resume and are curious but do not want to invest the time to obtain your writing samples by postal mail or set up an interview without knowing more about you.

The mere fact that you have a Web site sends the right message to many employers. It demonstrates that you understand technology and know how to use it for practical purposes. If you are otherwise evenly matched with another candidate, this could be the decisive plus.

Establishing Web sites is inexpensive and easy. Many Internet service providers, including CompuServe and AOL, include Web server space at no additional charge. HTML editing software like Claris Home Page and Adobe Page Mill makes the technical aspects of page design simple. These factors mean that there is little reason not to establish a site to aid in your job search.

However, take heed: In the job search context it is better not to have a Web site than to have a poor one. Avoid tacky graphics and multimedia effects. Remember that less is more. Spend the time to proofread everything at your Web site and make sure that all links work properly.

Networking

Most people who are not law review editors or graduates of a top-twenty law school (as well as many who are) find legal jobs through personal networking. The Internet can help in developing contacts that can lead, directly or indirectly, to a job.

Learn the gathering places on the Internet for people interested in the type of work you want to do. Do you want to work in environmental law? Subscribe to some of the many mailing lists devoted to the topic. Are you looking for a job in Missouri? Subscribe to the Missouri Attorney mailing list. Post short, intelligent comments and questions. In some ways, this type of participation is better than a job interview. It's less stressful, and you select the time and the topics on which you want to comment. Even if you don't get a job directly, you are likely to learn information that will be useful to you.

Make sure that you use a signature block that tells people how to get in touch with you (including the URL of your resume site). If you create something that might be of interest to the other list members, perhaps a memo or article that's relevant to a question someone asks, post a short note describing it. Offer to send a copy or provide a Web site URL where they can find it.

Why tell someone that you have initiative, intelligence, and writing skills when you can *show* them? In ways that can't easily be duplicated in any other medium, intelligent use of the Internet can give you the opportunity to demonstrate to potential employers why they should hire you.

Finding Employees

Law firms seeking to hire lawyers, librarians, paralegals, or support staff through the Internet can use their own Web site or Internet-based recruitment services or try more targeted approaches.

Using Your Firm Web Site

Recruiting through the firm's Web site makes it easy for potential recruits to do factual research. About a third of the law firms with Web sites have sections devoted to recruiting. Not surprisingly, these sections are very popular. The recruiting section of the Venable, Baetjer, Howard & Civiletti Web site, http://www.venable.com, is historically visited more than any other part of the site. In some cases, like Cravath, Swaine & Moore http://www.cravath.com, recruiting is the major purpose for the site. Other firms with significant recruiting Web site sections include Brobeck, Phleger & Harrison, http://www.brobeck.com; Perkins Coie, http://www.perkinscoie.com; and Clifford Chance, http://www.cliffordchance.com.

The recruiting advantage of an Internet presence is not that it attracts a large volume of interested candidates. There are many ways to do that, and in today's legal market it is definitely not a problem. The real advantage that Web site recruiting gives you is an edge in attracting the top prospects, the elite group that you would most like to hire.

For years the U.S. Army has found its "Be All You Can Be" advertising slogan very effective. It has attracted a higher percentage of the right kind of recruits, ones motivated by a desire to challenge themselves, not just to draw a paycheck every month. A similar dynamic is at work with Web sites and law firm recruiting. An increasing percentage of today's top law school graduates understand the Internet and know how it can be used in the practice of law. If you have a good Internet presence and your competitors do not, this will give you an edge in recruiting this top group.

Dealing with a Recruitment Service

When it comes to Internet recruitment services, don't be dazzled by reports of thousands and thousands of search hits per month. Most law firms are already inundated with more resumes than they can read. Ask the right questions before signing up with a recruitment service, including:

- How many lawyers has the service placed?
- How many lawyers use the service?
- How many of those lawyers meet your firm's normal criteria (class rank, law review, etc.)?

Targeted Recruiting through the Net

The Internet can be used to recruit both lateral hires and new recruits. One method is posting announcements in specialized forums likely to be read by the candidates you are seeking. Many mailing lists that frown on "commercial" notices welcome job vacancy announcements. For example, if you are looking for a law librarian, try the Private Law Library mailing lists. If you are trying to recruit a legal ethics instructor, try the Legal Ethics mailing list. If you are trying to recruit a law firm marketing specialist, try the Lawmarketing discussion group mentioned earlier.

Resources

A range of online resources are included throughout this chapter. Don't, however, forget about the bookshelves. Here is a sampling of the better books about factual research on the Internet:

Netscape Guide to Internet Research, 2nd Edition, by Tara Calishain and Jill Alane Nystrom, (Coriolis, 1998).

Net Research: Finding Information Online, by Daniel J. Barrett (O'Reilly, 1997).

net.spy: How You Can Access the Facts and Cover Your Tracks Using the Internet and Online Services, by Michael Wolff (Wolff New Media, 1996).

Researching on the World Wide Web, by Cynthia N. James-Catalano (Prima, 1996).

The Internet Research Guide, by Timothy K. Maloy (Allworth Press, 1996).

PART *THREE*

Marketing

CHAPTER **TEN**

Law Firm Marketing on the Internet

HUNDREDS OF THOUSANDS of American businesses use World Wide Web sites for marketing. Thousands of law firms have Web sites and the number continues to increase.

Most of the potential clients in this expanding segment of the legal marketplace take the Internet and its marketing value for granted. Lawyers and firms who don't themselves have Web sites have little credibility with this segment of the market.

The Mayo Law Firm Web site (http://www.mayolawfirm.com) is a good example of a simple Web site for a small law firm. The site, shown in Figure 10-1, focuses on nonprofit organizations, philanthropy, and land conservation. It was the high scorer in the Redstreet Consulting rankings (http://www.redstreet.com) of the top small and midsize law firm Web sites. While all sizes of law firms can benefit, Web sites can be particularly effective at helping small law firms and solos level the playing field.

However, any lawyer considering Internet marketing should have a copy of *The Lawyer's Guide to Marketing on the Internet,* by Greg Siskind and Tim Moses (American Bar Association: Law Practice Management Section, 1996). Even if you already have a good Web site, that excellent book can probably show you how to get more benefit from it.

While minimizing overlap with that book, in this chapter and the next three, I cover some of the basics of law firm marketing on the Internet, discuss some recent developments, and add a few of my own perspectives. Web sites are not the only way to market on the Internet, but because they are so visible, they are the focus here and in the next two chapters. Chapter 13 discusses lawyer marketing through discussion groups.

FIGURE 10-1. Mayo Law Firm Web Site

Attracting New Clients

A Web site's power in servicing your existing clients can make it a good investment regardless of whether it brings in new clients. Nonetheless, for many law firms the major motivation for a web site is attracting new clients.

It's difficult to gauge how many law firms are achieving quantifiable results from their Web efforts. Firms are generally reluctant to disclose their financial and marketing strategy information to the view of potential competitors. Most firms that are successful on the Internet are probably reluctant to have it become known: Why encourage competitors to enter the arena? With this disclaimer in mind, my impression is that a handful of firms are getting many new clients from their Internet marketing efforts, but at the other end of the spectrum, most firms now on the Internet are getting few clients directly attributable to their marketing efforts there.

Why are many firms disappointed? There are two main reasons:

1. The firms had unrealistic expectations.
2. Most law firm Internet Web sites are poorly planned, poorly designed, and poorly promoted.

Unrealistic Expectations

It's naive for lawyers in most areas of practice to think that Web sites standing alone, no matter how well done, are going to attract significant numbers of new clients. A great Web site might be enough in a few specialty areas, like immigration or high-tech law, where the potential clients are already accustomed to communicating mostly by the Internet—but these practice areas are the exceptions. While a few people and some sophisticated corporate clients are presently willing to hire a lawyer largely on the basis of e-mail use and other electronic contacts, electronic contact alone is not enough for most clients.

If your goal is to attract new clients, you should view a Web site primarily as a means of generating new contacts that you would not get otherwise. It merely gives you a *chance* to obtain the business. In the vast majority of cases, you must still eventually make personal contact the old-fashioned way.

Poorly Executed Web Sites

Law firms are rushing to jump on the Internet without advance planning and market analysis of who and where their potential clients are and how, in concrete terms, the Internet site will help the firm reach them.

It's not unusual to come across firm sites whose primary content consists of lawyer resumes. Some sites do not even contain an e-mail address for the firm. It should not be surprising that such sites do not bring in many new clients. Working with a Web site design firm that understands the practice of law is the best approach. At the end of this chapter is a checklist of factors to consider in drafting Web site development contracts. In addition, *The Internet Lawyer* magazine maintains a list of Web site designers with some experience in Web site design:

http://www.internetlawyer.com/webdir.htm

On the other hand, you can't expect good results by hiring a consultant and then going to sleep. As Greg Siskind observed in an e-mail discussion group:

> Ultimately, I think that if you want a Web page to succeed, you need to plan on devoting significant time to making the site worthwhile. Hiring a knowledgeable consultant can help a lot, but you cannot rely on that [consulting] firm to do much of what needs to happen if you want your site to succeed. At least one person in your firm is going to have to take the responsibility for becoming an Internet expert.

A few lawyers will want to try developing their own Web sites. Some may relish the technical challenge. Other candidates may be solo practitioners with more spare time than clients, as well as those whose needs will be met by very simple Web sites. Whatever the motivation for constructing your own site, don't underestimate the commitment required.

Fortunately, Web site design software has come a long way. Programs like Microsoft FrontPage make it possible for even novices to include features that were difficult for design professionals a few years ago. Even with the help of such programs, most lawyers designing their own Web sites should consider subcontracting the most technical aspects, like graphic design and common gateway interface (CGI) script development (which is needed for interactive features).

Setting Web Site Objectives: A Business Card or Destination?

A law firm considering a Web site must have a clear understanding of its objectives. While there is some value in having a mere "cyberspace billboard," the equivalent of a firm brochure or even just a business card, your page will be much more beneficial to you if you can use it to provide something of value to the community. Give people a reason to visit your site, and while they are there, they will learn about the services available through your firm.

Mark Welch, a California solo practitioner who created an excellent site emphasizing estate planning (http://www.ca-probate.com), posted an essay there describing how he came to establish a Web site. Here is an excerpt:

> When I first began "surfing the Internet" in the fall of 1995, I was quite disappointed at the large number of attorneys who created Internet web sites that served as nothing more than "business card" advertisements.

Perhaps this represents the philosophy of those law firms, or perhaps it is an offshoot of the fact that many attorneys and law firms hire outside PR companies to create their web sites without regard for consumers' interests and needs.

My law practice has thrived based on a policy of generously giving away information that clients can use to evaluate their own estate planning needs, and I had developed a number of written materials to disseminate basic information about estate planning. Since those materials were already on my computer's hard disk, and since I quickly recognized that a "web page" is nothing more than a text document coded the same way as most word processor files, I knew it would be relatively easy for me to create a web site using existing materials.

Advertising vs. Public Service vs. Client Service

Law firm Web sites should comply with bar association regulations concerning advertising. It is, however, a mistake for lawyers to think of their Web sites merely as a form of advertising. If done properly, a Web site can bring in new business more effectively than most forms of conventional advertising, but the Web site is more likely to be effective if lawyers approach it as a form of *public service*. The right mental approach will lead them to "stock the pond" with the kind of material that will attract visitors—and potential clients.

Although Web sites are much more flexible and powerful, they are more like *faxback* machines than conventional advertising in concept. With faxback machines, you call a specific phone number and request that information be sent back to you by a special automated fax machine. Is this "advertising"? While it is definitely a form of marketing, it is a world removed from the intrusiveness of what we normally think of as advertising.

Having a high-quality Internet site can help a law firm establish or maintain a reputation for understanding business and high-technology and how they work together. If you are in a corporate law practice, many of your clients will have Web sites. In a few years, if not sooner, they may begin to wonder why you do not. As Roger Mahach, a manager at Iridium, LLC, a satellite phone company, advised this author:

> When I first got into the phone business, everyone had telex and fax numbers on their business cards. Now they all have Web sites and e-mail addresses. Telex and fax are dead.
>
> All the companies I deal with at work have Web sites. At home, my bank has a Web site, my credit card company has a Web site, and so on. It's a customer service/convenience thing. If a company didn't have a

Web site, I'd be suspicious just like I would be of a potential supplier who quoted a price too low. It makes you wonder if they are a marginal operation, or trying to cut corners.

It is difficult to know precisely how many clients could be gained (or not lost) as a result of this issue, but it is nevertheless a real concern, and you should factor it into your decision-making process.

Time and time again, I hear lawyers say that having a Web site will not help their firm because the senior in-house counsel at large law firms and other executives who are their target market are older and do not understand the Internet or "surf the Web." This is certainly not true of all executives, as Larry Bodine, Director of Communications for Sidley and Austin, explains:

> One of our firm's existing clients had used a law firm in Baltimore for a certain type of case, but the company wasn't happy with that law firm. The General Counsel of that client visited the Sidley & Austin Web site (http://www.sidley.com) and found information about Sidley's practice concerning this type of claim. As a direct result, Sidley & Austin now represents the client in this new type of claim, which could result in a significant amount of work.

Furthermore, in many cases the de facto decision maker will not be the top executive or general counsel but rather a junior staff member assigned to make a list of recommended firms. The target of good promotion is sometimes not the ultimate decision maker but instead key opinion *influencers*.

Understanding the Internet Marketing Environment

Before you begin marketing your law firm on the Internet, you need an understanding of its culture, and of netiquette.

Country clubs are considered good places for law firm marketing. However, you won't be well received if you accost everyone you see on the golf course and thrust your business card in their face. A few lawyers have already tried analogously crude techniques on the Internet, and the results have been what you would expect.

No discussion of law firm marketing on the Internet would be complete without mentioning the "Green Card Lawyers." In 1994, a small Arizona law firm named Canter and Siegel made itself nationally infamous overnight by spamming the Internet. The firm distributed an advertisement for its immigration law service through thousands of Usenet newsgroups. Usenet newsgroups are gathering areas for electronic messages that are supposed to be limited to specified topics. The Green Card posting was the equivalent of junk mail—only worse.

It is similar to junk faxes (now outlawed), where the recipient of the advertisement is forced to bear the cost for the privilege of receiving communications he or she did not ask for and does not want. Many Internet users pay for their connections by the minute. Moreover, there is a significant intangible cost to being unable to find your regular e-mail inside a stream of junk. Each junk e-mail ad may cost the recipient only a few cents, or just a fraction of a cent, but cumulatively the ads represent a major expense.

Many Internet users have resorted to various forms of vigilante action to protect the system. One form of this is *mail bombing.* Some advertisers include an e-mail address at which prospective purchasers can contact them. People who are annoyed by ads then set up automated mechanisms to send enormous volumes of e-mail to that address. Such quantities of mail will shut down the receiving computer, and will usually result in the advertiser being kicked off the system by its service provider.

Vigilante actions are not the answer. Hard-core spammers use temporary or phony addresses. In addition, pranksters have distributed phony spam with the address of someone they wish to injure. Legislation is needed. The best approach is probably to treat junk e-mail like junk faxes.

What is the lesson for lawyers? Never initiate contact with anyone on the Internet without a legitimate reason for doing so. Absent unusual circumstances, a commercial solicitation is not a legitimate reason.

A major advantage of law firm Web sites is that they avoid these problems. No one ever sees a Web site unless that person decides to visit it. For this reason, it's probably a mental trap to consider your firm Web site a form of "advertising."

It's true that even with Web sites, the potential clients are subsidizing the cost of their receipt of your promotional information. If your Web site is successful, the cumulative cost of the time and money spent by users accessing it will be many times higher than your expenses in designing and maintaining it. However, the Web site visitors are all making a voluntary decision that they want to see your site. If you have a bad Web site, your visitors may be disappointed with what they see, but no one can say that you forced it on them against their wishes.

The nonintrusive nature of Web sites is highly appealing for many lawyers and a major plus in the calculations of many firms that consider conventional advertising unprofessional or inappropriate for their image. This nonintrusiveness is, however, a two-edged sword. If you are not personally interfacing with potential clients, then you have to let them know where you are (i.e., your URL) and entice them into visiting your site. Once they get there, you will have a chance to tell them your story in detail. The big problem (and one discussed in the following chapters) is how to get them there.

The Gift Culture

Lawyers who want to market on the Internet must understand what has been called its "gift culture." This refers to the widespread expectation that things should be free on the Internet. Most successful law firm Web pages look more like public service materials than advertisements. The law firms are literally giving away their stock in trade—information.

Imagine that you were visiting a primitive tribe in South America that expected visitors to provide gifts. If you tried to do business there and didn't give away gifts, you wouldn't do very well. It's just like that on the Internet. People visiting your site will be disappointed if they don't find something of at least nominal value, some information or some sort of simple service that's available for free. Noted Web designer David Siegal (http://www.killersites.com) refers to small giveaways as "fishbait," but in this situation more largess may reap more benefits to the giver.

Internet newcomers are often puzzled by this generosity. They wonder how businesses can afford to give these services away, and why they would want to do so. The answers lie in Internet culture and economics. People expect to find something useful. They won't revisit your site unless you give them a reason.

Once you have compiled some information, the additional cost of making it available on the Internet typically is relatively small. If you don't do it, it's likely that one of your competitors will, thereby gaining goodwill and possibly eventual market share at your expense. It works. If you can entice many people to visit your Web site repeatedly, you gain public awareness, or "mind share," and get the opportunity to sell those visitors other products or services related to those you have given away.

Most law firms with Web sites have used techniques that are less colorful than those used by other businesses but that are probably more appropriate for law firms. The classic approach is publishing memoranda of law and newsletters that showcase the firm's lawyers' talents. More original approaches are possible.

Several firms offer collections of lawyer jokes. I do not necessarily endorse this marketing approach, but it went over well with at least one potential client (who's quoted below). You can check it out at the home page of Buckley Montgomery Le Chevallier & Lindley P.C., at http://www.teleport.com/~bmll/

> *One of my favorite law firm Web pages has an area with lawyer jokes. It's a page I visit now, and I barely knew the firm's name two weeks ago. All things being equal, I'd be inclined to give them the first call the next time I need a lawyer in the Northwest.*
>
> —Barry Levinsky, General Counsel, Inland Steel Industries, in *The American Lawyer*

The key rule in this area is to attract the type of visitors that *you* want by providing the type of material that *they* want.

A few firm Web sites make some information free to all visitors but require visitor registration before giving access to other data. Certainly there is value in obtaining as much information as possible about visitors, but before requiring even the minimal "cost" of registration, ask whether the risk of turning off potential clients makes it worthwhile. This is a judgment call, but unless you have truly compelling content that you're sure people will want to register to receive, it's probably a good idea to make sure that you have enough good free information available without registration to attract repeat visitors.

Why Not Web?

Many lawyers are afraid of throwing a lot of money away on something they don't understand. Developing a Web site need not be exceptionally expensive. Even if you have bad luck with your site and it's a total flop, you won't lose much if you showed good judgment in setting up the site.

Furthermore, the expense of Internet marketing should be kept in perspective. Does your law firm presently contribute to high-profile charities in your community? Do your lawyers devote their time to serving as board members for various organizations? Do you have firm accounts at expensive restaurants? Do you have luxurious furniture liberally scattered around your reception areas? Do you wine, dine, and entertain summer law clerks? Do you pay thousands of dollars a year so your key lawyers can be members of various associations? It's difficult to judge whether these expenditures are cost-effective, but many firms engage in them to help maintain an image of success, know-how, and competence. An Internet presence can help accomplish this objective more effectively, while at the same time providing concrete benefits for your firm. Surprisingly, a high-quality Web site may cost less than any of these other types of law firm promotion.

At a minimum, most lawyers should have a basic "business card" type of site with contact information, including phone and fax numbers, a street address and directions, and an e-mail address that someone will answer. This can be done so cheaply that there is no reason not to have one. Many organizations will host a site like this at no charge. One of the best such free hosting sites is at FindLaw, http://firms.findlaw.com.

Pricing a Web Site

Suppose that you want a site that will be more likely to bring in new business. How much should you expect to pay? Price one like you would a stereo system. How much you should pay depends on how elaborate a setup you need and how much you are willing to spend.

A five hundred dollar boom box is a more-than-adequate stereo system for most people. A few audiophiles won't be satisfied with less than the most esoteric high-end stereo system costing tens of thousands of dollars. Oddly, the boom box may turn out to be more reliable in the long run—and sometimes even sound better—than the high-end system. The story is no different with Web sites.

Some law firms spend hundreds of thousands of dollars. On the other hand, with some "sweat equity," you can have a reasonably good Web site with no out-of-pocket expenses. Easy-to-use Web page design tools make it possible for even those with little expertise to create their own sites. Many Internet service providers will host a Web site at no extra charge if you have a regular account with them.

There are good and bad law firm Web sites in all price ranges. Some of the most expensive are among the very worst. Spending a large sum of money is not a guarantee that you will have a good Web site. On the other hand, if you are careful, you can spend just a little out of pocket and wind up with an excellent site.

The content of your site is much more important than the technical aspects. Let's return to the stereo system analogy. Which sounds better, a $500 boom box or a $50,000 audiophile stereo system? It depends, doesn't it? Suppose that the boom box is playing a CD of the Philadelphia Orchestra doing Beethoven's Ninth Symphony, and the ultraexpensive system is playing a cassette of "You Deserve a Break Today" and other commercial jingles? The content makes all the difference. It's exactly the same on the Web. As long as your Web site passes a certain minimal level of quality (the Web equivalent of the boom box), few will care about extra technical flash.

How can you ensure that your Web site features the equivalent of the Philadelphia Orchestra playing Beethoven? That is the tough question, and most professional Web site design firms are unlikely to offer much useful assistance in answering it. There is really no substitute for the judgment of a lawyer who understands your target market and what will appeal to it. Compelling content is the big hurdle, not graphics and technical issues.

The biggest expense in developing an effective Web site should not be the out-of-pocket expense but rather an indirect cost—the time spent in planning what you want to do substantively with your site. The trick is not in being a technical wizard. It is in understanding your segment of the legal market and determining what you can do to appeal to that market.

This is the challenge, this is where most poor Web sites fail, and this is where most general-purpose Web design firms are ill equipped to help law firms. A law firm cannot be marketed as if it were a bookstore or a pizza parlor. Chapter 11 has some tips to help get you headed in the right direction.

Web Site Contract Design Checklist

Web sites differ from conventional media and multimedia in critical respects, and the law in this area is still developing. For this reason, the language of the contract is critical. Law firms need to understand Web site development issues both to address their own business interests and to be able to advise clients intelligently. The following checklist is intended to alert you to a few of the key issues. It does not purport to be exhaustive.

- **Who owns the copyright in the site?** Because the work-for-hire doctrine does not apply to independent contractors, such as most Web site designers, the site will be owned by the designer unless there is contractual language to the contrary.
- **Who owns the domain name?** Many developers automatically register the domain name for all sites they design in their own name. If the developer is also the Web site host, it is a good idea to include in the contract a requirement that the developer make reasonable efforts to cooperate in moving the Web site to a new host if the business commissioning the Web site decides to move it.
- **Who will obtain needed licenses?** Many site designers routinely incorporate preexisting content, often from third parties. For example, clip art may be incorporated into an expensive new logo or image map. This can create a problem if the clip art was not licensed for Internet usage. Similar problems can arise with using Java applets and CGI scripts, which are used to add interactive features. Some developers of applets and scripts willingly release them into the public domain. Many others do not.
- **Does the developer have to indemnify for infringements on third-party proprietary rights?** The developer is in the best position to know or ascertain the source of material incorporated into the Web site.
- **Is there a noncompetition clause?** The client may wish to restrict the developer from creating competitors' sites with a similar "look and feel." The look and feel at issue should be described in the contract and can include, among other things, particular graphics styles, themes, organization, and layout.
- **Exactly what is due under the contract, and when is it due?** Does the contract clearly specify what is included in the Web site? Is the developer to provide the computer files that make up the site, including graphics and HTML files, CGI scripts, Java applets, ActiveX controls, and so on? Schedules for completion and delivery of various components and payments should be established.
- **What warranties are given concerning site design quality?** It may, for example, be desirable to seek a guarantee that the page will be viewable and usable on older browsers like Lynx, Cello, and Mosaic, or that the graphics on specified pages will not exceed a certain size or will have no more than a certain number of colors (which is important to prevent many viewers from experiencing ugly "dithering" effects).

- **Who has editorial and artistic control?** Deciding what constitutes a "tasteful" graphic is a subjective process. Does the contract specify who makes such decisions? Does the contract specify who has the final say on things like the formats to be used for pre-existing graphics?

- **Are there any provisions for guaranteed uptime and bandwidth?** If the Web site developer is also to be the Web site host, is there any provision for guaranteeing uptime (i.e., the percentage of time that the site is accessible to visitors via the Internet) or a certain level of available bandwidth? Effective bandwidth is notoriously difficult to measure. One approach for purposes of contracting is to specify a minimum response time for user requests, based on a specified number of users contacting the site simultaneously.

- **Will the developer receive credit for its work?** To promote their business, developers will often seek a credit line and hypertext link back to their business site. Whether to allow such credits and, if so, where and with what level of prominence is a judgment call that should be specified in the contract.

- **What provisions have been made for handling confidential information?** Especially in developing intranets and extranets, the developer may be given access to confidential information. The contract should define what information the parties consider confidential and should require that the site designer use reasonable measures to prevent disclosure of such information. This could include nondisclosure or noncompete agreements when appropriate.

- **Under what circumstances can the agreement be terminated?** Developing a significant site can take months or even years. Anyone hiring an outside developer should seek to retain the right to terminate the agreement in the event of a change in plans or dissatisfaction with the developer's performance.

- **What provisions are made for backing up the Web site?** Does the contract require the developer to keep backups of all material at the Web site so that the site can quickly be installed on another server if the first crashes, possibly with loss of data? Does the contract require the developer to provide the client with a current copy of all material on the Web site? The latter will be handy if the client decides to change site hosts. If there is no such contractual provision, the client is well-advised to make its own backups.

- **Who is responsible for updates and maintenance?** Significant time can be involved in correcting changed hypertext links and updating content.
- **What, if anything, will the designer do to promote the site?** Publicity is discussed in Chapter 12. The contract should recite the parties' expectations.

Additional Information on Web Site Development Contracts

For more pointers on how to work with professional Web site developers, consult the following resources:

- Gary A. Kendra, Wise & Marsac, P.C., has a series of articles on the topic at http://www.icle.org/techlink.
- Geoffrey Gussi's article "Website Development Agreements: A Guide to Planning and Drafting" is at http://www.digidem.com/legal/wda/toc.html.
- Richard Raysman and Peter Brown's "Key Issues in Web Site Development Agreements," an article originally published in the *New York Law Journal,* is at http://www.ljx.com/internet/website.html.
- The law firm of King and Spaulding, as a public service, has placed the Web site development contract for its firm Web site online at http://www.kslaw.com/menu/agr.htm.

CHAPTER **ELEVEN**

Planning a Law Firm Web Site

THE NEWS MEDIA'S continuing infatuation with "cyber-anything" and the extraordinary increase in the number of Internet users have convinced many that the Internet must be a marketing gold mine. All you have to do is open up an Internet site and then sit back to count the money, right?

Unfortunately, it's not that simple. Poorly designed or promoted law firm Web sites will provide little benefit. Yet sites correctly promoted and designed to appeal to targeted audiences can provide a major boost. The effectiveness of a Web page depends on a number of factors, including the following:

- The firm's location
- The type of practice
- The potential clients the firm is trying to reach
- How well the page is designed
- How well the firm promotes the page

At a minimum, having a Web site helps a firm establish or reinforce an image as an innovative organization that knows how to use technology to keep up with or surpass its competitors. As Josh Blackman, editor of *The Internet Lawyer,* observes, "Online marketing by its very nature expresses forward thinking." This is particularly valuable when dealing with more sophisticated clients, or anyone who is already online themselves. This may be the reason that firms that handle (or would like to handle) intellectual property and high-tech legal matters tend to be among the first to establish Web sites.

Determining the Site's Purpose

As explained in the previous chapter, the largest expense associated with a law firm Web site is the indirect cost of the time spent planning the substantive content and keeping the site updated. Before you can begin the design process, you need to think carefully about how you expect the site to benefit your firm. You need to ask yourself the following questions about the Web page's purposes and your expectations:

1. Do you want the Web site to provide a service to the firm's existing clients?
   - If so, how will your existing clients learn about the site?
   - What services or information will you make available to them there?
2. Do you want the Web site to attract new clients to the firm?
   - If so, how will prospective clients learn about the site?
   - Can you come up with compelling content that will make prospective clients decide to (1) visit the site initially, (2) return to the site, and (3) contact the firm for assistance?

If you cannot answer these questions satisfactorily, then your firm is not ready to benefit from a Web site. Establishing one will probably be a waste of your time and money.

The major exception to this is the minimalist contact information-type sites. These don't provide large benefits, but they cost so little that they can still be cost-effective.

Coordinating Internet Marketing with Other Marketing

Unless you are in the right practice area or have a well-promoted Web site with dynamite content, don't expect it, standing alone, to do much for you. A Web site's biggest marketing value is that it reinforces other promotional work.

Therefore, your Internet marketing efforts should be coordinated with your conventional marketing at every opportunity. Each should strengthen the other. As Larry Bodine, Sidley and Austin's director of communications and cofounder of the Lawmarketing discussion group, explains:

> Many law firms don't get the most mileage out of their Web site because they fail to incorporate it into the rest of their marketing efforts.

For example, the firm's Web site URL should be reproduced on lawyer business cards, in advertising, on newsletters and other mailings, and even on stationery. Furthermore, a firm's newsletters, articles, press clippings, awards, and lawyer appearances should be set out and referenced on the firm's Web site. There is a tremendous benefit in this synergy.

Bodine's examples are a good start, but there is room for much more. The next two sections concentrate on just two of the many other areas in which law firms can obtain a synergistic effect by coordinating their marketing on and off the Internet:

- Speeches by a firm's lawyers
- Specialized directories and award lists

Marketing Synergy with Speaking Engagements

Most law firms encourage their top lawyers to speak before influential groups that contain potential clients. An Internet presence is a high-tech way of boosting the effectiveness of this traditional marketing technique.

The first boost that a Web site can provide in this area is helping the speakers obtain invitations. The New Orleans firm of Adams and Reece uses a section of its Web site, http://www.arlaw.com/SpeakersBureau.html, just to promote its lawyers' availability as speakers.

Getting the invitation is only the beginning. By giving the audiences a convenient way of obtaining further information about the speaker's subject, a biography of the speaker, or even a copy of the speaker's remarks, a Web site reinforces the favorable impression made by the lawyer.

Your firm immediately begins to realize the latter benefit when your speaker says, "You can get more information about the topic of my speech at our firm's Internet site at the following address. . . . " Even if no one in the audience ever takes your speaker up on the offer to visit the Internet site, the speaker has already aided your firm by delivering an unarticulated but extremely convincing message: "My law firm and I understand high technology and how to use it to give our clients choices and convenience."

Yet this is only the beginning of the benefits. Most likely, a certain percentage of the audience will visit your firm's Web site. Which ones are most likely to take such follow-up action? It will be the ones who are most interested in the topic of the speech, the ones most likely to retain a lawyer to help them with problems of that type—in other words, the ones who are most likely to be potential clients. Web sites provide *targeted* marketing.

This self-selection is one of the key reasons that Web sites are such an attractive marketing tool. Many more people would see a magazine or television advertisement, but the overwhelming majority would probably not be interested in hiring your firm, for one reason or another. By contrast, fewer people will visit your Web site, but if you have designed and promoted it properly, a much higher percentage of the visitors are likely to be potential clients owing to this self-selection factor.

It gets even better. For every person who does visit your firm's Web site because of the speech, you have a chance to tell your firm's story *in depth*. Those who want more detailed firm information can find it at their fingertips. Contrast this with the shallow impact of a television or magazine ad.

In addition, by having your speaker distribute his or her e-mail address on-site (perhaps in a handout with biographical information and the firm's URL) and making it available on your Web site, you make it easy for people to get in touch for follow-ups. A growing number of people are so fed up with phone tag, voice mail, and busy signals that they prefer to communicate by e-mail whenever possible. Having an e-mail address and Web site sends exactly the right message to this group.

The benefits continue. An Internet presence can also expand the audience for a topic beyond the immediate group of people who hear the presentation in person. If the presentation is on a high-interest topic, people will actively search for it online. Some of those people will be potential clients.

For example, one lawyer posted the slide show and outline of one of his presentations on a Web site. Two months later, the Web site had attracted *more than ten times* the number of people who had attended the original presentation. A year later, it was still attracting visitors. There was almost no extra expense or effort for the additional exposure. The lawyer invested a lot of time putting the presentation together, but once that was accomplished, he used the presentation software to convert it to HTML (the standard Internet format) automatically. Modern presentation programs like Lotus Freelance Graphics, Microsoft PowerPoint, Corel Presentations, and Astound will automatically translate the computer-generated slide shows used by many speakers into Internet publishable format.

When you factor in the low cost, it's not a question of why you should put your lawyers' presentations on the Internet but, instead, why not?

Could you put such presentation materials on your Web site even though you have yet to give a presentation on the topic? Certainly you could, and many law firms have done so. The Web presentation, however, is more effective when your credibility has been vouched for by respected third parties who invite you to speak—another illustration of the synergy between Web sites and conventional marketing that should be your goal.

Marketing Synergy with Web Site Directories and Awards

Creating a specialized directory at your Web site can cultivate leads that you can use to market your firm off the Internet.

For example, perhaps you would like to have more insurance companies as clients. You might further this goal by compiling a list of hypertext links to Web sites particularly valuable for that target market. If you do a good job, this would attract potential clients to the site, but that's only the beginning of the potential benefits.

The directory can be used for conventional marketing as well. While generally there is no requirement to obtain a Web site owner's permission to build a link to the site, it is considered polite to do so. You can do this by contacting the Webmaster at each site via e-mail. This approach is efficient, but it may be better to send paper letters to the relevant contacts at each linked-to site that is run by a potential client. A follow-up phone call by one of your lawyers would be appropriate. This is a way of letting potential clients know who you are and the type of law that you practice.

If you do a good job of building the directory, you can get more mileage out of it by sending press releases to newsletters likely to be read by your target market. Again, this is a way of getting out the word about your law firm. If it is valuable, the Web site directory is "news." It gives editors a good reason to run a story about your firm.

Having your firm honor particularly valuable Web sites is a variation on this technique. Instead of just listing resources, single out those worth special praise and label them as prizewinners. This gives you all the previously listed benefits and more. If a directory list is news, then a list of awards to Web sites in a particular industry is even more newsworthy. Of course, representatives of the prizewinners are likely to be even more receptive to follow-up contact by your firm's lawyers.

For optimum effectiveness, give out your awards only on merit. If they are merely a list of clients that you would like to attract, the awards may be dismissed as solely a marketing device. The extraordinary flexibility you have is one of the attractions to this approach. You and only you decide on the list of eligibles and the winners.

You can use the awards program to boost traffic to your Web site by having a graphic artist design an appropriate icon and making it available to the prizewinners, along with directions on how they can build a hypertext link back to your site.

Giving out awards has an additional subtle benefit. It is a form of almost subliminal marketplace positioning, helping create an image of your firm as the "experts among experts," the lawyers who are best qualified to distinguish the best from the best.

Marketing Your Net Law Expertise

In his treatise *Cyberlaw: The Law of the Internet* (Springer Verlag, 1997), Jonathan Rosenoer related two experiences that convinced him that expertise in the Internet law area would be valuable:

> [In 1993 an] in-house lawyer for a Silicon Valley computer company told me that his company had received a threatening letter from a person who had been "flamed" in an Internet newsgroup by a company employee who sent his posting via the company's e-mail system. The "victim" of the flame was seeking to hold the company responsible. The lawyer called one of the best-respected law firms in Silicon Valley, but was dismayed when told that they had no attorneys who knew anything about this. A little while later, attorneys working for two of the largest commercial online services complained to me that they simply could not find an attorney to call about online issues who could answer their questions without embarking on forty-hour research projects at their expense.

Years later, clients outside of Silicon Valley are asking such questions with increasing frequency. Lawyers who can handle these questions with assurance are even more in demand. This demand will only grow as Internet use becomes ubiquitous. If you hope to compete for this growing segment of the legal marketplace, make sure that your Web site supports your marketing efforts.

Garnering Other Marketing Benefits

A Web site can be used to maximize the benefit from favorable non-Internet publicity that a firm receives. Favorable newspaper stories or other mentions in the press are usually ephemeral and quickly forgotten. With a Web site, such stories can be "in print" and benefiting your firm for as long as you like.

Mailing to a prospective client a copy of a five-year-old magazine profile about one of your firm's partners might look tacky. The nature of the Web, with its flexible structure that puts the user in control, changes things. Put such stories on your Web site, after checking for copyright problems. If people want to read them, fine. If they are not interested, that's fine, too, but you haven't made a bad impression like you might have if you had mailed a paper copy. On a well-designed Web site, the visitor controls what to view and what not to view. (Check out the many reprints at the Siskind, Susser, Haas & Devine Web site at http://www.visalaw.com.)

While it does happen occasionally, most firms should expect to get few, if any, new clients from those who stumble across their firm for the first time while surfing the Net. If, however, prospective clients are trying to decide which of several firms to go with, the customer service and convenience of a Web site can be a decisive advantage with those who are technologically literate and on the Web. The number in this category is increasing exponentially, as mass market services like America Online, Prodigy, and CompuServe change the Internet from a techie-only haven to a Middle America phenomenon.

A Web site may also facilitate a move into a more lucrative practice area. A young lawyer handling mostly petty criminal cases may have few clients with Internet access. Maybe someone in this situation should be thinking about attracting a more affluent class of clients. An Internet site focusing on defense of white-collar criminal cases could be a key step toward upgrading a client base.

The Memphis and Nashville-based immigration law firm of Siskind, Susser, Haas & Devine is a good example of a firm that is well placed to take advantage of the Internet and knows how to use it to good advantage. Using their Web site (http://www.visalaw.com) and an Internet mailing list about immigration, they have been able to expand into a national practice. In less than a year, the firm's Web site has expanded its practice to the point where two-thirds of the new clients are now from outside the state of Tennessee.

In addition, cross-marketing is a significant potential benefit. Well-designed sites make it easy for visitors to one section to learn about the law firm's other departments.

The home page of the Columbus, Ohio, firm of Bricker & Eckler (http://benet-np1.bricker.com) attracts thousands of visitors per week. Many of the firm's clients had requested that Bricker & Eckler add links to their own Web sites. Now visitors to the Bricker home page can also link to the Internet sites of the firm's key clients with a click of the mouse. In effect,

Bricker & Eckler is referring potential customers to its clients, a service that builds goodwill with existing clients.

Some law firm marketing books devote a great deal of space to explaining ways in which you can get journalists to consider you an expert in a particular area of law so that they will call you for quotations. The hope is that clients will read the stories and remember your name. Most of this advice seems to consist of innovative techniques for buttering up reporters. Maybe this roundabout approach works for some people, but it seems like a time-consuming approach that would be of dubious effectiveness for most lawyers.

Why not take a more direct route? Demonstrating your expertise via the Internet is a more dignified and effective way to develop or enhance your reputation as an expert and to gain new clients. Lew Rose, of Washington, D.C.'s Arent Fox Kinter Plotkin & Kahn, is an example. His page on advertising law at http://www.webcom.com/~lewrose reinforced his standing as a leading expert in the field, bringing him at least a dozen new clients in just the first few months of operation.

I know from personal experience that journalists, including some from publishers like BNA, the *Washington Post,* and the *Seattle Times,* use the Internet to find experts. If you think that being quoted in the media will help in marketing your firm, ask yourself this question: Is the best way to reach that objective buttering up journalists through demeaning methods? One marketing book suggests directing an associate in your firm to write letters to reporters lauding your expertise. Isn't it more dignified and befitting your professional status to use the Internet and other means to establish yourself as an expert, so the press will want to seek you out *and* be able to find you easily?

Including Effective Content to Attract Web Site Visitors

As you can gather from the previous discussion, good Web sites emphasize strong content. Ideally, you want your target audience members to like your site so much that they create a bookmark in their Web browsers and visit your site repeatedly. Providing substantively interesting and useful information is the way to attract repeat visitors.

Make sure that you include a carefully drafted disclaimer along with your substantive material. Review other law firm sites, your state professional responsibility rules and Chapter 14 for ideas on how to do this effectively.

Some law firms use specialization to make them stand out on the World Wide Web. The Consumer Law Page (http://www.consumerlawpage.com) and The Whistleblower's Home Page (http://www.whistleblowers.com) are good examples of specialized sites. The low cost of putting up a Web page, and the fact that some firms can aim for a national practice, make niche markets profitable for many law firms. A major advantage is that the specialized appeal can make a site easier to promote. For example, designers of high-traffic sites that appeal to bicyclists look for links that will be of interest to their visitors. Most would love to include a hypertext link to a high-quality law firm site containing information on legal issues relating to injuries sustained in bicycling accidents.

Even if you are a general practice firm, you may be able to take advantage of the same dynamics. Almost every law firm has one or more practice areas suitable for promotion in a specialized Web site. Arent, Fox's site is a good example of specialization used to advantage for marketing purposes. In addition to a general law firm page, it has a section on Qui Tam (aimed at executives of businesses with government contracts). The Qui Tam section (http://www.arentfox.com/features/quitam/) alone contains more high-quality substantive material than the entirety of many firm's Web sites.

Such niche marketing can also lead to additional marketing bonuses. For example, defense or health industry newsletters for executives will occasionally run Internet tips articles and will mention Web resources like the Qui Tam site. Such alerts are a service to the magazines' readers, and they are a form of endorsement that gives your firm credibility that you cannot buy.

FAQs as Marketing Tools

FAQs—those lists of frequently asked questions with corresponding answers—are routinely used to provide Internet newcomers with basic knowledge in a particular area. Examples of numerous FAQs are collected at The Ohio State University site at http://www.cis.ohio-state.edu/hypertext/faq/usenet/FAQ-List.html.
The Internet FAQ Consortium is another good resource: http://www.faqs.org/
Since the format is familiar to most Internet users, FAQs can be a particularly effective law firm marketing tool as Web site content. Because of the traditional use of FAQs on the Internet, a document titled "FAQ" is more likely to be viewed favorably by Internet users than one titled "Essay" or "Memorandum" containing exactly the same material. Moreover, if your

FAQ is genuinely valuable, others will publicize it (and therefore your legal practice), since other Internet sites serving people interested in the same subject (i.e., potential clients) will refer them to your FAQ.

Some firms find FAQs useful for saving time by distributing basic information to clients. In some areas of law, such as domestic relations or bankruptcy, lawyers spend much of their work week repeatedly explaining the same elementary points of law to new clients. While it's desirable to spend some time explaining such information to build rapport with clients, many clients who have Internet access may prefer to receive certain information in an online format. Once you've prepared the information electronically, the additional cost of publishing it on the Internet is minimal.

In addition to serving existing clients, the FAQ format can also be used to market the law practice. Beth Bertelson, a solo practitioner, includes several employment law FAQs at her Web site at http://www.primenet.com/~bertlaw.(see Figure 11-1)

A wide variety of subjects are appropriate for FAQs, such as, for example, "Avoiding Employee Termination Disputes," "Your Rights as an Accident Victim in Virginia," "Your Children's Future: Estate Planning Basics," "Dissolving a Partnership in Pennsylvania," and "How to Have Your Views Considered During EPA Rule Making." Many lawyers try to promote their practices by drafting articles on subjects like these but publish them in paper publications of limited circulation. A FAQ can reach a much wider audience than the typical journal. Moreover, your FAQ will not go out of print until you decide to take it off your site.

Kevin M. Saavetz, author of several popular FAQs, advises selecting a limited topic to keep the FAQ short. He also suggests publishing a new edition every month, so the FAQ will look fresh.

It's important to be totally objective in your FAQ. Avoid any type of overt commercial pitch, although it's fine to mention that you are a lawyer and to give your e-mail address and Web site URL. Include a notice about when the file was last updated. Include a copyright notice that specifically authorizes reproduction and redistribution of the FAQ, on the condition it is distributed intact, including the copyright notice and your identifying information. You will know your FAQ is successful if people copy it and distribute copies to their friends and colleagues. The last thing you want to do is discourage such implied endorsements.

Include a suitable disclaimer, something like this one:

> Laws change, and the answers to legal questions often turn on fine questions of fact that require a skilled professional's questions to uncover. This FAQ merely provides an overview of a few general principles of law. It is not intended to and does not substitute for the advice of an attorney. You should consult your attorney if you have a specific legal

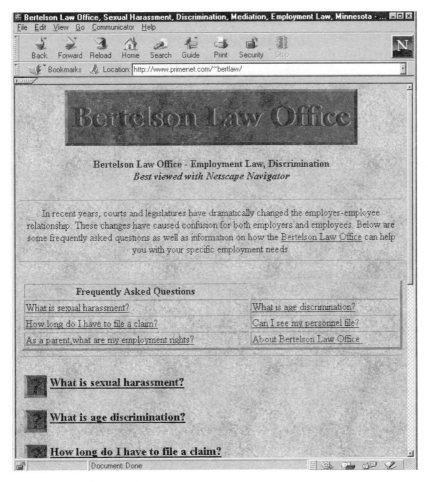

FIGURE 11-1. Bertelson Law Offices Web Site

question instead of relying on this FAQ, which may be dated by the time you receive it, contradicted by the laws of your particular jurisdiction, or not applicable to your particular problem.

You can learn more about drafting an effective FAQ by referencing Russell Shaw's *The FAQ Manual of Style* (MIS Press, 1996) or studying the examples in the newsgroup NEWS.ANSWERS or FAQ repositories like these:

http://www.cis.ohio-state.edu/hypertext/faq/usenet

http://www.faqs.org

To be effective, the FAQ should be publicized as widely as possible. Many FAQs are outgrowths of a newsgroup or mailing list. If you can have your FAQ so sponsored, this will provide built-in publicity and make it easy for you to have the FAQ included in repositories like those at Ohio State and MIT. If there is an existing newsgroup or mailing list related to your subject that does not already have an FAQ (and 90 percent of them did not at last count), post a message suggesting the possibility of one and offer to draft the FAQ.

You may be able to have some association or organization adopt and sponsor your FAQ. For example, it is possible that a group like the National Organization for Women could adopt a well-written FAQ on breast implant liability. The American Society of Hospital Pharmacists or the Institute of Scrap Recycling Industries could adopt an FAQ on legal topics of interest to their membership. These organizations have paper publications, and it's probable they will soon have Web sites if they don't already. They will be seeking high-quality substantive information that will help their members. A well-written FAQ by a lawyer with expertise in the area could be exactly what they're seeking. Needless to say, having an organization like this adopt and distribute a FAQ you've written could provide a major boost to your credibility and marketing.

If your FAQ is not officially sponsored by a newsgroup, mailing list, or other organization, there are other ways of publicizing and distributing it. You can begin by posting it on your own Web site, like Arthur Baker's Bankruptcy FAQ. Put the FAQ into hypertext format, with the questions at the top joined by hypertext links to the answers. You should also provide it in a straight ASCII text format to make it easier for people to download and redistribute it. Using PDF from Adobe is yet another formatting option. Many businesses distribute their specialized FAQs by e-mail, often through the use of auto-responders that mail them out in response to an e-mail request directed to a certain address.

You should send announcements of the FAQ to relevant (and only relevant) newsgroups and mailing lists. A reference to it in your e-mail signature block can serve the dual purposes of promoting the FAQ and giving you credibility as an expert on a particular topic.

Aggressively search for Web pages that your potential clients might read, and ask the Webmasters to include a link to your FAQ. They will be much more likely to create such a link to an FAQ on a subject of interest to their readers than to a law firm site that does not contain such material.

Interactivity

Try to engage the visitors of your Web site with interactive features like surveys, nonlinear slide shows, a site-specific search engine, or other interactive features.

One of the best examples of this is the "CyberBarrister Quiz" at the prize-winning Satterlee Stephens Web site, **http://www.ssbb.com**, shown in Figure 11-2.

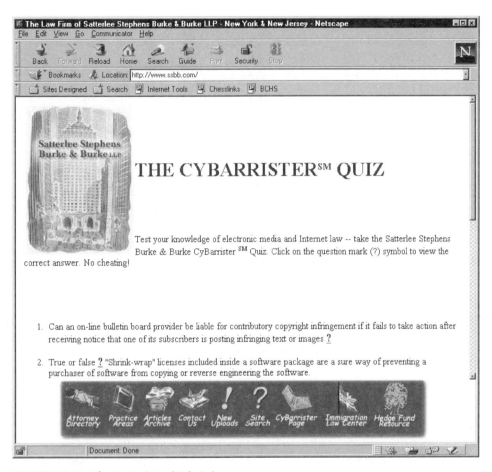

FIGURE 11-2. The CyBarrister (SM) Quiz

Using Domain Names for Law Firms

If you were looking for the best possible securities lawyer, would you be more comfortable with one whose business card had a Hackensack, New Jersey, address or a Wall Street location?

The Hackensack lawyer could well be the superior lawyer, but that's not the impression his business card creates. To people who are comfortable in the online world, your e-mail address says as much about you as the location of your physical office. On the Internet, any law firm—regardless of its size— can obtain the equivalent of a Wall Street address easily and inexpensively.

Systems like America Online are easy to use and they market to people with few technical skills, with great success. As a result of this, people who use some of these systems, especially America Online and Prodigy, are stereotyped as rather unsavvy by many other Internet users. Like most stereotypes, this one is not generally well grounded in reality. Unfair though it may be, however, many people hold this view.

What are the chances that this stereotype could hurt a lawyer whose only e-mail account was on one of these systems? It depends on the location and nature of the lawyer's practice. If you practice law in a small rural community and your clients are mostly middle-class, it's probably not a factor. If, on the other hand, you represent sophisticated business clients, or would *like* to represent them, telling them that your e-mail address is jsmith@barrister.com is preferable to telling them that it's smithja499@aol.com.

The most prestigious type of Internet address is one with your own *domain name*. This is the part of the e-mail address to the right of the @ symbol. If the name of your firm is Smith, Jones & Thomas, for example, you can arrange for all the lawyers in your firm to have an address in this format:

jsmith@sjt.com *or* john.smith@smith.jones.thomas.com

Any number of variations on this theme are possible. Experienced users tend to prefer the shorter formats. The *.com* extension indicates that you are a business. The part after the @ symbol will be the same for every lawyer in your firm with an e-mail account. If you eventually decide to open up a Web home page, you can set it up so that the URL, or address, is:

http://www.sjt.com *or* http://www.smith.jones.thomas.com

An alternative to a variant of the law firm name is selecting one or more domain names that indicate the type of practice. Many of the obvious choices, like *visalaw.com,* are already spoken for, but there is still room for creativity.

It is possible to have more than one domain name that points to the same Web site, a process known as *aliasing.* You can also have different domain names for different sections of the same Web site. For example Smith, Jones & Thomas might wish to have sjt.com as the default entry to its Web site, from which visitors should be able to reach any subsection. There might, however, be marketing benefits to letting users with specialized interests bypass the generic entry point and jump directly to the corporate law section by using corplaw.com or to the labor law section by using laborlaw.com. This is a way of showing that the firm is serious about its commitment to a given practice area. It might also make it easier to persuade other relevant sites to build a hypertext link directly to that section, as explained in the next chapter.

You can use the InterNIC Web site to determine whether someone else has already registered a domain name that you are considering. The site's URL is http://www.internic.net.

If someone else has already registered your first domain choice, you normally have two options:

1. Selecting another name
2. Working out a deal with the prior registrant

The New Orleans firm of Phelps Dunbar, for example, successfully negotiated with a small business that had previously registered the domain name phelps.com. On the other hand, West Publishing Company was not successful in persuading a prior registrant to give up the rights to west.com, so they use westpub.com instead.

There is a third possibility *if* you have registered a trademark on a potential domain name. You may be able to prevent someone else from registering a domain name in your trademark. This is a developing area of law, with more information available at http://www.patents.com.

Many law firms that have no immediate plans to get on the Internet are registering their domain names. A few years ago, only 10 percent of the largest law firms in the country had established World Wide Web sites, but 60 percent of them had registered domain names. Some law firms are registering domain names related to areas of law. For example, the name whistleblower.com now belongs to a San Francisco firm that specializes in False Claims Act cases.

Another advantage of having your own domain name is that it provides more flexibility and negotiating leverage in dealing with your Internet service provider. If you do not have your own domain name, your e-mail is routed to you "in care of" your ISP, be it America Online or a local company. That's what the @ symbol means. Suppose that you have a falling out with that ISP? If you change providers, what will happen to the e-mail that's sent to your old address? Will it be forwarded, and if so, for how long? You could get hurt during a changeover.

While there might still be a few hassles, having your own domain name makes a changeover simpler. The new ISP can arrange for all your e-mail to be forwarded to your new account. To your clients, you're still at the same familiar electronic address.

Some law firms register multiple domain names to reinforce "branding," a projection of expertise. Robinson & Cole has registered deregulation.com, statetaxes.com, landtakings.com, and bostondevelopment.com. As Mark Pruner of Web Counsel, LLC, has pointed out: "Businesses, other firms, not-for-profits and government agencies will be more likely to contribute material and associate their names with sites that do not directly promote the sponsoring firm and are part of a virtual community." Of course, the sponsoring law firm benefits nonetheless.

What is needed to register a domain name? It merely requires an application, a small fee (seventy dollars for the first two years and thirty-five dollars for each subsequent year), and a computer on the Internet that will respond to the domain name when the registration organization tries a test contact. It doesn't have to be your computer, just one set up to answer with the electronic equivalent of "Present" when the roll is called. Most ISPs will help you for a nominal fee.

A few ISPs and Web site designers maintain that customized domain names are an unnecessary affectation that only appeals to vanity and snobbishness. When assessing the strength of this argument, remember that most of these people own Web site hosting businesses that do not offer customized domain names to their customers. While these businesses have their own distinct, easy-to-remember customized domain names, they are at the same time trying to convince customers that the customers *do not* need one. Is there something wrong with this picture?

Having your own law firm domain name is not an issue of vanity (although it does feel nice) but rather one of intense practicality:

- Does it make sense to lock yourself into a long-term business relationship with one Web hosting service that has so much bargaining leverage over you?
- Do you want to give clients who understand the Internet the inadvertent impression that you are a marginal operation?
- Do you want more sophisticated clients who understand the benefits of owning a domain name to question the business judgment you use in your own firm's affairs?

If the answer to any of these questions is no, then your firm needs its own domain name.

Enhancing Client Service through the Web

The most obvious reason for a law firm to establish a Web site is to expose the firm to potential new clients. This, however, is far from the only reason to have a Web site. For some firms, it is not even the main reason.

Law firm marketing experts typically advise investing a high percentage of your effort in two areas:

1. Retaining existing clients
2. Generating more business from them

The 80/20 rule is often cited: Spend 80 percent of your marketing efforts on your existing clients and 20 percent on attracting new clients.

While an Internet presence can be useful in bringing in new clients, conventional Web sites can benefit you just as much, and probably more, by helping you retain existing clients and increase your billings from them. For some of these uses, a simple Web site will suffice. For other uses, a secure extranet-type of Web site will be required.

If you regularly include material of interest to your clients, they will continue to visit your Web site and learn about areas in which your services can benefit them. This is why providing memoranda on legal topics has been a staple feature of law firm Web sites such as the trailblazing Venable, Baetjer, Howard & Civiletti home page at http://www. venable.com. Although your primary intended audience may be existing clients, if the Web site is public, an incidental benefit is possible: others may come across it and be impressed enough to become clients.

Carl Oppedahl, a leading patent lawyer, says that his firm's Web site (http://www.patents.com) was set up to respond to people contacting the firm for basic information, such as what it costs to obtain a patent, how to obtain copyright protection, and the like. He estimates that each lawyer in the firm spent an average of one hour a week or more responding to such inquiries. A Web site made sense to his firm because many of those making inquiries would rather get such information from a Web site.

In another practical use, the San Francisco-based firm of Brobeck, Phleger & Harrison (as discussed in Chapter 9) uses the Internet to make its law library a profit center. Clients can request billable research projects directly from the Web site.

Even if only 25 percent of your clients are comfortable using the Internet, distributing information via the Web can still save you money because it can be so inexpensive. Furthermore, if 25 percent of your clients have Internet access this year, it's likely that the number will be more like 50 percent next year and higher in subsequent years.

You can make available much more information at a Web site than is practical to give clients in printed form. Some clients prefer to receive large volumes of material in electronic form instead of in paper. Making an electronic version available is considered "value added" because it can be manipulated more readily.

With the consent of the bankruptcy court, the law firm of Camhy Karlinsky & Stein used its Web site (http://www.camhy.com) as the primary means of distributing a reorganization plan to eight thousand creditors in the Fruehauf Trailer Corporation's bankruptcy. Creditors without Web access could pay twelve dollars for a paper copy of the plan.

For some firms, the attractiveness of being able to distribute information to clients easily and inexpensively is in itself enough to justify moving to the Web. The Web site of Boston's Hale & Dorr (http://www.haledorr.com) is a good example of this philosophy. As that firm's former director of client services, Mara Aspinall, explained to *legal.online* magazine:

> We looked at a home page primarily as a way to get basic information to current clients. We needed to give clients as many communication possibilities as we could. A client can go to our home page and look at the biography of an attorney they never met, or look at the practice areas they are not familiar with. We've had a lot of feedback, all positive, that clients like having the access, like having it in real time.

Distributing information via the Web normally does not require a secure Web site, but if the material is extensive or sensitive, law firms may not want to give it away. In that event, a secure Web site will be needed. Only users who have been given passwords will be allowed access.

Extranets for Client Service

While static Web sites can be used to provide many client services, interactive features provided through extranets can provide more ambitious features. This chapter focuses on extranets as marketing and client retentions tools chapter 18 provides more information.

The Los Angeles-based law firm of Latham & Watkins is a pioneer in using the Web for client service.

The Regulatory Flexibility Group, an advocacy organization made up of fourteen Southern California companies concerned with manufacturing emissions regulation, is one of Latham & Watkins' major clients. Before setting up their extranet, its fax, phone, and copying charges for notifying fifty-four individual participants about new laws and technology were about $2,000 a month. Partner Robert Wyman decided to establish a private, password-secured Web site to distribute this information more rapidly and inexpensively. He was able to set up a site within one month, and it has been extraordinarily successful. The clients appreciate the extra speed and convenience as well as the reduced costs.

As explained in *Amlaw Tech* (Shoket: "Latham's Lawyer-Driven Approach," p. 50, Spring 1997.), the Washington, D.C. branch of the same firm established another extranet for another group of clients concerned with technology issues, the International Environmental Network (IEN). One motivation was complaints by clients about receiving large amounts of material in paper instead of electronically. One client said that he had accumulated twenty-six unwieldy three-ring binders of newsletters and regulations from Latham. According to Latham partner David Hayes, "The real value of the site is that it has given the firm a cachet that has led to about four new IEN members since the site's launch." Possibly the best thing about satisfied clients is that they lead to new clients.

Uses of this type are best reserved for secure extranets. A sophisticated extranet makes it possible to restrict the client's access to material the law firm has decided to make available. A client's confidential information should never be accessible except by authorized personnel.

How many firms make standard forms available to clients? How many of those clients are using a copy of a copy of a copy of a form that their lawyer gave them years ago? With a Web site, you can make the newest version of your forms available twenty-four hours a day, seven days a week, at the client's convenience. If you have a sophisticated Web site, you can set it up to bill the client for each document downloaded.

An extranet can be used to give clients access to material like this:

- Files related to that client, including briefs, memos, depositions, and other work product
- Internal docket sheets, time sheets, and relevant sections of lawyer calendars
- Memoranda analyzing new or pending legislation or regulations or significant cases that may be too detailed or sensitive for distribution on a public Web site
- Announcements of seminars or other events of interest to the client

Do you want a client to review some documents before a fast-approaching hearing? Making them available via an extranet may be the most convenient way for you and the client.

Of course, extranets can work both ways. If a law firm does extensive work for a major client, it may be appropriate to give the law firm access to the client's network through an extranet, possibly one operated by the client's in-house counsel. The client can save money by making voluminous databases available in a manner that is convenient for both client and law firm.

Not all law firms will feel comfortable providing this type of access and level of service. However, in today's economic environment, where clients are less loyal than they were twenty years ago, this type of interlinking can be a powerful way of enhancing client loyalty and tightening relationships between firms and their most valuable clients.

Building Client Relationships in Other Ways

Mark Pruner suggested a few other ways in which a Web site can be used to build relationships with clients and prospective clients in a presentation for the Practicing Law Institute, now archived at http://www.webcounsel.com:

- Once you have a Web site, you not only have the ability to link to anyone, you can also publish to the world. Your clients may not want to put up certain kinds of information on their Web sites (e.g., litigation or regulatory agency's enforcement actions), so you can provide an appropriate site.
- Firm lawyers may be actively involved in charity work. Offer to host the charity's Web site on your Web site. Everyone who comes to the site will be typing the firm name in the URL. You need not link to the charity from your home page. Give the group a sub-domain such as http://www.firmname.com/~charity.
- If you are going to serve as a special master in complex litigation, offer your Web site as a clearinghouse for information. If your firm is in a multiparty litigation, you can also set up a password-protected Web site-based clearinghouse for information for all the counsel on your side. Your firm will then be at the center of the information flow.
- If you have a referral network, you can provide a short Web page to each of these lawyers to strengthen these relationships. Ask these referring lawyers what other Web-based resources you can supply via your Web site.

Mark's examples merely scratch the surface. The only limits are ethics rules and your imagination.

As Greg Siskind has observed, "Marketing is about building relationships." In the long run, this may be the most effective law firm marketing philosophy of all.

Resources

Online

Red Street Consulting's site reviews: http://www.redstreet.com. A wonderful site designed by Erik Heels and Rick Klau, authors of *Law Law Law on the Internet* (American Bar Association: Law Practice Management Section, 1998). It contains many reviews of law firm Web sites. Hypertext links to each of the reviewed sites make this site a veritable textbook for lawyers concerning what to do and what to avoid. No teaching method provides the impact of real-world examples, and the insights sprinkled liberally throughout these reviews and the authors' excellent book are priceless to both Web site novices and veterans.

The Internet Lawyer magazine's site reviews: http://www.internetlawyer.com/firms.htm. Mark Pruner, another respected Web site designer, provides short reviews of law firm sites.

Richard Granat's "Creating Your Own Web Site": http://www.digital-lawyer.com/websites/new_page_4.htm. An excellent practical overview.

Mark Pruner's "Creation, Marketing, Disintermediation, and Ethics": http://www.webcounsel.com/plipaper.htm. An outline of a Practising Law Institute presentation.

Matthew Mandell et al.'s "A Web Hosting Primer for Law Firms": http://www.technolawyer.com/technopost/winner3-27-98.html. From *The Techno-Lawyer* (March 27, 1998).

In addition, prize-winning Web sites can make good models. Here are some lists of prize-winning law firm sites:

- Webbernaut Awards: http://www.webcounsel.com/wbrntlst.htm
- legal.online magazine: http://www.legalonline.com
- Greg Siskind's Top 20 Picks:
  http://www.lawmarketing.com/cgi-bin/law/display.pl/appendB

In Paper

HTML Publishing on the Internet, Second Edition, by Brent Haslop and David Holzgang (*Coriolis* 1998). The single best one-volume general Web site design tutorial and reference book that I know. It includes clear explanations of important topics ignored or glossed over by most authors.

Teach Yourself Web Publishing with HTML in a Week, by Laura Lemay (*Sams.net* 1994). Lemay's original best-selling book. It provides a simpler introduction to the topic than the previous recommendation. This book has gone through many subsequent revisions and has spawned a whole line of books marketed using Lemay's name, some of them written by other authors who emulate Lemay's clear style and simple explanations.

The Lawyer's Guide to Creating Web Pages, by Kenneth E. Johnson (American Bar Association: Law Practice Management Section, 1997, 159 pages). One of the best legal technology authors around provides an overview of technical aspects of web site design and web site design tools. The author's web site is also worth a visit:

http://www.wwwscribe.com

CHAPTER **TWELVE**

Publicizing a Law Firm Web Site

If a tree falls in an empty forest, does it make a sound?

—Zen Buddhist Koan

AFTER CENTURIES of debate, the jury is still out on this philosophical riddle. There is, however, a clear answer to a modern-day counterpart: Your Web site will definitely not help you if no one knows about it.

Few people are likely to stumble upon your site while aimlessly surfing the Internet. Next to poor substantive content, poor promotion is probably the biggest reason why many law firm Web sites do not live up to their owners' expectations. To make your site successful, you must promote it aggressively.

Inadequate publicity is an Achilles' heel for most Web site design companies. If they offer any assistance at all, it is likely to be an automated registration service. These sound impressive to novices because they promise to register your site with hundreds of search engines and directories. Yet all this involves is sending a form e-mail announcement to a mailing list of search engines. Because they are limited in their customizing ability, these services have marginal value at best. In some cases, they can even be counterproductive. You are flirting with failure if you rely on these automated services instead of taking more realistic measures to let the world know where your site is and what it has to offer.

The promotion process has five general steps:

1. Planning a promotable site
2. Making your site easy to find
3. Promoting the site off the Internet
4. Promoting the site on the Internet
5. Using feedback to improve promotion

Designing a Promotable Site

Do not wait until your site is up and running before thinking about how you will promote it. This issue should be one of your top priorities during the design phase.

Try to include material that will be attractive to journalists and other key opinion influencers for your target market. The Vacatur Center at Anderson Kill and Olick's site, http://www.andersonkill.com/vacatur.htm, is a great example of this. The practice of allowing litigants to bury unfavorable judicial precedents through postjudgment financial settlements is controversial, and will be for the foreseeable future. Including these court decisions on their Web site was a groundbreaking idea, and guaranteed that sophisticated editors and journalists would not ignore this as they would a garden-variety Web site. In just a few months, the site garnered Anderson Kill and Olick favorable coverage in many news stories, including a major write-up in the business section of the *Washington Post,* the newspaper favored by many of those in Anderson Kill's target market group. Moreover, journalists will probably be writing stories about vacatur for decades to come. The Web site helps raise awareness of Anderson Kill's expertise in this area and will make many journalists want to seek comments from Anderson, Kill lawyers in future.

If you want to use a Web site to promote your firm, do not ask yourself, What will be safe and make our Web site have the same bland, comforting ambiance as hundreds of others? Instead, ask yourself, What will make us stand out from the competition and catch the attention of mainstream journalists?

Structure your site so that it has discrete sections that can be promoted separately. Each section can be an independent entry point into your firm's Web site. People with little understanding of the Internet often say, "But I want all the visitors to my site to enter through my main entry point, so I can control their experience." What they actually mean is that they want the first thing every visitor sees to be the nice graphic on their opening screen, and they definitely don't want any visitor to miss the great photo of the senior partner, etc.

This kind of thinking results from misunderstanding Internet dynamics. In a well-designed Web site, the user is in control. If you don't give visitors what they want, and give it to them fast, they will not stick around. They will go to better sites to get the information they are seeking.

Counsel Connect president Mark Obbie explained how to structure a Web site in a forum on the invaluable Counsel Connect online service (http://www.counsel.com):

> Lots of law firm home pages have heeded the call that "content is king," but they're burying their content—sometimes excellent articles— beneath several layers of marketing junk. . . . Tell me why I should spend any time looking at this. And tell me this very, very quickly. That means that the little "Publications" or "Newsletters" button tucked away at the bottom of your home page should become the top page itself, except with more sizzle—better headlines, reader-oriented angles on topics, etc. Then, and only then, will your readers be ready for "Partner Biographies," "Our Firm's History" and the ever-popular "Message from the Chairman."

If you put the substantive content up front, and do a good job with it, visitors who are favorably impressed will actively seek out your marketing material. They will be in a much more receptive mood when they do get around to reading the "Message from the Chair."

Establish different entry points for different practice areas of your firm. Allow the regulatory group a section, the estate planning lawyers a section, the environmental lawyers a section, and so on. You can do the same thing even if you are a one-person firm. Do you advise associations? Include a section on association law. Do you have several clients in the trucking industry? Include a section on issues of interest to those in that industry. All these sections are potential entry points.

Every different entry point should have navigational icons at the bottom of every page to make it easy for visitors to find your main entry point and your marketing materials. In Internet indexes and subject matter organizers, promote each section independently as a site about regulatory law, or estate planning, or environmental law, or whatever the topic. In this way, you can attract much more traffic and, more importantly, attract visitors who are more likely to be potential clients.

Including External Links

Be judicious in building links to external sites. One of the most common mistakes in poor law firm Web sites is including external links for no reason. A common example is highlighting the name of a lawyer's alma mater in her or his biography and making a hypertext link to the school. Web surfers have notoriously short attention spans. If your site is good, you've probably invested a significant amount of time designing and publicizing it. You want visitors to stay and look around for a while. Does it make sense to show your visitors the door as soon as they've arrived? Unless your site is intended purely as a public service site, with no intention to benefit your marketing, don't include an external link without first asking whether it benefits you in some way. Well-chosen external links can help by making your site more attractive to visitors, but thoughtlessly sprinkling hypertext links throughout a site is counterproductive.

On the other hand, if you have good reasons for linking to an external site, don't be afraid to do so. Here are some general approaches to external links:

- With permission of the client, it can be beneficial to link to client Web sites.
- You can indirectly benefit by providing visitors with links to unusually helpful resources. For example, many of your Web page visitors may be pleasantly surprised to learn that they can get free information from the SEC's EDGAR database. They may be grateful for your thoughtfulness in including such a link, and impressed with your knowledge of the Internet. (The Brobeck, Phleger & Harrison firm includes a link to the SEC site under a button reading "The EDGAR Connection." See http://www.brobeck.com to see how they do this and pick up some other tips from a well-designed site.)
- Some firms can amass collections of links so comprehensive and so useful that they become a strong reason to visit their Web sites. It takes a great deal of work to design a trailblazer page that will act as a magnet, but if you are willing to invest the time, this can be a viable strategy.

Use discretion in including external links:

- Don't continually make it too tempting to leave your Web site: Many visitors will take you up on your invitation.
- If your site has a lot of external links, mention it on the opening page and suggest that visitors bookmark your site initially so they

can always find their way back to your home page. Then list some of the more important links to other sites you've provided for them.

◆ Once you've established links to external sites, periodically check all those links to verify accuracy and location.

Making Your Page Easy to Find

All the sophisticated Web search engines use numerical scoring systems to rank sites by relevance to a typed-in request. If someone conducts a search for documents containing "(toxic AND tort) and (attorney OR lawyer)" hundreds of results may be returned. The scoring system decides which results appear at the top of the list. A particular scoring system might weigh how many times key phrases appear at your site and where they appear. Other weighting factors are explained in more detail in Chapter 5.

When designing your site, keep search engines in mind. Think carefully about the keywords that potential clients trying to find a firm like yours would use, and make sure that these keywords appear repeatedly and prominently at the appropriate parts of your firm's site.

Some automated Web indexing tools rely on what are called META tags being inserted in the HEAD section of the HTML markup. These are not visible to casual visitors, but they are used by search engines.

Some Web page designers also include repetitions of key phrases in places where the automated Web search engines will pick them up, but the phrases won't be obvious to visitors to your page. One such place is inside the HTML title block, as in the following example:

<TITLE> Smith And Jones Law Firm: Toxic Torts.
Environmental Law Environmental Law Toxic Torts
Environmental Law Toxic Torts Environmental Law Toxic
Torts </TITLE>

Casual visitors would see only the first part of the page's title, but some search engines will pick up the extra repetitions of the key phrases (*Toxic Torts and Environmental Law*) and give this page a higher rating as a result.

Overdoing keyword repetitions will annoy sophisticated Internet users, some of whom call listing extraordinary numbers of repetitions of keywords **index spamming**. Some search engines now detect attempts to manipulate the system and may penalize pages for doing so, or even altogether ban sites that are too aggressive. Use moderation in applying such techniques, and monitor what any outside Web consultants you may employ are doing in this area.

Some search engine ranking-manipulation techniques may be unwise, unethical, or both. Some Web sites, for example, try to raise their hit counts by including hidden search terms related to sex. This would not raise the credibility of a law firm foolish enough to try it.

One Web site tried to boost its ranking by including in its META tags the names of the partners in a law firm well-known for its expertise in intellectual property law, Oppedahl and Larsen, http://www.patents.com. When such tactics are discovered, they can result in litigation and embarrassment.

Promoting Your Site Off the Internet

The key rule here is that your Internet site should be integrated into nearly all your off-the-Net marketing, and vice versa. Once you have this idea firmly in mind, other things logically follow. For starters, include the Web site URL and your e-mail address in the following:

◆ All business cards, letterhead, and fax cover sheets
◆ Every issue of any paper newsletters you distribute
◆ Any law firm brochures you use
◆ Any handouts distributed by your lawyers at their speaking engagements

Announcements similar to those sent out by firms to herald new associates or new partners could also be used, as could notices to newsletters published by legal groups to which firm members belong. It's extremely important to send out paper press releases about the Web site. These should be sent to publications most likely to be read by your potential clients. If, for example, the site deals with advertising law, try *Imprint, American Advertising,* or *Advertising Age* magazines. If your legal experience would make you marketable to dealers in rare artwork and you have relevant material on your Web site, try *Dealer Communicator* or *Manhattan Arts International Magazine.* One of my clients does a great deal of tax law work for universities. Having his Web site featured by the *Chronicle of Higher Education,* the leading trade paper for his target market, was a major boost.

During the design process, think about what will impress the relevant journalists. If your site is just a cyberspace billboard for your firm, the equivalent of a vanity press autobiography with no substantive content, few print publications will be interested in it. You will get a more positive reaction in industry newsletters and other potential client referral sources if you have information at your site that is useful to your target market. I can't say it often enough: It all centers around content.

Promoting Your Site on the Internet

At the end of this chapter are three law firm Web site publicity checklists. The first provides a general checklist for promoting a law firm Web site on the Internet. The other two checklists facilitate registering with search engines and directories, both general and legal specific.

Many vendors will take your announcement and forward it to other indexers and search engines. Here are two of the better ones:

Submit It at http://www.submit-it.com

The Postmaster at http://www.netcreations.com/postmaster/

If you want maximum exposure for your site, vendors like these save time, but if you want to get the best possible publicity for your site, it is a mistake to rely on them exclusively. While the "multiple listing services" are convenient, it's best to submit information about your site manually, at least to some of the key directories and search engines. The better multiple submission sites allow some flexibility, but they are not as effective as visiting the indexes and submitting the information yourself. At Yahoo, for example, you can improve your chances of obtaining a good listing and possible cross-listings in more than one relevant area if you post your announcement manually.

Announce the site in appropriate Usenet newsgroups and mailing lists. The newsgroup comp.infosystems.www.announce is an obvious starting point. Check out the group's charter to see how to format your announcement.

Do not limit yourself to newsgroups and mailing lists that are designed for new Web site announcements. When you stray beyond those few, however, use extreme caution. Unless your site has obvious value to the readers of the particular newsgroup or mailing list, and you make it clear what that value is without playing up the commercial element, such announcements will be counterproductive.

In addition to formal announcements of a new site, look for other opportunities to pass along the word about your site in newsgroups and mailing lists. You *must* tie the information about your site to a topic legitimately discussed in that forum. For example, you could answer a question by noting that relevant information is at your Web site.

Remember that, in addition to promoting their Web site's default entry point (i.e., the home page), most law firms can benefit by promoting significant subsections and attractions. This increases traffic because sections can be designed to appeal to niche audiences. If the site is well designed, someone entering at any part of your Web site should immediately know whose site it is and be able to find your main entry point and marketing materials easily.

Signature Block Usage

It's a very good idea to include the URL of your site in your signature block for e-mail and Usenet newsgroups. If there are any mailing lists or newsgroups that are particularly relevant to your firm's site, someone from your firm should participate so that others will frequently see the signature block (along with an appropriate disclaimer). If your lawyers post intelligent comments, the curious will check out the Web site to learn more about them.

Customized Links to Your Site

It's critical to have highly visited Web sites build hypertext links to yours. The most effective links you can have are those from sites that your potential clients might visit. For example, a number of university sites link to The College and University Tax Page, http://www.universitytax.com. The link acts as a sort of referral, or implied endorsement, giving you instant credibility with the referred party.

It sounds like a pretty good game, right? To get into it, it's important to have a "promotable" site. If your site is good, other Web site owners will consider a link to it to be a valuable service to their own visitors.

Some Web site owners will learn about your site from the rest of your publicity campaign and decide to add links to it, if you have good content. You can get other such links by sending e-mail to the owners of suitable sites and asking them to link to you. Many of them may ask for a reciprocal link from their site, which may or may not fit into your Web site marketing strategy. As noted earlier, a hypertext link can be interpreted as an implied endorsement. If your site is valuable enough, the other site owners may not need or even ask for a reciprocal link.

How can you locate sites whose owners will be interested in linking to you? One method is to find a good site that is appealing to your market, possibly a strong competitor's site, and then learn who is linking to that site. AltaVista (http://www.altavista.com) is one of the search engines that allows this. For example, if you want to find out who is linking to the ABA Web site, enter the following search request:

   +link:abanet.org -url:abanet.org

The second part (-url:abanet.org) of the search request is simply a time-saver: it excludes internal links within the ABA Web site. AltaVista will respond to this search request by returning a list of sites that have linked to that domain name. If these site designers thought it was worthwhile to build a link to a site that appealed to your market, they will probably want to build a link to yours as well, if, once again, you have created a promotable site.

More Mileage from Your Memos

An innovative way of increasing Web site traffic is to publish some of your content at sites owned by other organizations—if they will provide a hypertext link back to your site. If you publish a legal memo at the Law Journal Extra site (http://www.ljx.com), for example, they will include a hypertext link back to your firm's home page. Since you can usually also post the article at your own site, you don't lose anything by publishing articles elsewhere.

Creative Sharing

Consider how to put some of your other work product to added use. The New York firm of Herzfeld & Rubin got extra use out of a computer database of personal injury awards it had prepared for a particular case by allowing the *New York Law Journal* to republish it at the journal's site at http://www.nylj.com/awards.

Malls and Directories

Some firms hope their sites will be more easily found if they are listed in online "malls" or commercial directories with other law firms. If there is little or no extra charge for inclusion in such a listing, it probably won't hurt you, but it is inadvisable to rely on such a listing instead of aggressively promoting your Web site in other ways. Some mall/directory operations like to boast of the high numbers of hits that their sites attract. Such claims can be misleading, as explained below.

It's also a good idea to be wary of mall operations that do not give you the option of having a customized domain name. They prefer to give you a directory listing under their own domain name instead. This generally results in a URL that is longer than it needs to be—and harder for clients to remember. Furthermore, without your own customized domain name it is more difficult for you to move to another vendor, thus reducing your future mobility and bargaining power.

Using Feedback to Improve Your Site

If you know the quantity and types of visitors accessing your Web site, you can gain valuable data for future improvements to it.

Server Log Statistics

Before you select a Web site host, ask about the availability of logs to track visits to your site. How extensive are they, and how much help does the host's software provide in analyzing visitor trends? Two relevant questions: (1) Where are your visitors coming from? (2) Which pages do they visit?

For an example of what computer-generated hit counts look like, check out http://www.abanet.org/stats. Some lawyers who operate Web sites set up their browser programs so that every time the programs are loaded, the lawyers go to their statistics page and see how many people have visited. This will probably be overkill for most lawyers, but it is a good idea to monitor the results from time to time.

If your Web site host does not provide visitor statistics, you can purchase third-party counting services. These generally rely on inserting a link back to a counter at a central location that the monitored site owner can access when desired. These services tend to be much less useful than the information provided by a good monitoring program installed directly on a Web server. If you operate your own web server, you can install your choice of logging and analysis software.

The Hit Game

Be aware that some people consider it as a separate hit (i.e., a request for a section of the Web site) each time any file is downloaded. Under this liberal interpretation, one person downloading a single page that included six pictures and one Java applet would account for eight hits: one for the text file, one for the Java applet, and six for the pictures. A single visitor could easily accumulate hundreds of hits during one ten-minute surf of a site. Don't equate hit counts with distinct visitors.

Links to Your Site

You should periodically check to see who is providing links to your Web site. When others have built a large number of links to your site, it is a good sign that you are on the road to success.

As previously explained, you can use search engines to check on such links. Some links may be undesirable from your point of view, and you may wish to ask that they be removed. Knowing what parties have linked to your site may give you ideas for further links or other promotional activities.

Read the text accompanying such links. Some may be complimentary and some critical. (After another site criticized me for having the letters J.D. and LL.M. after my name, I decided to delete them.) If your site is included on a list of the ten ugliest, take it as a hint.

Some novice Web site owners become agitated when they discover that other sites have built links directly to their content (e.g., articles written by the firm's lawyers) instead of going through their default main entry point. This practice has been called "deep linking." They have a vague suspicion that such direct linking is an unethical or otherwise improper exploitation of intellectual property. A few will even request that links be made only to their default entry page.

Generally, if your Web site is well designed, *any* hypertext link to any part of your site is beneficial to you. It gives you a chance to capture the attention and interest of more visitors than you would otherwise have gotten. It is your responsibility to take advantage of such a boon. Make sure that a visitor coming into any part of your site knows where he or she is and has easy access to information about you and your firm.

There are a few exceptions to the desirability of links, the most important being when someone builds a hypertext link that puts your site in a *frame* on that party's site. Frames allow one Web site's image to appear inside a section of a screen image from another site. Frames can make it difficult for visitors to leave the referring site and to concentrate on your material, and they can sometimes even mislead visitors as to the ownership of your site. If you don't like the way a framing site presents yours, it is appropriate to ask to be removed.

Figure 12-1 illustrates how framing works. The excellent Lawguru legal research site, http://www.lawguru.com/search/lawsearch.html, uses a frame at the top of the screen to display various destinations in a frame at the bottom of the screen. In the illustration, a search engine operated by the Government Printing Office at the University of California is shown in the frame at the bottom of the screen.

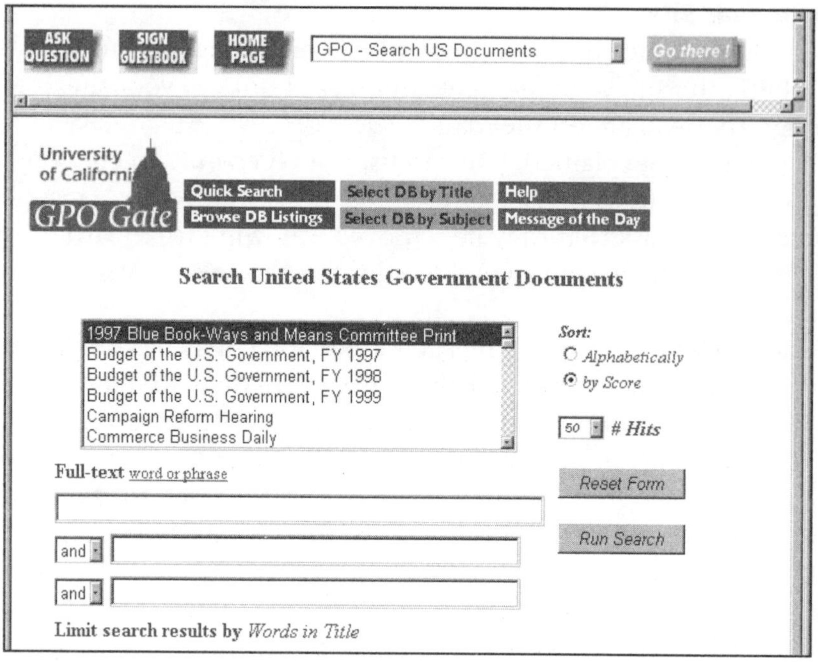

FIGURE 12-1. Example of Site Framing

Using the Publicity Checklist Forms

The following checklists are designed for use in publicizing law firm Web sites. To make sure you have the latest version, to make it easier to use the hypertext links, and to facilitate customizing these forms for your own use, check out this book's Web site at http://www.abanet.org/lpm/netbook. The site has the newest versions in hypertext and word processor file formats.

Law Firm Web Site Publicity
Master Checklist

URL _____

Site Name _____

Law Firm Name _____

Law Firm Contact _____

E-mail Address _____

Preparation		
Item	***Date Completed***	***Date Checked***
Keywords META tag		
Description META tag		
First words of text on page: Do they describe the firm?		

Publicity Campaign		
Target	***Date Completed***	***Follow-up***
General search engines/directories **(See separate checklist)**		
Law-specific Web directories **(See separate checklist)**		
Automated promotion services (Optional)		
Lawyer-oriented discussion groups for states and cities where firm practices		
USENET (comp.infosystems.www.announce)		
Other relevant discussion groups		
Research of relevant special indices to request links		
Web site rollout inside of firm		
General e-mail press releases		
General paper press releases		
Press releases targeted to particular markets		
Personal contact with key editors/journalists		
Personal contact with key opinion influencers		

NOTE: This form is intended to serve as an overall guide to a law firm publicity campaign. Not every checklist item will apply to every campaign. For example, if your target audience is highly specialized, you should disregard general e-mail and paper press releases in favor of targeted news releases and personal contacts. The next two forms are to assist in particular aspects of the campaign.

Checklist of Major Search Engines and Directories

Search Engine	URL	Contact	Follow-up
AltaVista	http://www.altavista.digital.com		
Excite	http://www.excite.com		
Hotbot	http://www.hotbot.com		
Infoseek	http://guide.infoseek.com		
Lycos	http://www.lycos.com		
Magellan	http://www.mckinley.com		
Webcrawler	http://www.webcrawler.com		

Checklist of General Internet Directories

Directory	URL	Contact	Follow-up
Yahoo	http://www.yahoo.com		
Snap	http://www.snap.com		
Point (Top 5%)	http://point.lycos.com/categories/criteria.html		
Starting Point	http://www.stpt.com		

Checklist of Law Firm Indices

Index	URL	Contact	Follow-up
Attorney Net	http://www.attorneynet.com		
Carswell (Canada)	http://www.carswell.com:80/LawDir		
Emory University	http://www.law.emory.edu/LAW/refdesk/lawyers		
FindLaw	http://www.findlaw.com/14firms/lawyers.html		
Hieros Gamos	http://www.hg.org/lawfirms.html		
University of Indiana Law	http://www.law.indiana.edu/law/v-lib/lawfirms.html		
LJ Extra	http://public.ljextra.com/lfonline.html		
Legal.Net	http://www.legal.net		
Seamless Web	http://seamless.com		

Note: If you operate a free lawyer listing service or directory of lawyers and would like to be added to future versions of this list, send an e-mail to info@netlawtools.com.

Resources

Online
Search Engine Watch is a wonderful resource for nuts and bolts information about promoting a site on search engines: http://www.searchenginewatch.com.

Cindy Chick's publicity overview for LLRX at: http://www.llrx.com/features/publiciz.htm

Internet Legal Marketing: http://internetlawyer.com/ilm. A consortium of three legal businesses that provides law firms with consulting services, targeted banner ads, and print advertisements.

In Paper
Publicity on the Internet, by Steve O'Keefe (Wiley, 1997). An excellent book about Internet publicity that lawyers will find quite useful.

Do-It-Yourself Public Relations, by David E. Gumpert (American Bar Association: Law Practice Management Section, 1995). Your Web site should be promoted off the Internet as well as on the Internet, and this book is an excellent primer on non-Internet marketing. Written expressly for lawyers, the book includes a floppy disk with press releases and other forms in word processor format.

The Lawyer's Guide to Marketing on the Internet, by Gregory H. Siskind and Timothy J. Moses (American Bar Association: Law Practice Management Section, 1996).

CHAPTER **THIRTEEN**

Marketing via Discussion Groups

Some OF THE MOST SUCCESSFUL law firm Web sites, in my experience, are operated in conjunction with Internet discussion groups. This is probably not a coincidence. Discussion groups can nicely complement Web sites or serve as independent marketing tools. Note that while sections of this chapter refer mainly to mailing lists, most of it applies equally to Web-based discussion groups and newsgroups. The Web site accompanying this book, http://www.abanet.org/lpm/netbook, contains links for subscribing to all the lists mentioned in the chapter.

The first thing to understand about firm marketing via discussion groups is that there's a right way and a wrong way to go about it. The wrong way is spamming, or shotgun-style posting of ads, similar to what the "Green Card Lawyers" did to thousands of Usenet newsgroups (as discussed in Chapter 10). While this tactic is not illegal, it is very contrary to the mores of the online community, and you can expect to receive many angry responses from people who are annoyed by ads. If your conduct is blatant or repeated, your Internet service provider will almost certainly cancel your account. What then is the right way? There are several more subtle and effective methods of marketing your services to the right groups.

While lawyers who participate in online discussion groups must exercise a certain amount of caution, I tend to agree with Counsel Connect president Mark Obbie:

> Despite common fears that any legal discussion is a liability risk—particularly those with non-lawyers—there is practically no difference between on-line legal discussions and their "real world" analogs: public

speaking, writing articles, or simple conversations at a neighborhood picnic or a PTA meeting, where people talk to you about the law because you're a lawyer. So long as you treat online discussions as if you were a CLE event speaker or cocktail party analyst, and note that you're speaking *generally* and not giving advice, you should be fine.

Including a Signature Block

The initial step toward effective marketing on mailing lists is a good signature file. All messages that you post should contain a signature block identifying you, your firm, and your contact information. This is a key tool for networking on the Internet. Blatant commercialism is unwelcome on practically all mailing lists, but signature files of reasonable length are acceptable just about everywhere. Here is one example:

Clyde Barrow, Esq.
Estate Planning
333-555-1234
dilly@barrow-parker.com
Barrow and Parker, 345 Main St., Metropolitan, XX 12345

The next example is a little more elaborate:

```
**************************************************************
Jerry Lawson, Esq.                INTERNET TOOLS FOR ATTORNEYS
lawson@netlawtools.com            http://www.netlawtools.com
Phone: (703) 978-9498             FAX: (703) 978-0680

"Make Tomorrow's Ideas Work Today"   ABA TECHSHOW 99
Chicago, March 18-20, 1999           http://www.techshow.com
```

The formatting in the second example looks better in a fixed-pitch font, as shown. The row of asterisks at the top distinguishes the signature block from the body of the message. If you are trying to promote a Web site, like the one for ABA TECHSHOW, be sure to include the http:// portion for the URL. Modern e-mail programs will thereby recognize the URL as a hypertext link and let visitors go there with a single mouse click. This makes it easy for impulse visitors to get to the site.

Having a Web site and listing the URL in your signature block is a significant help. It lets people who want to get more information about you and your firm do so rapidly and conveniently.

Make sure that your e-mail signature file conforms to any rules that your state bar has on letterhead and signature blocks. For example, Mr. Barrow might need to say that "The state of X does not certify legal specializations." It is also a good idea to set up your signature file to include other disclaimers, as explained in the next chapter.

After you have composed a signature file, the next step is to do some reconnaissance to learn which lists are going to be most effective as marketing forums. They fall into two broad categories:

1. Interactive discussion groups to which any subscriber can post messages
2. One-way lists that serve to distribute information just as paper newsletters do

Using Existing Interactive Discussion Groups

Depending on your area of practice, you might use lists read mainly by lawyers as a source of referrals. I have referred clients to lawyers I came to know through mailing lists, particularly specialists whose postings impressed me with the lawyer's knowledge. Sometimes lawyers looking to refer a case will seek candidates by posting a notice on a list.

Discussion groups oriented toward specialized nonlegal audiences are an appealing alternative to the lawyer-oriented groups. If you were duck hunting, would you be likely to find more ducks at a National Rifle Association meeting or a game reserve? The association meeting could be a great place for hot tips on the best shotguns, but you're not going to find many ducks there.

If you want to stay on top of the law, the lawyer lists will be fine, but if your objective is marketing, go where the potential clients are. If, for example, you want to stay current on real property law developments, you might subscribe to DIRT, where discussions are tilted toward real property law. Many of the subscribers are law school professors. If, however, you want to develop new clients or stay on top of industry trends, you could monitor RESIDENTIAL-REALESTATE, which is described as a list for "full-time real estate brokers, investors, management companies, developers, or institutions; networking/dealmaking forum."

The big exception to my "duck hunting" rule is if your area of legal practice is such that you can readily expect to receive referrals from other lawyers. If you are in this category, lawyer-oriented discussion groups will be right for you.

FIGURE 13-1. Prairelaw.com, Which Hosts Web-based Discussion Groups for Consumers

Counsel Connect (http://www.counsel.com) is not a mailing list but a paid Internet service for lawyers. Among its features are two online discussion groups designed to make it easier for those in need of legal services to find lawyers who suit them: the Corporate Counsel Inquiries and Law Firm Inquiries sections. The former is primarily for corporations looking for outside counsel. General counsel post their requirements and lawyers who are interested to respond. The Law Firm Inquiries section is geared more toward lawyer-to-lawyer referrals. Here's an example of how the Corporate Counsel Inquiries section works.

One Saturday at 9:42 somebody from a large corporation posted the following request:

Need counsel in Philadelphia area for potential acquisition.

The following [edited] reply was posted at 11:49 the same morning:

> I suggest very strongly that you contact my partner . . . in our Philadelphia office—he can be reached at 215-123-4567, or by e-mail at charlie@abc.com. Charlie is the Vice Chair of our Business Department, and if you like, you can read more about him and the department on our Web page, at http://www.abc.com. If you contact Charlie, please tell him that I pointed you in his direction as a result of your posting an inquiry on Counsel Connect. If you have any questions today, please feel free to e-mail me directly at . . . or to call me at . . . .

There are many other Counsel Connect discussion areas that are not dedicated to legal marketing but may provide referral opportunities. In general, these can be divided into geographic areas or substantive areas of law. For example, someone in New York seeking an environmental lawyer in Austin may post a request to the Environmental Law or Texas discussion groups instead of, or in addition to, posting to one of the dedicated marketing discussion groups.

Counsel Connect is one of the best forums for this type of marketing, but there are others. You can sample a particular discussion group long enough to get a feel for it and then decide whether it will be a good source for referrals, clients, or both. If all the other subscribers on the list are lawyers, most of whom practice in the same field of law as you, it could be a great list for networking and education but you're probably not going to get many referrals. You will probably have better marketing results with something that's a little off the beaten track for lawyers.

Remember that the opportunity to answer questions posted by other subscribers is a chance to demonstrate your expertise in a favorable forum. Here are a few pointers:

- ◆ Be quick. A short reply that gets there fast is better than a magnum opus that arrives after the questioner has retained another lawyer.
- ◆ While e-mail is great, it's not always the best way to build a relationship. Ask yourself whether a phone call will be better than an e-mail reply.
- ◆ Especially when participating in public forums not restricted to lawyers, avoid giving any answer that could be construed as specific legal advice. This applies no matter how carefully you have drafted your disclaimer.
- ◆ Avoid one sentence replies like, "Call me and I'll be happy to talk to you about this issue." Call the questioner, or use the opportunity to show that party why she or he should call you.
- ◆ Consider whether it is better to post your response publicly or only to reply privately. Sometimes I do both, with a general reply to the

whole list and more detailed comments to the requestor. Remember that if you press the Reply button, most software will route your answer to all participants in the discussion, which could be embarrassing. You usually must take some other affirmative action to send a private reply.

◆ If you have it handy, consider providing additional material that you have written, possibly something posted at your Web site. I like to volunteer to send potential clients more lengthy information, possibly a memo or article I have on hand, by e-mail upon their request. This is more likely to lead to a dialog than merely sending a lot of information up front.

◆ Do not be aggressive in pursuing business in a discussion group. This will backfire. Never try to push yourself on a prospective client. Try to gain the respect of the other subscribers. If you succeed, they will come to you or refer their colleagues when they need a lawyer in your area.

As Mark Obbie explains, "The most successful online rainmakers are those with the patience (and good taste) to form relationships before expecting to reel in a new client. Relationships come through interactions in discussion groups, not just 'billboards' on the Web."

This form of marketing is not for everyone. It can be time intensive, and not everyone is in a specialized or "national" area of practice that can be effectively displayed on a mailing list. If you meet the prerequisites, though, this can be a very effective marketing tool.

One example is Mark Sanor, an associate who works in the Russian practice area with the Cleveland firm of Hahn Loeser & Parks. He subscribes to a number of lists that relate to Russia, including the Eastern European Business Network. Through participating in this list, he developed a large network of contacts with expertise in Russian law and business. When preparing for a three-month stay in Moscow, he posted a message to the list asking for help in finding an apartment or a potential joint venture or trading partners for his firm's clients. He received more than 150 replies, which led to his finding a "perfect apartment" as well as credible referrals for business relationships.

If they relate to your legal practice, you could try to develop new clients by subscribing to lists like NRCH (described as the "National Report on Computers and Health's Hospital Information Systems issues list; open discussion of management, operations, and technical issues facing health care information systems executives"); COMMERCIAL-REALESTATE ("for professionals involved in sales, acquisitions, management, and development of commercial property"); TELECOM-TECH ("forum for discussion of technical aspects of telecommunications, including legislation and regulations"); and HOA-LIST ("Home Owner Associations, for owners and associations, as well as lawyers, accountants, and managers working with HOA"). There are hundreds of other possibilities.

In sum, the way to use interactive discussion groups as marketing tools is to look for promising candidate lists and then to participate as a "good citizen" in the life of those mailing lists. As you become known to the participants, you can expect to make some contacts that could lead to new business—if you have chosen your lists well. Furthermore, even if you never obtain a client directly through a particular mailing list, monitoring one that is closely related to your practice can benefit you through education concerning new developments and potential clients' views of their industry.

Using Mailing Lists to Distribute Newsletters

Some law firm mailing lists serve not as two-way communication tools but more as inexpensive ways for firms to distribute information that would normally be distributed in a paper firm newsletter. E-mail mailing lists are cheaper, faster, and in a sense, closer to the client than the conventional paper newsletters on which many firms rely. The lists invite responses that can develop into additional work for your firm. It is easier for a potential client to reply to an e-mail message than it is to write a letter or to call on the telephone.

If your practice tends to focus on one or more groups of people with common interests, they may be candidates for subscribing to a mailing list run by you on that topic. For example, suppose that you represented many medical services providers in their disputes with third-party payors. Some firms with this type of practice publish paper newsletters for their clients. As e-mail becomes more and more accessible in the corporate world, use of Internet mailing lists to supplement or replace paper newsletters becomes increasingly attractive.

Another good candidate for a one-way e-mail mailing list might be a tax firm that periodically sends out announcements of tax law changes. Distributing this type of public service information to people who have asked to be on your list is an effective form of law firm promotion that fits in perfectly with Internet culture.

Newsletters are more likely to be effective if you can target them to different categories of clients and prospective clients. The law firm of

Fried, Frank, Harris, Shriver, and Jacobsen has at least five different e-mail newsletters: "21st Century Banking Alert," "The Fair Lending Alert," "FraudMail Alert," "Government Contracts Alert," "SecMail," and "Y2K Alert." You can get more information at the firm's Web site: http://www.ffhsj.com.

Debevoise & Plimpton, http://www.debevoise.com, maintains eighteen newsletters that, like Fried, Frank's, are oriented toward corporate clients. To the best of my knowledge, Hughes, Hubbard, and Reed, http://www.hugheshubbard.com, is the reigning champ among law firms, with twenty-seven different newsletters.

Solo lawyers and small law firms can also use newsletters effectively. Sharon Nelson, of Fairfax, Virginia, the heart of the would-be "Silicon Valley East" Washington, D.C. area, has had success with her technology-oriented "Bytes in Brief" monthly newsletter, at http://www.nelsonwolfe.com.

Part of the beauty of e-mail newsletters is that (as long as they provide timely, useful information) they are a way of binding your existing clients closer to your firm and generating more new business from them.

They are closer to some members of your target audience than other forms of communication and more convenient for them. It's awfully easy for potential clients to hit that Reply button when they need help with a problem. This is particularly effective with busy executives like in-house counsel, CEOs, and CFOs who, like many of us, are tired of playing telephone tag and talking to voice mail systems.

Many people who have their secretaries screen paper mail, including law firm newsletters, still read all their incoming e-mail personally. For a sophisticated e-mail user with a good program, it is enormously easier to store and search through old e-mail newsletters than old issues of your paper newsletters (which probably get tossed, not stored).

Starting Your Own Discussion Group

By this time, some of the more astute readers may be asking, "If mailing lists are such effective law firm marketing tools, why haven't I heard much about them?" The answer is simple: Most consultants ignore them because it is difficult for vendors to make a profit on them. They'd rather sell you an expensive, flashy multimedia Web site. Starting a mailing list, by contrast, requires some "sweat equity" but little out-of-pocket expense.

Such lists can be either one-way newsletter-type lists or interactive discussion groups. Lew Rose, of Washington, D.C.'s Arent, Fox, Kinter, Plotkin & Kahn, one of the first lawyers to open his own site on the

World Wide Web, also operates AD-LAW, a list about advertising law, as well as a Web-based discussion group on the same subject.

Many mailing list host alternatives are available. Good general-purpose e-mail software may be enough for small lists. You can also purchase e-mail software that will install on a PC for higher-volume lists. Paralegals or secretaries can handle the administrative chores.

For a larger list, find an experienced third-party host. Webcom, http://www.webcom.com, is one of a number of Web site hosts that include free mailing list hosting for their Web site customers. Lsoft, http://www.lsoft.com, is one of the more expensive options, but it is a reliable choice, especially for mammoth lists.

If you start a mailing list, consider adding a form on your Web site making it easy to subscribe. Figure 13-2 shows what the Siskind Susser & Haas form looks like.

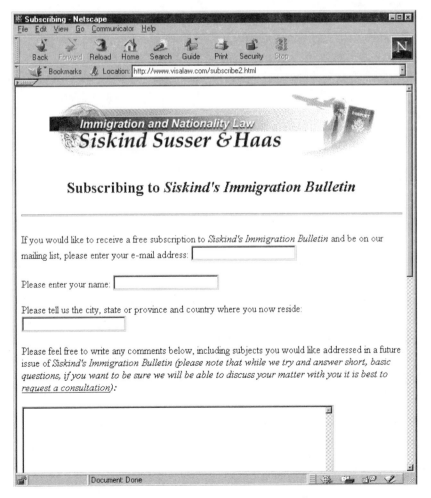

FIGURE 13-2. Siskind Susser & Haas Discussion Group Subscription Form

When asked at ABA TECHSHOW which section of his award-winning Web site was the most valuable, Greg Siskind singled out the interface to his e-mail newsletter mailing list. Web sites get all the glamour, but mailing lists may provide more practical benefits for your firm in the long run.

Starting Your Own Push Channel

A major drawback of Web sites is that they rely on visitor initiative. Even if your site is great, someone may visit it once and forget about it. Push technology is a promising way of overcoming this problem. Push channels can be used to broadcast updated Web-type content on a continuing basis.

Chapter 4 discusses push technology as a time-saving way to collect research information. Lawyers can subscribe to push channels and have information sent to them in a browser or browser-type format.

Law firms with something to say can go beyond being information consumers and become information providers. Firms with expertise in particular areas (e.g., labor law) can broadcast relevant material through push channels. In this context, push channels are an alternative to e-mail mailing lists.

New push technologies make things possible that are impractical with e-mail mailing lists. If a law firm wanted to market to corporate in-house counsel, for example, it might sponsor a Corporate Counsel Update channel. While an e-mail newsletter that appeared too frequently would be annoying, the Corporate Counsel Update channel could be updated as frequently as hourly and include well-laid-out tables, spreadsheets, or graphics if desired. As higher bandwidth becomes widely available, it will become practical to include a recording of highlights of a special speech, or even a video clip.

You should expect only a few of your Web site visitors to subscribe to a push channel, but once again, a self-selection process is at work. Those who do subscribe will tend to be the ones most interested in the channel's topic, who are frequently the ones most likely to become clients.

Marketplace positioning is a major attraction of establishing a push channel. Giving visitors the option to subscribe to a push channel at your Web site sends a subliminal message. CCN, *The New York Times,* and many other major organizations have push channels. If you also have one, you are sending a message that you are in their league. It reinforces the impression that your law firm is established, legitimate, important, and definitely worth paying a premium to retain.

There are some drawbacks to push channels. They are not worth much unless you have frequently updated, high-quality content. In addition, there is no single accepted standard for push technology as of this writing, so the audience is fragmented. You either have to set up multiple channels using different technology or hope that the audience you want to reach is using compatible software.

For these reasons, push technology has not been as widely adopted as expected by its most enthusiastic boosters, with the exception of its most primitive form, e-mail newsletters. It is too early to make a decision on the concept's long-term viability. However, establishing a Netscape or Internet Explorer channel is not particularly difficult, and if it doesn't work, there is little downside, so this is a good place for experimenting.

More information on setting up push channels is available at the web site accompanying this book: http://www.abanet.org/lpm/netbook

Resources

Online

CINET's overview of establishing push channels:
http://builder.cnet.com/Authoring/Push

In Paper

net.gain: Expanding Markets through Virtual Communities, by John Hagel III and Arthur G. Armstrong (Harvard Business School Press, 1997).

Delivering Push, by Ethan Cerami (McGraw Hill, 1998).

The Lawyer's Guide to Marketing on the Internet, by Gregory H. Siskind and Timothy J. Moses (American Bar Association: Law Practice Management Section, 1996).

PART FOUR

Ethics and Security Issues

CHAPTER **FOURTEEN**

Net Legal
Ethics Issues

THE INTERNET IS NOT some type of ethical free-fire zone where any-thing goes. Professional responsibility and malpractice rules apply to lawyer conduct on the Internet just as they do anywhere else. Lawyers who overlook this fact act at their peril. This chapter is intended to help lawyers identify ethics issues arising from Internet use. Because e-mail security is such an important topic, it is treated separately in Chapter 15.

State ethics rules vary, often significantly. While most state codes are based on the *ABA Model Rules of Professional Conduct,* often with substantial variances from the ABA version, about one-fourth of the state codes are based on the older *ABA Model Code of Professional Responsibility.*

Until Internet awareness spreads more among the organized bar, it's probably best to go out of your way to avoid overreaching in your Internet-based promotion efforts. Keep in mind that even many ex-cellent judges and members of ethics review boards may not be famil-iar with the Internet. A few may bear residual hostility toward any form of advertising, particularly technology-aided advertising that they feel gives one law firm an unfair advantage over less-technologi-cally savvy competitors. They may tend to decide that if they are go-ing to err, it will be in favor of what they perceive will best protect the public and the legal profession's image. Be conservative. It's no fun being the test case.

Conflicts of Interest

Many law firm Web sites contain direct e-mail links to individual lawyers. Some contain client intake forms that directly ask for potentially sensitive information. Aside from the potential communications risks, these practices heighten the risk of conflicts of interest. Similar risks arise if lawyers undertake to answer legal questions in Internet forums such as chat rooms or "Ask a Lawyer" forums connected to Web pages.

You should integrate Internet communications with your existing conflict-checking mechanisms. If you have a Web site, one way to facilitate this is by arranging it so that all hypertext links to send e-mail to the firm go through a single address, not the browser's built-in general e-mail. This way, e-mail from prospective clients who contact the firm through the Web page can be routed to someone who will check for conflicts of interest before forwarding the e-mail to a responsible lawyer.

This technique also has some other advantages. Your e-mail form can contain a warning of the dangers of e-mail insecurity and make your public key for encryption available, if you have one (explained in Chapter 15). In addition, since many lawyers don't read their e-mail routinely, a "funneling mechanism" like this can make it less likely that an important message to the firm will fall between the cracks, thereby running afoul of the duty to reply to client inquiries promptly.

These techniques are illustrated at The Northern Virginia Law Page, http://www.farr-law.com, designed by Fairfax, Virginia, lawyer and popular CLE speaker Evan H. Farr. The site is shown in Figure 14-1.

Diligence and Promptness

"Perhaps no professional shortcoming is more widely resented than procrastination," notes the comment to MRPC 1.3, on diligence and promptness.

The Internet opens up new vistas for procrastination. E-mail does not seem as "real" as a phone call or letter to some lawyers, but if you hold yourself out as using e-mail, failing to read and answer it can cause the same sort of problems as failing to return phone calls or to read and answer your paper mail.

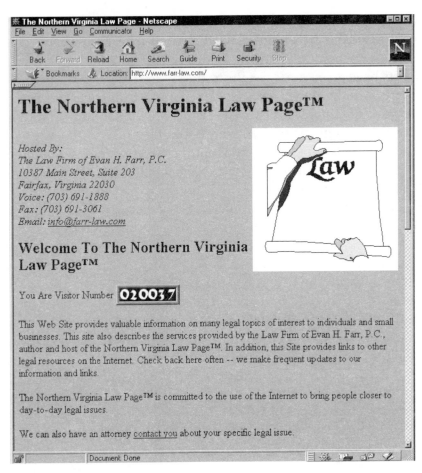

FIGURE 14-1. Northern Virginia Law Page™ Web Site

Unwanted Lawyer-Client Relationships

Lawyers participate in Internet discussions via Usenet newsgroups, mailing lists, and Web-based forums. Laypeople participate in some of these discussions. Can a lawyer's comments in such a forum give rise to an unwanted lawyer-client relationship? The question is important because if so, ethical requirements of zealous representation arise, the lawyer could be subjected to liability for malpractice, and the lawyer could even be subjected to unauthorized practice of law charges if the unwanted client is in another state. Similar issues can arise when lawyers address legal topics through articles posted on Web sites. (See Peter Krakaur, "The Ethics Of Giving Casual Legal Advice Online," at http://www.ljx.com/newsletters/internet/1998/1998_05_00.html.)

This issue is the subject of heated debate, with some lawyers insisting that the circumstances should make it obvious to any reasonable person that no lawyer-client relationship is formed. Others note cases in which the courts have given great weight to the subjective belief of the putative client as to whether there was a lawyer-client relationship. The case of *Togstad v. Vesely, Otto, Miller & Keefe,* 291 N.W. 2d 686 (Minn. 1980) is frequently cited in support of the latter proposition.

There is similar disagreement about the effectiveness of disclaimers in such situations. Some insist that a disclaimer will always protect a lawyer, while others say that boilerplate disclaimers are next to worthless.

Regardless of the theoretical niceties, as a practical matter it is safe to say that a lawyer who provides specific advice in such a forum is running a risk, regardless of how well drafted a disclaimer is used. Many lawyers use signature blocks to say things like, "Nothing in this message constitutes legal advice," and this practice is advisable. However, if in the body of your message you tell someone, "The statute of limitations in most states in cases like yours is five years," when it is in fact one year in the recipient's jurisdiction, you may have done something that will make your malpractice insurance carrier very unhappy.

Chat rooms feature live, real-time typed multiparty conversations, similar to telephone party lines. These are sometimes organized on an ad hoc basis, and sometimes focused on one guest who may give a virtual lecture and interact with the audience. The same dangers of unwanted lawyer-client relationships as those just discussed can arise in these forums as well. Be careful about what you say in such a forum, just as you would exercise caution at a cocktail party, in giving a speech, or participating on an in-the-flesh discussion panel.

Firm Web Site Issues

Because Web sites are so different from conventional advertising, lawyers might assume that bar association rules on lawyer marketing do not apply to Web sites. One difference is that the client must actively seek out the Web site to view it, unlike television advertisements, for example. However, note that bar rules definitely apply to Yellow Pages ads, which clients also would not normally see without conscious effort.

Some commentators devote a great deal of discussion to the issue of whether Web sites are advertisements for purposes of ethics rules. For practical purposes, no extended discussion is necessary—you should assume that your Web site is an ad unless unusual circumstances apply.

Some lawyers argue that their Web sites are protected from regulation by the First Amendment because the sites are not commercial but "public service" type of announcements, educating the public about the law. The case law does not appear to support such an argument. In *Zauderer v. Office of Disciplinary Counsel,* 471 U.S. 626 (1985), the lawyer communication consisted mainly of accurate factual information about IUDs and related litigation. Despite this, the material was held to be an ad that was subject to regulation.

The ethics rules in most states are written broadly enough to cover most forms of "commercial speech," a concept that is broader than advertising. Therefore, you should comply with state rules on lawyer advertising, including subjects such as using disclaimers, retaining a copy of the Web site materials, including the firm's physical location (not just an e-mail address and phone number), and labeling the site as "advertising material." Some states impose even more restrictions and requirements, covering areas such as obtaining prior or concurrent review of information, using client testimonials, implying specialization, using illustrations, and the like. Iowa imposes such strict requirements on ads (including forbidding anything calculated to evoke an emotional response) that lawyer advertising in that state is relatively rare.

If ethics rules prohibit you from doing something in your advertisement off the Internet, you shouldn't do it on the Internet. This sounds obvious, but it's overlooked with surprising frequency. For example, ethics rules restrict puffery, use of statistics that may raise unjustified expectations, and an implication that the lawyer can obtain results through other than appropriate means. All these violations can occur with advertising off the Internet as well as advertising on the Internet. If problems like this seem to occur more frequently on lawyer Web sites than in print or television ads, there are probably two reasons:

1. A Web site allows the lawyer to be more expansive, thus giving more opportunity to make a mistake.
2. Many Web sites are established without intermediaries like ad agencies or others with experience in the constraints on lawyer ads.

As Susan Ross, of Piper and Marbury, has noted, some lawyers seem to get so caught up in the excitement of the new technology that ethics rules are the last thing on their minds.

Many of the rules on lawyer advertising are not intuitive. Here is a brief summary of some of the ethics rules on ads that are not unique to the Internet but frequently seem to cause problems on law firm Web sites:

♦ **Ads must be truthful and nondeceptive.** Compliance with this can be harder than it might seem at first glance. Even citing your court track record or client testimonials or endorsements could create unjustified expectations. Puffery is prohibited. For example, the phrase "serving all your legal needs" could be a violation if your firm does not handle divorce or criminal cases. Subjective words like "experienced," "trustworthy," and even "competent" have been held to be misleading.

♦ **Ads must have no material omissions.** For example, ads that say "no recovery, no fee" have been held to be deceptively incomplete. Some states, including Georgia, require specific, conspicuously placed disclaimer language if similar phrases are used.

♦ **Ads must comply with any state-specific requirements.** For example, some states require that lawyer ads be labeled as such. Some require that ads be screened in advance of or concurrently with their dissemination to the public, or that fees be paid to the review board. Many states place limits on stating or implying that a lawyer specializes in a particular field of law. Some states require that every ad contain the name of a responsible lawyer or the location of a physical office. Restrictions on saying or implying that a lawyer is a "specialist" are common.

♦ **Ads should not identify clients without first obtaining the clients' permission.** Some law firm Web sites feature lists of representative existing clients (similar to those found in Martindale Hubbell listings). In some states the identity of a client can be a protected "secret" that should not be disclosed without prior permission.

Low-Tech Rules in a High-Tech Era

Some advertising ethics rules are difficult to apply in an Internet context. Record-retention requirements are one example. What must be retained where Web sites are concerned—paper printouts or the underlying HTML coding? The entire site or just the marketing-specific sections?

The problem becomes trickier when you consider dynamic pages that can present a unique experience to different users, based on user input or even the time of day the visitor arrives.

Some state rules require that notices be a particular size or even in color. How do these rules apply on the World Wide Web, when font sizes and colors are controlled by the capabilities of software, hardware, or the user's choices?

At least one state imposes special requirements on what it terms "The Home Page First Screen." How should this type of rule apply to sophisticated Web sites, which frequently have multiple entry points? For example, on the College and University Tax Page, http://www.universitytax.com, is "The Home Page First Screen" or is it at the one that gives information about the sponsoring law firm? Alternatively, is it the FAQ page, which could also be logically promoted as an entry point? (See Figure 14-2.)

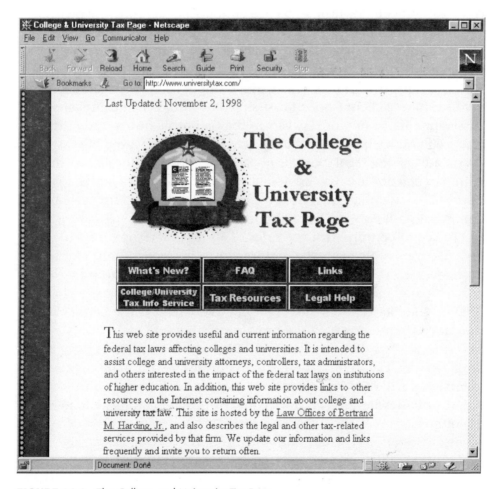

FIGURE 14-2. The College and University Tax Page

In some cases, rules are drafted and interpretations issued without adequate understanding of the effect of unique Internet features. In such circumstances, lawyers should respond accordingly:

- Reason by analogy and use common sense.
- Try to protect yourself with appropriate disclaimers.
- Point out inconsistencies to the appropriate authorities and request guidance.
- If you are knowledgeable about the Internet, consider volunteering your services to work on the appropriate boards or committees to help them do a better job.

Choice of Law and Unauthorized Practice of Law

The most difficult law firm Web page ethics issues are those involving multiple jurisdictions. A likely scenario in which such issues can arise is when a firm in one state files a complaint after losing a major client to a firm in another state as a result of the latter's Web marketing.

Consider a situation in which, as a result of its Web site, a California law firm gains a client from a Mississippi law firm, which complains in Mississippi. If one or more lawyers in the California firm are admitted to practice in Mississippi, they could be charged with violating Mississippi's lawyer advertising regulations. If no lawyers in the California firm are admitted to practice in Mississippi, unauthorized practice of law charges are a possibility. In either case, the prospect of defending against such an action in a distant forum is not pleasant.

Trying to comply with the rules of all fifty states is a difficult, and perhaps impossible task. The requirements are inconsistent and sometimes even contradictory. If twenty-three states require filing a copy of advertising material, are you supposed to send each state a copy? What if you change your site's content every day, as the better Web sites do? Compliance with the most restrictive rule in every state would result in a Web site that would have very little marketing appeal, anyway. Even if you were successful in meeting state requirements, you still might not be safe. What about foreign countries that might not allow any legal advertising, or might even make it a criminal offense?

Bar associations and law firms must keep the issue in perspective. Would we discipline a Maryland lawyer whose television ad complied with the law of Maryland but not that of Virginia? Some large firms and lawyers with specialized practices run ads in paper publications that are circulated nationwide, and even internationally, and no eyebrows are raised.

There are commonsense ways to avoid ethical difficulties arising from a law firm Web site. Until the entire situation can be hashed out by the organized bar, lawyers who want to establish Web sites should take measures such as the following to minimize any risk that might exist:

- Make sure that your site complies with the rules of the state in which your law firm is located, including states where the firm has branch offices. If it's unclear how a particular rule should be applied to a Web site, ask your state board of professional responsibility for guidance.
- Above and beyond that minimal compliance, do a commonsense check of your site and eliminate any "lightning rod" provisions that would be likely to attract the ire of a regulatory body in another state. For example, even if your state would not prohibit it, do not suggest that you have been endorsed by some celebrity or make inflammatory emotional appeals.
- Follow the lead of sweepstakes advertisements that include the disclaimer "Void where prohibited by law." Several variations on this theme are possible:
  1. Many lawyers will be satisfied to say that they are only licensed to practice law in State X and will only accept clients from that state.
  2. Others, like immigration or bankruptcy lawyers, may say that they practice federal law and are not licensed to practice law in any state except State X.
  3. Firms that want to be more aggressive in seeking business can leave open the possibility of attracting clients in other jurisdictions by saying that they will not accept any clients if the formation of a lawyer-client relationship as a result of the Web site would violate the laws of the prospective client's state. If someone from out of state wants to hire them, and it looks like a case worth taking, they would first check that state's rules.

Think carefully before accepting clients in states where none of your lawyers are licensed to practice.

Solicitations

"Solicitation" is an effort to recruit a client that is directed toward a specific recipient, unlike "advertising," which is directed at the public more generally. Solicitation is heavily restricted by ethics rules. The rules often distinguish phone contacts, in-person contacts, and paper mail contacts. It is unclear how these distinctions will be applied to e-mail or chat room contacts.

Arguably, e-mail should be handled under the more liberal rules governing "written communications" because it has less potential for overreaching than phone or in-person contact. In addition, e-mail is arguably easier to police because there is normally an identifiable electronic "paper trail."

In any event, lawyers need to be exceptionally careful about soliciting clients on the Internet. Whereas no one visits a Web site unless he or she specifically decides to do so, e-mail can be, and often is, unwanted. Owing to the widespread hostility toward spam, e-mail solicitations are more likely to trigger consumer complaints to disciplinary boards than paper solicitations are. The state of Tennessee disbarred Laurence A. Canter, one of the "Green Card Lawyers" who created a national controversy in 1994 by spamming Usenet newsgroups. This was not quite as offensive as personally directed unsolicited commercial e-mail, but close enough.

Chat rooms appear to fall somewhere between e-mail and telephone conversations. Chat rooms are unlikely to be a useful promotional medium for most lawyers except in unusual situations like live question-and-answer sessions held in conjunction with special events.

Referral Services

Many lawyer referral services have opened up shop on the Internet. Most of them are for-profit ventures, often run by non-lawyers. MRPC 7.1 and *Model Code of Professional Responsibility* 2-103(B) forbid lawyers to pay for referrals. States impose a variety of other restrictions, such as requirements that the referral services be formally approved by the state or that the referrals be rotated among the panel of participants. Some states even ban for-profit referral services. Don't participate in a referral service without verifying that it complies with the requirements of your state and the state in which it is located.

Continuing Legal Education and the Duty of Competence

Lawyers have a duty to maintain an acceptable level of professional competency, a duty that is acknowledged in some states by a requirement for continuing legal education (CLE) program attendance.

The Internet's flexibility and depth of resources make it a convenient alternative to local CLE providers. Using the Internet, you can take a course when you want, on a topic that you want. Even better, Internet CLE can offer features not customary in conventional CLE delivery mechanisms, such as interactive hypertext and associated discussion groups. A few states with mandatory CLE already accept courses conducted via the Internet. There is a list of Internet CLE providers at http://www.netlawtools.com/cle.html.

The American Bar Association has been a leader in this area. One of its projects is CLE Now!, a team effort with CLE Group, which has a Web site at http://www.clegroup.com/aba. This site offers CLE using state of the art online audio-streaming technology, accessible through ordinary Web browsers with the RealAudio plug-in.

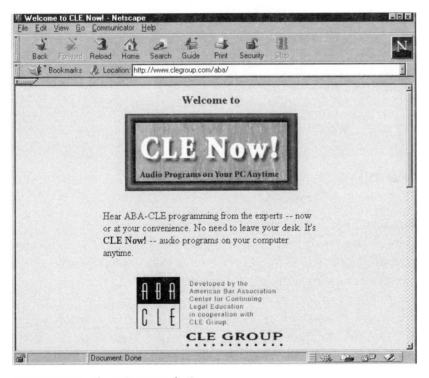

FIGURE 14-3. The ABA-CLE Web Site

Michigan ICLE, one of the nation's more innovative CLE providers, uses its Web site at http://www.icle.org (see Figure 14-4) to boost its programs in many ways. This includes its "Online Partners" program, which makes special services, including hundreds of forms, extensive legal updates, and discounts on ICLE products, available to subscribers.

FIGURE 14-4. Michigan ICLE Online Web Site

Virginia CLE leveraged the Internet to increase its visibility and better service its customers by becoming the first free supplier of Virginia appellate court decisions over the Internet. Its site is located at http://www.vacle.org. It also sponsors an e-mail discussion group for Virginia lawyers.

Many other vendors have entered the market as well. Counsel Connect, http://www.counsel.com, the Practicing Law Institute, http://www.pli.edu, and CLE Online, http://www.cleonline.com, are just a few of the reliable online CLE providers. Law Info, http://lawinfo.com, delivers programs in partnership with the San Diego County Bar Association.

In addition to serving as an independent communications mechanism, the Internet can be used to supplement other forms of CLE delivery. The ABA's Lawyers Communication Network uses direct satellite broadcasting to bring CLE programs to lawyers' offices and homes and a Web site (http://www.abalcn.com) to provide course manuals and otherwise supplement video offerings.

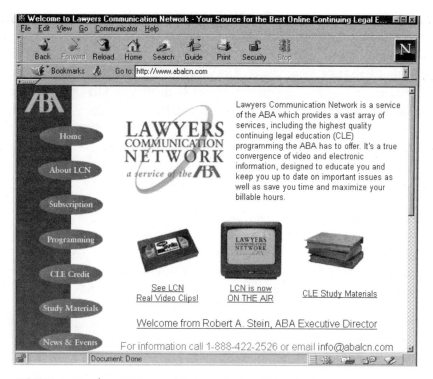

FIGURE 14-5. The ABA Lawyers Communication Network Site

Other Competency Issues

A lawyer shall provide competent representation to a client. Competent representation requires the legal knowledge, skill, thoroughness, and preparation reasonably necessary for the representation.

— Model Rules of Professional Conduct 1.1

A lawyer shall not [h]andle a legal matter which he knows or should know that he is not competent to handle. . . .

—Model Code of Professional Responsibility 6-101(A)(1)

The Internet is rapidly becoming an integral part of American life, and of American business in particular. It is changing the way that law is practiced and what clients expect from their lawyers.

The decision in *Whirlpool Financial Corp. v. GN Holdings, Inc.,* 67 F.3d 603 (7th Cir. 1995) was widely reported to impose a "duty to browse" the

Internet as a part of due care on the part of litigants in certain securities cases. Examination of the language of that decision reveals this comment to have been dicta. There is yet no standard accepted methodology for conducting Internet searches, so any attempt by the courts to impose a "duty to browse" would be unwarranted at this time. On the other hand, you would be wise to take advantage of the Internet's research resources in situations where they would benefit you and your client. In the not-so-distant future, a failure to use the Internet may even be considered a violation of professional responsibility rules, as noted by Professors Lanctot and Maule of the Villanova Law School:

> A lawyer with access to the Internet who fails to take advantage of that resource when it would advantage the client arguably could violate the duty of competency [under Pennsylvania Rule of Professional Conduct 1.1]. It may well be that as use of the Internet becomes more widespread within the profession, a lawyer who has not developed the requisite expertise and skill will not be using "the methods and procedures meeting the standards of competent practitioners [quoting the commentary to Rule 1.1]." Although it is doubtful that such a standard would apply today, the rapid expansion of Internet access within the last two years suggests that such a standard is not outside the realm of possibility. Compare the standard use of LEXIS/WESTLAW today with that of fifteen years ago.

Catherine Lanctot and James Maule, "The Internet—Hip or Hype? Legal Ethics and the Internet" ⟨*http://www.law.edu/vcilp/MacCrate/mcle/lanctol.htm*⟩ (No date).

(Cf. Barbara Folonsbee-Moore, "Ethical Concerns in Doing Legal Research," ⟨*http://www.llrx.com/features/ethical.htm*⟩ (Posted July 22, 1997; archived September 1, 1997).

Consider the following questions:

1. Lawyer A has a commercial law practice and is at a deposition when the other side begins asking about a relevant PGP-encrypted e-mail message or a digital signature. He has no idea what this is all about and fails to ask the appropriate questions. *Query:* Has lawyer A provided competent representation?
2. Assume that law firm A bills its clients tens of thousands of dollars a year for courier services. Firm B saves its clients thousands of dollars because its lawyers understand how to use Internet e-mail attachments and encryption when necessary. Firm B's information routinely arrives faster, more reliably, and (because it is

encrypted) more securely. *Query:* Is law firm A providing competent representation to its clients?

3. Traditionally, intellectual property lawyers have behaved reactively, swinging into action only after their clients have received a report of infringement. Innovative intellectual property lawyers have begun to use the Internet to search proactively for activity that harms their clients' interests. *Query:* Are clients whose lawyers don't provide such services receiving competent representation?

4. Some law firms are reducing costs and providing better representation for their clients through using collectives known as intranets or extranets that pool research results, exhibits, databanks, and the like. *Query:* Are clients whose lawyers don't use such mechanisms receiving competent representation?

5. A law firm loses a civil trial because it did not know how to find information easily available on the Internet that would have impeached the other side's expert witnesses. *Query:* Did the law firm's client receive competent representation?

The bodies that enforce ethics rules focus mainly on making sure that all lawyers meet a minimum standard. Lawyers generally have nothing to worry about unless they fall below what is usually a fairly low standard of competency.

Lawyers who fail to use the Internet to represent their clients more effectively, as in the preceding hypothetical situations, or through other techniques discussed in this book, are probably not in danger of disciplinary actions for the foreseeable future. Whether their clients are receiving the level of competent representation they deserve, however, is a question that deserves discussion.

Lawyers who aspire to provide the highest possible quality of representation for their clients will be among the first to embrace the Internet and to use it to improve the way they practice law.

Resources

The best place to go for up-to-date information about Internet legal ethics issues is the Internet. The following two sites contain links to most of the relevant articles and opinions.

Georgia lawyer Jeff Kuester's excellent Netethics site is at:
http://www.kuesterlaw.com/netethics

San Francisco lawyer Peter Krakaur's Legalethics.com site is even more comprehensive and includes an online discussion forum at:
http://www.legalethics.com

CHAPTER FIFTEEN

E-mail Privacy
for Lawyers

Privacy is as apple pie as the Constitution.

—Philip Zimmermann, Developer of PGP
(the best-known encryption program on the Internet)

INTERNET E-MAIL BRINGS new conveniences, economies, and efficiencies. It also brings new dangers. Just as phones can be tapped, e-mail can be intercepted in transit. People with access to other computers on the network with which you're communicating can set up *sniffer* programs to scan all traffic. They can surreptitiously make a copy of any messages that contain certain keywords, such as a person's name or a case number.

Some lawyers argue that Internet e-mail is so insecure that prudent lawyers should never use it. Others insist that e-mail is at least as secure as the telephone, so no special concern is necessary. The truth is probably somewhere in between.

The Hacker Threat to E-mail

In the movies, any young hacker can penetrate any computer system in the world and access anyone's e-mail within a couple of days. It's not quite like that in real life. However, if people who know what they are doing are sufficiently well motivated, have the right resources, and want to intercept your e-mail, there's a chance they may well be able to do so.

Some lawyers who access the Internet through dial-up accounts suffer from the misconception that it is no more or less difficult to intercept e-mail than it is to intercept a phone conversation. In fact, after the information from the account user gets to the ISP, it typically does not pass over regular phone lines again unless it is picked up at the end of its journey by another dial-up account user. In some ways Internet e-mail is less secure than voice phone calls, while in other ways it is more secure.

One key tool in the hacker's arsenal is the *packet sniffer.* This can screen all traffic passing through a certain point and make copies of any messages containing certain words, such as a client name or case number. Further, Snoops can now use commerically available software, with technology originally developed for U.S. intelligence agencies, to analyze large volumes of captured e-mail, much faster and more effectively than humans could. See, http://www.assentor.com, for example. This ability to automate the snooping process allows it to be done on a large scale relatively easily, and it arguably makes e-mail interception qualitatively different from phone wiretapping.

Aside from packet sniffing, there are a number of other means that can be used to gain improper access to e-mail. Many of them involve password attacks. For more on this, see Bryan Pfaffenberger's book, *Protect Your Privacy on the Internet* (Wiley, 1997).

It's difficult to judge how common e-mail interception is. Some people argue that it must be rare because there are few if any criminal prosecutions for such crimes. This is not a particularly persuasive argument, for several reasons:

- People who intercept e-mail are unlikely to let it become known because it is a federal crime (under 18 U.S.C. § 2511).
- E-mail tampering is a difficult crime to detect, since, compared to other snooping crimes, the culprit is less likely to leave behind physical evidence.
- The people in the best position to observe evidence of the crime, ISP system operators, have strong motivations not to report it. Bad publicity about security could cause them to lose customers, and they could be liable for civil damages if their negligence contributed to the interception (as is usually the case).

Most of the documented cases of e-mail interception I know about did not involve random snooping. The hackers targeted specific people, usually looking for information with economic value.

The Legal Background

The first step in analyzing the issue is to understand clearly that three distinct but interrelated elements are involved:

1. **Attorney-Client Privilege**—This is an evidentiary concept. It controls whether information can be admitted at trial or released through discovery.
2. **Ethical Duty of Confidentiality**—Lawyers can be disciplined by the appropriate state bodies for failing to exercise proper care in safeguarding client information. The duty of confidentiality is broader than the attorney-client privilege in some ways.
3. **Malpractice Liability**—A client who suffers damage through his or her lawyer's failure to safeguard the client's information may seek compensation through a malpractice action. In some states, breach of an ethical rule (like the duty of confidentiality) will be rebuttable evidence of malpractice.

It is important to keep the three issues distinct because the legal standards are different. For example, consider the language some lawyers are adding to their e-mail signature blocks, similar to that long in use on fax cover sheets:

> This e-mail message contains confidential, privileged information intended only for the addressee. Do not read, copy or further distribute it unless you are the addressee. If you have received this message in error, please call us (collect) at xxx-yyy-zzzz and ask to speak to the message sender. Also, please send the message back to us by replying to us and then deleting it. Thank you for your assistance in correcting this error.

In some states such notices have been held effective in determining whether a miscommunicated fax waived the attorney-client privilege. ABA Formal Ethics Opinion 92-368 (1992), "Inadvertent Disclosure of Confidential Material," holds that a lawyer receiving an inadvertent communication so labeled has an ethical duty not to read the message and to follow the instructions. Some jurisdictions take a contrary view. See, for example, District of Columbia Ethics Opinion 256 (1995).

Regardless of how a particular jurisdiction treats such a notice for purposes of resolving attorney-client privilege issues, such a notice is unlikely to help the lawyer who sent the misdirected message when it comes to a disciplinary proceeding or malpractice action. In fact, it might even be used as evidence against the lawyer. Key issues in such a disciplinary proceeding or malpractice action would be whether the method of communications used by the lawyer was insecure and whether the lawyer knew that it was insecure. Using such a form notice would arguably be circumstantial evidence that e-mail is insecure, and direct evidence that the lawyer knew it to be insecure and chose to try to protect it by an ineffective method (bluster) instead of an effective method (encryption). Encryption means scrambling the text while in transit so that only the intended recipient will be able to read it.

E-mail interception violates 18 U.S.C. § 2511, but the possibility of criminal sanctions may not be an adequate deterrent if large amounts of money are involved.

Some have argued that the existence of such a statute means that lawyers do not have to worry. For example, "The area is, therefore, susceptible to a bright line rule: If the interception is criminal, the lawyer has not violated the ethics rules, has not waived any privilege, and has not subjected herself to civil liability," writes William Freivogel in "Internet Communications—Part II, A Larger Perspective," *ALAS Loss Prevention Journal* (Vol. 7, 1997), republished at http://www.legalethics.com.

It is uncertain whether the courts will accept this theory. This is another situation in which the results under the rules of attorney-client privilege may differ from the results in a disciplinary action or a malpractice suit. If you leave your briefcase containing confidential information in a place where it is foreseeable that it will be stolen, the intervening criminal act may arguably mean that there was no waiver of the attorney-client privilege, but it is much less likely to be a defense against a disciplinary or malpractice action.

System Administrator Issues

By far the most likely spots for e-mail interception are near the message's origin or destination points. It is technically a trivial matter for systems administrators who operate e-mail systems at a message's origin or destination points to read any messages passing through their systems. This should not necessarily be a barrier to using e-mail:

- ◆ Standard contracts for courier services like Federal Express and UPS reserve for them a right to inspect all packages. No one contends that sending a package by one of these services raises a confidentiality issue.

- Perhaps more to the point, certain phone company personnel have long had the ability to monitor calls, but no one claims that there is no expectation of privacy in ordinary voice land-line telephone calls.
- The Electronic Communications Privacy Act of 1986, 18 U.S.C. § 2510 et seq., limits the system's operator's ability to monitor messages passing through the system. Watch for waivers of this statutory protection, allowed by 18 U.S.C. § 2511(2)(c), as many ISP contract forms include waiver provisions.

While the mere possibility of system administrator access should not be a barrier to lawyer e-mail use, there are still some unresolved issues:

- Would the result be different if a lawyer negligently selected a service provider, or saw evidence of possible improper interception and failed to investigate or take protective measures?
- Do lawyers have a duty to negotiate confidentiality provisions in contracts with their ISPs? If so, what about the confidentiality of the ISPs of the persons with whom the lawyer communicates? Does a law firm have a duty to monitor the ownership or employees of its ISP or their backgrounds?
- What would be the legal consequences if an opposing party bought your ISP and gained access to backup tapes containing old e-mail belonging to you or your clients? This question is not as unlikely as it might seem, since most ISPs are small local operations. Would there be a duty to seek a protective order, or would the statutory restrictions be adequate?

Safety through Encryption

You can make your communications more secure by using an encryption program to code your messages before transmitting them.

Some applications like word processors and spreadsheets include optional encryption. You can use them to restrict access to a file to someone who knows a password. Use of one of these programs would probably be enough to avoid an argument that you had waived the attorney-client privilege by sending material via the Internet. It would show that you *intended* for the message to be kept private and had taken some steps to ensure that privacy.

The encryption routines built into these application software packages, however, are probably inadequate to protect your information from a sophisticated snooper. The encryption modules in these programs are deliberately kept weak, mainly for two reasons:

◆ To allow the manufacturers to accommodate customers who have lost a password or had important information encrypted by a malicious employee who destroyed the password

◆ To comply with government restrictions on exporting strong encryption programs

Free software to crack many commercial encryption programs is available. There is also a company in Orem, Utah, named Access Data that specializes in selling utilities to decode the password-protected files created by many popular programs, such as WordPerfect, Lotus 1-2-3, and Microsoft Excel. An Access Data programmer has been quoted as saying that he had to put "delay loops" in the program so the code breaking would not look too easy to the customers. He had to slow it down so it would *look* hard and the customers would think they had received their money's worth.

Because the federal government restricts the export of strong encryption programs, some companies sell programs with strong encryption domestically and weakened versions abroad. Others sell only a single, watered-down version for domestic and foreign use.

Modern Encryption Alternatives

Traditional encryption systems use only one password. This technique is known as the *symmetric key,* or *secret key,* approach. Modern encryption systems achieve greater security than older systems primarily by using more secure algorithms and longer keys. They also achieve greater convenience by using a concept known as *public key* encryption.

With conventional encryption, you need to have access to a separate, secure method of communicating with message recipients to send them a password. This can be inconvenient, and in some circumstances, impossible. By contrast, with modern public key encryption, you don't need to send a secret password to a message recipient for that person to decode your message. The public key encryption system uses dual keys, one *public* and one *private.* The fundamental principle of the system is that a message encrypted with either key can only be decrypted with the other key.

The private key is kept secret. The public key can be, and usually is, made widely available. Some people include their public key in an e-mail signature block that they routinely append to all their e-mail correspondence. There are a number of public key repositories on the Internet that keep easily accessible, open databases of public keys.

If you encrypt mail using the recipient's public key, only someone who knows the recipient's private key should be able to read it.

Here's an analogy to illustrate how public key encryption operates. Imagine that you are the ruler of a land with untrustworthy couriers. You don't trust anyone, not even the members of your court, but you want to make it possible for anyone in the kingdom to communicate with you privately. You have your locksmith design many special lockboxes that anyone can lock, but once locked, they can be opened only with a special key. You keep the only copy of the special key. You have the lockboxes distributed throughout the kingdom. Anyone who wants to send you a private message can put it in one of the boxes and have it delivered to you.

The special lockboxes are like copies of your public key. You can distribute them anywhere you want, and you don't care if your nosiest enemy gets ahold of one. They are useless without the special private key.

In our hypothetical, a determined snoop who intercepted one of your locked message boxes would simply smash it open. Of course, real-life snoops try the same thing. This is called trying to "crack" the message by unscrambling it. Here's where the analogy breaks down. The strongest physical lockbox can eventually be broken by someone sufficiently determined. However, a message properly encrypted, using good software is exceptionally difficult to decrypt, even using the most powerful computers available today or for the foreseeable future.

This is why strong encryption frightens governments. Criminals and terrorists can use it for invulnerable secure communications. Honest citizens, businessmen and lawyers concerned about their privacy also use it for legitimate purposes.

Benefits of Public Key Encryption

Public key encryption is the dominant choice among sophisticated Internet users for two reasons:

- ◆ **Better key management**—Suppose that you want to order some merchandise from a merchant you have never met, using an unsecured method of communication. This could be the Internet or, for that matter, the telephone or fax. You can contact the merchant and obtain that party's public key (the "first password").

It can be safely transmitted over an unsecured channel. You then use the public key to encrypt your message (including your credit card number). The encrypted message can be safely transmitted over an unsecured channel like the Internet because only someone who knows the merchant's private key (the "second password") can decode the message. The bottom line? You can have secure communications with someone whom you have never met. There is no need to have some separate, highly secure alternate method of communication to transmit passwords.

♦ **Digital signatures**—This feature allows checking for sender authentication ("who sent the message?") and message integrity ("was the message altered in transit?"). These are discussed in a later section.

Upon exposure to knowledge of some recent technological advances, it becomes apparent that the transition to paperless commerce actually offers an opportunity to raise our level of security expectations far beyond what we have come to expect in the paper-based world.

—Charles Merrill, Partner, McCarter & English

More on Public Keys

A public key is a long, random-looking block of numbers and letters that people can use to send secure messages. The first time you run the popular program PGP (for "Pretty Good Privacy"), it leads you through the steps to create a public-private pair. Here's what a public key looks like:

```
-----BEGIN PGP PUBLIC KEY BLOCK-----
Version: 2.7

mQBtAy9OaHoAAAEDAMO8EwnPG8yCYBKnCT8viqLdZP4XdI2fFXUx/tdS/3nR2UFK
fpLKjhANgEovdQfPlkLbuUZnrrZuKRR8o3G7rIfuyYvkqbsMnVQjEJ3eWGmT/FsY
FqMRSFOvDWCpbRpcSwAFEbQqU3VuYnVyc3QgQ29uc3VsdGluZyA8c3VuYnVyc3RA
bm92YW51dC5jb20+
=o//l
-----END PGP PUBLIC KEY BLOCK-----
```

With modern software, you should never have to type a key. Your software should handle it for you. When you want to send secure messages to the key owner, your encryption software will take this information and use it to encode the messages. Because good software handles it automatically, you don't have to retype the public key. This is a valuable convenience, since one small typo would prevent the key from working properly.

A few lawyers include their PGP public keys in their e-mail signature blocks. This is not recommended. It will be a waste of bandwidth to most message recipients. Furthermore, instead of making people think that you are careful about security, it may have the opposite effect on encryption-savvy Internet users. People who are really serious about security prefer to distribute their public key in a way that causes less concern about the possibility of it being altered in transit. Instead of including your public key in full with every message you send, just let people know how they can get it.

Another option is to include your PGP Key at your Web site. (See Figure 15.1, from the Rice and Stallknecht web site, **http://www.rsrlaw.com**.) Yet another method is through directories called public key servers. The MIT version is at **http://pgp5.ai.mit.edu**.

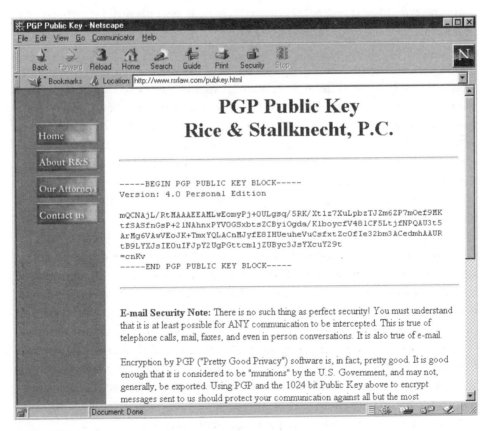

FIGURE 15-1.

Practical Implementation of Encryption Techniques

In the near future, encryption will be incorporated seamlessly and transparently into Internet e-mail packages and possibly other forms of communication as well. Encryption is already built into some cellular phone systems. With programs like the Eudora Pro e-mail software coming from the factory with built-in, easy-to-use strong encryption options like PGP, we are well on the way to this. Further, all the major Internet Web browser programs already incorporate encryption intended for the limited purpose of exchanging secure information with specially designed sites to facilitate merchandise orders using credit card numbers. This encryption operates seamlessly, without user intervention, using the browser to communicate with a secure Web site.

The latest e-mail software includes the option to encrypt e-mail. The two most common types are S/MIME and PGP. PGP and the stronger versions of S/MIME are catagorized as a munitions under World War II vintage statutes, and it is illegal to export them from the United States. You could be considered to be "exporting" them if you merely take them out of the country on your laptop computer without having first obtained a license.

PGP has a reputation for being particularly strong. Although certain elements within the federal government would prefer to discourage the widespread availability of PGP, it is now and always has been perfectly legal to use the program in the United States. For years, the developer of PGP, Phil Zimmermann, was under investigation on allegations that he was involved in "exporting" his creation by allowing it to be placed on the Internet, where people from other countries could download it. This controversy never affected the legality of PGP use inside the United States, and the investigation was eventually dropped.

Is PGP unbreakable? No encryption system in common use is considered absolutely unbreakable, but PGP is considered one of the strongest. Scientists have demonstrated the theoretical possibility of "cracking" PGP by using indirect methods (such as "timing attacks") instead of direct brute force (trying all possible key combinations using high-speed computers), but none of these appear to be very practical in the real world.

One of the best endorsements of PGP is the fact that it is used by the Computer Emergency Response Team (CERT) at Carnegie Mellon University, the organization that coordinates the national response to major computer security breaches. If PGP satisfies CERT'S experts, it should be good enough for the most sensitive law firm uses.

The security of most encryption systems, including PGP, depends on a number of factors, especially these:

- **How well the users guard their private keys.** This is solely under the control of the users. For many years, the former Soviet Union had no need to directly attack the U.S. Navy's sophisticated encoding algorithms. The Walker spy ring provided the Soviets with copies of the Navy's encryption keys.
- **The quality of the underlying mathematical formulas.** The algorithms used in PGP are highly regarded by experts.
- **The length of the key used for encoding.** PGP allows you to choose the length of the key that will be used.

Key lengths are normally stated in computer terminology, in terms of *bits* (the smallest unit of information handled by computers). The most common key-length categories are classified as casual (384 bits), commercial (512 bits), and military (1,024 bits). Keys of 512 bits (equivalent to 154 digits) are considered possibly breakable by the intelligence agencies of larger nations.

To illustrate, here are some practical examples. Present U.S. policy prohibits the export of encryption software with a key length of 40 bits. It is not exceptionally difficult to break messages encrypted with key lengths this short. In 1995, a French college student broke such software using two supercomputers, supplemented by about a hundred powerful workstations. Longer keys are not immune from attack. In 1993, a team of computer specialists cooperating over the Internet broke a message with a key of 400 bits. Using about a thousand powerful computers, it took about one year.

Decrypting a 1,024-bit message is much more difficult than decrypting a 512-bit message. Barring extraordinary increases in computing power or the development of unforeseen techniques of mathematical analysis, 1,024-bit keys (equivalent to 308 digits) are believed to be unbreakable for at least the next few decades. The newer versions of PGP give the option to use 2,048-bit keys.

A site at MIT distributes free copies of PGP for private, non-commercial use:

http://web.mit.edu/network/pgp.html

In 1996, Phil Zimmermann joined with some others to form a company to sell enhanced, easier-to-use versions of PGP. Their URL is what you would expect:

http://www.pgp.com

Some software (like the Eudora Pro e-mail program) includes a built-in copy of PGP.

Alternatives to PGP

While PGP is popular, it's hardly the only form of encryption. The latest high-quality Web browsers often come from the manufacturer bundled with a form of encryption based on what is called S/MIME. Instead of generating their own public and private key pair, users purchase them from trusted third parties, such as Verisign or the U.S. Postal Service. These encryption features don't work automatically. You need to obtain a public-private key pair and invoke the encryption mechanism to be safe. Get the domestic version (128 bits), not the weaker export version (40 bits) of the program, unless you need to travel abroad.

The forms of encryption discussed above require both parties to have compatible software, which can be a problem when dealing with un-sophisticated clients. Some non-public key encryption programs, like DataSafe and WebCrypto, can encrypt a file so that it will decrypt itself if the recipient has the password. These programs can be very useful, but users still have the administrative chore of communicating the password by some alternative secure channel. Further, this method is probably not as secure as the PGP.

In addition to the methods of encrypting e-mail only, another form of public key encryption is also built into the better World Wide Web browsers. This feature works only for information being sent to and from a secure site. As a user, you never see the public keys being exchanged. An icon on screen will indicate whether a site is secure. *This form of browser encryption does not protect e-mail.* E-mail is transmitted differently from information sent between Web sites.

Some vendors rely on built-in browser encryption to secure commu-nications. The sender uses a Web browser to send the information to a se-cure site operated by the vendor, where the recipient can pick it up. This technique has the advantage of allowing a third party to certify that a particular message was sent and received, and when. It also does not re-quire both sender and recipient to use the same brand of software. Any of the latest Web browsers will usually do.

Noncompatibility between the different types of encryption pro-grams is presently the biggest obstacle to more widespread use of e-mail encryption. If you know that you will only be sending or receiving sensitive information to and from a limited, predictable group, it's not particularly difficult to get everyone on the same brand. Most of us, however, want the flexibility to communicate securely with as many other people as possible. For this reason, consider the popularity of an encryption program before selecting it.

PGP is presently the leading encryption program among those serious about encryption. If browser-bundled e-mail programs become standardized and compatible in the future, they may become the preferred alternative, even though they are not as secure as PGP.

Key Escrow

Because good encryption programs can be extremely difficult, even impossible, to break without knowing the keys, as of this writing, the federal government has strongly encouraged what is called key escrow. A copy of the private keys for all strong encryption programs would be stored in secure repositories. Upon a proper showing, government investigators would be given access to the private key. This form of government-mandated key escrow is controversial.

All law firms using encryption should institute their own internal key escrow systems, so they will be able to access the encrypted files of employees who die, lose keys, and so on. This is critical because without a copy of the key, the law firm may otherwise be unable to access the data.

When to Encrypt E-mail

When should you use encryption for e-mail? This issue is heavily debated. Some lawyers argue that it would be a mistake to advocate routine encryption of e-mail, since this would become the standard to which lawyers would be held.

The admiralty case of *The T.J. Hooper*, 60 F.2d 737 (2nd Cir. 1932), is cited by many commentators, including Lance Rose in his excellent book *Netlaw: Your Rights in the Online World* (Osborne 1995). In that case, the issue was whether a tug operator was negligent in failing to have a radio on board, even though it was not then the industry standard to have radios. Judge Learned Hand denied the defendant's motion for summary judgment, stating that "there are precautions so imperative even their universal disregard will not excuse their omission." Most lawyers today don't use encryption, but those who like to cite this case argue that a future tribunal could decide to set a new "industry standard" just like Learned Hand did.

The consensus of the best-informed commentators seems to be that while encryption is seldom needed by most lawyers, it is sometimes necessary. Even William Freivogel, quoted earlier, who argues aggressively in favor of a "bright line" no-encryption-needed rule, would admit of an exception for "confidences so valuable that the client will want to take extraordinary steps to protect them. . . . The key is to recognize these extraordinary situations and then take extraordinary measures." The problem is how lawyers are supposed to identify material that is sensitive or extraordinary enough to require encryption.

The test set forth in a subsequent Learned Hand decision, *United States v. Carroll Towing Co.*, 159 F.2d 169 (2nd Cir. 1947), is probably more useful for analyzing such questions than *The T.J. Hooper* case. In *Carroll Towing,* Learned Hand stated that the defendant would be negligent if the burden of taking precautions was less than the product of the seriousness of the potential harm and the likelihood of the potential harm.

This test states the relevant factors. Despite the fact that Learned Hand stated it in the form of an algebraic equation, the factors involved cannot be weighed with mathematical precision. Nevertheless, Learned Hand's formulation provides a useful framework for analyzing such issues. How does it apply in the context of e-mail? Here are some points to consider:

1. The more sensitive the information being transmitted, the greater the need for encryption.
2. Lawyers routinely dealing with high-dollar matters (like mergers and acquisitions) might be held to a higher standard, since not only would the potential harm be greater but so would the likelihood of injury (because hackers would be more likely to target them).
3. Perhaps most important, encryption software is rapidly improving and becoming easier to use. This reduces the "burden" of taking precautions under Learned Hand's formula. *The trend toward easier encryption will increase the likelihood of lawyers being held liable for failure to encrypt their sensitive messages.*

Practical Advice

Though most lawyers will seldom need to encrypt their e-mail, there are good reasons for any lawyer using e-mail to have the capability to send and receive encrypted e-mail:

- You can't predict in advance when a situation might arise in which you might need to send or receive secure e-mail on short notice. If you have the software and a public-private key pair, you will be ready.
- Giving your clients the option to communicate securely with you, and letting them know that they have that option, provides you with a form of insurance. In the event that something does go wrong, and a client complains, you have set yourself up to make a waiver defense: "The client had the option to use a secure communications method, but, knowing the risks, for his own convenience, he chose to use an unsecure method instead." There is no case law dealing with this argument in an e-mail context yet, but this sounds like a persuasive defense.
- Demonstrating that you understand how to use technology to protect clients' interests and give them choices makes you that much more attractive to sophisticated clients, even clients who may not use encryption themselves.

Digital Signatures

Digital signatures are critical to practical Internet commerce. They allow recipients to verify who sent a particular message. Further, they can allow verification that a message has not been altered in transit.

Digital signatures are made possible because of public key encryption. As previously explained, if someone encrypts a message using his or her private key, then only his or her public key will be able to decrypt it. If a person's public key will decrypt a message, you know that it must have been encoded with that person's private key. This lets you verify that a message came from a particular person. This is a very useful tool in commercial situations.

Here's what a digitally signed document looks like:

```
-----BEGIN PRIVACY-ENHANCED MESSAGE-----
Proc-Type: 2001,MIC-CLEAR
Originator-Name: webmaster@www.sec.gov
Originator-Key-Asymmetric:
    MFgwCgYEVQgBAQICAf8DSgAwRwJAW2sNKK9AVtBzYZmr6aGjlWyK3XmZv3dTINen
    TWSM7vrzLADbmYQaionwg5sDW3P6oaM5D3tdezXMm7z1T+B+twIDAQAB
MIC-Info: RSA-MD5,RSA,
    WqQsKpTDrqlaLZm4FPSlsf0ubj8u52KFSaTJb+m3296XtUmXyuyRYehh8DP0OdW
    pvG6SpGP916CZWMW1nwllA==
```

```
[The body of the digitally signed message goes here]


-----END PRIVACY-ENHANCED MESSAGE-----
```

The random-looking string of letters and numbers below the "Originator-Key-Asymmetric" block is a unique string that's generated using information from the body of the text *and* the sender's public private key. If a would-be forger tried copying the header information into another message, the recipient's software would detect the forgery. This particular example was taken from the SEC's Edgar database. The SEC digitally signs disclosure documents filed there, so the public can be confident that the documents are legitimate.

There's a variation on the digital signature technique in which the program uses a mathematical function called *hashing*. This allows you to verify not just that a message was sent by a particular person but also that it was not altered in transit. Good software makes digital signatures and message authentication easy.

> *The digital signature is one of the great innovations in the history of cryptography. The recipient of a signed message knows that the message is in fact from the alleged source and that the message hasn't been altered in any way after it was signed. The digital signature makes possible a whole range of security services that are impractical using conventional encryption.*
>
> —Dr. William Stallings, A Leading Encryption Expert

It is probable that digital signatures would be held to meet the broad definition of a binding signature under Uniform Commercial Code Section 1-201(39), even in the absence of a more explicit statutory blessing. Nevertheless, to reduce uncertainty and encourage electronic commerce, some states have enacted, and others are considering, legislation approving digital signatures and public key encryption.

A common theme is establishing a licensing program for the certification authorities who will, among other things, verify the authenticity of public keys. Among its other provisions, the Utah statute provides that a "digitally signed document is as valid as if it had been written on paper."

The ABA's Section of Science and Technology has published Digital Signature Guidelines, which are available at http://www.abanet.org/scitech/ec/isc/dsgfree.html.

Conclusion

Ordinary Internet e-mail is probably secure enough for the vast majority of messages that most lawyers will send or receive. There is a security risk on the Internet, but there are also risks in discussing information over telephones (which can be tapped) or in faxes (which can go astray or be intercepted in transit).

Considered in this light, the most remarkable thing about transmitting information on the Internet is that through encryption, it is much easier to secure Internet communications than it is to ensure that your phones are not tapped or that your faxes are not intercepted. Few lawyers will want to encrypt all their e-mail correspondence, and even fewer will have a need to do so. All lawyers, however, should weigh the risks before using Internet e-mail for sensitive information without encrypting it.

Many lawyers have avoided encryption programs over the years owing to fears that encryption would be hard to use. This is no longer a good excuse, since these programs have now added graphic interfaces and become easier to use. Make a public key available for use by those who want to send you sensitive information, and encrypt any sensitive e-mail you send over the Internet.

> *Soon any child old enough to use a computer will be able to transmit encoded messages that no government on earth will find easy to decipher.*
>
> —Bill Gates, *The Road Ahead*

Resources

Online
Monte E. Sokol and Philip P. Andriola's "E-Mail Adds Twists, Raises Questions, Regarding Privilege" (*New York Law Journal,* April 13, 1998): http://www.nylj.com/tech/041398t2.html

RSA FAQ: http://www.rsa.com/rsalagbs/faq/

Usenet newsgroup: alt.security.pgp

In Paper
Protect Your Privacy: The PGP User's Guide, by William Stallings (Prentice Hall, 1995).

E-mail Security: How to Keep Your Electronic Messages Private, by Bruce Schneier (John Wiley & Sons, 1995).

The Lawyer's Quick Guide to E-mail, by Kenneth E. Johnson (American Bar Association: Law Practice Management Section, 1998).

CHAPTER **SIXTEEN**

Net Security and Privacy Overview

These Yankees don't have the slightest idea about security. Who is at fault? Obviously, the North Americans are not very clear on the security of their systems if a kid from South America can enter them. I would be ashamed to admit it.

—Julio Rafael Ardita, Father of the twenty-two-year-old Buenos Aires man who used the Internet to break into computer systems at Harvard, the NASA Jet Propulsion Laboratory, Los Alamos National Laboratory, and many sensitive Department of Defense facilities

T HERE IS A SECURITY RISK involved in using *any* computer. The risk increases somewhat if you network computers together internally. The risk increases a little more if you connect that network to the Internet. This doesn't, of course, mean that you should never use computers, network them internally, or connect to the Internet. Computer networking, including Internet use, is essential to modern business success. This chapter explains the threats and shows some ways to reduce them.

Law enforcement personnel who specialize in computer security report that, while a few years ago a high percentage of hackers were thrill-seeking kids, there is now a trend toward professionalism. (This partly results from the fact that as hackers age, they become more interested in monetary gain than in cheap thrills and ego gratification.) The danger is increased by the fact that hackers often work in gangs or loose ad hoc alliances. This can multiply their operating effectiveness. In many cases, one sophisticated hacker directs an attack, while others with less technical skill perform the time-consuming grunt work, such as trying various log-in names and passwords. Hackers trade information to gain status among their peers. Sometimes requests for particular items of industrial intelligence are posted in discussion groups used as hacker gathering places. Skilled hackers write easy-to-use programs that automate the hacking process—to make it simple for amateurs. "RootKit" is the name of a popular suite of hacking tools that is widely available.

The Hacker Threat to Firms

Hacker intrusion is mainly a threat to larger law firms that have permanently connected their internal firm computer network to the Internet. If you are using individual computers and dial-up Internet accounts, the risk is probably much lower, for several reasons:

Terminology Note: The word *hacker* did not always have the negative connotation that it has today. Originally, it was an entirely positive term, used to describe someone whose superior knowledge, inventiveness, persistence, or intuition made it possible for that person to improvise solutions to computer problems readily. Some people object to using the term *hacking* to describe malicious activity and would prefer to substitute the word *cracker* to describe a maliciously inclined person. To avoid confusion, however, I follow the prevailing negative usage that has attached itself to *hacker*.

- The target is less attractive to hackers, since there is less for them to gain.
- The window of vulnerability is smaller, since your system is not on-line twenty-four hours a day, seven days a week. Hackers, and their automated cracking software, must try to guess when you are coming online and to break through during the relatively short time that you are online.
- It may be more difficult to crack your system, since most dial-up Internet accounts now use what is known as *dynamic addressing*. This means that you are not permanently assigned an Internet Protocol (IP) number. Instead, each time you connect, you are randomly assigned a different one from a pool of IP numbers. This is frustrating to the would-be hacker because the IP number usually is used to get a fix on a targeted computer.

A direct attack on a dial-up Internet account is not impossible, but it is less likely than an attack on a system that is permanently connected to the Internet.

While connecting an internal computer system to the Internet does introduce some new security risks, computer security is not just an Internet problem. Regardless of whether you connect to the Internet, your internal computer network (and thus your firm's secrets) is vulnerable to penetration by outsiders. This is particularly true if you allow access to it through dial-up connections by lawyers working at home. Some hackers use *war dialers,* computer programs that dial phone numbers at random. When the program detects computer tones, it records the corresponding number so the hacker can attack it later.

The Inside Threat to Firms

While the rogue hacker threat is real, one of the most frequently overlooked facts in computer security is that, in many cases, the biggest threat is posed by *insiders.* Some experts estimate that as many as 90 percent of all computer security breaches are made by insiders.

How well do you screen employees given high-level computer access? How quickly do you deactivate the passwords of employees who leave your organization, especially those who leave involuntarily? Think twice before retaining any terminated employee as a consultant. If you do decide to retain one, don't automatically give that person the same level of access that he or she had before.

> ▼ ▼ ▼ ▼ ▼
>
> *Computers are capable of protecting information in such a way that even the smartest hackers can't get at it readily unless someone entrusted with information makes a mistake.*
>
> —Bill Gates

Disgruntled or dishonest employees, especially ones who are knowledgeable about computers, can do as much or more damage as the most skilled and determined hacker—and in many cases, you may never suspect the source of the injury.

Risk Assessment

Most experts believe that just about any networked computer system, on or off the Internet, can be penetrated by a determined, knowledgeable attacker with sufficient resources and time. You must assess the risks and the precautions that can be taken and then balance them against the benefits to be gained. After performing these calculations, most sophisticated organizations will conclude that the potential benefits of networking, including networking via the Internet, are so large that they make some risk exposure worthwhile, especially if that exposure can be reduced through appropriate precautions.

The first step in establishing a computer security policy is to determine the level of threat that you face. Based on the type of law that you practice, which of the following are realistic threats for your firm?

1. Casual snoopers who know a little about computers
2. Individual hackers or small organizations with some knowledge of how to attack computer systems
3. Well-financed experts with high motivation to attack your computer system and the skills and resources to mount a strong attack

The level of security measures you need to adopt will vary according to your threat level. If you are in category 1, minimal precautions will probably suffice. If you are in category 3, make security a top priority. This means being prepared to get out your checkbook and fill in a lot of digits to hire top security consultants and to buy some fancy hardware and software. It also means being prepared for a lot of aggravation resulting from the use of "one-time password" systems. Fortunately, most of us don't have to ward off this type of threat.

Social Engineering

Hackers are sometimes stereotyped as misfits who overcompensate for their lack of social skills with their brilliant computer programming ability. The reality is that many of the most successful hackers are little more than slick con artists.

Everyone connected with your organization, not just the computer users, should understand a key hacker tool: *social engineering.* Social engineering means personal interactions geared toward getting information to help break into a computer system. This can be done by letters, faxes, phone calls, or even in person, if the hacker is bold enough. Hackers have been known to go through garbage, pose as security guards, and even stand in the lobbies of buildings conducting fake surveys, asking about pet names, hobbies, and so on and then using the information to try and guess passwords or otherwise further an attack. One feature article in *2600: The*

Hacker's Quarterly explained how to go about obtaining a job as a janitor in a company whose computer security you want to attack. (This magazine, which also contains more technical articles, is readily available at newsstands. The number 2600 in the title refers to the frequency of a computer tone used to abuse phone systems illegally.)

One social engineering technique is to get inside the targeted organization and post forged signs purporting to give the new telephone number of the organization's technical support staff. When company employees dial the "new" phone number, the hacker answers.

A favorite hacker objective is to obtain a copy of an organization's internal phone directory. This can be used to further an attack in many ways, including figuring out which supervisors could be impersonated over the phone or whose name could be invoked to add credibility to some request for other information.

Another approach is to call and pose as a computer repairperson who needs information about the system to fix a problem. A variation on this technique is posing as a new or temporary employee who knows nothing about the system, and calling the computer support office. The hacker's spiel would go something like this:

> "Well, Mr. Jones told me if I didn't get that project out today, he'd fire me. Tom had the file I need, and I can't get into his computer. Tom had an accident, and he's in the hospital. If I don't get that password, I'm in big trouble. You sound like a nice guy. You know how Jones is. I need this job. You don't really want me to get fired, do you?"

Password Problems and Solutions

Computer hackers have ready access to free programs that can go through dictionaries and try out all the words in an attempt to break into a system. If left to their own devices, many computer users will select passwords that are trivial for such an attacker to discover. A Purdue University study showed that 5 percent of computer users selected passwords of four letters or less in length. To even a semiserious hacker, this is hardly an obstacle—and remember, a hacker needs just one password to get into your system. If you have thirty people on your network, you probably have one or more with passwords that are easy marks.

Longer passwords, however, are not necessarily secure. Good computer hackers can often guess passwords. They are not clairvoyant, they

▼ ▼ ▼ ▼ ▼

Where to Get Help: The Computer Emergency Response Team (CERT) at Carnegie Mellon University is a government-funded organization that coordinates responses to computer security threats. It handled more than 2,000 incidents in 1994 alone. CERT has a twenty-four-hour hot line, (412) 268-7090, and a Web site: http://www.cert.org.

Another resource is the National Institute of Standards and Technology computer security Web site: http://csrc.ncsl.nist.gov.

Commercial incident response teams are also available. One of the better companies is Global Integrity Corp. http://www.globalintegrity.com.

just observe human behavior well and think systematically. A few of the words from the password guessing list of hacker Robert Morris, Jr. (author of the famous 1988 "Internet Worm") include: beowulf, aaa, mozart, and scotty (Star Trek-related names are popular among computer buffs). Other hackers say they have good luck by guessing sex-related passwords.

In one study, an experimenter collected actual encrypted password files containing nearly 14,000 user-selected passwords. Experienced computer security experts using standard automated attack techniques were able to crack nearly one-fourth of that number. Using computers, they first tried the user's name, initials, account name, and other personal data. They tried 130 different permutations of this information. Where this did not succeed, they used password dictionaries and tested them in an automated guessing pattern. Where this did not work, they tried variations of the dictionary words, such as making the first letter uppercase or substituting a zero for the letter O. All these attacks can be carried out in a surprisingly short time with a high-powered computer and the right software—if someone's attacking a system whose users do not understand the importance of password selection.

What makes a good password? It can be tough to balance security against ease of user memorization. Computer-generated mixes of random letters and numbers are the safest, but users who don't understand the risks involved may balk at memorizing them. Even worse, they may store the hard-to-remember password in a convenient desk drawer or even tape it to their computer monitor.

One approach is to let users select their own passwords but to review the passwords periodically with a password-cracking program. If the password can be cracked, the user is required to change it.

A better approach is to use a proactive password checker, which is a program that rejects all user-proposed passwords that don't comply with a set of rules concerning length and the like. The following rules are recommended by Errol Weiss, of Global Integrity Corp.:

- All passwords must be at least six characters long.
- All passwords must contain a mix of alpha and numeric characters.
- Passwords that contain nonalphanumeric characters (like $ or #) are even better.

Using the first letters of the words in a sentence will work: "I'd like some fries with my hamburger, please," gives us "Ilsfwmh,p.", surely a hard to guess password.

Regardless of how good your passwords are, they should be changed regularly. You should require all your users to change their passwords at specified intervals.

Alternate Password Systems

A more secure approach to password security is *token identification,* which I prefer to call by the more descriptive name of the "one-time password system." When someone tries to log on, the host computer issues a challenge number. Authorized users have specialized calculators called *tokens* that take the challenge number and compute a corresponding response according to a secret formula shared by the host computer and the user's device. If the response number matches the result of the host computer's calculations, the user is admitted.

This type of system can enforce security considerably, and it is not outrageously expensive. In my experience, the biggest drawback is that users complain about the inconvenience.

Biometric devices are coming onto the market at reasonable prices. They identify users by fingerprint, retinal scan, facial pattern or other physical characteristics.

Other Security Measures

Call-back systems can improve security for those who have legitimate users who need to call into your local area network (LAN) from remote locations. You can set up your system so that when an authorized user calls in, the host modem hangs up and then calls a prearranged number, which could be the remote user's home phone, a hotel room phone, or any other prearranged number. This makes the password useless to the hacker, because the target computer is not programmed to dial the hacker's number.

Keep a computerized record of all logins and logouts on your network. Review it from time to time to look for suspicious events. If a

breach of security does occur, such logs can be invaluable if you are trying to track down a hacker intrusion.

Require that everyone log off your network before leaving for work
every evening. If you want to be very careful, you can require logging off
during lunch hours. An unattended account can be exploited by a hacker.

LANS and Firewalls

If you are connecting your firm's internal network to the Internet, you
should probably have what is known as a *firewall*. This is a system involving one or more computers with special software that are placed between
the public Internet and the system to be secured. All traffic from the
Internet is routed through these computers, which are expected to screen
out and repel attacks by unauthorized personnel on your computer network. A properly configured **router** (device that acts as an interface between computers or networks) can act as a decent firewall.

Firewalls are not perfect. Sophisticated attackers can get through
them by a number of means, including *IP spoofing*. This means disguising
an unauthorized intrusion so that it looks to the firewall like something
legitimate. One way to minimize the damage if your firewall is breached
is to partition your internal networks. Even if an intruder gets into your
administrative section, you might be able to keep that party out of your
research and finance sections.

SATAN is a free set of utilities designed
for the purpose of helping organizations
find Internet security weaknesses so they
could be fixed. Ironically, the SATAN
program is now a favorite tool of hackers,
who use it to zero in on the weaknesses
that it discovers.

Web Sites

You can avoid one of the biggest danger areas rather easily. Unless you
have an extremely capable computer
security staff on hand, don't operate a
World Wide Web site on a system
that's connected to your internal
computer network. This is a major
risk because Web sites are visible and
obvious targets that can attract the attention of casual vandals who don't
like lawyers.

Even worse, ordinary Web sites are notoriously insecure, especially if
they provide users with access to any interactive features, such as
searches of a database supplied by the firm. The main threat is not that a
hacker will disrupt your Web site, though such attacks have occurred, but
that the hacker will use its vulnerability to gain access to confidential information in the rest of your system.

Fortunately, it is easy and cheap to rent space on a commercial server for a Web site. Let the ISP take the risk of being attacked. There is little risk of harm to you even if a hacker were to penetrate to your Web materials on your ISP's server. You shouldn't be keeping anything on your Web site that you don't want the world to know, anyway. The idea is to prevent hackers from using a Web site as a point of entry to your internal network.

Make certain that no one in your firm is running an unauthorized Internet server on your LAN. This is more of a risk than you might think. Even an unsophisticated user can use software suites like Internet Chameleon that contain programs to run anonymous FTP servers on personal computers. Sophisticated users might even try to set up their own Web servers. Such servers offer hackers another potential access point into the rest of your system. To further reduce your vulerability, configure your firewall to allow only the services that are required. For example, if your lawyers only use e-mail and access the Web, turn off FTP and Telnet.

Modems are another possible point of LAN vulnerability. As Errol Weiss, a former National Security Agency employee who has done "white hat" hacking, told this author: "Often, I find a remote access package, such as PC Anywhere, installed without a password, or an easy to guess password, and voila, we are inside the network." White hat hacking, sometimes known as "tiger team" testing, involves authorized testing of computer security to find vulnerabilities so they can be repaired.

Weiss concludes: "Just because you have a firewall, you should not feel like you are invincible."

System Use Policies

How do you think your local newspaper would react if it discovered that messages from your firm's Internet domain name were being mailed to a pedophile discussion group? It is essential to establish clear policies on what is and what is not an acceptable use of the Internet, to put those policies in writing, and to make sure every employee understands them and the penalties for violating them. Software packages that monitor the Internet activity of employees on a LAN are available.

Destroy any expectation of personal privacy that employees may have in their use of law firm computers by explicitly warning them that all use of firm computers is subject to monitoring by the firm. Some firms do this by the use of warning banners that are displayed periodically or even every time the computer is started up. Failure to have such a warning can leave you vulnerable to lawsuits if you have to monitor your employees' computer network use to track down a hacker. (Appendix F contains a sample law firm Internet use policy.)

How should you react if a security breach does occur? Be careful about looking for a fall guy to blame. If the situation is handled poorly, other employees might become afraid to step forward and report security holes that they have discovered.

Some firms pay small bonuses to employees who report security weaknesses. This can be a good idea, as long as you and any employees who are reported on keep minor breaches in perspective and don't overreact. Overreacting can be counterproductive.

Training

Training firm personnel is critical. Several elements are involved. The first is training your technical staff. Send them to the appropriate seminars, and have your more technologically sophisticated lawyers debrief them after the training.

Don't stop there. Your technical staff, or someone who understands the issues and is a better teacher than your technical staff, should provide training on computer security basics to every staff member who uses a computer. Staff members don't need to understand how to configure a firewall, but they do need to know that they should report a mysterious message that appears on their computer screen and thanks them for changing their password when they did not change anything. They need to understand the risks in sending unencrypted e-mail. They need to have a basic understanding of how to avoid computer viruses.

Everyone on your staff, not just those who use computers, needs to understand that things like an attempt to obtain a firm phone directory or an odd phone call can be the sign of a "social engineer" in action.

Backups

Regardless of whether you use the Internet, a sound backup policy is an essential component of computer security. Hackers can intentionally or unintentionally destroy files. Fires and other natural catastrophes are not unknown. Computer malfunctions or human errors make it all too easy to lose information that can be replaced only at great expense, if at all.

Compared to the cost of rebuilding from a computer disaster, good backups are very inexpensive. Here are some points to keep in mind:

- Select reliable, easy-to-use backup hardware and software. Remember that if you don't use it, it won't do you any good.
- Test your backups. It is surprisingly common for a law firm to make backups and then to discover when they're needed that they fail, owing to some malfunction in the backup system. Run tests when you set up your backup system—and at regular intervals thereafter—to ensure that this does not happen to you.
- Keep some backup copies off-site. Don't allow them to be destroyed in the same catastrophe that takes out your main system.
- Keep historical copies. If a hidden, hard-to-eradicate virus infected all your files last week, you have a problem if your most recent backup is three days old—it contains the virus as well. Balance the need for historical backups against the added vulnerability to discovery requests. Some businesses are limiting retention of e-mail in particular because of the high potential for embarrassment.

Conclusion

Many law firms believe that they can buy their way into computer security. They feel safe because they have invested thousands of dollars in the newest firewalls or a one-time password system. While there's nothing wrong with having those tools, this attitude is almost certain to lead to disaster. The best password security system can be worthless if a temporary employee reveals a password to a social-engineering hacker.

A debacle can also result from something as simple as a failure to change default passwords. Many security systems come from the factory with such passwords. Studies have shown that a surprisingly high number of users, even a few system administrators (who should be your first line of defense against intruders), never change the default passwords. How many halfway-decent computer hackers in the country don't know those default passwords?

In addition, experts say that a high percentage of expensive firewalls provide no security because they are not properly configured or monitored.

No hardware or software will protect your system unless the people in your law firm use it correctly and consistently. Computer security is not something you buy once and then forget about. It is something you do every day.

Resources

Protect Your Privacy on the Internet, by Bryan Pfaffenberger (Wiley, 1997).

@Large: The Strange Case of the World's Biggest Internet Invasion, by David H. Freeman and Charles C. Mann (Simon & Schuster, 1997). Combines simple explanations of hacker techniques with entertaining narrative of the exploits of a particularly successful real-life hacker.

The CPA's Guide to Information Security, by John Graves and Kim H. Torrence (AICPA 1997).

Web Security & Commerce, Simson Garfinkel with Gene Spafford (O'Reilly 1997). Excellent overview of technical issues likely to concern lawyers working on electronic commerce issues.

CHAPTER **SEVENTEEN**

Computer Viruses and Other Malicious Code

It all depends on human stupidity, you know. It's not the computer's fault that viruses spread.

—"The Dark Avenger," Bulgarian author of
the notorious "virus mutation engine"

COMPUTER VIRUSES ARE not a threat that is unique to the Internet. In fact, even if you are a very active user of the Internet, your greatest risk of virus infection is probably from other sources. Therefore, regardless of whether you're on the Net, you should be taking *at least* the minimal precautions against computer viruses. If you have a good virus protection program in place, you should not need additional protection when adding an Internet connection. This chapter explains the nature of the computer virus threat and the elements of a good protection program.

Terminology and Origins

Malicious code is a catch-all phrase used to describe software that infects a computer system and that is used for some nefarious purpose, such as vandalism or spying. Viruses are the best-known type of malicious code. They are small computer programs that can "reproduce" electronically and spread from computer to computer.

A *Trojan horse* is a virus that appears to be a legitimate program but causes damage after it gets into a system. *Logic bombs* are programs that monitor the activity of a system and perform some type of destructive action when triggered by a specified event (e.g., the tenth time a spreadsheet is loaded, or the computer being booted after 9:30 a.m.). *Worms* are programs that can travel from computer to computer via a network. Some of them try different password combinations and look for vulnerabilities in target systems. Although it is theoretically possible, as of this writing, there are no known worms that attack personal computers. They target larger machines.

Who creates viruses, and why do they do it? Most virus writers have initially been motivated mainly by the intellectual challenge or the same impulse that motivates people to proclaim their identity and power through graffiti. A fringe element of self-styled philosophers considers viruses a new form of life that has as much right to exist as any other "creature" on the planet. Most of the viruses written under this type of motivation are relatively harmless. Their authors would like to see their creations spread as widely as possible. Making them cause serious damage would work against this objective, since people hit by a damaging virus are more serious about eradicating it and preventing its spread to others.

A classic example of a virus written under this type of motivation is the "Saddam Virus," discovered in 1991. Its negative effect, or payload, is to display intermittently on the user's computer screen the message "HEY SADAM LEAVE QUEIT BEFORE I COME." (Its author was apparently better at computer programming than spelling.) The "Cannabis" virus displays the message "Hey man I don't want to work. I'm too stoned." While it would be annoying if such a virus infected your computer, for most people no enormous damage would be caused by having to view these messages a few times before a virus removal program could be run.

Unfortunately, not every virus designer has benign intentions. Indeed, a few want to see just how much damage they can cause. The "Ripper" virus, for example, randomly swaps pairs of numbers on your computer spreadsheets. This is not the sort of thing you want to happen to your firm's accounts receivable.

Viruses can be used as tools of industrial sabotage. There are frightening but unconfirmed anecdotal reports of very sophisticated custom-built viruses designed to infiltrate a particular computer system to obtain certain information or cause specific damage. It is widely believed that the U.S. military is developing viruses as weapons to attack enemies' information infrastructures. A number of computer programmers in Eastern Europe, who can't get jobs in the nearly nonexistent computer industry there, design viruses either out of frustration or as a perverse means of attracting recognition of their programming skills.

In addition, just because a virus designer doesn't intend a creation to cause serious harm doesn't mean that it will not. The notorious Robert Morris "Internet Worm" in 1988 (which, by the way, hit only UNIX systems and not IBM compatibles or Macintoshes) was said to have been an innocently intended experiment that spread beyond its creator's intentions.

Paranoia Reduction

A healthy respect for the virus threat is good. Unfortunately, many computer users harbor irrational fears. You can begin to put the problem in its proper perspective by understanding the ramifications of a simple fact: *A computer virus can only be spread through "executable code."*

You cannot get a computer virus from a text file, or a graphic, or a spreadsheet, or the vast majority of file types. A virus has to be in a *program* or *executable code* that can perform some action. Programs normally have file name extensions of **.exe, .com,** or maybe **.dll** or **.bat** and a very few others in an IBM-compatible environment. Macro viruses, discussed in the next section, are the big exception to this rule.

This should be reassuring because text files are by far the most common type of files that most lawyers will receive via the Internet. All e-mail is text. Even if it has an executable program as an attachment in a MIME, Binhex, or UUENCODED form, it's still text when it is received. Any attachment is harmless until it's decoded. Most modern e-mail programs decode attachments automatically, but this is not a major problem because, even though virus code may exist in a file on your computer, it can't do anything until the program containing the virus is executed. This means that you can download an executable file and check it out. Even if it contains a virus, your machine will not become infected as long as you delete the file without running the program.

The Macro Virus Threat

Some software allows users to create *macros,* or sequences of computer commands that automate various processes. As macro languages became more complex, malicious users began to use them to create macros that operate as viruses.

This threat is particularly insidious if the software allows macros to be stored inside a data file. Most lawyers seldom need to exchange stand-alone macros with clients or other lawyers, but they frequently need to exchange data files. This means that macro viruses can spread readily.

As of this writing, an estimated 80 percent of all computer virus infections come from macro viruses. Microsoft Word viruses are particularly common.

Viruses that take advantage of scripting features in sophisticated e-mail programs are the newest type, with the first being publicly disclosed in July, 1998. Check with the web site of the manufacturer of your e-mail program for patches.

Levels of Risk

The threat of viruses is not a reason to stay off the Internet. However, it is foolish for computer users not to take some precautions against infection. The appropriate level of precautions will vary according to a number of factors.

The first step in establishing a virus protection plan is to assess the level of virus threat and the risk that you can tolerate. Are your computers so "mission critical" that having them go down even for a short time would cause major problems? Does anyone ever add executable code (basically, programs) from sources about which you are not absolutely sure? Do you have a LAN? Do you have a good backup system in place, and do you enforce it?

You must balance the risk and weigh the time and money that would be spent on protective measures against the benefits to be gained. Some computer users can probably get by with few precautions. Those whose computer systems are mission critical may have to exercise extraordinary care. Most people will fall somewhere in between these extremes.

Having a LAN instead of stand-alone computers tends to alter the cost-benefit equation radically. With stand-alone computers, if one goes down temporarily owing to a virus, you might not lose that much productivity. If the virus spreads to shut down all the computers on a LAN, you could be looking at a disaster. Cleaning up one computer is usually no big deal, especially if you have a good backup system. Cleaning up fifty computers, while the people who should be using them are twiddling their thumbs, can cost a fortune in lost productivity.

Elements of a Virus Protection Plan

There are several factors to be addressed in an effective computer virus protection program. If you have not already done so, take precautions now. Don't wait for a virus infection.

Preparing for the Worst

Back up your system regularly. A sound backup system is critical, and not just because of the possibility of computer viruses. Every hard drive is guaranteed to fail. It is only a question of when. Tape drives and removable disks like Iomega Zip and Jaz drives have become so inexpensive that there is no excuse for failing to have a thorough backup system in place.

Do a virus scan of your hard disk *before* backing it up. It is a good idea to keep multiple sets of backups that extend over a fairly long time. You don't want to lose all the data on your hard drive because of a virus only to discover that your only backup has the same virus.

Keep a clean, write-protected boot disk. *Stealth* viruses, once active, take measures to conceal themselves. If you start up as usual from your hard disk, your antivirus software may not be able to locate such a virus. Even worse, some viruses can spread themselves by using an antivirus program. A *fast infector* virus infects every executable file that is opened when the virus is active, even if the file is not executed. If an unsophisticated user gets a message that a virus is active on his or her machine, the user might start up the virus scanner to see what the virus is. In such a case, the virus would automatically spread to every program on the hard drive. You can avoid this nightmarish result by booting from your clean boot disk *before* running the virus checking program.

Programs like PC Tools and Norton Utilities have routines to create such boot disks. If you use disk compression software or anything that requires its own drivers, include them on the boot disk.

Avoiding Infection

Be careful about where you get your software. This step will reduce your risk—but it will not eliminate it. You may think that you can avoid all risk of viruses by ensuring that the only programs ever installed on your machines come from brand-new commercial software distributed by reputable commercial companies. You would be wrong. There are multiple documented cases of viruses being distributed through shrink-wrapped retail software, including software from major manufacturers. Even disks sold as blanks have contained viruses.

If your computers are mission critical, you should routinely screen any files or disks that go into your computer, regardless of their source, be it a commercial online service, a neighbor or a friend, or the Internet. If your computer system is critical and you can't afford any downtime, use one or more good virus checking programs on *all* executable files and disks that come your way.

A speaker at an Internet conference I attended had been a serious computer user for many years, downloading hundreds of files of various types from the Internet and other sources. During all those years, he had received *one* virus infection. He traced it back to a floppy disk he had received by postal mail from a respected national legal organization.

Another example of an unexpected source of infection: computer repair technicians. Watch out for computer repairpeople who run diagnostic software on your equipment. This is a common method by which viruses are unintentionally spread. Another potential source is salespersons running demo software from your equipment. Check your machine for viruses after either event.

Much new software is compressed on the installation disk, and your virus scanner probably won't pick up the compressed viruses. If you really want to be safe, run the scanner program again after you have installed the new software.

No virus scanner detects every virus 100 percent of the time. Consider using more than one brand of scanner to increase your chances of finding any viruses. Just remember to reboot the machine between tests because fragments of virus signatures left in memory by one program can cause false positive readings by the second. You should also stay current with updates issued by your antivirus software manufacturers because new viruses are discovered regularly. The best antivirus programs will download updates from the Internet automatically.

Does being careful about where you get your software mean that you can never use files downloaded from the Internet? Definitely not. You should check them out, just like files from any other source, but it would be foolish to impose a *per se* rule.

If you have a CD-ROM drive, buy your software in that format whenever possible. A virus can't be added to the discs after they leave the factory. If you have to install software from floppy disks, make sure they are physically write-protected. On a 5.25-inch disk, this involves putting a piece of tape over the write-protect notch. On a 3.5-inch disk, it involves pushing the write-protect tab toward the edge of the disk. If you're already unknowingly infected by a virus, write-protecting will prevent the virus from contaminating the new disks. You can use the same technique if, for some reason, you must insert your own disk into another computer that might have a virus.

If possible, install new software on an isolated test computer first and run it there for a few weeks before installing it widely throughout your organization.

If you have a LAN or WAN, consider establishing controls to prevent unauthorized users from installing software. Train your users and establish a rule against using nonapproved software to deter people from trying to evade your access controls. It's a bad idea to be too draconian in your rule enforcement, however, because this could deter users from reporting a virus infection, thus giving it time to spread to still more machines.

You can use the ATTRIB command in DOS to make all your **.exe** and **.com** files read-only. This will protect against some unsophisticated viruses, but it has the drawback that some programs will not run in read-only mode.

Most of the commercial antivirus software can be configured to run continuously in the background, automatically scanning files copied from floppies, e-mail attachments, and Internet downloads before copying them to the hard drive. As Errol Weiss, a leading computer security expert with Global Integrity Corp., advised me: "This is quite a useful feature and one that has saved me many times."

Detecting the Symptoms

Despite your best efforts, a virus may get into your system, so you need to remain alert for signs of infection. The symptom could be something blatant, like the message to Saddam Hussein mentioned earlier, or it could be more subtle, such as the following:

- Hard or floppy disk drive lights come on frequently for no apparent reason
- There is a radical change in the amount of free RAM or space on the drive
- The computer operates unusably slowly
- The date or time stamp on files or programs changes oddly

Most DOS viruses cannot run under Windows. They can, however, infect Windows programs and stop them from running. This makes it easy to detect the infection.

Using Antivirus Software

Antivirus programs use one or more of four basic approaches:

- Scanning disks for telltale signs of known viruses
- Monitoring computer activity for suspicious behavior
- Detecting suspicious changes in files
- Disinfecting once a virus is discovered

Some products perform all four functions. You can improve the effectiveness of your antivirus software by frequently obtaining and installing the newest files of virus signatures. New viruses are being discovered constantly. While some scanners have "heuristic" features that let them ferret out some new viruses, don't expect a scanner to find a virus that it doesn't know about.

If you do discover a virus, it is important to try to track down its source. You need to avoid the risk of reinfection from the same source, and you may need to warn others of the virus.

Some antivirus software purports to "disinfect" an infected file, removing the virus so that you can use the file as if nothing had ever happened to it. No antivirus program does this accurately with every infected file. It is better to delete the infected file and replace it from the original or a backup disk that you know is safe.

New Forms of Malicious Code

Java, JavaScript, and ActiveX are used to add interactive features to Web sites:

- Java is a feature that allows the small programs called applets to be downloaded from the World Wide Web and run on your computer automatically.
- JavaScript (not as similar to Java as the name implies) uses a simpler scripting language coded into the actual Web pages to provide interactive features.

- ◆ ActiveX is a set of techniques developed by Microsoft to allow Web sites to interact with programs on visitors' computers.

All these features have legitimate purposes and, as of this writing, none of them has yet given rise to rogue uses as common as viruses.

The designers of these features have taken pains to add security measures to their products. However, with any complex and powerful new technology, it is safe to predict that security flaws will be found. For example, a hacker group in Germany has demonstrated an ActiveX application that can search the hard drive of a Web site visitor, find the bank account password in the visitor's Quicken program, and send it to the hacker by e-mail.

From a security point of view, using Java, JavaScript, and ActiveX is analogous to allowing housekeepers from a temporary service to have keys to your home. Even if the overwhelming majority of housekeepers are honest, just as most Java, JavaScript, and ActiveX applications are safe, there is some risk in such a practice.

Law firms that need a high level of security should consider restricting the use of such features by their network users. The latest browsers provide some built-in protection measures, including warnings and "signing" by authors to identify safe applications. If you want to be very careful, you can set browsers to disallow any use of Java, JavaScript, or ActiveX. Some antivirus program vendors have begun to include some protection against these new threats in their products, but it is unclear how effective they will be.

As Java and ActiveX (which are both more powerful and hence more dangerous than JavaScript) mature, they will be used more frequently to provide substantive benefits instead of animated graphics and the like, and the inevitable security flaws will be patched. As the risk-to-benefit ratio changes, a more liberal attitude toward Java and ActiveX may be appropriate.

Conclusion

Viruses pose some danger to computers, on or off the Internet, but it is important to keep the matter in perspective. Assess your situation and the level of risk you can tolerate, then implement the appropriate level of security measures. Don't let irrational fears keep you from taking advantage of the Internet.

Resources

F-PROT, an antivirus program developed in Iceland that gets consistently high ratings from independent testing organizations:
http://www.DataFellows.com

Computer Virus Myths: http://www.kumite.com/myths

Information on known computer viruses:
http://www.av.ibm.com/InsideTheLab/VirusInfo

PART FIVE

Putting It All Together

CHAPTER **EIGHTEEN**

Collaborative Tools

THE INTERNET'S ABILITY to facilitate work on multiperson projects is one of its great strengths. Improved cooperation brings with it the promise of increased productivity, higher quality work on large projects, and decreased costs.

The basic Net collaboration tools are e-mail, public discussion groups, and public Web sites. Yet even simple "e-mail pager" technology like Instant Messaging (which lets you contact people connected to the Internet immediately instead of waiting for them to pick up their e-mail) can make life easier for those working on team projects.

Intranets and a subset, extranets, are a type of collaborative tool that deserves more attention.

Bill Gates's Epiphany

In his famous 1995 "Tidal Wave" memo explaining to his employees his intention to turn Microsoft into an "Internet company," Bill Gates observed that "Amazingly, it is easier to find information on the Web than it is to find information on the Microsoft Corporate Network."

Gates was neither the first nor the last corporate manager to make such a discovery. He and many other sophisticated managers decided that if Internet tools were more efficient than conventional network software, it made sense to bring Internet tools inside the company. Executives like Gates tired of wondering why it was easier for them to locate information on another company's Internet server in Moscow or

Singapore than it was to locate information on their own company's local or wide area networks. Spoiled by the ease of use and power they discovered on the Internet, they decided that they wanted the same power and flexibility in their internal operations.

This is the essence of an intranet, a sort of private Internet. Information is made accessible via Internet technology—especially Web browsers—to selected groups, usually within one organization. Because the TCP/IP protocol used on the Internet can run simultaneously with the Novell, Macintosh or Microsoft networking protocols in use on most business networks, most organizations can add an intranet to their existing network without extensive hardware upgrades. Today more Web server software is being sold to use in intranets than to establish conventional public Web sites.

Intranet Advantages

Intranets are relatively inexpensive to establish and operate because they use commonly accepted standards, which facilitates competition and interchangability. As Lee Glickenhaus, a former litigator who is now president of T Lex (http://www.tlex.com) notes, "Open standards allow users to select from many compatible products and take a modular approach to developing the functionality they need." Burgess Allison estimates that it is an order of magnitude less expensive to distribute data internally via an intranet than via a custom, proprietary database.

Many intranet benefits are supposed to be available through a category of software called *groupware*. Lotus Notes and Novell Groupwise are two popular examples. Intranets provide all or most of the benefits of proprietary groupware products and have a number of advantages:

- Intranets are simpler.
- They are platform independent (i.e., can be accessed with Macintosh or UNIX computers, as well as DOS, Windows 3.1, Windows 95 and 98, and Windows NT systems).
- Intranets are more flexible because they are not tied to one particular vendor.
- They are easier to connect to other systems.
- They require less processing power, hard disk space, and bandwidth.
- They are easier to expand, and it is simpler to add other functions to them.

◆ They are better at decentralization and empowerment of ordinary personnel, and it is easier to create useful Web pages than to add comparable value in a proprietary system.

If these advantages are not enough, intranets reduce training time significantly. Anyone who can use a Web browser should be able to use an intranet or an extranet.

Intranet Content

What might a law firm put on an intranet? Here are some starters:

◆ Policies
◆ Announcements
◆ A firm directory
◆ Calendars for lawyers and other key personnel
◆ Collections of resources related to particular practice areas
◆ Customized lists of links to useful Web sites
◆ Checklists
◆ Brief banks and legal memoranda files
◆ Lists of FAQs or similar references
◆ Forms
◆ Court rules
◆ CLE and other training materials
◆ Information on new clients
◆ Financial reports
◆ Profiles of judges the firm has encountered

An intranet can include an amazing range of other things that would save time or otherwise make the firm's personnel more productive. Certainly, information like this can be distributed through other mechanisms. However, as Bill Gates learned, Internet-type technology makes things easier to find, and people are more likely to use it than a proprietary system that requires extensive training.

Intranets are not limited to static collections of information. An intranet lets users operate Web browsers to access programs like the following:

◆ Calendar management programs
◆ Databases

- Specialized programs that relate to the firm's practice, such as tax computation software
- Conflict-checking programs
- Threaded announcement or discussion programs for social events, employee awards, and the like

Features like these allow users to do two key things:

1. Quickly find the information they need
2. Easily add to (or annotate) existing information

Less time is devoted to reinventing the wheel, so more time is devoted to improving the quality of service provided.

An intranet may be the best step you can take toward significantly reducing the flow of paper through your law firm. Moreover, considerable cost savings and increased efficiencies can result. As Carl Middlehurst notes about the Sun Microsystems legal department intranet (see the Web site http://www.sun.com/sun-on-net/Business.on.Internet/legal/intranet.html):

> We used to distribute policies in hard copy. Quality printing was expensive and distribution was cumbersome. Often, within weeks, these policies were out of date. Similarly, we would make hard copies of agreements available to clients and that same version of the agreement would be photocopied and used for years. With the web, your publication costs are reduced greatly while your client access to your information is greatly enhanced. In addition, the content can be easily updated on a regular basis. When changes are made to policies or when more recent versions of an agreement become available, it is a simple matter to update the web site. [Users] are trained to rely only on the web site to access the information, not other hard copy versions.

Peter Krakaur, a San Francisco lawyer and leading intranet designer, says "I see intranets as acting as a single source, one-stop shopping for legal information within the firm or company." Sabrina Pacifici, director of library services for Sidley and Austin, uses her firm's elaborate intranet to implement a similar philosophy of one-stop shopping for legal research resources. Lawyers can select from customized collections of links to and searches of Internet resources, Westlaw or LEXIS database links, Folio databases on CD-ROM, and the firm's collection of memos and other documents, all broken down by practice area. Unlike some intranets, it does not include administrative functions or information like personnel manuals but rather concentrates solely on legal research.

The Los Angeles firm of Latham & Watkins was quick to see the value of intranets for litigation management. As partner Julie Wilson Marshall told *Amlaw Tech,* "The intranet is a way for us to leverage what are our strengths. We can tap into a knowledge base that is strictly Latham & Watkins in a matter of seconds." The *Amlaw Tech* story goes on to note:

> Marshall put all the pleadings, research, memoranda, and imaged documents for one of her cases on the firm's intranet. Using Netscape on their computers, all of the lawyers involved in the litigation—two partners, three associates, and five paralegals in the firm's Los Angeles, San Diego, and Chicago offices, as well as two local counsel and two in-house lawyers—will have immediate access to all the company documents and lawyer work product generated in the past year of litigation. (Ann Shoket, "Latham's Lawyer-Driven Approach, *AmLaw Tech* (Spring 1997))

Firms whose lawyers travel extensively can also benefit from the Internet's global reach through a firm intranet. From literally anywhere in the world, one of your lawyers who has access to a World Wide Web browser can be given access to all the information on your firm's intranet. This is much more convenient and cheaper than using telephones and dial-in access programs like PC Anywhere.

The trend toward intranets is one reason that so many software companies are adding Internet functionality to products like word processors, spreadsheets, databases, presentation programs, personal information managers (PIMs), and the like. These features will work just as well on an intranet as they do on the public Internet.

Components for Building an Intranet

A simple intranet might have the following hardware and software. If you have a LAN, you already have the first three up and running:

- **A server computer.** A basic setup would involve a 486 CPU machine with at least 16MB of RAM and a 500MB hard disk. (If you plan to use the server for other purposes, get at least a Pentium 90 and 32MB of RAM. Otherwise the intranet performance will slow significantly when the server is being used for other purposes.)
- **Operating system software.** One of the beauties of an intranet is that the computers on the network need not all be using the same type of software.

- ◆ **Network adapters and cabling.** The adapters and cabling are used to link the computers on the intranet together.
- ◆ **Web browsers for all users.** Available at no charge.
- ◆ **Web server software.** This software responds to user requests for information. Basic Web server programs are available at no charge.
- ◆ **Internet software tools.** This includes HTML editors and site management software. Depending on how elaborate you want to be, you might also want database management, calendaring or other specialized software. Microsoft FrontPage, which includes its own Web server software, retails for approximately $150.

In addition, if the firm does not want every user to have access to every area, both intranets and extranets (discussed later in this chapter) can incorporate user access rights. The intranet or extranet can be set up so that it recognizes a user's login name and password and restricts access to only those sections to which that particular user has been authorized to have access.

Going to an intranet is not an all-or-nothing proposition. A firm that is wedded to a proprietary groupware program can operate an intranet side by side with that program. For example, you could use a Web server for your intranet but continue to rely on Novell Groupwise for e-mail and scheduling.

While many firms have designed intranets using only in-house resources, some firms will prefer hiring a consultant. Lee Glickenhaus, the former litigator who runs the T Lex intranet-extranet consulting firm, provides some suggestions: "Hire someone good who you feel simpatico with. If a company is committed to a project, they can delegate a lot but they still have to be involved. Appoint one person whose job it is to be a nudge, to be the 'producer' in-house and the interface with the contractor/consultant. Be patient—even great systems take time to catch on. Think big, but take small steps."

Outsourcing can be particularly attractive to smaller firms. As Peter Ozolin, of Legal Anywhere (http://www.legalanywhere.com), explains, "With a turnkey intranet hosted at our site, our customers do not have to start from scratch or 'reinvent the wheel.' Rather, each of our customers benefits from collective feedback from all our customers. In this way, small and medium-sized firms gain economies of scale even greater than those enjoyed by large firms with vast resources."

Some consultants, like Internet Legal Services, market services specifically designed to be used in conjunction with intranets (see their Web site at http://www.legalethics.com/brochure.htm). Internet Legal Services' Intralaw is a licensed program and database of Internet legal resources that is designed to be customizable. Services like this can save time and

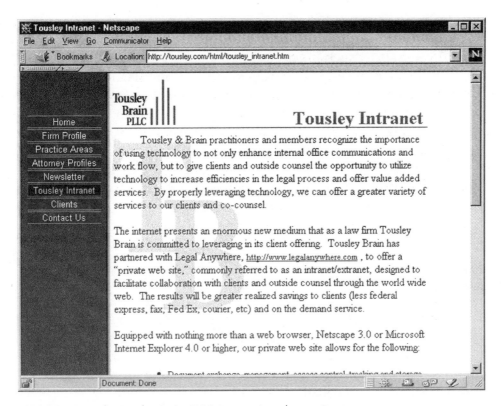

FIGURE 18-1. The Tousley Brain, PLLC, Intranet Introductory Page

improve the quality of an intranet, especially for smaller firms that do not have law librarians on staff.

Intranet Yellow Lights

Valuable though they are, intranets are not perfect. There are several caution areas.

It is no easier to find and work with your key information on a disorganized intranet than it is on a conventional LAN. Accordingly, give some thought to organization. One possibility is to structure your information to parallel the law firm's structure or practice areas. For example, have a section for your litigation group and one for your corporate group.

While cheaper than proprietary groupware products, intranets are not cost free. The hardware and software costs may be much lower, but inputting the information and setting up an intranet requires some "sweat equity," and possibly the use of a contractor.

The biggest intranet benefits come through using it to facilitate your firm's day-to-day performance, including mission critical functions. What if you transfer such functions to the network and it goes down? Do you have an alternate way of getting those jobs done? Plan ahead so that you can perform necessary functions without the intranet if it is temporarily unavailable because your LAN or WAN goes down.

Connecting your intranet to the public Internet increases its utility by making the associated resources readily accessible to your intranet users, but it also introduces new security risks. Thus, firewalls and other protective measures are necessary. Appropriate measures are discussed below and in Chapter 16, "Net Security Overview."

Extranets

Clearly intranets can offer major productivity and convenience improvements inside an organization. Is there any way to leverage these advantages over more than one organization? *Extranets* provide a private (and often secure) environment for individuals from multiple organizations to share information and collaborate on projects.

To some extent, the traditional practice of law has been a type of cottage industry, involving very expensive, custom-designed products. Law firms have maintained their own legal brief and standard pleadings files but had no access to such material compiled by other law firms. Extranets can change this in a radical way.

Extranets can contain highly specialized information, including databases of information on witnesses or opposing counsel, exhibits, pleadings, literature libraries, and shared legal strategies.

In-house counsel tend to be big extranet fans. As the counsel for a major nursing home chain explained, "We used to spend a lot of time reinventing the wheel in every case. We made it absolutely mandatory that outside counsel be hooked up to an extranet, and you could see the savings almost immediately."

Like intranets, extranets are platform-independent, which facilitates the task of connecting people from multiple organizations (and multiple computing platforms). Before extranets came along, some organizations used dedicated leased phone lines, frame relay, or other expensive communications links to transfer information between organizations. Extranets are an attractive replacement for such arrangements because no private communications line is necessary. You can use the public Internet infrastructure—as long as you take appropriate security precautions.

Three basic types of law-related extranets are common:

1. Extranets used by law firms to provide better client service, such as distributing voluminous databases or making available up-to-date billing and status information (as discussed in Chapter 11, "Planning a Law Firm Web Site").

2. Extranets associated with some legal organization. The National Association of Criminal Defense Lawyers (NACDL) site is at http://www.criminaljustice.org. The Association of Trial Lawyers of America operates ATLA Exchange at http://www.atlanet.org. Even some state trial lawyers organizations are beginning to get into the act, including the Texas Trial Lawyers Association, at http://www.ttla.com. All these sites contain some sections that are open to the general public, while other sections are restricted to members through the use of passwords. Members have access to custom-designed lists of hypertext links and online newsletters, as well as more significant resources like brief banks and document libraries (including research memos, hard-to-find published cases, and government documents). Some have calendars, audio libraries, and private Web-based discussion groups.

3. Multifirm cooperatives. TrialNet, headed by Mike Curreri, a partner in the Richmond, Virginia, firm of Wright, Robinson, Osthimer & Tatum, is a leading example. TrialNet specializes in the business of setting up extranets for litigation management for large-scale litigation and mass torts. TrialNet's URL is http://www.trialnet.com. (see Figure 18-2.)

TrialNet is organized into a number of separate sections called *tracks.* Each track revolves around a particular corporation, product, or subject matter. For example, a large corporation that employs many outside counsel could have its own track. Another track could be devoted to breast implant litigation. Through the use of a set of passwords, a TrialNet member is given access to only the tracks to which he or she has been authorized. Some material may be duplicated across more than one track.

Here's one example of how an extranet can save money and improve the quality of legal services at the same time: One law firm was strikingly successful in defending "failure to timely diagnose" malpractice claims in breast cancer cases using one particular theory. At the direction of the TrialNet track sponsor, an insurance company, this firm uploaded an explanation of how it handled the defense of such cases, including links to

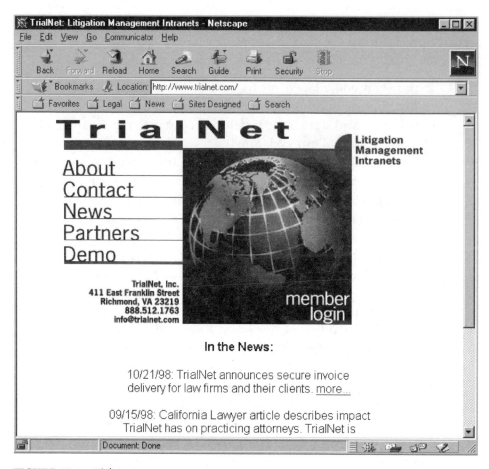

FIGURE 18-2. TrialNet

supporting briefs, medical literature, and expert witnesses. Now other law firms who are members of the same extranet can present the same defense at a fraction of the cost it took the first time. Even many of the original exhibits can be recycled.

The extranet makes it easy to coordinate uniform positions, such as responses to discovery requests, which is a major problem with large organizations that must coordinate litigation in many jurisdictions. By requiring outside counsel to subscribe to an extranet, the client can make its policies and updates easily available to its lawyers at any time and in any locale with Internet access.

Some lawyers may wonder why law firms that normally consider each other to be competitors would willingly cooperate by contributing material to an extranet. In some cases, their clients require it. Further, effective use of the extranet can make a law firm more attractive to clients. Extranets sponsored by large corporations that employ many outside counsel can operate

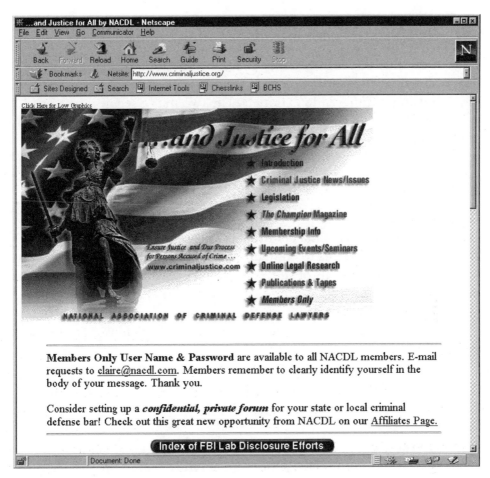

FIGURE 18-3. The NACDL Extranet

as a sort of marketplace of ideas where firms can compete for recognition. The track sponsor can easily monitor how often and how well outside counsel are using the extranet. A firm that makes significant contributions can expect to get more business from the extranet sponsor as well as referrals from other participating law firms that learn to respect expertise.

The increasing use of fixed-fee programs and other fee arrangements that shift all or part of the burden of inefficient representation to law firms make extranets more attractive to some firms. Some are beginning to tout their membership in extranets, and their willingness to use them, as a selling point to potential clients.

In addition, extranets can offer small firms and solos a way to combine resources and compete with larger organizations on more even terms.

While we are only beginning to realize extranets' potential to make major changes in the way we practice law, it is already clear that major benefits are achievable.

Security Concerns with Intranets and Extranets

The ethical duty of confidentiality and concerns about waiving the lawyer-client privilege make security a major concern for lawyers interested in using intranets and extranets. The two major security concerns are authentication (allowing only the right people to access the extranet) and channel security (preventing interception of information in transit). In both cases, the system administrator must balance security measures and ease of use.

Authentication

There are several ways to make intranets and extranets secure. The most basic is for administrators to configure their Web servers to restrict access to certain sites or portions of sites. This can be done through requiring a password to obtain access to those areas or to restrict access to users accessing the site from certain IP addresses.

Firewalls and proxy servers provide a "perimeter defense" around the Web server against outside intrusions.

Identifying information contained in "cookies" of the Web browsers is another security measure. Like a password, it helps the server distinguish between authorized and unauthorized users.

Channel Security

Some Web servers permit encryption of data in transit to protect communications with encryption-capable Web browsers. This protects information sent to and from the Web server. Nearly all newer browsers contain such encryption features. If you are not sure, check the documentation. A lock or key in the corner of the screen is frequently used to indicate whether you are communicating with a secure server. If the lock or key is unbroken, your communications at that site are secure.

Server or browser encryption is a necessity with an extranet where sensitive information may be transmitted using Web browsers. Encryption keeps information secure while in transit over the public Internet.

Virtual private network (VPN) is a popular buzz term but not the world's most specific concept. As Steve Steinberg observed in *Wired* magazine, "The wonderful thing about virtual private network is that its myriad definitions give every company a fair chance to claim that its existing product is actually a VPN."

The basic idea underlying all VPNs is fairly simple: Information is encrypted before it leaves its destination and is decrypted by the recipient.

Modern public key encryption systems that don't require the exchange of private passwords make this practical for widespread commercial use.

Many lawyers have heard that browser programs have built-in encryption and mistakenly believe this encryption automatically protects their e-mail. This is not accurate. Some e-mail programs bundled with browsers have an e-mail encryption option, but it must be invoked separately. Chapter 15 has more information on e-mail security.

Qualified Extranet Personnel

If sensitive information is available on a law firm extranet, security is an issue. Achieving the level of security needed to operate an extranet is not a job for amateurs.

Operating an extranet in house may be appropriate for some law firms that have extremely well-qualified personnel on board, but most firms will probably be better off hiring outside experts or contracting with an extranet operator that already has extranets up and running. Economies of scale and the benefits of accumulated experience mean the latter option is often not just cheaper but safer, whether for intranets or extranets.

Other Collaborative Tools

Intranets and extranets are not the only ways to take advantage of the Internet's power for facilitating teamwork.

Real-time Conferencing

Group conferencing software is very promising. These programs support real-time meetings through features such as the following:

- Built-in "chat" (i.e., users see what each other are typing in real-time)
- Built-in Internet phone features for voice conference calls over the Internet (which requires a sound card, speakers, and a microphone)
- "White boards" that let you share chalkboard-type scribblings, graphics, spreadsheets, charts, and so forth
- Features that make it easy to set up meetings over the Internet

The major web browser suites from Netscape and Microsoft contain software with this capability. In the past, conferencing software from one manufacturer would usually not be compatible with that from other manufacturers. With the recent adoption of the International Telecommunication Union (ITU) H.323 standard, this should change. A conferencing program built to this standard should work with others built to the standard.

As Kevin Manson, a lawyer and instructor at the Federal Financial Fraud Institute, has pointed out, the issuance of warrants is one of many logical uses of Internet conferencing for lawyers. Rule 41 of the Federal Rules of Criminal Procedure permits telephonic and fax warrant applications under appropriate circumstances. The language appears broad enough to support Internet conferencing as well, since it may fairly be characterized as merely a more sophisticated form of telephone call. The judge can use the white-board feature to see the supporting evidence and application. It's easy for the judge to ask questions, and all the information can be recorded automatically. Prosecutors will appreciate the fact that no more evidence will be suppressed because the judge forgot to include in the authorization some of the evidence that was in fact presented.

Counsel Connect, http://www.counsel.com, offers the ability to set up private conference areas. These require no special software in addition to a regular Web browser, so some lawyers may find them suitable alternatives to conferencing software.

Chat

The traditional Internet chat medium is IRC, or Internet relay chat. IRC features real-time teletype-like "conversations," much like America Online's chat rooms. Chat features are being built into other types of software, including interactive Web sites and Internet conferencing programs. Many proprietary chat programs are available as well. Some Web sites feature chat rooms as a way to build a sense of community among users in hope of drawing repeat visitors.

Chat has a reputation for being a time waster, and it has not been used very much for serious business purposes. However, this may change. FindLaw is trying to lead the way with its chat area: http://chat.findlaw.com.

A transcript of a law school class discussion is available at the Texas Tech Law School site at http://www.law.ttu.edu/cyberspc/cybses2.htm.

More information about chat is available at http://www.icq.com.

Internet Phone

You can make free long-distance calls to anyone in the world with an Internet connection. There are tens of thousands of users already. The sound quality is not yet as good as Ma Bell's, but it's sure to improve as the technology advances and more bandwidth becomes widely available. As of this writing, you can only communicate with another Internet user who has compatible software and is logged onto the Internet when you call. To save money on long-distance calls, some people make a traditional call to alert the person they want to talk to, then hang up and finish their conversation via the Internet.

Teleconferencing

People have predicted for decades that teleconferencing would become a mainstream application, but high cost and inflexibility kept it mostly on the shelf. The Internet will make it a reality.

Internet video cameras cost approximately one hundred dollars. The picture quality and reliability are not very good, but they will certainly improve as the technology matures and higher bandwidth becomes available.

Some lawyers are already using Internet teleconferencing to communicate with clients. This will become much more popular over the next ten years. In response to lawyer demand, courts will begin using video-conferencing for hearings on motions and other routine appearances. As noted by Eugene Volokh, "At some point, lawyers may find it hard to justify to a client why they spent a day, or even a few hours, traveling for half an hour of oral argument."

Resources

Online

Mark Gibbs's "Build Your Own Secret Intranet" (*PC World*, March 1997): http://www.pcworld.com/software/networking_workgroup/articles/mar97/ 1503p109.html. Gibbs uses the term "secret intranet" to make the point that the impetus for an intranet sometimes does not come from top management or information systems personnel but from workers who are close to the job and want the additional tools an intranet provides.

Sabrina Pacifici's Articles on Intranet Design for the Law Library Resource Xchange: http://www.llrx.com/features/intranet.htm

In Paper

Extranets: The Complete Sourcebook, by Richard H. Baker (McGraw-Hill, 1997).

The CPA's Guide to Intranets, by John Graves and Jacqueline Justice (AICPA, 1997). Yes, we can learn from our professional cousins. Excellent nuts and bolts advice on intranet design.

CHAPTER **NINETEEN**

Thinking About the Net

"**A**TTITUDE IS EVERYTHING," a popular advertising slogan tells us. While I wouldn't go quite that far, it is certainly true that attitudes are frequently more important than aptitudes in determining who succeeds and who does not. This chapter describes some attitudes and concepts that have only one thing in common: their potential to assist you on your way to becoming an Internet power user.

Selecting Internet Tools

Choosing products for use on the Internet involves some considerations that will be new to many lawyers, even those with some technical savvy.

If you are a solo practitioner with no compelling need to share personal information with others, you are pretty much free to select whichever PIM you like—Sidekick, Microsoft Outlook, Lotus Organizer, it makes no particular difference. The same flexibility applies to word processors, spreadsheets, graphics programs, and so on. By contrast, when selecting software to use in a "networking" situation, where you must interface with others, your choices are more constrained. You are better off if your software, in the kindergarten teacher's phrase, "works well with others."

These restraints apply particularly to Internet software choices. While the Internet is blessed with some common standards, like the use of the Simple Mail Transport Protocol (SMTP) and the Post Office Protocol (POP) for e-mail servers, its open nature means that many incompatible and proprietary standards are in common use for things like encryption. There are literally scores of encryption products on the market, and the vast majority of them are worthless unless the sender and recipient of an encrypted message are using the same software.

Here are two key factors to be considered in selecting Internet software that must interface with other software to be usable:

- Does the product comply with open standards?
- If it uses a proprietary standard, is it likely to be supported by a critical mass of users, to make it viable?

Open standards are nonproprietary specifications, generally promulgated by some body of experts. SMTP is an example. The methods used to transmit e-mail under SMTP are specified in an Internet Request for Comment (RFC), which is a defined specification established by key Internet decision makers and adhered to by consensus. The widespread acceptance of standards for e-mail is a key reason why e-mail services and software are relatively free from compatibility problems and also cheap. No one owns the SMTP standard and no one can charge you a license fee to build it into your products.

While some people support open standards with a pure, almost religious fervor, a more flexible approach is probably more sensible. Support open standards whenever possible because they are generally in the long-range best interests of the community as a whole. However, there are situations in which proprietary solutions are the best pragmatic choice. The popular PGP encryption program, for example, is a proprietary program, even though versions of it are given away at no cost.

Understanding Metcalfe's Law and Its Consequences

By now, most people have heard of the conjecture called Moore's Law, named after Gordon Moore, a senior Intel Corporation executive:

> *Computers tend to double in power, or drop by half in price, every eighteen months.*

This rule of thumb has been an accurate predictor, with the exception that in the past few years, the cycle has been even faster, closer to twelve than to eighteen months.

Metcalfe's Law, named after Bob Metcalfe, the inventor of the Ethernet networking standard, applies to networks:

The value of being a member of a beneficial network increases as the square of the number of users.

It makes sense when you think about it. The first fax machine in the world was useless. When the second fax machine was built, it made the first one worth something. Today, with millions of fax machines in use, they are so useful that it is very rare to find a lawyer without a fax number on his or her business card.

Metcalfe's law has an interesting side effect: As being on a network becomes more valuable because the number of users is growing, economies of scale mean network membership tends to become cheaper.

This result may seem paradoxical if we naively try to apply conventional economic principles. Normally, when something becomes more desirable, we expect it to become more expensive, right? The highest quality car is usually the rarest and most expensive. The more common cars tend to be cheaper and less desirable.

However, the dynamics of networking lead to a totally different result: When it comes to networks, "rare" means not just expensive, but worthless as well. It is the most common products that tend to be both cheaper and more valuable.

This, too, makes sense, once you analyze it. Years ago, fax machines cost thousands of dollars. Moreover, because they were relatively rare, they were not all that useful for many people. Today, fax machines are dirt cheap, but paradoxically, they are much more useful than they were twenty-five years ago. As Kevin Kelly has pointed out, "When you go to Office Depot to buy a fax machine, you are not just buying a US $200 box. You are purchasing for $200 the entire network of all the other fax machines and the connections between them—a value far greater than the cost of all the separate machines."

Metcalfe's Law is commonly cited as a rule why Internet growth has increased exponentially in recent years and will continue to increase rapidly for the foreseeable future. When there were relatively few Internet users, there was not much reason to go on-line. Furthermore, getting a connection was difficult and expensive.

As the number of users and the amount of useful information on the Internet increased, the case for getting a connection became more compelling, and getting a connection became both easier and cheaper.

Metcalfe's Law and Software

Metcalfe's Law applies to software as well as to physical connections and equipment. All those using a particular type of encryption software, for example, can be considered to be a sort of closed network. They can communicate securely only with those in the same network, that is, those using compatible encryption programs.

Imagine that instead of one universal fax machine standard, there were scores of different types of fax machines using incompatible standards. Rational consumers in such a market would tend to buy the brand that had the greatest market share, unless they knew for certain that they would only need to communicate with parties using a less popular brand.

When networking products are incompatible, choosing the market leader will generally give the biggest bang for the buck. This rule applies to encryption, videoconferencing software, voice over IP (Internet telephone) equipment, chat software, and some other Internet software. For example, it does not apply to browser software or e-mail programs. With a few exceptions (like "Marquees" in I.E. Explorer, and "Return Receipt" in Eudora Pro), they are built to conform to open standards.

The so-called "tipping point rule" reinforces this preference for market leaders when the use of proprietary standards is unavoidable. Experts generally agreed that the Sony Betamax standard was technically superior to VHS. Yet today, Betamax is nearly dead while VHS thrives. Why? Superior marketing made it easier to buy and rent VHS tapes. The trend to VHS reinforced itself, giving VHS so much momentum that at some point buying the technically superior but rarer product no longer made sense. Economists call that point in time the *tipping point*. When a tipping point is reached, it becomes inevitable that one product will come to dominate a market. While an "orphaned" word processor, one abandoned by its manufacturer, will continue to function well for many years, an orphaned network product will usually have a shorter useful life span.

If the use of a proprietary product is unavoidable, going with the market leader has other advantages. Other vendors are more likely to produce enhancements and add-ins for the market leader. It is also easier to find inexpensive technical support from third parties and other sources, like Internet discussion groups.

Metcalfe's Law helps us understand why marketing strategies that would be nonsensical off the Internet make sense in the networking environment. Microsoft does not give away its flagship word processor—but it makes perfect sense to give away its Internet browser. If you can establish your program as the Internet leader, profit will follow, since you will then be in a position to sell related products and services.

20 Million Frenchmen Can Be Wrong

Sometimes there are good reasons to shun market leaders. For example, at one time, the Microsoft Antivirus Program was the world's most widely distributed, being bundled with MS DOS and early versions of Windows. Yet it was lousy. As Michael Alexander explained in *The Underground Guide to Computer Security* (Addison Wesley, 1996): "In every test of MSAV, it has ranked at the bottom for accuracy and speed in detecting viruses. Folks, this is a rabid dog of a program you should steer clear of."

One of the most reliable ways to stay away from poor performers is by following recommendations from trusted sources like G. Burgess Allison's "Technology Update" column in the ABA's *Law Practice Management* magazine. In October 1997, for example, when America Online had 10 million users and was the top recommendation of mass market computer magazines, Mr. Allison was explaining in convincing detail that while AOL might be acceptable for grandparents in Dubuque and teenagers in Santa Monica, it was a bad choice for most serious business users. (The article is available at http://www.abanet.org/lpm/magazine/tu977.html.)

He pointed out that while "easy to use" had been AOL's major selling point,

> When you can't get connected when you need to, when your e-mail is getting lost and delayed, when your e-mail inbasket fills up with junk mail, and when the Internet gateway is so slow that key Internet services are almost unusable, then it's not easy to use any more.

> (It's just easy to install.)

> I believe that current business users of AOL should be actively considering other alternatives, and that they should take a long hard look at what AOL is actually delivering.

> And for new users, I now believe that AOL is a mistake.

Before making a key decision, look for knowledgeable, objective expert advice. You can learn about the products to avoid by talking to technically savvy lawyers and checking out the magazines and Internet discussion groups listed in Chapter 9. Over time, you will learn who you can trust and who you can't.

Specific Product Recommendations

Benjamin Franklin told us that "Dead fish and visitors stink in three days." Internet product recommendations have a somewhat longer life span, but I wouldn't be inclined to put much faith in ones that were more than three months old. By the time this book makes its way into your hands, Netscape Navigator may have been supplanted as the top browser program, PGP may no longer be the best encryption choice for a high level of security, and it is even possible that AOL may have upgraded its service significantly.

Books are not the best place for specific Internet product recommendations. A current list of my favorite products in various categories is available at: http://www.netlawtools.com/picks.

Looking for Force Multipliers

The Holy Grail of modern military planners is the *force multiplier,* a weapon or tactic that can enable a small force to defeat a larger one. One of the most exciting things about the Internet is its force multiplier potential. It can help solos and small firms compete more evenly against those with more people and money but less savvy. For example, the Brief Reporter database, at http://www.briefreporter.com (shown in Figure 19-1), gives small firms access to a brief bank that rivals those of the country's largest firms. Subscribers can download a full brief for ten dollars.

This force multiplier effect applies to many aspects of Internet use, such as the following:

- ◆ Extranets and private, specialized mailing lists can help solos and small law firms pool their resources and expertise.
- ◆ A five-lawyer firm can afford a Web site that looks just as nice and attracts just as much attention as one for a five-hundred person firm.

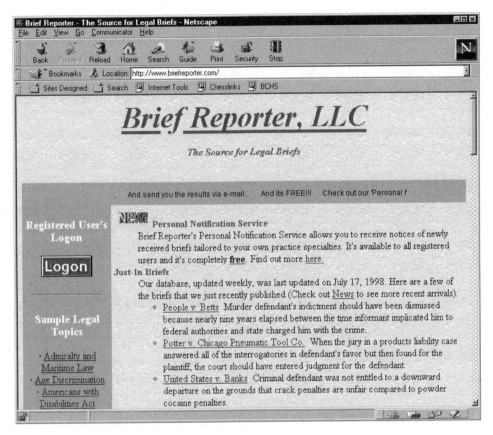

FIGURE 19-1. Brief Reporter, LLC

◆ The Internet reduces the need to have a large on-site technical support staff that only a large firm can afford. It does so through technical support from vendor Web sites, software that can diagnose problems on a remote computer without the technician's physical presence, software that downloads upgrades and bug fixes and installs them automatically, and personalized advice from on-line discussion groups.

◆ Internet e-mail neutralizes a major communications advantage that private e-mail links have given larger firms in recent years.

Many large law firms have established private e-mail connections with favored clients. Until rather recently, only large firms could afford the expense, but they calculated it was worth it because the clients would appreciate the convenience and cost savings. Now, encrypted Internet e-mail gives even the smallest firm similar functionality, at very little cost.

Nowhere is the force multiplier effect more evident than when it comes to Internet research, particularly factual research. Small law firms cannot afford to hire armies of investigators. Here again, the Internet can help level the playing field for those who understand how to use it.

The Virtual Law Firm (VLF) Network (shown in Figure 19-2), begun by Parry Aftab and Nancy Savitt, is a consortium of mostly small firm business lawyers. Located at http://www.vlfnetwork.com, it shows how the Internet can be used to combine forces for networking, better client service, and marketing.

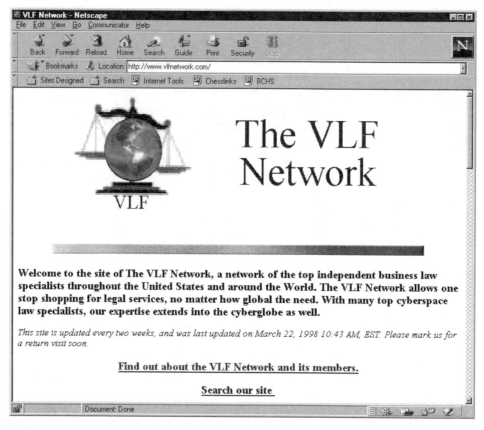

FIGURE 19-2. The VLF Network

Intranets and extranets hold particular promise as force multipliers. For example, Legal Anywhere (http://www.legalanywhere.com) offers a "turnkey" intranet/extranet. This model is designed to enable smaller firms to enjoy the benefits of Internet collaboration without incurring the high costs of designing, developing, and maintaining such a system. John Battin, director of client development for Tousley Brain, PLLC, of Seattle, comments on his firm's experience: "As a firm of twenty lawyers, we do not have the resources to implement and support a custom intranet/extranet system in-house. We consider our intranet/extranet to be not only a productivity tool, but also a marketing tool because it tells our clients that we are conscious of the costs of doing business, and that we intend to improve the quality of our services through the use of technology."

Understanding the Net and Quality of Life for Lawyers

When I studied computer programming as an undergraduate, nearly thirty years ago, computer time was treated as if it were more valuable than human time. Because the college's IBM 1130 was used for administrative purposes during normal working hours, students could use it only at nights or on weekends. It wasn't unusual to find students staying up so they could run their programs at 3:00 a.m. We were so pleased to have any access to the computer's power that we didn't consider arranging our schedules around the computer's availability to be a sacrifice. In some ways, we behaved as if the computer were the master and we were its slaves.

Today's average desktop computer is enormously more powerful than the computers we used then, and computers seem to be ubiquitous in the business world, including law offices. Computing power is inexpensive and abundant. Despite this, too many lawyers still behave as if they subliminally believe that their computer is the master and they are the servants. Changing this attitude may be the biggest step you can make toward increasing your productivity on the Internet, and with computers in general.

If your computer is making your life harder instead of easier, something is wrong. Look for every opportunity to shift as many of your work burdens as possible onto your computer. Even a few seconds saved on each task can add up to very large productivity increases over the course of a day, and even more over the course of a year.

A great place to start is reducing the time you have to spend on e-mail. Get a good e-mail program and master its time-saving features. Let your computer take over as much of your work as possible. For example, don't manually type in your signature block. Set one up and let the computer do it for you. Don't waste time sorting and filing incoming e-mail messages. Set up a directory system (including a separate directory for each mailing list you use, for each person you correspond with frequently, and for each of your major projects) and a set of filters that automatically files incoming messages in the proper location. If you do this well, don't be surprised if out of two hundred messages, all but fifteen or so are usually filed for you automatically. Some lawyers use their e-mail programs as their primary personal filing system. When they learn something they need to remember, or a Web page with particularly useful information, they send themselves a copy by e-mail and store it in their e-mail program's filing system.

Instead of searching for information, let it come to you. Find and subscribe to high-quality push channels that broadcast information relevant to your legal practice, like constantly updated news on your client's takeover candidate. Pointcast lets you monitor news on up to 25 companies or up to 10 industries of your choice at a time: http://www.pointcast.com.

Learn and use your browser's time-saving features. Keep a well-organized bookmark file so that your computer keeps track of the URLs instead of your having to do so, or worse, having to use a search engine every time you want to revisit a site. Create desktop shortcuts and browser toolbar shortcuts for going to your favorite sites quickly. If you have one particular site that you visit more often than any other, make it the home page in your browser, so you never have to type the URL.

Instead of wasting time while waiting for a slow page to download, open additional browser windows and do something productive instead of twiddling your thumbs.

You may increase your Internet productivity substantially by purchasing a larger monitor. Larger screens are more than a luxury. They're a practical benefit because they let you display much more information on your screen at one time and reduce the time wasted through scrolling or opening and closing windows to conserve screen space. Technology guru Burgess Allison is right on the money when he recommends 17-inch monitors as the minimum size for serious business use.

As the product category matures, look for *intelligent agent* software to reduce your workload. Agents are computer programs that operate like very sophisticated macros that a user can easily program to perform tasks on his or her behalf. They are like a personal secretary or assistant who can learn your preferences and come to anticipate your needs. We are already seeing the first generation of such products. WebCompass, by Quarterdeck, is one example. It is designed to relieve an Internet researcher of much of the drudgery involved in tracking down information. It will take a search request to multiple Internet search engines, collate the results, and help structure them to make it more likely that the ones you're interested in will be near the top of the results list. Future agents will perform more difficult tasks and work even more efficiently. See IBM's Intelligent Agents site: http://www. networking. ibm.com/iag/iaghome.html for a glimpse of the future.

Even today's relatively primitive agents can make our lives easier. Do you hate setting up meetings? Agents can handle this chore. You tell the agent who should attend and your preferences as to when and where, and it will swing into action. Several new personal information management programs can do this over a LAN or over the Internet.

Excite's Newswatcher will monitor the news and deliver updates on topics you specify by e-mail. As you tell the software which sites you like, it refines your search request to zero in on the precise things in which you are interested. It's located at http://nt.excite.com.

In the future, you'll be able to give a software agent purchase parameters for something you want to buy, and it will be able to seek out the product on the Internet, negotiate the terms, and, if authorized by you, bind you to a sales contract. Lawyers have already begun speculating about how such creations will fit into the existing body of agency law.

These examples merely scratch the surface. The key is to always remember that you are the master and the computer is your servant, not the other way around.

Panning for Internet Gold

The struggle to get useful legal information from the Internet is like panning for gold nuggets in California in 1849. It's hard for pioneers to find reliable maps, and there aren't many other amenities out there on the frontier. The most striking similarity is the difficulty in locating your objective amid the mountains of worthless mud.

Gold prospectors who were having trouble finding nuggets could try to improve their results in three ways:

1. Change location (move upstream or downstream)
2. Change tools (get a better pan or bigger shovel)
3. Change technique (try moving the pan differently)

A lawyer trying to get more benefit from the Internet can try changing the same three variables.

Location

You could change your Internet "location" by accessing the Internet through a different route.

For example, if you have an account with a commercial on-line service like AOL, MSN, or CompuServe, you may be frustrated by the slowness or the lowest-common-denominator approach they frequently adopt in search of a mass market. You may be ready to move from the online services (which often offer only Internet gateways) to a real Internet service provider.

You may already have an account with an ISP that doesn't have enough modems (thus causing busy signals when you call) or enough bandwidth (thus causing information to be transferred too slowly). If so, it's time to look for a better ISP.

Maybe your bottleneck is the capacity of the phone line connecting you to your service provider. You might be better off with a high-volume ISDN line, a cable modem, or a direct satellite Internet link instead of a regular analog dial-up connection. If your law firm is large, maybe you need the speed and reliability of a T1 line.

Simply moving away from a dial-up modem connection to any of the other types just mentioned may benefit you more than you might expect. The faster downloading speed once you are connected is a plus, but the biggest benefit may derive from the fact that initially establishing a connection is so much faster.

Once your computer is booted up, it typically takes a minute or so to dial up an ISP and access the Internet with a conventional modem, but with more sophisticated techniques, it may only take a few seconds. If you haven't experienced a full-time Internet connection, this may not seem like a big deal, but in practice the difference is significant.

For example, before I got an ISDN line in my home, if I needed to review an article I had read in that morning's newspaper or that week's *Virginia Lawyers Weekly,* I would normally try to find the physical copy. I did not want to wait the minute that it would take me to dial up my ISP and log on. With ISDN, the connection is open and idling in the background at all times my computer is on, so no "dial up" delay is necessary. It is now much easier for me to access the *Washington Post* or *Virginia Lawyer's Weekly* Web sites than it is to walk into the next room and find the paper copy. The online version is faster to find, and the Web sites' search engines and other features make them easier to use and more complete (including the Web archives) than the paper version. It can be faster to look up words in an online dictionary you have bookmarked in your browser than to pull your paper copy off the shelf.

Having nearly instant access to the Internet can produce changes in your work habits that make you surprisingly more productive.

Tools

If your Internet connection is not the problem, maybe your tools are holding you back. Try different hardware or software.

For example, a 386 PC with 4MB of RAM can access the Internet, but it won't work very well with modern GUI software. More RAM and a faster processor will make a difference.

Would a 56K modem be better for you than a 28.8K model?

If your modem is behaving erratically, maybe you need to upgrade to a high-speed serial port (16550 UART or compatible).

Does your software have a good balance of ease of use and power? For most lawyers, the most important pieces of Internet software are the Web browser and e-mail package. If you're still using Mosaic 1.0 for your Web browser, you are living in the Internet version of the Dark Ages. Modern Web browsers have redefined this software category.

Some lawyers try to save a few dollars by using Eudora Lite, a free e-mail program. There is a full-strength commercial version called Eudora Pro. As a lawyer, your time is valuable. If Eudora Pro's powerful extra features save you five minutes a day (a conservative estimate), its cost of fifty dollars or so will be an excellent investment. A good alternative is Pegasus Mail, which is a free program that's about as powerful as Eudora Pro but a little harder to use.

Are you having a hard time finding files on your local hard drive? Download a program like AltaVista Discovery which will index your hard drive and let you use sophisticated search engine type tools on it. Available free at http://www.altavista.com.

Tired of typing e-mail addresses into your address book? Look for an e-mail program like the newer versions of Eudora Pro or Outlook that will automatically add an address from incoming mail. Better yet, get a program like Lotus Organizer 5.0. You highlight a complete address, and press an icon. The "EasyClip" feature creates a new entry in your Contact directory.

Techniques

If your location and tools are all right, perhaps you need to try some different techniques.

If, for example, you are overwhelmed by a high volume of e-mail, learn how to use the automated filtering features on your e-mail software.

If high-volume legal mailing lists are a problem, switching to the digest version could be the answer.

If you are having trouble finding things on the World Wide Web, start your searches in a different place. Yahoo's directory approach is excellent, but it's not the best way to approach every research problem. The search engine with the largest database may not be the best if its search software is poor or too difficult to figure out.

Maybe you should learn more about how your favorite search engine implements Boolean searching, field restrictions, and other powerful techniques to help narrow your search requests. Print and review the on-line help files supplied by your favorite search engine.

Lastly, you might pick up some new techniques by attending CLE courses on the Internet or checking the other resources referenced throughout this book.

The two most important pieces of advice for Internet prospectors are these:

1. **Ask for advice when you run into a problem.** Your colleagues on the Net will be a lot more forthcoming about sharing leads than were California gold miners who considered prime locations state secrets. Don't be afraid to ask questions, on mailing lists for lawyers (like NET-LAWYERS or ABA LAWTECH) or elsewhere.
2. **Be willing to experiment with different locations, tools, and techniques until you get the results you want.** Finding the binary gold you are looking for on the Internet may not be easy, but with some perseverance and a willingness to be flexible, most lawyers can make the Internet pay off in a big way.

Avoiding the Mental Trap

The Internet . . . THE Internet . . . THE Internet

Many lawyers learning to use the Internet get caught by a subtle psychological pitfall. It's caused partly by the human tendency to generalize and partly by the necessary use of the phrase "the Internet."

We're stuck with this terminology because there *is* only one global computer network like "the" Internet. However, while using the word "the" is accurate (and, in English, pretty much unavoidable), it is also subtly, almost subliminally misleading. It helps create an expectation that once you are connected to "the" Internet, your experience will be like that of anyone else who is connected to "the" Internet.

This expectation is very wrong. It can seriously hinder you as you try to make the maximum constructive use of the Internet in your legal practice.

Bill Gates has noted that the phrase "information highway" is similarly misleading: "The term *highway* also suggests that everyone is driving and following the same route."

The Internet is almost unimaginably large and complex. There are many different ways to connect to it, types of software you can use, and ways to proceed once you have a connection. Experiences and productivity levels vary wildly.

It's like the parable of the blind men who were asked to describe an elephant. Each was given a brief opportunity to touch a different part of the elephant. The one who touched the elephant's leg thought it was like a tree. The one who touched the elephant's tusk thought it was like a curved, smooth spear. The one who touched its trunk thought it was like a snake.

Your impressions of the Internet and its usefulness will vary widely depending on how you are connected, the software you use, and the areas of the Internet you access.

A high percentage of the lawyers with some Internet experience never understand this.

- Perhaps they started out accessing the Internet through a commercial on-line service, and the underpowered software and slow connection convinced them "the" Internet was inappropriate for serious legal work.
- Perhaps they had a UNIX shell account when they were university students and never really learned how to use it.
- Perhaps they had access to a powerful, easy-to-use Internet account but had no one to teach them how to use it, and they eventually gave up on it.

Today, all these lawyers will most likely tell you that "the" Internet has little value for law firms. Their initial experiences disappointed them, and they were misled by the subtle implications of the phrase "the Internet." They think that if "the" Internet did not help them, it must not help any lawyer.

Many other lawyers fall into a more advanced version of the same trap. They have some success with the Internet, and they then assume this must be what "the" Internet is like. Content with the benefits they have found, they stop trying to learn new ways to gain further benefits from it.

You can avoid this trap by being unwilling to settle for small benefits from Internet use. The potential benefits are extraordinary, so don't settle for a small piece of the pie.

The Japanese have a word, "kaizen," which translates into "continual striving for improvement." The Internet's extraordinary range of large and small potential benefits make it a fertile field for those who understand kaizen. The most successful law firms will be those that never stop experimenting with new ways to benefit from the Internet.

CHAPTER **TWENTY**

The Future of
the Internet

"There's no one who can hold this thing back."

—Bill Gates speaking to Tom Brokaw
about the Internet

I BELIEVE LAWYERS TODAY are like blacksmiths a hundred years ago. Technology is getting ready to turn our profession inside out, but we've only begun to see how it will happen.

How many blacksmiths looked at horseless carriages and imagined the impact that things like the Interstate Highway System, M-1 tanks, motorized farm equipment, Honda Civics, eighteen-wheelers, Harley Davidsons, and sports cars would have on their profession? While some blacksmiths had trouble adapting to the internal combustion engine, others prospered, some far more than they might have dreamed possible.

I believe the Internet's most significant effects will be economic. Some of the trends will parallel changes we're already seeing in the "off the Net" global economy, including displacements and increasing gaps between those at the top and the rest of the heap. The saying goes "A rising tide lifts all boats," but I believe this particular tide will capsize a few and lift some much higher than others.

I stress that I am not necessarily advocating or predicting all of the consequences suggested in the following sections, some of which may cause considerable disruption to many people working in legal jobs. However, I suggest that economic pressures like those already being experienced in other lines of work may make some of these changes inevitable and that it is best to understand what may be coming and to prepare for it. For some this may mean preparing for a rainy day, while for others it will mean taking advantage of new opportunities.

The Strange World of Network Economics

The previous chapter considers Metcalfe's Law. The benefit of being a member of a network increases as the square of the number of members. This is illustrated in the flowchart in Figure 20-1. The horizontal axis shows the number of users. The vertical axis reflects the value of being on the network. The more people on a network, the more benefit there is in being a member of that network.

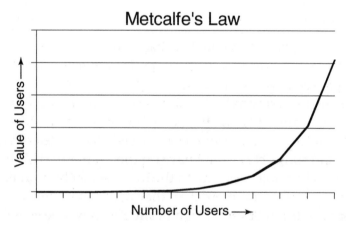

FIGURE 20-1. Metcalfe's Law

Metcalfe's Law, as discussed in Chapter 19, affects software selection, but its effects go well beyond that. The number of Internet users will continue to grow for the foreseeable future. This will have some consequences that may not be apparent at first glance. Conventional economic theory leads us to assume that scarcity leads to high value. This is not necessarily true where networks are involved. The more common products tend to be not only more valuable but less expensive as well. Consider how this applies to fax machines:

Number of Fax Machines	Cost of Each Fax Machine (Price Owner Pays)	Value of Each Fax Machine (Benefit to Owner, Not Cost)
One	Very expensive	None
A few	Less expensive	Some
Ubiquitous	Very inexpensive	Large benefits

The same phenomenon applies to the Internet. As the number of Internet users increases, the value of being on the Internet increases, and the cost tends to drop. (See Kevin Kelly, "New Rules for the New Economy," printed in *Wired,* September 1997, and archived at http://www.wired.com/wired/5.09/newrules.html. Viking Press published Kelly's book with the same name in 1998.) When few lawyers were on the Net, it didn't matter that much whether or not you were connected. In a world where most of your clients, colleagues, and competitors are on the Net, you will need to be as well.

It's no coincidence that the e-mail signature block of legal technology guru Burgess Allison contains a wry takeoff on a familiar Shakespearean passage, attributed to "Skippy Shakespeare, Will's smarter brother": "The first thing we do, let's connect all the lawyers."

Income Stratification

Several factors mean that the Internet may create some downward pressure on legal fees:

- The Internet makes it easier for non-lawyers to access the legal resources that lawyers use to ply their trade. Despite unauthorized practice of law rules, this may increase the level of competition lawyers face.
- The Internet will reduce the significance of geography, intensifying competition among lawyers living in different states, and in a few situations, even in different countries.
- In more efficient markets, where buyers and sellers are well informed, prices tend to be lower. Historically, the legal services market has not been very efficient. Internet features such as Web sites, e-mail, and searchable lawyer databases like those operated by Westlaw and Martindale-Hubbell will make it easier for consumers of legal services to inform themselves, thus encouraging lower prices.

As John Hegel and Arthur Armstrong observe in their book *net.gain,*

Virtual communities [made possible by the Internet] are likely to turn these traditional marketplace dynamics [in which sellers usually deal from a position of superior knowledge] upside down by creating "reverse markets"—markets in which the customer, armed with a growing amount of information, uses that information to search out vendors offering the best combination of quality and price tailored to his or her individual needs.

Even if there is no reduction in the total amount of legal fees, it is likely that the Internet will tend to increase income stratification in the legal profession. Economists Robert H. Frank and Philip Cook have pointed out that "developments in communications, manufacturing, and transportation costs have enabled the most talented performers to serve an even broader market, which increased the value of their services." (Robert Frank, Talent and the Winner-Take-All Society, "*The American Prospect* (Spring 1994), pp. 97–107. Note: Frank's *ideas* were incorporated into a book with Philip Cook, The Winner-Take-All Society (The Free Press 1995).)

At the same time, the Internet makes it easier for elite lawyers to become known and for prospective clients to gravitate toward them, in many cases despite geographic boundaries. As E. J. Dionne observes,

> The best entertainment lawyer in Los Angeles can—thanks to airlines, telephones, computers, and fax machines—quickly become the best entertainment lawyer in Bombay, New York, Paris, London, and Moscow, displacing many other lawyers in the process. In different areas of expertise, companies all over the world compete for the services of the best in their professions, no matter what country they call home. (E.J. Dionne, *They Only Look Dead* (Simon & Schuster 1996).)

These effects may further push the legal profession toward a profile of a relatively few highly paid stars versus everyone else, which Frank and Cook call the "winner-take-all-society." The Net is another technical tool that, like cellular phones and jet planes, helps those who master it leverage their time and accomplish more.

Economist Paul Krugman notes, "Television does not take the place of hundreds of struggling standup nightclub comedians. It allows Jay Leno to take their place instead." The Internet may do for a few talented lawyers who master it the same thing television does for Jay Leno. Indeed, I have already seen the first signs that this phenomenon has begun.

Disintermediation: A Threat and an Opportunity

Disintermediation is a fancy word that means "cutting out the middleman." It is one of the most significant ways in which the Internet will disrupt the lives of many people—and create great opportunities for others. Those who deal primarily in information are particularly vulnerable to disintermediation. Here are a few examples:

- Legal secretaries are somewhat vulnerable. Most people who send e-mail do it themselves, without relying on a secretary, as they would if they were sending a paper letter. To the extent that a law firm can move toward greater reliance on e-mail, it may be able to do without as many secretaries.
- To some extent, traditional journalists are also being disintermediated by the Internet. As Scott Rosenberg, editor of *Salon,* an on-line journal, observed in the *Washington Post,* "as the new medium matures, many Internet news junkies are quickly learning to shoulder some of the old journalist's job of evaluating sources."
- By distributing on-line versions via the World Wide Web, newspapers like the *New York Times* (http://www.nytimes.com) and the *Washington Post* (http://www.washingtonpost.com) are positioning themselves to disintermediate, when the Internet becomes ubiquitous, their many employees involved in physically printing and distributing paper copies of their publications. Whereas today paper copies are sold relatively cheaply, to help the papers maintain high circulations that justify high advertising rates, in the future consumers may pay a premium for the luxury of holding an ink-stained piece of newsprint in their hands.

Legal-related businesses are not immune from the trend toward disintermediation. As leading business consultants Larry Downes and Chunka Mei have noted, the Internet makes commercial services like LEXIS and Westlaw prime candidates:

> Much of these companies' actual data, moreover, are public data (laws, court opinions, and other government publications). These competitors have been so focused on matching feature and function with each other, implicitly agreeing not to compete on price, that they appear to have completely missed the killer app coming right at them: the Internet's superior user interface and exploding public databases. . . . It won't be long before someone takes these fledgling experiments [by Cornell University, the House of Representatives, the Securities Exchange Commission, and others], puts them together, and wipes out the information empires of both LEXIS/NEXIS and West.

Of course, lawyers are also vulnerable to disintermediation. Many legal professionals now make a good living by basically taking publicly available information (e.g., environmental regulations or tax law changes), repackaging it, and selling it to clients. With the Internet making it easier and cheaper to access such information, some clients may be tempted to cut out the middleman by having much of this work performed by someone willing to work for lower pay, like junior accountants or young employees with MBA degrees.

Organizations like the innovative People's Law Library of Maryland (http://www.peoples-law.com) also stimulate disintermediation of lawyers by making it easier for citizens to represent themselves pro se. Figure 20-2 shows the introductory page of the organization's electronic library.

FIGURE 20-2. People's Law Library of Maryland

The Fading Allure of the Personal Touch

Some lawyers insist that disintermediation is not a serious threat for the legal profession: "There is no substitute for the skill and personal touch of an experienced lawyer." However, underestimating the threat disintermediation poses to many legal professionals may be no wiser than emulating blacksmiths who scoffed at the new horseless carriages.

The "personal touch" of lawyers may not be enough to protect many of them from new sources of competition, just as other "personal touches" have not prevented travel agents from suffering through competition from "book it yourself" services like Travelocity (http://www.travelocity.com) or prevented brokers from suffering through competition from services like E*trade (http://www.etrade.com).

In their book *Unleashing the Killer App,* Downes and Mui compare the average overhead of transactions in retail banking. If handled by human tellers, it's $1.07. If handled by an ATM, it's $0.27. If handled via the Internet, it's $0.10. Numbers like these, combined with high rates of satisfaction among consumers banking on-line, led the CEO of Nationsbank to predict that within fifteen years, 95 percent of all U.S. homes will be banking through the Internet or on-line services. That translates into a lot of former bank employees looking for a different line of work.

Tellingly, these new on-line services are not being forced on consumers. Many consumers *prefer* on-line alternatives to human service for most transactions.

Unlike human professional services, assistance via the Internet is available at the customers' convenience, in the comfort of their homes, twenty-four hours a day, seven days a week. The Internet makes it unnecessary for the prospective client to take off a day from work, make an appointment with a busy professional, then fight downtown traffic and struggle to find a parking space.

Many consumers are not just willing but eager to deal with a discount service like Auto-by-Tel (http://www.autobytel.com) or a Web site selling discount insurance instead of having the "personal touch" of an auto or insurance salesperson.

In addition to often being more convenient for the consumer and cheaper than their off-line counterparts (and more profitable to those who sell them, due to lower overhead), services delivered via the Internet are frequently of higher quality.

A human travel agent may be baffled by the airlines' constantly changing prices, but computers with access to the right databases can seek out the lowest price reliably, every time. Web sites less frequently do the equivalent of putting you on hold, and a well-designed interactive Internet service will never have a cold or a headache, or treat visitors in a surly manner.

Despite these examples, some lawyers remain skeptical: "All this computer stuff might be a threat for travel agents and salespeople, but it will never replace the judgment and empathy of members of the learned professions, like doctors and lawyers."

In fact, some doctors are already complaining about being disintermediated. As Texas physician Tom Ferguson told the *Washington Post,*

> We're in the early stages of a great power shift from doctors to savvy patients. Doctors aren't the gatekeepers in health care anymore. When I was in medical school, I was trained never to let the patient know you don't have a 100 percent answer to a question. We reduced medicine to oversimplified formulas. Now, consumers have access to the same information. They can go online and find the best doctors and the best treatments.

When doctors, who pride themselves on their bedside manner, complain about the effects of the Internet on their profession, it is time for lawyers to realize that the threat of online competition may be more threatening to purveyors of "the personal touch" than it might appear at first glance.

Disintermediation: Fighting Back

The best way for middlemen (including lawyers) to avoid disintermediation is to concentrate on providing unique high-quality services that cannot be easily replaced by computer-delivered services or human competitors using the Internet.

After outlining the previously quoted threat to LEXIS and West, Downes and Mei go on to prescribe a defense:

> There is a winning digital strategy for these information providers. Although they charge based on access, the real value they provide is enhancing the raw information they collect with commentary, indexing, and organized notes services. Instead of access, the companies could sell their expertise on a subscription or a transaction basis (for example, answering specific tax questions). Doing so would ultimately bring them into competition with their current customers, lawyers, and accountants, but without the considerable markup the professionals add in answering legal and regulatory questions for their clients. (Downes and Mui, *Unleashing the Killer App*, Harvard Business School Press, 1998.)

Lawyers too will need to adapt to the digital era by looking for ways of adding value and making themselves irreplaceable middlemen.

For some lawyers, this will be a means of survival. For those with more vision, it will be a route to new opportunities. Greg Siskind, for example, parlayed the success of his firm's immigration law-focused Web site, http://www.visalaw.com, into two spinoff ventures, http://www.visajobs.com and http://www.visahomes.com. These provide job placement and home-finding assistance for would-be immigrants with marketable skills and their prospective employers. The one stop-shopping approach is a way of taking advantage of the "visalaw" brand name and adding potentially lucrative new product lines.

Personalization

Personalizing services is another way that law firms can add value and make themselves less vulnerable to disintermediation. New technology enables providers of goods and services, especially those who deal in information, to customize their products to a degree that was impossible a few years ago. Here are examples:

- The *Wall Street Journal* site (http://www.wsj.com) allows subscribers to set up a "personal journal" to customize their own mix of *Journal* features, columns, topics, and companies.
- PointCast (http://www.pointcast.com) is a free screen saver that can be personalized in the same way. It will automatically provide an up-to-the-minute mix of information, organized according to the user's specification, provided by, among others, Reuters, Standard & Poors, the *Los Angeles Times,* and the *Boston Globe.*
- To make themselves "sticky" (i.e., hard for users to abandon), on-line "portals" like My Yahoo, My Excite and My Netscape allow a high degree of personalization.

This trend led Downes and Mui to claim the following (emphasis in original):

> *Market targeting is to the friction-free economy what the assembly line was to Henry Ford.* Like mass production in earlier times, targeting makes it possible to deliver products that satisfy [client desires]. It is yet another mechanism that delivers better products at lower prices. But unlike earlier times, "better" today means "customized." (Downes and Mui, *Unleashing the Killer App,* Harvard Business School Press, 1998.)

Law firms are beginning to get into the personalization game. The cutting-edge Morrison & Foerster Web site at http://www.mofo.com, shown in Figure 20-3, allows visitors to indicate their preferences on the first visit. Whenever the visitor returns, the Web site recognizes them and automatically customizes itself to their tastes.

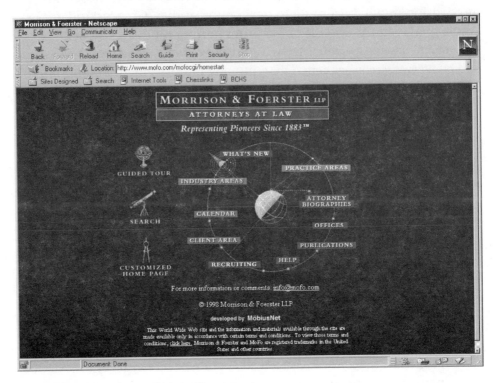

FIGURE 20-3. Morrison & Foerster Site

The Morrison & Foerster site illustrates customization as a marketing tool. It can also be used as a means of providing new forms of billable client service. For example, a major attraction of the interactive domestic relations database discussed in the next section would be its ability to customize its responses to the questioner's situation.

Using the Internet, a firm could provide frequently updated, customized legal information to key clients, such as general counsels of major corporations, personalized to address their particular interests.

Lessons for Lawyers from "Ask Ernie"

A sophisticated, aggressive law firm that wanted to attempt to use the Internet to dominate the market for a particular type of service in a particular area might imitate the management consulting firm Ernst & Young. A similar approach might be used to attract business clients (like the Ernst & Young target market), but for purposes of the discussion here, assume that this hypothetical law firm wants to establish itself as the clear leader in domestic relations cases in a certain state, and then, through a network of affiliates or branch offices, to expand gradually into market leadership in other states across the country.

The Ernst & Young "Ask Ernie" Web site, http://ernie.ey.com, is a Web-based question-and-answer service that costs $6,000 for a one-year subscription. Ernst & Young's superior knowledge base and industry experience enable it to make money though selling "Ask Ernie" subscriptions even at such relatively low (by Ernst & Young standards) prices.

More important, the subscriptions generate business for much more expensive on-site teams of Ernst & Young consultants. The "Ask Ernie" subscriptions are feeders for new, often poorly capitalized businesses that develop respect for the Ernst & Young brand name and will eventually need, and be able to pay premium prices for, more sophisticated consulting services.

A law firm that wanted to imitate Ernst and Young might begin by compiling a comprehensive legal analysis of the most commonly occurring issues in domestic relations cases and then setting up elaborate decision trees. These decision trees could end in specific conclusions in many cases. For example, in some situations they might recommend that the party contact the police to seek enforcement of a no-contact order, while in others they might recommend that the party contact a lawyer for personalized advice. Compiling such a legal analysis for a particular area of law like domestic relations would not appear to be significantly more difficult for experts in that area than compiling the summaries of all a state's significant laws, which many large firms compile for inclusion in Martindale Hubbell digests. See the Independent Contractor vs. Employee Interactive Flowchart at The Tax Prophet Web site for a simple example: http://www.taxprophet.com/apps/active2/.

After this legal analysis has been accomplished, the law firm would contract with computer programmers to turn the analysis into an interactive program that could be accessed via the Internet. This would not seem to be significantly more difficult than designing one of the interactive tax preparation programs now on the market.

The resulting computer program would interface with a detailed questionnaire completed online by visitors to the Web site. Downes and Mui refer to this method of data entry as "outsourcing to the customer" and note, "The data you collect has far fewer errors because it has been handled only once, and then by the originating source. Cost savings on your end can come quickly and they are significant."

After a visitor completes the questionnaire, the interactive computer database would use the information to provide answers to specific questions about the visitor's legal situation. The answers given by the database could be monitored by the firm's lawyers, just as human beings control the information distributed through the "Ask Ernie" Web site. If the interactive database were well designed, however, there might be little need for such monitoring. The information gathered by the questionnaires could be used to prepare any pleadings the client might need, interfacing with document assembly programs.

The Interactive Web Site Approach: Prognosis for Law Firms

Establishing an interactive Web site like "Ask Ernie" would open up new economic opportunities for law firms. A firm might be able to make a healthy income by charging small fees for access to the interactive database, or even for the answers to specific questions. The development of "digital cash" based on encryption technology will make "micropayments" practical. This will make it possible to make money on the Internet by selling a large volume of products or services (like the answer to a particular question) at very low prices (one dollar, fifty cents, or even less).

"Do Your Own Divorce" books and software have been around for a long time, but the Internet versions have much more potential for a number of reasons. Disintermediation of conventional book and software publishers would allow the law firm to retain a much higher percentage of the retail price. The "author" of such a program would not be limited to the 10 to 15 percent royalty payment typical for book authors or software developers. Further, intelligent use of the Internet can greatly expand the potential market, particularly as Internet access becomes ubiquitous, as well as reduce advertising expense, distribution costs, and other overhead.

However, the optimal marketing strategy for the Internet version of such an interactive database may not be the high-volume, low-cost model. The best strategy might be to make access to all or most of the information in the firm's interactive domestic relations database available at no charge.

The most lucrative segment of the market might be the well-heeled, sophisticated clients who are able and willing to pay a premium for the best divorce lawyers. The Web site would serve as a feeder for the law firm operating it, just as the "Ask Ernie" Web site serves as a feeder for Ernst & Young's more expensive consulting services.

It is important to realize that in some ways a well-designed interactive database could provide a level of service superior in some respects to that received by many clients in divorce cases. There is a limit to how much time most divorce lawyers can or are willing to put into answering the same basic questions repeatedly, especially in cases where little money is involved.

While some clients would probably still prefer "the personal touch," the experiences of travel agents, bank tellers, and automobile and insurance salespeople suggests that for at least a few segments of the legal market, well-designed on-line services will be enthusiastically received replacements for some types of legal services.

Would such a venture run into ethical problems? Certainly conflicts of interest would be a danger, but it would not appear to be insurmountable. If the interactive database were well designed, it would not appear to be "practicing law" any more than one of the "Do Your Own Divorce" books or computer programs on the market. Further, the promise of drastic reductions in the price of high-quality, reliable legal advice may make legislative or regulatory restrictions on the development of such services politically impractical.

Again, I do not necessarily advocate or encourage law firms to move into such activities. While they might make a few firms much better off than they now are, such activities could have the effect of disrupting the lives of many lawyers who presently make a living on divorce cases. Yet just as the development of the assembly line inevitably reduced the market for hand-made automobiles, the Internet may make automation of some types of legal practice inevitable.

Large corporations and government agencies with geographically dispersed offices are logical markets for similar systems. For example, the Department of Defense employs thousands of lawyers and other specialists whose major duty is interpreting and applying the voluminous, and often arcane, rules that apply to government contracting. These employees are spread from Seoul to Fort Benning to Bosnia. An expert system interactive database available over the Internet that enabled the Department of Defense to reduce the number of employees devoted to such endeavors by even 20 percent would result in major cost savings. Similar expert systems could be used in many other legal practice areas.

Virtual Organizations

Ronald H. Coase won the Nobel Prize for economics in large part because of his theory that large business organizations became necessary owing to transaction costs involved in creating, selling, and distributing goods and services. According to Coase, market inefficiencies made complex, geographically dispersed organizations practical and necessary in the business world.

To take a simple example, it is impractical for each individual employee in an organization to buy his or her own pencils, paper, paper clips, and personal computer, or to deal with governmental agencies as if each employee were a separate entity. Similarly, while a publishing company needs authors and editors, it also needs a large capital investment in physical plants and an expensive, complex infrastructure of type-setters, printers, and salespeople.

A number of scholars and businesspersons have noticed that the Internet can reduce transaction cost inefficiencies and their accompanying overhead. This may enable organizations to reduce their layers of bureaucracy.

The Internet reduces the "friction" of transaction costs. For example, it makes it easier to buy items as simple as paper clips and as complex as computers. It makes it possible for authors to sell their works without the large infrastructure and high overhead of conventional publishers.

Downes and Mui argue convincingly that:

> A truly frictionless economy needs no permanent firms. [While new technology, including the Internet will never make our economy completely "frictionless," the] nature of the firm will change, however, and indeed, it is already changing. The concept of a firm as a physical entity, defined by its permanent employees and fixed assets, is giving way to what some call a "virtual organization," where employees may be part time or contract workers, where assets may be jointly owned by many organizations, and where the separation between what is inside and what is outside the firm becomes increasingly hazy. (Downes and Mui, *Unleashing the Killer App*, p. 42, Harvard Business School Press, 1998.)

Trends in these directions are already visible in many business sectors, and there is no reason to believe that law firms will be immune.

New ways of approaching the practice of law are emerging. I know two law firms that merged even though no partner of either firm had ever had a physical meeting with any partner of the other. Although their offices were geographically separated, through using e-mail, video-conferencing, and other Internet techniques, the partners of the merged law firms may have actually known each other better and been able to work together more efficiently than some lawyers who share physical offices.

The Internet makes it easier for law firms to reduce overhead and improve the quality of service through:

- Increased use of telecommuting
- Outsourcing of support functions

In the future, firms may rely increasingly on work-at-home employees, including law librarians, paralegals, secretaries, technical support staff, and many other personnel in addition to lawyers. They may still be regular employees of the firm, or they may be freelance or independent contractors. The basic core of employees could be smaller and be expanded by temporaries or freelancers as needed for particular projects.

This trend is not merely a way of reducing overhead. It can also result in a higher quality of service. For example, a medium-size law firm may not be able to employ one of the best computer system administrators in the country on a full-time basis. However, instead of keeping an average system administrator on staff full time, it may be better off hiring a much better qualified expert as a part-time consultant. One top-quality talent may be able to handle the firm's needs on a part-time basis better than a mediocre employee could full time. This trend will tend to increase income disparities, since the top performers in various fields (including the best lawyers) will be in demand and make much more money. This is another example of what economists Frank and Cook call the "winner-take-all society."

The lower overhead and greater efficiency of virtual organizations may also make them more attractive to some of the most sophisticated clients in the new networked world. Business like the on-line book retailer Amazon.com have achieved much of their competitive advantage by operating as virtual organizations themselves. They may be averse to subsidizing the large, expensive downtown offices and fixed payroll expenses of traditional large law firms.

In today's environment, luxurious downtown offices and large permanent staffs may provide marketing advantages, including an impression of solidity and reliability. In the not-so-distant future, sophisticated, potentially lucrative clients who themselves avoid such high overhead items may prefer to avoid patronizing law firms that indulge in such expensive and ostentatious displays.

The Reduced Significance of Geography

Our improved physical transportation system (e.g., container ships) has increased the potential for competition from those located in remote places. Automobile manufacturers can easily locate plants in low-wage locations, for example. The Internet's ability to transport information more efficiently means that "information workers" like lawyers are also now more vulnerable to competitors in distant places.

For example, some law firms already employ companies that handle legal research on a contract basis. In addition to facilitating such outsourcing domestically, the Internet expands the geographic range of practical competition for this market.

U.S. computer software companies already outsource computer programming to employees located in low-wage nations like India and Russia. How much of the work done by junior associates in prestigious Wall Street law firms is more intellectually challenging than computer programming? "Law clerks" located abroad with good Internet access, including the Westlaw and LEXIS services (now available through the Internet) could reduce the need to hire so many high-priced associates.

There are many brilliant men and women in places like the Ukraine and Bangladesh capable of learning enough in a short time about particular parts of the U.S. legal system to produce high-quality legal work product. Some of these people would be quite eager to do such work in their home countries, where they can maintain an opulent lifestyle for a fraction of the salary of a junior associate at a prestigious U.S. firm. Would U.S. clients accept such work product? Most likely, if the price is right, and the quality is guaranteed by a "name brand" law firm.

As I read the ethics rules, they do not bar lawyers in the United States from using work product generated by non-lawyers or researchers located in other countries. Further, the prospect of lower turnover may mean that the overall expense in training a permanent "law clerk" in Moldavia, let's say, may be less than the expense of training a series of associates located in the United States.

As mentioned previously, I do not necessarily advocate or endorse such trends, but economic pressures like those that resulted in U.S. factories moving to low-wage countries abroad may eventually make lower-paid workers abroad using the Internet competitors for some law-related jobs in the United States.

Virtual law firms can have flexibility and low overhead that give them a competitive advantage for some types of legal work. The same rapid pace of change, competitive pressures, and lesser significance of geographic boundaries that push other businesses into similar types of arrangements make virtual law firms attractive to some lawyers and clients.

Digital Cash

Forms of "digital cash" using public key encryption and digital signatures make possible the reliable, anonymous transfers of large amounts of money. Companies now working to develop digital cash include Citicorp, Microsoft, Digital Equipment Corporation, and Nomura. This is widely touted as a mechanism for making the Internet more attractive for direct sales to consumers, but it also has broader economic implications.

Federal Reserve Board chair Alan Greenspan, not one known for engaging in wild flights of fantasy, has predicted that digital cash will give rise to private currencies, forms of money not issued or backed by any government. As Josh McHugh explained in his article "The Siege on the Greenback" (*Forbes Magazine,* September 9, 1997, available through the archives at http://www.forbes.com):

> The Internet's global reach solves the acceptance problems that private currencies used to encounter in the 19th-century days of free banking. And the Web is the perfect place to post a rating newsletter that could tell potential users whose currency is the most trustworthy or widely accepted.

> Robert Hettinga, who runs the Boston Digital Commerce Society, predicts that digital cash will first gain currency as a medium for small on-line transactions, such as payments for downloading inexpensive software. Once people gain confidence in the banks that issue digital money and the software that moves it, they will trust them with larger sums.

Wired magazine maintains an archive of articles about "The Future of Money" at http://www.wired.com/collections/future_of_money.

With about the same ease in which you can set up a corporation in Delaware, you can incorporate and establish an Internet presence in a foreign jurisdiction like Anguilla. Nations in the Caribbean, the Isle of Man, and Vanuatu compete for foreign corporations by using low taxes and secrecy laws, and the Internet makes them more attractive. Among the results? Ian Goldberg, the Canadian graduate student at Berkeley who demonstrated how to repair significant weaknesses in the Netscape flagship Web browser's 40-bit security, predicts that "Taxes will have to be based more on physical things like land—assuming one believes in taxation at all. With encryption, not only can you hide your transactions, but your assets as well. Intellectual property can be hidden easily."

Lawyers who don't understand the Internet will be poorly equipped to deal with a digital economy.

Online Communities

The Internet's ability to foster interactive special interest groups based on affinity, not geography, is one of its most powerful features. Discussion groups, focused Web sites and extranets can produce something that is more powerful than the sum of its parts:

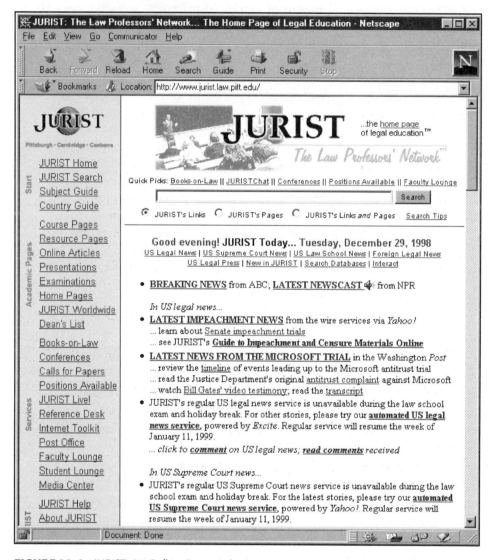

FIGURE 20-4. JURIST: An Online Community

- The JURIST Project, started by University of Pittsburgh law professor Bernard Hibbitts, is one example: http://www.jurist.law.pitt.edu. Starting from a modest beginning, it is now a leading focal point for law professors nationwide.
- Neil J. Squillante's Technolawyer project combines e-mail discussion groups, a focused web site, live chat sessions and more into a unique resource for lawyers: http://www.technolawyer.com.

- That National Association of Criminal Justice Defense Lawyers extranet empowers its members: http://www.criminaljustice.org.

Online communities will be even more important in the future.

Don't let the ease with which the Internet allows us to access computer databases deceive you. The biggest value of the Internet is not that it lets you talk to computers. The Net's biggest value is that it lets you use computers to communicate more efficiently with other *people.*

Your New Frontier

The Internet is here today, it is real, it is ready for you to use for your benefit. Though it is not science fiction, the Internet's possibilities are as exciting as anything Gene Rodenberry or Steven Spielberg could imagine. Good luck on your explorations.

Resources

Wired. Some of my friends swear by this magazine. I mostly swear at it. The insistence on cutting-edge (some might say bizarre) typography and layout make this magazine hard to read, and the "trendier than thou" hipness of many articles can be off-putting. However, if you can tolerate these quirks, it is a good place to preview Internet trends. Online version: http://www.wired.com.

Richard Granat's address to ABA TECHSHOW 98, "Retraining Lawyers for a Digital Age," including the accompanying PowerPoint presentation: http://www.digital-lawyer.com/retrain.html.

Unleashing the Killer App: Digital Strategies for Market Dominance, by Larry Downes and Chunka Mui (Harvard Business School Press, 1998).

The Friction-free Economy, by T. G. Lewis (Harper Business, 1997).

"Technology and the Future of Law," by Eugene Volokh, *Stanford Law Review,* Volume 47 (1995).

PART SIX

Other Voices

Other Voices

WELCOME TO MY FAVORITE section of this book, which is devoted to condensed suggestion lists from top authorities on the Internet and the legal profession—the best from the best.

Of course, YMMV, or, as translated for the Internet newcomer, "Your Mileage May Vary." I don't necessarily agree with every statement from these guest contributors, and I'm certain that not all of them would endorse everything in the rest of this book.

The tips cover a number of areas, ranging from predictions on how the Internet will change our profession to Web resources for specific practice areas to pointers for conducting legal research and designing your Web site. There are even lists written for law librarians and paralegals.

Some suggestions appear on more than one list, or overlap with the rest of the text. As noted in the invitation sent to the contributing experts:

> I don't think some overlap will be bad. In fact, it will probably be beneficial. When reading movie critics' "Ten Best" lists every December, it is fun and sometimes educational to see idiosyncratic selections, but there may be more value in seeing the areas of expert consensus.

When you see a suggestion on multiple lists, it's probably one worth special attention.

I learned plenty from these experts, and I hope you do too.

David Johnson's Ten Ways the Internet Will Change the Legal Profession

1. Because we'll do research in an online "case space" rather than a law library, our basic materials will be increasingly available to laypeople and nonlawyer competitors.

2. We'll find new business through the online marketplace—and the best way to attract clients will be to publish helpful, substantive Web pages and to respond helpfully to online queries.

3. Groups of experts will produce continuing legal education courses and "just in time" substantive publications via online asynchronous threaded discussions.

4. Online treatises that organize information concerning the issues in various practice areas will evolve continuously, will hyperlink down into primary materials, and will send you an e-mail when they add something new that you ought to read.

5. We'll argue some motions and even try some cases by jointly authoring a complex hypertext. Advocates will point electronically to each other's arguments and to the evidence. The judge's decision will be a series of pointers to the most pertinent and persuasive portions of an online record, compiled over time by the parties.

6. We'll use new types of graphical interfaces to work with interactive forms, consult with expert systems, explore options, negotiate with opposing parties, train in legal simulators, and create new rules. The screen will become the place where we do much of our billable work.

7. Those representing corporate clients will be required to join legal extranets and intranets through which all inside and outside counsel representing the client confer on a regular basis.

8. As commerce moves to the Net, we'll create a new "law merchant" that establishes distinct sets of rules for various online spaces. Lawyers will have to track and understand such evolving rule sets on a global basis.

9. Lawyers and engineers will need to work more closely together because optimal solutions to online conflicts may often be the thoughtful deployment of new technologies.

10. Global electronic commerce will require use of contractually based dispute resolution and decentralized rule making. Lawyers will have to rethink and reengineer the litigation process, the adversarial system, and sovereignty. Much of the legal profession will no longer derive its role from a monopoly on the right to appear before local courts but rather from its collective problem-solving skills and its ability to engineer stable and value-enhancing relationships between parties with conflicting interests, on a global basis.

David R. Johnson is the Leader, E-group, Wilmer, Cutler and Pickering: djohnson@wilmer.com.

Lynn Chard and Mary Ellen LeBlanc's Ten Tips for Lawyers New to the Net

1. Start your search for information using a search engine. The top search engines are continually searching and indexing Web sites. Examples include:
   - InfoSeek at http://www.infoseek.com
   - Lycos at http://www.lycos.com
   - AltaVista at http://www.altavista.com

   To search using several search engines at once, try MetaCrawler, a Web site that sends your query to multiple search engines, at www.metacrawler.com.

2. Find the most recent state and federal court decisions, often within twenty-four hours of publication. Go to FindLaw at http://www.findlaw.com or Cornell at http://www.law.cornell.edu for a complete listing.

3. Access company information, including company profiles and the latest quarterly earnings. Try Hoover's Online at http://www.hoovers.com for company profiles and EDGAR at http://www.sec.gov/edgarhp.htm for the latest SEC filings.

4. Find the addresses and phone numbers of individuals just about anywhere in the United States. Examples include:
   - American Directory Assistance at http://www.lookupusa.com/
   - Lycos People Find at http://www.whowhere.lycos.com
   - Find a Friend (a fee-based service) at http://www.findafriend.com

5. Look for prior statements and information about expert witnesses on the Web. A comprehensive list of expert witness resources is available through the Washburn University School of Law at http://lawlib.wuacc.edu/washlaw/expert/expert.html.

6. Join an e-mail discussion group in your practice area to hear about the latest legal developments—where to find new legislation, regulations, and forms and their implications for your practice—and to find out how other lawyers approach issues in your practice. See Law Lists at http://www.lib.uchicago.edu/~llou/lawlists/info.html for a list of legal mailing lists.

7. Find technical help twenty-four hours a day. Many hardware and software vendors provide technical support at their Web sites, along with software fixes and the latest product information.

8. Find the latest legal and business news (including financial and stock information). Examples include:

- Law Journal Extra at http://www.ljextra.com
- The *New York Times* Business Page at
  http://www.nytimes.com/yr/mo/day/business
- The *Wall Street Journal* (a subscription service) at
  http://www.wsj.com

9. Find current legal and government forms, including the latest IRS tax forms, at http://www.irs.ustreas.gov.

10. Don't limit your research to Web sites—investigate your case through the archives of Internet discussion groups covering thousands of topics. You may find information relevant to your case in these online forums. Go to DejaNews at http://www.dejanews.com, which has organized and archived these discussions.

Lynn P. Chard is the director and *Mary Ellen LeBlanc* is the Web site manager of The Institute of Continuing Legal Education, Ann Arbor, Michigan, which is on the Web at http://www.icle.org. ICLE recently published *The Internet Guide for Michigan Lawyers* and provides a series of technology training courses for lawyers.

Bob Ambrogi's Ten Worst Internet Pitfalls for Lawyers

The Internet can boost your law practice in lots of ways, from enabling you to conduct low-cost research to providing you with a forum for broad-based marketing. But for the uninitiated, the Internet also presents hazards—not of the ethical or tortious variety, just common pitfalls that can blemish your image, cost you money, or waste your time. Here, in no particular order, are ten Internet don'ts.

1. Don't make a fool of yourself. It's one thing to commit a gaff; it's far worse to do it on the Internet, where thousands can read it. The greatest sin: billing yourself as an expert, then saying something that proves you are anything but. Be judicious both on your Web site and in discussion groups.

2. Don't waste your money. Hiring an Internet consultant can be money wisely spent or thrown away. Shop around. Look for law firm experience, then compare work products and prices. For a simple, low-maintenance site, don't be afraid to do it yourself.

3. Don't waste your time. Let's face it, the Internet is way cool. You can play chess with a stranger in Taiwan or watch live pictures of

someone's fish tank. You and your associates can easily fritter away hours. Don't. Make sure your firm has an Internet use policy, and enforce it.

4. Don't forget where you live. Sure, the Internet makes us all part of a global virtual community. But most of our business will still come from that real community just outside the front door. If you plan to market your services on the Internet, keep this in mind. Announce your Web site in local newspapers, find listservs dedicated to local concerns, and speak to the local Chamber of Commerce about legal issues in electronic commerce.

5. Don't proceed without a plan. Marketing without a plan is like sailing without charts: no matter how fair the wind, it will never take you where you want to end up. Before creating a Web site, decide what you hope to achieve, who you hope to reach, and how best to proceed.

6. Don't forget your profession. You're a lawyer, and your Web site should say so. Avoid glitz and glamour in favor of information and ease of use.

7. Don't ignore how visitors come to your site. Many are the Web sites with beautiful front pages but forgotten back doors. Few visitors will first enter your site through the home page—more likely they've come for some inside article. Make sure every page tells who you are and what you do.

8. Don't forget why people visit your site. Your picture and accomplishments displayed prominently on your home page will impress your parents, but no one else. Fresh, practical content is what visitors seek.

9. Don't fail to answer e-mail. Answering e-mail is like returning phone calls—do it and do it promptly. Far too many lawyers who say they're on the Internet don't even regularly check messages.

10. Don't forget the real world. With all the neat technology, it's sometimes more fun to play Web master than lawyer. And in the vast reaches of cyberspace, it's easy to forget the mundane matters of real-life clients. Repeat after me: "I am neither Web master nor Web guru. I am a lawyer whose clients pay my bills."

Robert J. Ambrogi, a lawyer in Rockport, Massachusetts, is editor of *legal.online,* a monthly newsletter about the Internet at http://www.legalonline.com. Mr. Ambrogi maintains an excellent archive of his articles on lawyer use of the Internet at http://www.legaline.com, his legal practice Web site. He can be reached by e-mail at rambrogi@legaline.com.

Diana Botluk's Ten Tips for Internet Legal Researchers

1. Find a good starting site to point you in the right direction. FindLaw, at http://www.findlaw.com, is a great overall index to law resources on the Web.

2. Use American Law Sources On-Line, at http://www.lawsource.com/also/usa.htm, when seeking state law resources. It provides links to a wide range of legal resources divided by state.

3. Looking for the U.S. Code? Look no farther than the House of Representatives Internet Law Library at http://law.house.gov/usc.htm or Cornell Law School's Legal Information Institute at http://www.law.cornell.edu/uscode. For updates on public laws, also try the following:
   ♦ The Law Revision Counsel's U.S. Code Classification Table at http://law.house.gov/tbl_cd.txt
   ♦ Thomas at http://thomas.loc.gov
   ♦ GPO Access at http://www.access.gpo.gov/su_docs/aces/aaces002.html

4. Thomas, at http://thomas.loc.gov, is a fabulous free collection of federal legislative history from the past couple of U.S. Congresses. For more extensive access to federal legislative history resources, spring for a subscription to CIS Congressional Compass at http://www.cispubs.com/compassweb/welcome.htm or LEGI-SLATE at http://www.legi-slate.com.

5. The C. F. R. can be searched at the National Archives and Records Administration at GPO Access, http://www.access.gpo.gov/nara/cfr. GPO Access also provides *Federal Registers* from the past few years, at http://www.access.gpo.gov/su_docs/aces/aces140.html.

6. Locate federal agency Web sites with Villanova's Federal Web Locator at http://www.law.vill.edu/fed-agency/fedwebloc.html or the Great American Web Site at http://www.uncle-sam.com.

7. FindLaw at http://www.findlaw.com/casecode/supreme.html holds the most complete free collection of U.S. Supreme Court opinions. Cornell's LII presents an informative page linking to the variety of Supreme Court resources online at http://supct.law.cornell.edu/supct. Listen to oral arguments at Oyez Oyez Oyez at http://oyez.nwu.edu

8. Begin your search for U.S. court of appeals decisions at the Federal Courts Finder at http://www.law.emory.edu/FEDCTS. If U.S. district court opinions exist online, you can find them by using American Law Sources Online, http://www.lawsource.com/also/usa.htm,

and looking in their corresponding state. Although current cases are fairly easy to find online, there are very few older cases. An extra-cost service like V., at http://www.versuslaw.com, provides a few decades worth of cases, but so far law libraries are still the best place to research the oldest case law.

9. Keep up with current developments by consulting an online legal newspaper, like *Law Journal Extra!* at http://www.ljx.com, or an on-line legal research-related newsletter, like *Law Library Resource Xchange* at http://www.llrx.com. Locate law-related listservs with Lyonette Louis-Jacques' Law Lists at http://www.lib.uchicago.edu/~llou/lawlists/info.html, or use Cornell's BigEar http://350/barratry.law.cornell.edu:5123/notify/buzz.html to spy on e-mail discussion group announcements of new Web sites.

10. Consult a guide to online legal research, such as The Legal List: Research on the Internet, at http://www.lcp.com/The-Legal-List/TLL-home.html, to discover what the Internet has to offer legal researchers. This guide provides instruction for novices, explanations for intermediate searchers, and lists of sites for advanced searchers.

Diana Botluk is a reference librarian at Catholic University Law School and has been teaching online legal research for fifteen years. Author of the most recent editions of West Group's *The Legal List: Research on the Internet,* she also writes a monthly column called "Finding Information on the World Wide Web" for the *Internet Law Researcher* newsletter.

Josh Blackman's Top Ten Web Sites for Factual Research

Because online data typically is not comprehensive, current, accurate, and citable, the Internet is currently better suited to factual than traditional (case law and statute) research. This doesn't mean that you can't use the Internet to retrieve traditional legal materials. In fact, in many situations, including keeping up on current issues or reading recent opinions and bills, the Net is an excellent and cost-effective (often free) resource.

The Net is even more useful, however, in the context of factual research. For example, you can find people and information about people, experts and evidence useful for impeaching experts as well as business, medical, and competitive intelligence data. Here are just a few of the many excellent (and in many cases completely unique and free) factual resources legal professionals will find on the Internet.

Finding News Sources
1. For a directory of links to online newspapers, magazines, radio, and TV, try Newslink at http://www.newslink.org/menu.html.
2. For an exhaustive, clickable directory of electronic publications, try the Association of Research Libraries Directory of Electronic Publications at http://www.qrl.org/scomm/edir/archive.html.

Finding Experts
3. The Northern California Association of Law Libraries offers an extensive collection of sources for expert witnesses at http://www.nocall.org/experts.html.
4. EXPERT-L is an Internet mailing list for those engaged in expert witness activities associated with litigation. It was inspired by the need experts have to communicate with each other about issues related to expert witness services. If you want to subscribe, send an e-mail to expert-l@lern.mv.com with the word SUBSCRIBE in the subject header.

Finding People
5. For a national phone book, try Database America, which offers a criss-cross feature. If you type in a phone number, you will get back a name and address. Find it at http://www.databaseamerica.com.
6. You can conduct geneology research at the Death Database, which provides several free databases, including the Social Security Death Index. Nearly 98 percent of the entire index contains individuals who died after 1962 (when the Social Security Administration began keeping the database on computer). The site, at http://www.ancestry.com, also includes an early American marriage database, listing nearly 75,000 American marriages before 1800.

Company Research
7. An excellent starting place if you're simply trying to track down a company is the Business Phone Books at http://www.companylink.com/. It pulls together several databases, including the Switchboard Directory, AT&T Directory, and GTE Interactive Yellow Pages.

8. One of the most comprehensive public company sites on the Net is Wall Street Research Network at http://www.wsrn.com. This site provides links to company home pages, SEC filings, and business news.

Medical Research

9. The AMA's comprehensive physician database is at http://www.ama-assn.org.

10. For a primary source describing symptoms, common clinical procedures, laboratory tests, and virtually all the disorders that a general internist might encounter, try the Merck Manual of Diagnosis and Therapies at http://www.merck.com/!!rJfJw0ayFrJfJw0ayF/ pubs/mmanual/html/sectoc.htm. If you are not in the mood to type a lengthy URL, just go to http://www.merck.com and select the menu choice for the manual. Merck provides the manual on the Internet in searchable, full-text form without charge.

Josh Blackman edits *The Internet Lawyer* newsletter at http://www.internetlawyer.com. He has written several books on Internet research. The most recent is one he wrote with David Jank, *The Internet Fact Finder for Lawyers: How to Find Anything on the Net* (American Bar Association: Law Practice Management Section, 1998).

Billie Jo Brooks's Internet Advice for Law Librarians

1. When requesting information from government agencies, ask whether the information is available through the Internet. Locating government documents on the Web saves time and money. The mammoth directory at http://www.fedworld.gov is a good starting point.

2. Learn to construct a basic Web page for your lawyers. You don't need anything fancy, just a list of Internet sites that your lawyers might like to access.

3. Use the Internet for company research, whether the company is Fortune 500 or a mom-and-pop shop. The Internet is available as an advertising medium to all.

4. Don't restrict searches to one search engine. Each search engine produces different results.

5. Provide introductory, advanced, and subject-specific Internet training to personnel in your law firm.

6. Take advantage of the wealth of statistical information available on the Internet by using such sites as http://www.fedstats.gov, which has links to statistics from scores of federal agencies. A broader set of statistical links is available at http://www.lib.umich.edu/libhome/Documents.center/stats.html.
7. Use online catalogs. They are a great source when preparing a bibliography on a particular practice area.
8. Use listservs such as PRIVATELAWLIB-l for interlibrary loans, reference questions, document retrieval, and to discuss library operation problems and techniques.
9. Stay up-to-date with Internet access issues.
10. Bookmark sites that provide an extensive list of subject-specific sites (e.g., every site on product liability, every site on immigration).

Billie Jo Brooks, a law librarian with Williams, Mullen, Christian & Dobbins in Richmond, Virginia, is a popular CLE speaker. She is on the Web at http://www.wmcd.com.

Genie Tyburski's Ten Don'ts When Using the Internet as a Research Tool

1. Don't conduct comprehensive case law research at official court Web sites or via any noncommercial means. Do retrieve individual recently issued opinions at official or commercial Web sites.
2. Don't expect to find complete public record information without expecting to pay for it. Similarly, don't attempt to perform thorough due diligence research online.
3. Don't exclude traditional information sources when seeking an expert. The Internet offers a variety of resources useful for locating experts, but it is not the be-all-and-end-all of expert-finding aids.
4. Don't conduct historical research with the expectation that you will find complete, accurate information. Beware of the information source and note the relatively recent advent of electronic data.
5. Don't perform complete legislative history research even if the law is a recent federal one. Do use official government sites like GPO Access to retrieve specific reports, memoranda, and other documents.

6. Don't expect to find complete legal texts. You may discover promotional sites that provide abstracts of recently published books or educational archives that offer complete texts for works in the public domain.

7. Don't stop searching if the SEC's EDGAR database fails to locate a public filing. Do check with a securities research firm such as Disclosure Incorporated or Global Securities Information, Inc., to determine the availability of the document.

8. Don't ignore traditional computer-assisted legal research services when looking for commentary. Do consider including relevant trade association sites when seeking such information.

9. Don't assume your word processing package can open the files you download. Many files require decompression utilities or proprietary software.

10. Don't attempt to conduct research on the Internet in the same way you would conduct research on LEXIS/NEXIS or Westlaw. The Internet is neither a database nor the Web. A series of keyword searches at search service sites may result in hours of unchargable time with little or nothing to show for your efforts. Consider using catalog sites or research guides.

Genie Tyburski is a law librarian with Ballard Spahr Andrews & Ingersoll in Philadelphia. She designed The Virtual Chase, a site devoted to research aids and tutorials, at http://www.virtualchase.com.

James Wheaton's Top Ten Internet Tips for Corporate and Securities Lawyers

1. Use Edgar. The SEC's Edgar site, at http://www.sec.gov/cgi-bin/srch-edgar, currently includes all documents electronically filed since 1995 (the oldest year rotates off the site each year). It is an all-purpose source for company filings, all types of document forms (use the exhibits routinely filed with various registrations and reports), merger and acquisition documents that the other side has used in prior deals, and general company information. The SEC also provides a link to a freeware utility that will convert "edgarized" documents into WordPerfect 5.1 format.

2. Subscribe to the *Wall Street Journal* online. The mere fact that the *Wall Street Journal* can be accessed by subscription from your

desktop at http://www.wsj.com should be enough, but the ability to personalize the *Journal* to organize the information that you receive each day is invaluable. Set up your "Personal Journal" as your default browser page, and your personal news selections will be the first thing you see when you open your browser in the morning.

3. Use the SEC site to keep abreast of important rule makings. Want to check on the status of a proposed rule change that you heard about a few months ago? Use the SEC's up-to-date rule-making page at http://www.sec.gov/rulemake.htm.

4. Go to the *New York Times* for business news and business links. The *New York Times* at http://www.nytimes.com has a comprehensive Web site. It also has a business links page that compiles a substantial number of links to stock markets, government agencies, financial news sources, and banking and other market information sources, at http://www.nytimes.com/library/cyber/reference/busconn.html.

5. If you are looking for an IPO, check out IPO Central. IPO Central, at http://www.ipocentral.com/features/search.html, allows you to search for recent and pending initial public offerings based on a number of criteria, including underwriter, business location, or industry. Once it retrieves a list of filings, it also provides direct links to Edgar filings.

6. For breaking business news, go to PR Newswire. PR Newswire's site at http://www.prnewswire.com allows you to check out breaking business news in a variety of industries. These are usually in the form of rewritten press releases, but if you have heard about a deal and want immediate access to the basic information, this is a good place to start.

7. If you have bank clients, you need *The American Banker.* Even if you don't do enough banking work to justify the full price of *The American Banker* print subscription, you can keep current with daily banking industry news with a limited online subscription to *The American Banker* at http://www.americanbanker.com. The least expensive online subscription gives you access to the *Daily Digest* for $50 per year and allows you to retrieve online articles for $1.95 each.

8. Use the Nasdaq page for company information. Nasdaq's site, at http://www.nasdaq.com, gives you access to a substantial amount of information about Nasdaq-traded companies, including trading histories, delayed price information, and links to news releases and company Web sites.

9. Keep federal regulations up to date by using the C. F. R. and Federal Register databases. The paper C. F. R. volumes are always a year behind, and the *Federal Register* is unwieldy, late, and poorly indexed. By contrast, the C. F. R. at http://www.access.gpo.gov/nara/cfr/index.html and the *Federal Register* at http://www.access.gpo.gov/su_docs/aces/aces140.html provide timely and accurate on-line information about regulatory changes.

10. Use your customizable Personal Toolbar to create personal button links for your most critical sites. Although bookmarks and favorites are nice, a button for each of your most-used Web sites is not only convenient, but serves as a visual prompt of the need to check those sites regularly (or at least daily) for breaking information.

Jim Wheaton is a corporate and securities lawyer in Norfolk, Virginia. He teaches a seminar on business entities at the University of Virginia School of Law and is chair of the Limited Liability Companies Subcommittee of the ABA Business Section's Partnerships and Unincorporated Business Organizations Committee.

Peter Chapman's Top Ten Internet Tips for Bankruptcy Professionals

1. Stay on top of the latest news at http://bankrupt.com/chap11.html, which offers daily news updates about the nation's high-profile bankruptcy cases.
2. Get tips and leads, share your successes, solicit ideas, and solve problems at http://bankrupt.com/discussion.html. This site features roundtable-style mailing lists hosting bankruptcy-related discussions.
3. If you just want the facts, get operating and financial data from the SEC at http://www.sec.gov/cgi-bin/srch-edgar. This site contains full-text electronic copies of SEC filings by public companies, with exhibits.
4. For a directory of the nation's bankruptcy clerks, with local paralegal contacts, try http://bankrupt.com/clerks.html.
5. Get to know your opponent by checking out the Martindale-Hubbell Directory at http://lawyers.martindale.com/marhub at no charge.
6. For bankruptcy law online, try http://www.catalaw.com/topics/Bankruptcy.shtml. This is a one-stop source for statutes, rules, some case law, and related items.

7. To help you harvest information from the Internet, use
http://webcrawler.com. Bankruptcy is a hotter topic on the Internet
than you might suspect.

8. To learn what people are spouting off about, check out
http://www.dejanews.com. Read what people post in public
newsgroups—about you or your client.

9. Online filing and retrieval of S.D.N.Y. bankruptcy documents is
a reality at http://www.nysb.uscourts.gov.

10. For a directory of the 100+ PACER bulletin boards for on-line
bankruptcy court docket sheets, try
http://www.uscourts.gov/PubAccess.html.

Peter A. Chapman of Bankruptcy Creditors' Service, Inc., Princeton,
New Jersey, is a co-host of the InterNet Bankruptcy Library at
http://bankrupt.com. The IBL—the oldest bankruptcy-related Web site on
the Internet—provides updates about significant Chapter 11 cases from
1994 to date and more.

Arlin Neser's Top Ten Internet Tips for Estate Planning Lawyers

1. Use estate planning "finding lists" to locate estate planning re-
sources on the Internet. These are some of the best of such lists:
   - Dennis Kennedy's Estate Planning Links at
     http://members.aol.com/dmk58/epl.html
   - Findlaw's Wills, Trust, Estates and Probate Home Page at
     http://www.findlaw.com/01topics/31probate/index.html
   - Mark Welch's Law and Estate Planning Sites on the Internet at
     http://www.ca-probate.com/links.htm

2. If you are thinking about switching your Internet service from
America Online or CompuServe to a different Internet service
provider (ISP), don't hurry to cancel your AOL or CompuServe
account. Occasionally, you may need to download a document
from the Internet when your ISP is either busy or down. In these
situations you'll be glad to have a backup source to the Internet,
such as AOL or CompuServe. AOL allows you to have a basic
Internet account for a minimal amount per month.

3. Search engines survey the Internet differently, so it's a good idea
to use more than one search engine when trying to locate Inter-

net resources. I like to start with Yahoo!, then try AltaVista, and finally HotBot. Each engine searches differently and yields different results. You may also want to try one of the "meta-search" programs, which use several different search engines simultaneously.

4. For the latest general information about computer hardware and software, point your browser to cnet: the computer network at http://www.cnet.com.

5. For a complete list of all state and federal substantive law currently on the Internet, try Substantive Law on the World Wide Web, at http://www.mother.com/~randy/law.html.

6. You can find a current and historical listing of applicable federal rates at the Tax Page maintained by the law firm of Pillsbury, Madison & Sutro, LLP, at http://www.pmstax.com/afr/.

7. Stay current with the latest trends in estate planning and probate by checking out the Web sites of professional estate planning organizations, including these:

    ◆ National Network of Estate Planning Attorneys at http://www.netplanning.com

    ◆ American College of Trust and Estate Counsel at http://www.actec.org

    ◆ National Academy of Elder Law Attorneys at http://www.naela.org

8. Be sure to join at least one estate planning listserv. Some of the more popular estate planning listservs are:

    ◆ Estate Planning List at estateplanning-request@northwest.com (in the subject area enter "subscribe estateplanning")

    ◆ ABA-PTL at listserv@home.ease.lsoft.com (in the subject area enter "subscribe aba-ptl")

    ◆ Elder Law Mailing List at listserv@topeka.wuacc.edu (in the subject area enter "subscribe elderlaw-l Your Name")

9. Take advantage of these inexpensive case law resources on the Internet: V. by Versuslaw at http://www.versuslaw.com and The LOIS Law Library at http://www.pita.com.

10. Remember that all major government agencies have Web sites. Some of them are actually very good and have a wealth of resources. For example, check out these:

    ◆ Health Care Financing Administration for information about Medicare and Medicaid at http://www.hcfa.gov

    ◆ Department of Labor's Pension & Welfare Benefits Administration Homepage at http://www.dol.gov/dol/pwba/welcome.html

    ◆ The IRS's Homepage at http://www.irs.ustreas.gov

Arlin P. Neser practices estate planning, business, tax, and real estate law and is a consultant in the areas of legal technology and online services for lawyers. He is also the author of *Law Office Guide to Online Courts,* published by James Publishing, Inc. For other information about electronic legal research, contact him on the Internet at arlinn@pacbell.net.

Joseph Matthews's Internet Sites for Trial Lawyers

Top Four Medical Sites

While there is still no easy or free Internet access to Medline, the full-text database of old and current medical articles created by the National Library of Medicine, the Internet offers access to medical journals and other information via some alternative sites, including these:

1. NLM's PubMed Medline Retrieval System, at http:/www.medmatrix.org, provides access to literature, citations, and links to their full-text versions at publishers' Web sites. This is an experimental service of the National Library of Medicine.
2. Healthgate, at http:/www.healthgate.com, provides free Web access to Medline for searching primary medical sources.
3. Medicine Net, at http:/www.Medicinenet.com, is a free medical resource written by physicians and continuously updated. It provides information on diseases, treatments, and medications and includes a medical dictionary.
4. Merck Manual (Merck & Co.), at http:/www.merck.com, provides extensive information on diseases, etiology, diagnosis, and treatment.

Top Six Product, Engineering, and General Sites

Here are some of the most useful Web sites for product liability research:

1. The National Highway Transportation Safety Administration (NHTSA) is responsible for reducing death, injuries, and economic losses resulting from motor vehicle crashes. Its Web site, at, contains all the NHTSA's years of research on motor vehicle safety. In the Web site you will find various databases.
2. The National Center for Statistical Analysis (NCSA) is responsible for providing a wide range of analytical support for NHTSA and the traffic safety community through data collection, analysis, and crash investigation activities. The NCSA Web site, at http:/www.nhtsa.gov/people/ncsa, includes the NCSA databases.

3. The National Transportation Safety Board (NTSB) investigates accidents pertaining to aviation, automobile accidents on highways, marine and pipeline hazardous materials, and railroads. Its Web site, at http://www.ntsb.gov, contains information on these various areas as well as the text of NTSB member speeches and testimonies on safety issues.

4. The Notice Company's page, at http://www.notice.com, provides information about class action lawsuits. This Web site covers such class actions as tobacco litigation, hemophilia HIVcompensation, and asbestos. In addition, the Notice Company also offers free e-mail notification of class actions and product recalls.

5. The U.S. Consumer Product Safety Commission (CPSC), an independent federal regulatory agency, helps keep American families safe by reducing the risk of injury or death from consumer products. The CPSC Web site, at http://www.cpsc.gov, contains information about all recalls of products that have been ordered by the CPSC or another government agency.

6. The National Climatic Data Center (NCDC) is a division of the National Oceanic and Atmospheric Administration (NOAA). The NCDC's Web site, at http://www.ncdc.noaa.gov, is the world's largest archive of weather data. The NCDC produces numerous climate publications you can use to prove weather conditions at the time of an alleged defect. Users can view other conditions of a specific day and see satellite images of weather on a particular date.

Joseph M. Matthews, an experienced trial lawyer, is a partner in the Miami firm of Colson, Hicks, Eidson, Colson, & Matthews.

Claudia Rast's Top Ten Sites for Environmental Law Research

1. What better starting point for the environmental lawyer? The U.S. EPA, at http://www.epa.gov, includes links to the EPA regional offices and labs, environmentally related regulations and legislation, and information on EPA programs and initiatives. Lots of good information is buried in this site. For example, following the links to regulations and legislation, you can ultimately find aids at http://www.epa.gov/docs/epacfr40/find-aid.info/state that will yield EPA approval status for programs (e.g., air, waste, water) on a state-by-state basis.

2. A bit different from the government's C. F. R. site, the Chemical Industry Home Page, at http://www.nvi.net/, mimics the way we would scan the C. F. R. if we had the document in hand, knew generally where to find the information, and just needed to verify the exact language. Title 40 is divided into its subchapters, which link to the relevant parts and subparts. If you are stumped about where to find a particular issue, use the general search term capabilities of the URLs mentioned below in items 3–5.

3. The National Archives and Records Administration: The C. F. R. (minus Title 29 and others, but including Title 40), at http://www.access.gpo.gov/nara/cfr/cfr-table-search.html.

4. Title 40 of the C. F. R. (brought to you by the U.S. EPA), at http://www.epa.gov/epacfr40.

5. Title 29 of the C. F. R. (brought to you by the Department of Labor and OSHA), at http://www.osha-sic.gov/OshStd_toc/OSHA_Std_toc.html. For OSHA-related environmental issues that are outside Title 40, this site covers the gap in the URLs mentioned above.

6. The *Federal Register* a la EPA, at http://www.epa.gov/fedrgstr, is another of those unglitzy but necessary URLs. It has become more user-friendly in recent months. If you'd rather not check out the site on a daily basis for what's new, consider subscribing to one or several of the environmental subsets of the Federal Register at http://www.epa.gov/fedrgstr/subscribe.htm. For example, you could subscribe to EPA-AIR, EPA-WATER, or EPA-WASTE to cover the basics, or EPA-SPECIES for information on endangered species. Just sit back and watch the e-mail notices roll in with the information.

7. GSU's College of Law—MetaIndex of Law, at http://gsulaw.gsu.edu/metaindex consists of a huge collection in one site of the traditional legal resources: U.S. Supreme Court Reports, all the Federal Circuit Courts of Appeals, the U.S. Code, and Federal Bills. They are searchable by text or bill number, general law search engines, and more.

8. Always a reliable and rich source of information, Cornell's Legal Information Institute on Environmental Laws, at http://www.law.cornell.edu/topics/environmental.html, includes links to the text of most federal environmental laws, state environmental regulations, recent U.S. Supreme Court opinions on environmental topics, federal agencies, and national environmental groups. Before the Web, Cornell had much of this information available in gopher format.

9. Described as a work platform for environmental professionals, the Virtual Desktop for Environmental Lawyers, at http://www.clay.net/ep1.html, a page on the clay.net Web site, purports to be

the all-encompassing virtual desktop of URLs for environmental lawyers. It's not too far from the truth. There are federal and state government sites, private organizations, commercial entities covering legal issues, news, jobs, seminars, and more. Another handy link through the clay site is its collection of state environmental agency sites at http://www.clay.net/statag.html.

10. The Environmental Treaties and Resource Indicators site is useful: http://sedac.ciesin.org:80/entri. Long-time Internet users will recognize the "ciesin" part of this URL. Known as the Consortium for International Earth Science Information Network (CIESIN), back in Internet gopher days, the ciesin gopher was a rich resource for environmental information then as now. It offers more than the usual "insert your search term" and "hit the seek button." It lists such questions as, "When did a treaty enter into force?" When clicked, the question generates a page with a scroll-down box of 430 treaties. You can select a treaty from the list as well as the date of adoption, the date entered into force, and the place adopted. It also lists official languages.

Claudia Rast is a partner with the Detroit firm of Dickinson, Wright, Moon, Van Dusen, & Freeman and director of the firm's sixteen-lawyer environmental practice department. The firm's URL is http://www.dickinson-wright.com.

Bertrand Harding, Jr.'s Top Ten Internet Tax Law Resources

1. One good site is Access to Tax Legislation at http://thomas.loc.gov.
2. You can find a wide variety of tax-related substantive, administrative, and professional information at http://www.taxsites.com.
3. For an excellent article containing a comprehensive list of tax-related federal, state, and international Web sites, tax discussion groups, directories of tax articles, and many other tax-related items, see "Tax Resources in Cyberspace: A Worldwide Web Update," by Richard J. Coppins et al., in the July 1996 *Journal of Taxation* (Vol. 85, No. 1).
4. Get information about determining independent contractor tax status in the IRS Training Manual on Making Employee/Independent Contractor Determinations at http://www.irs.ustreas.gov/prod/bus_info/training.html.

5. Also, check out the IRS Daily Digital at http://www.irs.ustreas.gov/prod/cover.html.
6. You can download IRS forms at http://www.irs.ustreas.gov/basic/forms_pubs/forms.html.
7. The IRS Newsstand, at http://www.irs.ustreas.gov/basic/news/index.html, is a useful site.
8. For IRS regulations in plain English, try http://www.irs.ustreas.gov/prod/tax_regs/reglist.html.
9. To get a summary of the latest tax developments, go to http://www.tax.org.
10. U. S. Tax Code On-Line is at http://www.fourmilab.ch/ustax/ustax.html.

Bertrand Harding, Jr. is a tax attorney in Washington, D.C., and owner of the College and University Tax Law Page, http://www.universitytax.com.

Evan Farr's Top Ten Internet Tips for Small Firms

1. Communicate with clients via e-mail. E-mail is cheaper than postal mail, and saves time by allowing you to type and send directly rather than wasting time printing, folding, addressing envelopes, stamping, and mailing. E-mail also can be more effective in some cases. For example, some executives whose phone calls or paper mail are prescreened receive their e-mail directly.
2. Communicate with other lawyers via e-mail—for the same reasons mentioned above.
3. Use encrypted e-mail for high security on your most sensitive communications. For sensitive or confidential client communications, sending encrypted e-mail is probably the most secure form of communicating—safer than telephone, fax, or postal mail.
4. Use e-mail discussion groups (mailing lists). Mailing lists provide a great way to keep on top of developments in the law and to do research on legal or factual issues.
5. Use mailing lists for networking. Mailing lists facilitate conversation with other lawyers on topics of mutual interest. They foster contact and cooperation among practitioners and academics. These functions are particularly valuable for small firms and solo practitioners, because the lists to a large extent equalize the playing field between large and small firms, allowing even solo practitioners to tap a vast network of expertise on any given area of the law.

6. Use mailing lists for marketing. E-mail newsletters are cheaper and, in some cases, more effective than their paper counterparts.

7. Market your services via the Web. The Web allows lawyers to establish a dignified presence in the on-line world, and for an increasing number of clients the Web is becoming the preferred method of locating a lawyer. A Web site designed by a small firm can be as good or better than a site designed by a large firm, evening the playing field between small and large firms.

8. Use the Web to better serve existing and potential clients. A Web site is an easy and efficient way to disseminate basic legal information and thereby reduce the time you would otherwise spend answering the same questions. Many clients actually prefer receiving basic information from a Web site because it is more convenient for them and they don't have to feel as if they are wasting your time.

9. Use the Web for legal research. Although its legal resources are not necessarily complete and not always up to date, the Web provides an enormous quantity of material that makes it a good starting point for many types of research.

10. Use the Web for factual research. This is probably an even better way to use the Internet's vast resources than using it for legal research.

Evan H. Farr is a principal in The Law Firm of Evan H. Farr, P.C., in Fairfax, Virginia, where he is the chair of the Fairfax Bar Association's Law Practice Management Section and a member of the Board of Governors of the Virginia State Bar's General Practice Section. His firm was the first general practice law firm in Virginia to establish a Web site—The Northern Virginia Law Page™, at http://www.farr-law.com.

Mike Curreri's Top Ten Reasons Why Corporations Use Extranets to Manage Litigation

1. An extranet can improve team-oriented collaborative behaviors of outside counsel by creating a "marketplace of ideas," where the best counsel compete for attention by providing the best ideas and work product.

2. Using an extranet can reduce expenses associated with "reinventing the wheel." It is an easy-to-use mechanism that enables counsel to share information about experts, product literature,

medical and technical literature, federal and state regulations, opposing counsel, defense strategies, other defense counsel, opposing counsel, and use of critical exhibits.

3. Use of an extranet can reduce repetitive communications and instructions to counsel regarding approved discovery responses and litigation procedures. By using automated systems that track and report compliance, counsel can better audit and manage outside counsel compliance with guidelines.

4. An extranet can minimize vendor expenses by requiring counsel to use low-cost Internet resources instead of expensive information vendors.

5. An extranet provides an electronic infrastructure to facilitate communication between counsel and client with threaded conferencing by subject matter, customized e-mail directories, and customized task-based billing mechanisms.

6. Extranet use provides counsel with collateral access to information-rich, economical Internet resources for better client and practice development.

7. In-house counsel and smaller outside firms with reduced resources can benefit from the information and expertise of the entire network of counsel.

8. An extranet provides a mechanism by which each matter can be tracked on a real-time basis. It links associated exhibits, pleadings, and correspondence and allows for performance-based comparisons of cases and counsel.

9. Leveraging counsel's work product and communications through the collaborative network can reduce wasted effort per case, vendor fees, and overnight express, fax, and copying charges, thus creating a win-win situation for both client and counsel.

10. Using an extranet can enable counsel to avoid contention caused by reducing hourly rates and transferring responsibility for expenses to outside firms.

Mike Curreri is a principal in the national litigation firm of Wright, Robinson, Osthimer & Tatum and developer and president of TrialNet, Inc., the nation's leading litigation management intranet/extranet provider. His practice focuses on civil litigation and litigation management, primarily in the areas of products liability and medical malpractice.

The Trialnet web site is at http://www.trialnet.com.

Debbie Steele's Top Ten Internet Uses for Paralegals

1. Perform legal research. Although still not a total substitute for other sources, the Internet can in many instances provide fast, accurate legal information. Two good starting points are http://www.findlaw.com and http://www.abanet.org/lawlink/home.html.

2. Conduct factual research. For example, an excellent starting point for health and medical research is http://www.healthfinder.gov. For consumer product safety information, try http://cpsc.gov.

3. Locate missing people, including defendants, witnesses, and heirs. Two good search tools are http://www.yahoo.com/search/people and http://www.whowhere.com.

4. Use the Net for professional development. One good starting point is the National Federation of Paralegal Associations at http://www.paralegals.org, which includes employment information, an online newsletter, and other resources.

5. When appropriate, use e-mail to communicate instead of phone, fax, or letter.

6. Locate information about lawyers and law firms through online legal directories such as Martindale-Hubbell at http://www.martindale.com/locator/home.html or West's Legal Directory at http://www.wld.com.

7. Use the Net to find information about courts. The Villanova Center for Information Law and Policy has two good starting points: the Federal Court Locator at http://www.law.vill.edu/Fed-Ct/fedcourt.html, and the State Court Locator at http://www.law.vill.edu/State-Ct.

8. Obtain corporate and other information from secretary of state offices, many of which are now online. For example:
   - Illinois at http://www.sos.state.il.us/home.html
   - Georgia at http://www.sos.state.ga.us
   - California at http://www.ss.ca.gov
   - Texas at http://www.sos.state.tx.us

9. Become a software guru by exploring sites related to the software your firm uses. For information about Microsoft products, try the Microsoft Legal Home Page at http://www.microsoft.com/industry/legal. For WordPerfect information, try Corel's site at http://www.corel.com/products/index.htm.

10. Develop a solid basic understanding of how your browser, probably Netscape Navigator or Microsoft Internet Explorer, and various search engines, such as InfoSeek, Yahoo, and AltaVista, work. This will enable you to conduct effective searches for new sources of information.

Deborah B. Steele is an attorney and legal educator in Charlotte, North Carolina. She can be reached at dbsteele@bellsouth.net.

Tom Strassburg's Tips for Starting and Operating a Mailing List for Lawyers

1. Select a service provider or administrator with proven ability to use mailing list software.
2. Provide clear instructions on how to subscribe to the list.
3. Advertise the availability of the list widely in both print and electronic media.
4. State the purposes and policies of the list in a welcome message, along with information on how to use the list and how to unsubscribe.
5. Make sure the service provider or administrator conceals the e-mail addresses of subscribers to make it difficult for those who might try to collect such addresses for commercial purposes.
6. Don't use the list for commercial purposes yourself.
7. Read all messages posted to the list and comment to the entire list if the discussion is not in keeping with the list's purposes and policies.
8. Be sensitive to any discussion that could be considered an antitrust violation.
9. Promptly warn (by private message) any subscriber who posts a commercial or other inappropriate message to the list.
10. Encourage subscribers to use private messages rather than messages to the entire list to respond to inquiries or requests for help that would not be of interest to other subscribers.

Tom Strassburg is assistant director for publications with Virginia CLE and is the "list owner" of the Virginia Attorneys Network mailing list. The Virginia CLE Web site is at http://www.vacle.org.

Ross Kodner's Top Ten Internet Networking Tips

The Internet offers lawyers in public, private, and corporate law practice the penultimate medium for interactive networking. It is better than Rotary meetings, better than being on one's church or synagogue board, and better than weekend kids' soccer matches. Why? Because it's a twenty-four-hour-a-day, seven-day-a-week virtual talkfest. Discussion happens everywhere all the time. The following tips are focused on how and where to network and what to say—or not to say.

1. Get on an e-mail mailing list. E-mail discussion lists, sometimes referred to as "listservs," are the ultimate collegial communications tool. A mailing list is a way to have a simultaneous ongoing discussion on specific substantive or practice management or legal technology topics with hundreds or even thousands of fellow lawyers.
2. Have a purpose. In other words, know what you want to accomplish. For example, your goal might be to find a group of lawyers you feel comfortable enough with to use for referrals on matters that you can't handle. Or you might want to get the word out that you're an expert on a particular substantive topic and can help people or accept referrals in a specific area.
3. Take it easy when signing up for mailing lists. The volume of daily messages that comes through on mailing lists can be absolutely staggering. For example, on the ABA's SOLOSEZ list, oriented to solo and small firm lawyers, seventy to one hundred messages a day are not uncommon. Sign up for four or five mailing lists and you can quickly find yourself swimming in a totally unmanageable sea, teeming with hundreds of messages in a single day. Start with one or two mailing lists. See if you like them, get used to the volume, then consider adding more or switching to other mailing lists that might be more pertinent to your needs.
4. Check out legal-specific usenet newsgroups. These can be somewhat neater, cleaner versions of listservs. Newsgroups are more like public bulletin boards—no e-mail is involved. You need "newsreader" software, such as Forte's popular Free Agent at http://www.forteinc.com. The software can also be built into Netscape Navigator/Communicator and Microsoft's Internet Explorer (if you add the Internet News component to IE). You use it to look at the postings on the virtual bulletin board and then reply to any of them. Others see your reply and post their own

responses. If mailing lists are a voluntary "push" product—with e-mails sent to you automatically if you voluntarily subscribe—then newsgroups are a voluntary "pull" system—you have to go to the messages, they don't automatically come to you.

5. Learn the tone, tenor, and "customs" of the mailing lists or newsgroup. You can't network if you're seen as the proverbial bull in the china shop. Many such discussion lists have evolved into genuine virtual communities where regular participants become quite friendly and develop a set of mores and communication standards. It can be very easy to alienate an entire group if you don't follow basic netiquette standards.

6. Do not confuse networking with spamming. Spamming is the ultimate breach of netiquette. In the case of a couple of Tennessee lawyers, it led to disbarment—yes, you read that correctly. Spamming is the process of sending unrequested, uninvited, and unwanted advertising to users via e-mail or posting the same to a newsgroup. People will hate you, publicly vilify you, and bombard you with nasty e-mails. So never post a message to a discussion group that says something like, "Hi, I'm John and I'm a great personal injury lawyer. If you've been hurt in an accident and are tired of getting the runaround from insurance companies, contact me NOW! And get a free key chain just for the call!" This is completely verboten.

7. Be helpful—build a reputation in your virtual community and business will come. If you are a helpful participant in discussions, give more advice than you ask for, and especially, if you take the time to provide well-reasoned, concise information to discussion group participants, your chances of being perceived as a credible expert worthy of a direct contact when services are needed increases substantially. Don't expect overnight miracles. It takes time to build a virtual reputation, but the Net effect can be quite powerful.

8. As with live networking, the key is to have people think of your name first in connection with whatever service you offer, or want to offer. So, for example, if someone has an environmental matter in northern Virginia, they immediately think of calling John XYZ because John XYZ is a lawyer in the area who is an active and apparently quite knowledgeable participant in an environmental law mailing list. It happens all the time.

9. To find law practice-oriented discussion lists, go to the ultimate source: Lyonette Louis-Jacques List of Law Lists at

http://www.lib.uchicago.edu/~llou/lawlists/info.html. This is a massive collection of information about legal listservs with descriptions of mailing lists focus and subscription information. It's also fully searchable by keyword with instructions at the site.

10. Above all, network patiently, but consistently. Persistence pays off, as with live networking. You need to build a positive reputation in the virtual communities you participate in. As when networking with "liveware" (also referred to as people), pushiness and blatant self-promotion are the ultimate networking turnoff. Credible helpfulness without obvious or direct self-promotion is always appreciated and will ultimately help you reap rich rewards.

Ross Kodner is a Wisconsin lawyer who saw the light thirteen years ago and formed MicroLaw, a nationally focused legal technology consultancy and systems integrator. He is also a founding principal, along with Susan Ross, of CLEgal, LLC, an organization focused on providing top-quality legal technology CLE seminars worldwide. He is a frequent national presenter and author on the whole range of legal technology topics and is the developer of the "PaperLESS Office" process. He can be reached via http://www.microlaw.com or rkodner@ix.netcom.com.

Greg Siskind's Ten Internet Marketing Tips for Lawyers

1. Have a well-developed Internet marketing plan that defines your market, your services, your target clientele, and your competition. Incorporate the plan into your firm's overall marketing plan.
2. Choose a domain name for your e-mail address and Web site that helps distinguish your firm. Consider using your firm name, geographic area, or area of concentration in your domain name.
3. Treat e-mails like telephone calls—have a policy of responding in twenty-four hours or less.
4. Use signature blocks in your e-mail and newsgroup messages that provide key marketing information—your name, phone number, practice areas, and Web address. Remember to include any necessary disclaimers.
5. Build a Web site and keep it fresh in content. Make sure you identify prominently the date of the most recent changes and have a "What's New" page letting people know where to find

the site's changes. Repeat Web site visits lead to name recognition. Name recognition leads to business.

6. Design a Web site that loads quickly and is easy to navigate. And avoid adding high-tech elements that are more tacky than useful.

7. Develop a content strategy that incorporates promotional, informative, and interactive elements. But more important, gear your strategy to the target audience—existing clients, referring lawyers, and potential clients.

8. Stay out of trouble by attentively complying with ethics rules and "netiquette" standards.

9. Fine-tune your marketing efforts by using a sophisticated server log to carefully measure your site's ratings.

10. Remember to publicize your Web site. Get your site linked by other sites and listed in search engines. Blend your online marketing into your traditional marketing—incorporate your Web and e-mail addresses into your letterhead, business cards, fax cover sheets, Yellow Page ads, and brochures.

Gregory H. Siskind is a partner at Siskind, Susser, Haas & Devine, an immigration law firm with offices in the United States and Canada. He practices out of the firm's Nashville and Memphis, Tennessee, offices. He was one of the first lawyers in the country to establish a Web site for his firm. His firm's immigration law newsletter, distributed via e-mail and at the Siskind, Susser, Haas & Devine. Home Page, is read by tens of thousands people every month. He is also the author of the ABA's *Lawyer's Guide to Marketing on the Internet.*

Guy Alvarez's Top Ten Tips for Lawyer Marketing via E-mail Discussion Groups

1. Find an electronic mailing list on a familiar topic or one in which you have particular expertise. To find such a mailing list, you may use Lyo's Law Lists at
   http://www.lawlib.uchicago.edu/cgi-bin/law-lists.

2. Get to know the mailing list before you start posting. See what kind of messages are being posted and by whom. Get a feel for the tone of the discussions.

3. Your first post should be an introductory post. Introduce yourself and your area of practice or expertise.

4. Make sure you have a signature file at the end of all your posts that includes your name, address, e-mail, phone, and URL. You may also want to have a catchy phrase or quote.

5. Check your e-mail frequently. There may be a post or question which may represent a perfect opportunity for you to demonstrate your expertise and your willingness to help others on the list. Being first to answer is always beneficial.

6. Find out if the list has an archive or FAQ file. Read the archives to find out what topics have already been discussed and by whom.

7. If the mailing list allows, send a "who is" or "review" command to find out who else is subscribed to the list and how many subscribers the list has. You may be interested to know who the other subscribers are.

8. If someone else on the mailing list has beaten you in providing a quick answer to a post, find a way to add to or enhance that particular answer. Whenever possible point to information that is already online, and if you do, always give the URL.

9. Be on the lookout for items of interest to those on the mailing list. Scan the daily periodicals and law journals for news or other items of interest and volunteer them to the mailing list.

10. Never use an auto-responder or post information that may be deemed self-serving or off the topic. Make sure you learn the rules of netiquette.

Guy Alvarez, an attorney and nationally recognized Internet expert to the legal profession, has written many articles on the Internet for lawyers. He is presently Director of Internet Operations for KPMG Peat Marwick, LLP: http://www.kpmg.com.

Kenneth Johnson's Top Ten Web Site Design Technical Tips

1. Avoid poor organization. A Web site that isn't logically designed is difficult to navigate and visitors to the site are unlikely to come back. Your site should be hierarchically arranged, dividing information into sections like chapters in a book, with each section made up of individual Web pages.

2. Don't put too much on the page. Individual Web pages should be small and focused on one topic, with links to related pages.

Large pages take a long time to download (and are difficult to read on screen), and some visitors may lose patience and go somewhere else.

3. Don't go overboard on graphics. Keep graphics short and sweet. Large graphics take a long time to download. Keep graphic size under 30K, limit the number of graphics per page, and use the same graphic on multiple pages—so that it only needs to be downloaded once.

4. Use alternate text for graphics. Alternate text is what displays in the visitor's browser when the browser cannot display graphics or the user has graphics turned off. The text should reflect what the graphic shows and its function, particularly if the graphic is being used as a link.

5. Avoid misspellings and grammatical errors. It's easy to overlook these word processing tools when dealing with HTML. But there is no excuse for these types of mistakes, which reflect poorly on your firm.

6. If you use blue pages, include text. Blue pages are pages of nothing but links, which typically show up as blue, underlined text. In addition to being hard to read, they provide no context about what the link is and why users might want to go there. Include some text.

7. Avoid out-of-date links. External links should be checked frequently to make sure they are still valid; if not, correct the URL or take it out completely. You're likely to be blamed when someone else changes their URL.

8. Don't use "under construction" signs. These are used to show that a page or section of the site isn't ready for viewing. If it's not ready, don't make it accessible.

9. Avoid designing your site for only one browser. Designing for only one browser can make pages virtually unreadable in others, and tells visitors they must use the browser you want them to.

10. Make sure to test the design. Broken links, bad formatting, slow downloading, and missing graphics show you didn't have enough professionalism to check the site before posting it.

Kenneth E. Johnson is the author of *The Lawyer's Quick Guide to E-mail* and *The Lawyer's Guide to Creating Web Pages,* both published by the ABA's Law Practice Management Section. He operates the excellent WWWScribe web site: http://wwwscribe.com.

Bernard Hibbitts' Top Ten Web Publishing Tips for Lawyers and Law Professors

1. Write brief articles, or "chunk" large articles into several separate files. Long scrolling is awkward, and large HTML files can take a while to download. Your Web publications will be more user-friendly if you keep them short, or at least chunk them into more manageable segments posted as separate, interlinked Web pages.

2. If you chunk a larger piece, provide an integral version for printing. Especially if your article or memo is lengthy, many users will prefer to print it rather than read it on the screen. If you have segmented your text into several different files, make printing easier by also providing an integral version that can be printed all at once. This version can be in HTML, in WordPerfect (allowing footnotes at the bottom of a page), or in a special format like Portable Document Format (PDF), which standardizes a document's appearance on differently configured systems. Better still, provide integral versions in all of these forms, thus allowing users to choose what's best for them.

3. Enhance text articles with relevant and helpful hypertext and multimedia. It's tempting just to dump existing print pieces on-line, but resist the temptation. Take advantage of the Web medium (and reward site visitors for using it) by using hypertext to connect them with helpful external sources of information. Use multimedia (as appropriate, of course) to add depth, heighten interest, and increase memorability.

4. Provide hypertext-based tables of contents and footnotes. Use hypertext to enhance navigability within your document. Footnote numbers should be hyperlinked to footnotes, and vice versa. In longer documents, a hyperlinked table of contents is also useful, allowing users to move instantly to any part of the document in which they might be particularly interested.

5. Number your paragraphs and anchor them. A Web document has no page numbers. To make it easier for readers and researchers to cite a particular segment of your work, number the paragraphs, either sequentially across the document or incrementally according to subsection. Also, remember that other writers might want to link directly to a paragraph rather than to the document as whole. You can make this easy by providing internal HTML anchors to individual paragraphs.

6. Provide an e-mail link to yourself. The Web is an inherently interactive medium. Don't forget to include your e-mail address on your document so that readers can get in touch with you with comments or criticisms. Ideally, provide both a "mailto:" HTML command and an obvious e-mail listing (unfortunately, many computers are not properly configured to send e-mail via their Internet browsers).

7. Provide a forum for feedback and dialogue. The e-mail you receive on an article or memo may be both useful to you, and of potential interest to others. Consider constructing a "Readers' Forum" where you can post messages (with permission) and publicly reply to them. You may find that the dialogue that ensues is in some respects more valuable than what you originally wrote.

8. Provide updated versions periodically and archive superseded versions. The Web is a dynamic medium. It's easy to post content, and it's easy to revise content. Revision can be useful to both publishers and readers; it allows authors to develop their ideas (even change their minds!) and it allows readers to gain up-to-date information. Revision is also one means of bringing readers back to your document even after they've read it once. But don't fall into the trap of throwing away the past. If you update a document, archive its predecessor(s) and make sure readers can access the archive online. Future researchers (not to mention your own conscience) will thank you.

9. Register your document with the appropriate search engines. If you write it, will they come? No. To draw readers to your work you should register it with the most prominent Web search engines and directories. My favorites are Hotbot, Excite, AltaVista, and Infoseek. If you've chunked a large article, consider registering each section separately (under a different subject-based title) so that searchers will be able to reach deep into your document even before they go to your site.

10. Inform related sites of your document's existence. The Web is just that—a connected latticework of sites and documents. Many Web authors find that in the long run most of their traffic comes not from search engine inquiries, but rather from other legal sites that collect links to certain types of documents or publications. If you post a document on, say, tax law, contact some other tax law sites and see if they will link to you. (They may ask for a reciprocal link, but you may actually find providing such a link useful.) The relationships you develop in this process not only will gain you readers, but also will be good for business.

Bernard Hibbitts is associate dean for communications & information technology and professor of law at the University of Pittsburgh School of Law. He learned the ropes of Web publishing by writing several Web-based articles. He also runs JURIST: The Law Professors' Network, an academically-oriented legal information and communications service at http://www.jurist.law.pitt.edu.

Elliot Chabot's Ten Favorite Free Tools for Web Site Design

All sorts of tools are available now to help develop and maintain Web sites—some available for free and some for a fee. These are my ten favorite free tools. In addition to being free, each of these is fairly easy to use and only one involves loading any software down to your machine.

1. For a site that checks to see if your HTML code conforms to various standards, including Netscape, Internet Explorer, HTML 3.2, and the draft HTML 4.0 standard, try WebTechs HTML Validation Service at http://www.webtechs.com/html-val-svc.
2. For a site that shows how your Web pages would look through a nongraphical Lynx browser, check out Lynx-me at http://ugweb.cs.ualberta.ca/~gerald/lynx-me.cgi. Remember, many people still view the Internet through nongraphical browsers.
3. If you need a site that spell checks and looks for broken links, go to Doctor HTML at http://www2.imagiware.com/RxHTML.
4. For a site that provides a basic analysis of the traffic on your Web site, including who is accessing your site, when, and how often, try Analog at http://www.statslab.cam.ac.uk/~sret1/analog. This is the only one of my ten free favorites that you have to install on your machine to use.
5. If you want a site that improves how efficiently your Web site stores and transmits images, go to GIF Wizard at http://www.gifwizard.com. With this tool, I have often been able to cut by half the amount of data I need to transmit an image—without losing any appreciable quality in the image.
6. For thousands of free images, check out Barry's Clip Art Server at http://www.barrysclipart.com. This is a great resource when you're not in a position to create original images.
7. To rate the level of sex, violence, commercialism, and other aspects of your site and then translate the rating into an HTML code, try SafeSurf PICS Label Generator at http://www.safesurf.com/classify/index.html.

8. Another useful site for rating purposes is RSACi PICS Label Generator at http://www.rsac.org.

9. Another rating site is Vancouver Web pages Rating Service PICS Label Generator at http://vancouver-webpages.com/VWP1.0/VWP1.0.gen.html. To some extent a response to the Communications Decency Act and similar legislation, these three sites all allow you to rate the level of sex, violence, commercialism, and other aspects of your site and then translate the rating into an HTML code. The codes use the SafeSurf, Recreational Software Advisory Council on the Internet, and Vancouver Web pages implementations (respectively) of the World Wide Web Consortium's PICS standard. Internet Explorer comes with an option (which may be available in Netscape and other browsers at some point) to lock out sites that lack an appropriate PICS label.

10. For an article on Web design, check out "Thoughts on Web Design" at http://law.house.gov/design/design.htm. A lot of articles have been written about good Web design. This is the one that I wrote. It contains lots of practical tips.

Elliot Chabot is a Washington, D.C., attorney known for his expertise at Internet legal research and skill at designing Web sites.

Randy Singer's Ten Internet Resources for Lawyers Using Macintosh Computers

1. The Law Office Software List for the Macintosh Computer features a list of all the available software for law office use on the Macintosh computer at http://www.macattorney.com.

2. The Mac-Attorney e-mail discussion list is the premier discussion list for legal professionals who use the Macintosh computer. This is the place to bring your questions, exchange tips, and meet other lawyers who share the Macintosh advantage. To subscribe send a blank message to: macattorney-digest@lists.macattorney.com. Be sure to turn off any automatic signature feature in your e-mail program. You can put anything that you want into the subject line of the message.

3. The MacLaw Admin list is for IS personnel at large Macintosh-only law firms. To subscribe, send a message to

requests@connecticutlawyers.net with the message body only
subscribe digest MacLaw Admin.

4. The American Bar Association's Apple/Macintosh Interest Group
   is among the ABA's most popular, at http://www.abanet.org/lpm/mac/
   home.html.

5. Order a free copy of The Macintosh Law Office Software Product
   Guide by sending e-mail to randy@mother.com. This is a 100+ page
   guide in Word format. Please be clear when ordering that you
   want a copy of the Macintosh Law Office Sofware Product Guide.

6. "Confessions of a Mac Attorney," by Bradley Handler, Esq., is
   an excellent article by a San Francisco attorney who decided
   to use a Macintosh in a large, otherwise all Windows/Intel-us-
   ing law firm. It contains extensive footnotes and hot links to
   references. You can find it at http://www.mother.com/~randy/
   confession.html.

7. Lawyers are not the only ones in the legal field who find the
   Mac makes practicing easier and more productive. For Macs and
   the Judiciary, go to http://www.halcyon.com/kegill/mac/uses/law.html.

8. The Macintosh is a major player in the law office market in
   Canada. I am told that three of the five largest law firms in
   Canada are all-Macintosh shops. Law Office Software For Cana-
   dian Macintosh Users, at http://www.terraport.net/lawyers/mac, also
   contains the fine article "Macintosh in the Small Law Office," by
   Peter Cusimano, at http://www.terraport.net/lawyers/articles/macoffc.htm.

9. Are lawyers who use Macs better and more productive lawyers?
   That is the experience of the New Orleans law firm of Adams &
   Reese at http://www.arlaw.com. With more than 120 lawyers in its
   offices, one of the largest law firms in Louisiana and the Gulf
   South uses Macintoshes for everything from legal research on
   the Internet to preparing briefs for the Supreme Court. Articles
   from *Computer Counsel* magazine about the use of Macs by
   lawyers are reprinted at the Adams and Reese Web site at
   http://www.arlaw.com/pubarticles/ccarticle/ccarticle.html.

10. What's that you say? No law firms use Macs? You might consider
    using a Mac if other firms used it? Check out these two links. A
    couple of listservs carried the question of how many law firms
    use Macintoshes. The responses were overwhelming. The Web
    pages below list several hundred such firms, some huge, some
    tiny. Plenty of law firms understand, and make use of, the Mac
    advantage. Check out http://www.mother.com/~randy/attylist.html and
    http://www.mother.com/~randy/attylist2.html. Honorable Mention:

MacInTouch home page by Rick Ford of MacWeek at http://www.macintouch.com. The premier source for getting the latest information about new Macintosh products, developments within Apple, and news of software and hardware issues for Macintosh users.

Randy B. Singer is an attorney practicing in San Francisco, California. He is an experienced civil litigator, one of the co-authors of *The Macintosh Bible* (the world's best-selling book about the Macintosh computer) and an Apple Legal Fellow.

Patrick Wiseman's Top Ten Ways the Internet Will Affect Legal Education

1. Students, other students, and their teachers will hold in-depth discussions of class material on class-specific e-mail discussion lists and Web sites. This will enhance the law school experience, as it will enable law teachers to monitor and guide their students' learning.
2. By participating in e-mail discussion lists such as Cyberia and Net-Lawyers, students will have easy access to practicing lawyers. This will give students a perspective on the practice of law not otherwise available. Both lists, and many others, are archived at Legalminds: http://www.legalminds.com.
3. Students will find primary legal information available on the Internet, at such sites as Cornell's Legal Information Institute at http://www.law.cornell.edu. They will rely less on proprietary sources of legal information such as LEXIS and Westlaw. This, in turn, will force LEXIS and Westlaw to improve their services.
4. Students will find primary and secondary sources of information, including course outlines, available for all of their courses at such sites as FindLaw, at http://www.findlaw.com. They will thus be better informed and better prepared than ever before.
5. Students will find other student work online at such sites as Law and the Internet at http://gsulaw.gsu.edu/lawand. While this may increase the risk of plagiarism, it will also create opportunities for students to share work with students at other law schools.
6. Syllabi and assignments will be posted on the Web, enabling students to retrieve their assignments while at home, and perhaps saving some trees in the process.

7. Students participating in online discussions will take more care in articulating their thoughts. This will lead to an overall increase in the quality of communication between student and student, professor and student, and eventually, lawyer and client.

8. Students will take exams from home over the Internet, at their own convenience. As a consequence, all exams will be legible, relieving teachers of the task of reading illegible handwriting.

9. Students will learn of and apply for jobs online. An example of an online jobs site is the GSU College of Law at http://gsulaw.gsu.edu/csojobs.

10. Professors will become accustomed to student use of technology. The teacher will be less a "sage on the stage" and more a "guide on the side." Use of these technologies will make students increasingly self-sufficient, and students will become increasingly intolerant of unwired teachers.

Patrick Wiseman is a professor of law at Georgia State University College of Law and the designer of the Metaindex for U.S. Legal Research, http://gsulaw.gsu.edu/metaindex.

Sherry Katz's Top Ten Antivirus Tips

1. Use virus scanning software, and keep it up to date.

2. If you have a particularly serious concern about viruses, use Windows NT rather than Windows 95. Because Windows NT does not allow programs direct access to the computer's hardware, it is less vulnerable to viruses. I've seen macro viruses spread on NT systems though, so it isn't immune.

3. Don't open unidentified e-mail attachments from strangers. Executables are particularly likely to spread viruses, but files containing macros are also suspect.

4. Don't boot with a floppy in the drive unless it is your emergency boot disk.

5. Set your hard drive to attempt to boot from hard disk first. Newer computers will allow the bios setup to be altered to allow for the boot sequence to begin with drive C:.

6. Share files with co-workers through the network, not through floppies. Floppies are particularly pernicious because they can reinfect repeatedly.

7. Don't leave your computer where strangers can get access to it. One office I worked in had a continuing infection problem caused by the night cleaning crew putting virus-infected floppies in the A: drives and booting the computers.

8. Be aware that even commercial software can come on virus-infected disks.

9. Keep a backup of your files in case you do get an infection that forces you to reconstruct your system.

10. Treat co-workers and employees with respect. The biggest threat to any system is a disgruntled employee.

Sheryl L. Katz abandoned a highly successful legal practice to become a technology consultant for law firms. She is a popular speaker at the ABA's annual TECHSHOW and regularly shares her depth of technical knowledge with the legal community in online discussion groups.

Samuel Lewis's Ten Ways to Protect Your Privacy on the Internet

1. Recognize that because e-mail is composed of plain text, it is a trivial matter for someone to intercept messages. Thus, e-mail has no inherent privacy or security.

2. Recognize that information is big business, and that hackers are becoming information specialists who sell information to the highest bidder. A healthy dose of paranoia and erring on the side of caution is typically safer than revealing sensitive information.

3. Don't send credit card numbers through e-mail. Despite the amount of e-mail that travels across the Internet every day, people referred to as "sniffers" will use software to find sequences of credit card numbers in your e-mail as it travels to its destination on the Internet.

4. Use a firewall. If your office is connecting to the Internet, make sure you use a firewall—a secure system that prevents unauthorized access from the Internet—between your Internet connection and the network in your office. Without a firewall, every computer on your office network is potentially vulnerable to an invasion by someone on the Internet.

5. Read the service agreement you have with your Internet service provider (ISP). Many people don't realize that their ISP may have the right to read their e-mail, monitor Internet activity, and even reveal information they discover to third parties without any liability. Most ISPs use some sort of agreement, even if you don't realize it.

6. Don't send plain-text messages. One way to protect the contents of your messages is to send them in binary form (i.e., a WordPerfect document file). The binary messages, when sent through e-mail, look like garbage. This is also referred to as the poor man's encryption. Note, however, that this method is not foolproof.

7. Use encryption. This is the only way to ensure your privacy on the Internet. Best of all, advancements in software in the past year or so give computer novices access to technology so sophisticated that the U.S. government doesn't want it exported. For more information about simple, military-strength encryption, take a look at the Pretty Good Privacy (PGP) Web site at http://www.pgp.com.

8. Understand what needs to be encrypted and what doesn't. Information that is not sensitive or private doesn't need to be protected (e.g., the time for your lunch meeting). Make your determination based on the contents of the message, and when in doubt, encrypt (always err on the side of caution).

9. Concern yourself with physical as well as virtual security. You may have the most secure e-mail in the world, yet someone can walk into your office, sit down at your computer, and read your sensitive information. If you are concerned with maintaining your privacy on the Internet, also concern yourself with maintaining privacy in your office and your home.

10. If you're in an office setting, hire a consultant who understands security. As quickly as methods are developed to protect your privacy, methods are also developed to invade your privacy. Make sure that the consultant you hire is not only able to put a security plan into operation, but also keeps up with the latest security updates.

Sam Lewis is an attorney with the firm of Romanik, Lavin, Huss & Paoli (http://www.rlhp.com), in Hollywood, Florida, an adjunct professor of law at the Shepard Broad Law Center, Nova Southeastern University, Fort Lauderdale, Florida, and a member of the Florida Bar Computer Law Committee. He may be reached at slewis@CompLaw.com and http://www.CompLaw.com/ ~slewis.

Susan Ross's Top Ten Internet Ethics Tips for Lawyers

1. Have an Internet and e-mail policy. Whether you include it in your computer use policy or put it under separate cover, be clear about who owns your internal and Internet e-mail, and then communicate that information to your employees. The same is true for use of the Web and other features of the Internet. Be aware that you may be compelled to turn over e-mail during discovery or under a court order. And recommend the same types of policies for your clients.

2. Remember that an e-mail spelling checker is not a proofreader. The spelling check feature on your e-mail can be a great time-saver for those of us who never made the finals of the spelling bee—but don't rely on it for anything more than that. A spelling checker cannot identify incorrect word choices that are properly spelled or identify missing words. For example, nothing is worse than sending an e-mail to a client saying that the buyer is liable when in fact the buyer is not liable.

3. Understand how technology is affecting the practice of law. The Internet is blurring state, federal, and international jurisdictional lines. The proliferation of e-mail is changing what to look for during discovery. The law is changing for personal jurisdiction, discovery, and contracts. Keeping up on the Internet may mean the difference between competently practicing law and a trip before your state's disciplinary board. The best place to keep up with some of these changes is through one of the many available electronic mailing lists, such as NET-LAWYERS. Alternatively, consider some of the publications that cover technology and the law, such as *The Internet Lawyer.* Even well-established publications, such as *Time, Newsweek,* and *Fortune* magazines address these issues.

4. Have antivirus software. Although you don't have to be on the Internet to get a virus, the Internet provides another avenue for a virus to invade your computer. Antivirus software, such as Norton's Anti-Virus or McAfee's VirusScan, may protect you, whether the sneaky little devil arrives via diskette or the Internet. By the way, as of this writing, you cannot get a virus from e-mail, but you can get a virus from e-mail with an attachment.

5. Keep current with new ethics opinions. State bar associations around the country have issued ethics opinions on the use of

the Internet in your practice, addressing everything from the propriety of advertising on the Internet to the security of e-mail to what a lawyer's standard of care should be when maintaining client information online. One of the best places to keep up to date on these issues is http://www.legalethics.com.

6. Don't keep your passwords for your Internet access, your computer, or for the various subscription Web sites where others can see them. Many of us can never remember the day of the week let alone a myriad of passwords. But leaving a password on a piece of paper taped to the computer is like leaving keys in the ignition of an unlocked car. Don't use obvious passwords, and change passwords frequently.

7. Be aware of the potential security risks of using e-mail and visiting various Web sites as well as the risk of allowing your lawyer to access your computer system remotely from your internal network. Maintaining a duty of confidentiality and the attorney-client privilege have become the prime directives for lawyers. Understanding the risks of having Internet access and using its features can help you maintain your clients' confidences.

8. Don't let the risks prevent you from getting online. Cars can get you to your destination quickly and safely. This doesn't mean that accidents don't happen, but the risks don't stop us from getting out on the road. We simply take appropriate precautions. The same is true with the Internet. And failing to use the Internet may be akin to failing to check the pocket parts in a paper reference book.

9. Always request any relevant electronic information during discovery. In the midst of discovery, failing to request e-mail or other electronic information may mean that you are missing many of the relevant facts for your client's case. As e-mail use proliferates, business communications will migrate from paper files to electronic ones.

10. Get some training. It's what some colleagues of mine and I call the "three and three rule": we took three years to get through law school, so it is worth taking three days now to learn how to surf the Net or how to encrypt e-mail.

Susan Ross is a lawyer with Piper & Marbury in Washington, D.C., http://www.pipermar.com. An engineer before becoming a lawyer, she is one of the country's most respected Internet trainers for lawyers and is known for her work in legal ethics issues arising from lawyer use of technology.

Peter Krakaur's Top Ten Internet Acceptable Use Policy Tips

1. Create a unique acceptable use policy. Your acceptable use policy (AUP) should be designed to addresses your firm's culture and technical infrastructure. There is no model AUP that you can adopt wholesale.

2. Define permissible and prohibited uses. Your AUP should define the permissible workplace Internet uses, prohibited uses, and general rules of online behavior. Define acceptable personal use, if applicable. The AUP should also address violations of the policy, including security violations and vandalism of the system.

3. Implement the policy. A policy that is not enforced is almost as good as no policy at all. Do not write the policy, distribute it, and let it lie on the shelf. Consider what mechanism you will use to ensure that employees have read and accepted the terms of the AUP. Anyone using a company's Internet and intranet should be required to sign the AUP and know that it will be kept on file as a binding document.

4. Address at least ethics, copyright, employment, and privacy issues. Legal professionals must comply with specific ethics rules. Internet technology, in turn, raises a number of unique copyright, employment, security, and privacy issues. Be aware of the source of the policy if you plan to fine-tune it to your needs. Many of the off-the-shelf policies available on the Internet today were drafted for libraries or universities, not law firms. Understand and address all rules of the jurisdictions in which all your legal professionals are licensed to practice.

5. Track compliance. Depending on the nature of your computer network and your firm's culture, you may need to implement a system to track compliance with your AUP. This may involve creating a system to track Internet and computer use or simply updating employees on additions to or modifications of the AUP.

6. Design the policy to protect employer and employee. Remember that AUPs protect both employers and employees. A properly designed AUP can go a long way toward protecting employers against harassment or privacy claims by employees and against vicarious liability for illegal uses. It also can serve as a guide for employee conduct.

7. Create an extra security layer. Viruses and frivolous use can negatively affect the network, perhaps damaging or destroying firm

and client files. Many security breaches are the result of poor security planning, not of malicious hackers. AUPs make the risks associated with passing confidential information over the Internet clear to employees and help protect the firm's network.

8. Make sure your policies are consistent. Are all firm policies (e.g., e-mail, Internet, communications, intranet, general discipline, workplace) consistent in their approach and implementation? For example, are your AUP's provisions regarding e-mail retention consistent with the firms practice? Craft the AUP to ensure a consistent approach.

9. Create a point of contact. Appoint one person or a committee to act as a contact for questions on the policy, to monitor compliance with the policy, and to update the policy in light of new developments with technology and within the firm.

10. Provide training. It is easy to get carried away with rules on security and employee performance. A properly trained staff will understand the issues better. This is likely to reduce the need to create detailed rules. The Internet and associated technology is relatively new. Don't assume that everyone understands the nuances and issues of this new mode of communication.

Peter Krakaur is an attorney and the president of Internet Legal Services. Among other Web sites, he designed and maintains the Legal Ethics site, http://www.legalethics.com.

Philip Harter's Ten Ways the Internet Will Change the Judiciary

1. Judges will use the Internet to research a wide variety of topics related to cases before them to obtain a better understanding of factual issues.

2. Judges will receive continuing judicial education online as new legislation is passed or new court rules are adopted rather than waiting for the annual judicial seminar.

3. Judges will present questions they may have to electronic mailing lists or Web-based discussion groups for judges and receive answers quickly from judges who may have encountered similar situations.

4. Judges will be able to access appellate cases within hours of the decisions being handed down.
5. Judges will receive materials, such as briefs, electronically and be able to select, copy, and paste portions of such materials into their opinions.
6. Judges will access libraries of information provided by other judges, including such things as specialized jury instructions, checklists, bench guides, etc.
7. Judges will communicate with other judges and attorneys by e-mail.
8. Judges will receive material in electronic format by e-mail which will enable them to immediately incorporate it into their work.
9. Judges will provide the public with information about their local court, local procedures, and the law through the development of court web sites.
10. Judges will have files scanned and digitally stored so that they may be accessed remotely by attorneys and the public moving closer to a paperless court system.

Philip Harter is a probate judge in Calhoun County, Michigan, and is Chair of the Michigan Probate Judges Special Committee on Technology.

Wendy Leibowitz's Top Ten Ways Lawyers Will Change the Internet

1. Lawyers will drag the courts into the twenty-first century and onto the Internet by insisting on easy access to court records, conveniences such as scheduling via e-mail, and, as bandwidth improves, live Internet videoconferencing to replace "docket calls."
2. User-friendly will really mean user-friendly: If lawyers can use it, anyone can use it.
3. Before someone copies and circulates a song, code, or essay from the Net, they will ask, "Is this copyrighted?"
4. Once lawyers master the technology, they will demand that it perform perfectly. Technical standards will struggle to meet lawyer standards.
5. Substantive thought and writing will at long last appear on the Net, complete with footnotes, to supplement the opinionated rantings that currently pass for Net thought.

6. Because most of us are bibliophiles at heart, we will teach others in cyberspace that books will never disappear. We'll use the Internet if our clients insist, and if we find that it improves our service to clients, but as long as lawyers are alive and well, there will always be a place for books, newspapers, newsletters, pocket parts, advance sheets, galley proofs, treatises, heavy volumes, indices, lengthy law review articles, notes, and Post-It notes.

7. After a few lawsuits, software reliability will improve—Windows 2010 will actually appear on January 1, 2010, and if it crashes, it will be replaced at no charge.

8. Internet legal humor will reach new heights: As lawyers, we can laugh at ourselves, but lawyer jokes by now have gotten old and lame. Jokes told by lawyers poke fun at the system, at human frailties, and at human pride and greed. Check out any legal elecronic mailing list for the finest in Internet humor.

9. Literary skills on the Net will improve. Spelling, grammar, punctuation, and sentence structure are now optional on the Net, but after you've had your Web site or Usenet posting dissected by a lawyer who notes that the absence of a semicolon blurs the distinction between two separate concepts, people may post in a more literate manner (after they flame the lawyer first).

10. Lawyers will perfect the disclaimer: People will be able to post freely and the exact status of their remarks will be clear, thanks to the fine disclaimers at the end of e-mail postings. My personal favorite, from Kevin J. Connolly of New York's Eaton & Van Winkle: "If this were legal advice, it would come with an invoice."

Wendy R. Leibowitz is the technology editor of the *National Law Journal*. Her columns are archived at http://www.ljx.com/tech/wendy/techarchive.html. Her motto is "Remember, even pencils break."

Appendices

APPENDIX **A**

Other Internet Tools

E-mail and the World Wide Web are far from being the only worthwhile Internet tools. This appendix highlights some other Internet features that can benefit lawyers. For a more detailed orientation, Fred T. Hofstetter's *Internet Literacy* (Irwin/McGraw-Hill, 1997) is a good tutorial. The book has an accompanying Web site, designed by Pat Sine, at http://www.udel.edu/interlit.

Telnet

Telnet is an Internet protocol that allows you to connect to a remote host computer on the Internet as if you had a terminal attached to that computer. Some libraries use it for access to card catalogs. At this time, for example, the Library of Congress catalog is available only via telnet. The address is: telnet://locis.loc.gov.

Other proprietary databases are available only through telnet. In some cases, you are given a UNIX command prompt after connecting. (This is similar to looking at a DOS C:\ prompt, circa 1984.) On other systems, including the Library of Congress catalog, you are given menus.

Telnet can be handy when you are away from home. If you can find a guest account somewhere, you can use telnet to contact most types of home accounts to retrieve your e-mail without incurring long-distance charges. If your firm's lawyers travel frequently, you can save money by establishing one or more accounts with an ISP like Netcom or a service like CompuServe or America Online that has a multitude of local access phone numbers (called POPs, for points of presence) across the country. When they are on the road, your lawyers can make local calls to access these accounts and then use telnet to access their home accounts.

Hytelnet offers a search engine for publicly accessible telnet sites. The URL is http://www.einet.net/hytelnet/HYTELNET.html. In addition, many Web browsers let you use telnet by entering a URL in this format:

telnet://telnetaddress.com

Microsoft Windows 95 and 98 have a built-in telnet program. (Try Start, then Run, then type in *telnet*).

At one time, all Internet users needed to understand telnet, but the need to learn it is lessening as more information is made available through the Web.

File Transfer Protocol

File transfer protocol, commonly *ftp,* is a method used to transfer files between distant computers on the Internet. Some computers with files available for transfer control access through requiring a user name and password, while others allow *anonymous ftp.* Use the word "anonymous" as the login name and your e-mail address as the password. These computers are open to the public. Some law firms run ftp sites that are restricted to those who know a specified login name and password. They distribute these login names and passwords privately to clients or others to provide those parties with file access.

You can use ftp from the UNIX command line if you have a shell account, but it requires typing in commands that will seem esoteric for most lawyers.

All Web browsers can download ftp files easily. Simply type in the name of the ftp site ftp://ftp.microsoft.com, navigate to the desired directory by pointing and clicking, then click on the name of the file you want. The software will ask you where you want the new file to be stored. Some Web browsers also allow you to upload files from your computer. Check the documentation.

Some non-Internet Windows programs, like the Norton Navigator file manager program and Word Pro (the flagship Lotus Corporation word processor), include ftp components. These usually are fairly intuitive.

Specialized ftp programs are available for those with heavy-duty ftp needs. The better ones have features like the ability to resume an interrupted download where you left off. Many people recommend a program called Cute FTP. It and other dedicated ftp programs are available at http://www.tucows.com. At that site, once you have selected a location near you, click on "FTP Applications" under "Networking Tools."

Gopher

Gopher is a way of organizing computer information that allows users to navigate and find information on distant computers with a system of text-based hierarchical menus.

Gopher is rapidly losing place to the flashier World Wide Web, which can do all the same things and more. For example, some universities that have gophers have announced that they will no longer be updating them. Some useful information, however, is still only available on gophers, so serious Internet users should know generally what they are.

The Washington and Lee Law Library has a link to all the gophers in the world: gopher://liberty.uc.wlu.edu/11/gophers.

There are two search programs you can use to find information on gophers:

♦ **Jughead**—Searches the full text of a gopher at a particular site
♦ **Veronica**—Searches the menus of gophers worldwide

Yahoo has a list of all Veronica servers at
http://www.yahoo.com/Computers_and_Internet/Internet/Veronica.

Separate gopher client programs used to be popular, but now most people just use their Web browser, which works fine as long as you type in the URL correctly.

Still More Internet Resources

Finger is a utility used to obtain information about organizations or people with Internet connections. For example, from the UNIX command prompt, you would enter: finger president@whitehouse.gov, and some corresponding information would appear. This will usually be bare-bones information, unless the person "fingered" has created a .plan file to make more information about themselves publicly available. For security reasons, many systems don't allow finger access. You can use finger via a UNIX shell account, via telnet to a UNIX shell account, or from the World Wide Web via a *finger gateway*. One popular finger gateway is at the University of Indiana: http://www.cs.indiana.edu/finger/gateway. There are also other uses for finger. Entering the command finger domain.com *may* lead to a directory of people with accounts on the system domain.com. For example, finger bu.edu leads to a directory at Boston University.

Internet radio and video broadcasting lets users listen to or watch "stations" that are not within broadcast reception range. Users can also use it to access archived recordings.

RealAudio, also known as *RealPlayer*, is the best-known audio software. It is available at http://www.real.com. It requires a sound card and speakers for your computer. Legal applications for this technology include the following:

- CLE programs—This is a natural application for RealAudio. Many providers already offer audio CLE programs via the Internet. The Indiana University School of Law offers a variety of RealAudio files at http://www.law.indiana.edu/law/realaudio. Other providers include CLE Now!, a project of the ABA Center for Continuing Legal Education and The CLE Group, http://www.clegroup.com/aba, as well as Law Info, http://www.lawinfo.com, which has many programs produced in cooperation with the San Diego County Bar Association.

- Supreme Court arguments—Recordings of U.S. Supreme Court oral arguments are available at a Northwestern University site, http://oyez.nwu.edu. What better way to learn about appellate advocacy than from masters of the art?

- Research—Some Internet archives contain recordings of interviews and investigative news reports on many topics of interest to lawyers. If, for example, you are litigating a newsworthy case, you may be able to find recordings of interviews with opposing parties, which could be used for impeachment or other purposes. A good collection of starting points is at: http://www.audionet.com.

- Niche marketing—The Internet makes it economically feasible to "broadcast" nationally or internationally with RealAudio to small markets that couldn't be reached otherwise. As the Internet develops, Real Audio broadcasts might become a great place for some lawyers to advertise. The most obvious appeal would be to niche markets, such as Korean-speaking businesspeople, would-be immigrants from China, or listeners to a weekly radio program about bicycling. (There is at least one lawyer in the country who specializes in representing bicyclists in personal injury cases).

Summary of Key Internet Features for Lawyers

Feature	Purpose	Drawbacks	Comments
E-mail	Method for easily sending and receiving electronic messages.	Can become flooded with unwanted messages.	Most valuable Internet feature for most lawyers. Can send and receive e-mail to and from other networks (CompuServe, etc.).
Mailing Lists	System under which e-mail sent to a central location is "echoed" to subscribers.	Can be difficult to learn about relevant lists. Some have low "signal to noise" ratio.	An important e-mail application. Useful for keeping in touch with others who are interested in the same topics. May be public or private, moderated or unmoderated.

Feature	*Purpose*	*Drawbacks*	*Comments*
World Wide Web	A "turbo-charged gopher" system. Easy-to-use point-and-click *hypertext* adds graphics, sound, and even video to the gopher text interface.	Operates slowly if graphics feature is used. It has grown so fast it is difficult to locate the minority of useful sites amid the great mass of worthless ones.	Sometimes called the "Swiss Army Knife of the Internet" because it can be used to access ftp, telnet, e-mail, etc. Easiest to use, most spectacular, and fastest growing Internet feature. You can speed up operations by turning off the graphics feature. Can be used to present information inexpensively to the public through posting of a Web page.
Newsgroups	Collections of e-mail messages on special topics	Most have low "signal to noise" ratio. There are many distracting topics.	Excellent way to obtain free technical support, do research, or get in contact with experts on specialized subjects.
Ftp	Method for transferring files to and from distant computers.	Can be difficult to use unless you have good interface software. Often it is difficult to learn about good files.	Way to download a wide variety of free files, including software updates and bug fixes, copies of Supreme Court decisions on the day of issue, etc.
Gopher	Finding aid that uses user-friendly menus to help locate Internet resources.	Can only use data that someone has linked to a gopher site.	Related search tools are called Jughead and Veronica. Has lost popularity and market share to the Web, which can do the same things and much more.
Telnet	Method for logging into a remote computer and operating it as if you were at a terminal directly connected to that computer.	Most destination computers that allow telnet access require the use of UNIX or other less familiar systems.	Only a few computers offer public telnet access. Can be difficult to navigate after logged into the remote computer.

APPENDIX **B**

Internet Addressing Outline

I. **Why it is desirable for lawyers to understand the Internet addressing system**
   A. So they can use the Internet intelligently. Internet addressing is key to understanding what is happening when you use the Internet. If you understand a few basic principles of the addressing scheme, you can avoid many mistakes and often do some simple troubleshooting when things go wrong. Understanding the addressing scheme is a major step in helping Internet users progress from feeling confused to being in control.
   B. So they understand the factual issues involved enough to function as advocates and advisors in a networked world. As millions of individuals and businesses move onto the Internet, legal and factual issues are beginning to arise in cases that at first glance appear to have nothing to do with the Internet. These frequently involve Internet addressing issues, directly or indirectly.

II. **Internet Protocol addresses**
   A. Internet Protocol (IP) addresses are unique numbers that are assigned to particular computers on the Internet (*hosts*). A typical one looks like this: 201.223.81.7
   B. The system uses these numbers to steer information between computers on the Internet.
   C. In a rare exception to the general Internet rule of benign anarchy, IP addresses (along with domain names, explained next) are allocated by a central authority. Some central control over this function is necessary because if more than one host computer had the exact same IP address, the results would be similar to more than one person having the exact same phone number.

D. IP addresses are occasionally referred to as "dotted quads" because they consist of four numbers separated by periods, or dots.

III. **The Domain Name System**

A. Domain names are assigned to specific Internet host computers that have IP numbers. For example, the National Archives and Records Administration's domain name is nara.gov, and Microsoft's domain name is microsoft.com. You can learn who is behind a certain domain name, including the party's address and telephone number, by searching the whois Web Gateway, operated by InterNIC, at http://www.internic.net/.

B. If domain names seem redundant, it's because they are. Domain names are used primarily because human beings find them easier to remember than the dotted-quad numbers that make up IP addresses.

C. The Domain Name System (DNS) involves computers that maintain databases matching domain names with IP addresses. When you enter a domain name, a computer looks up the corresponding IP number to route your request.

D. Inside of the United States, the three-letter extension at the end of the address gives you an idea of the type of organization with which you are dealing. These are called the *top-level domains*:
   - com refers to a business
   - edu refers to an educational institution
   - net refers to a computer network
   - mil refers to a military body
   - gov refers to a government body
   - org refers to a nonprofit organization

E. Outside of the United States, addresses end in a two-letter extension that identifies the country. For example, au is Australia, de is Germany ("Deutschland"), and hk is Hong Kong.

F. The general rule on domain names is first come, first served. You can't be legaleagle.com if someone has already registered that domain name. A possible exception is if you could show that the prior registrant's usage infringed on your preexisting trademark.

G. Troubleshooting tip: If you receive a "failed DNS lookup" error message when you enter a domain name, try entering the IP address (the numerical equivalent of the domain name), if you know it. It is possible that the error was caused by a failure of the DNS computer. If so, you may be able to bypass the problem by entering the IP address. You can find the IP number that corresponds to a particular domain name in the InterNIC DNS lookup database: http://www.internic.net/cgi-bin/whois/.

H. As of this writing, seven other top-level domain names have been proposed for implementation: firm, store, web, arts, rec, info, and nom.

IV. **E-mail addresses**
   A. This is an example of how e-mail addresses are formatted:
      president@whitehouse.gov. Here is an analysis:
      1. The @ symbol separates the individual identification from the domain.
      2. The part after the @ symbol represents the organization, and some-
         times a particular computer in that organization.

V. **Uniform Resource Locators**
   A. The Uniform Resource Locator (URL) system is a special way of format-
      ting Internet addresses that is used primarily with the World Wide Web.
      This is an example: http://supct.law.cornell.edu/supct/html/96-511.ZS.html. This
      URL leads to a copy of a Supreme Court decision stored on a Web server
      operated by Cornell University Law School.
   B. Here is an analysis of the URL's components (using the preceding ex-
      ample from Cornell University):
      1. The *protocol*. In this case, it is http://, meaning use the Hypertext
         Transfer Protocol. With modern Web browsers, you can often omit
         this part of the URL. However, it is a good idea to include it when
         you are identifying a URL that you want to promote, such as in a
         listserv message or in your signature block. Some software will then
         recognize the address as a Web site, and this makes it easier for others
         to visit it.
      2. *Directions* for navigating in the distant computer (not always used).
         Cornell University has many computers connected to the Internet,
         accessible through the domain name cornell.edu. The section supct.law
         indicates the part of the Cornell system to be accessed, in this case,
         the section of the law school's machine where Supreme Court deci-
         sions are stored. For World Wide Web sites, the most common entry
         here is www. The law school, however, apparently uses a different ma-
         chine from the main Web server.
      3. The *domain name* (explained earlier), in this case, cornell.edu, which is
         owned by Cornell University.
      4. A particular *directory and/or subdirectory* under the particular domain
         (not always necessary). In this example, the desired directory is
         /supct/html.
      5. A particular *file* inside that directory. In this case, you want the file
         96-511.ZS.html. This contains the text of the Communications De-
         cency Act case *Reno v. ACLU*.
         a. It is not always necessary to specify a particular file name. If you
            don't specify a particular file name, the host computer will look
            under the requested domain name or in the specified directory
            for a default entry file. By convention, these are often named

index.html or home.html, or their three-letter extension versions, index.htm or home.htm.

    b. If no file with the default name for that system is present, your browser will usually see a list of all files in that directory, along with information about the files. You can sometimes use this feature to help locate a hard-to-find file. This technique will only work if the directory you are accessing does not contain a file with the default entry file name for that system.

    c. You can make your Web site URL shorter and easier for visitors to reach by giving to the file you want visitors to see first the default file name for your system (index.html or the others listed previously). In this way, you can advertise your law firm's URL as http://www.barrister.com, instead of the longer, less-inviting http://www.barrister.com/welcome.html.

6. Optional URL parts are the *user name* and *password*, which are not needed or included very often. If needed, you insert them between the name of the protocol and the destination, with an @ symbol in between. For example, if you want to use telnet to get to a computer at a destination called cais.com that requires a user name and password, you can add them to the URL, which would then look like this: telnet://username:password@cais.com. Passwords and user names are supported by the protocols that use two forward slashes (e.g., http://, telnet://, ftp://) but by not the others (e.g., mailto:, news:).

7. Another URL part that is usually optional is the *port number* on the computer you are trying to reach. Unless you are trying to reach a host computer that is set up in a nonstandard way, the browser should default to the correct port number, so you don't normally need to enter this information. If needed, append it to the end of the URL after a colon. For example, if you were told that the ABA Web server was operating on port 81 instead of the customary port 80, you would enter the URL as follows: http://www.abanet.org:81.

C. URLs are primarily employed when using a Web browser program (Netscape Navigator, MS Internet Explorer, etc.). Web browsers can be used to access many other Internet areas in addition to the World Wide Web. Different URL headers are used to indicate which type of resource you want to access. Following are examples of URL types:

1. **Gophers**—Gophers are computers on the Internet that structure information in hierarchical text-based menu structures to make it easier to locate. An example is gopher://gopher.nara.gov. This will take you to the main National Archives gopher menu.

2. **File transfer protocol (ftp)**—This is a method of transferring information between computers on the Internet. An example is ftp://ftp.microsoft.com, which leads to a site used to distribute bug fixes and free software.

3. **Telnet**—This is a protocol to let an Internet user at one computer log into a distant computer and perform tasks on it. An example is telnet://lawnet.law.columbia.edu, and the password "lawnet" will get you into a Columbia University Law School System.

4. **E-mail**—An example is mailto:president@whitehouse.gov.

5. **Usenet newsgroups**—An example is news:misc.legal.computing. This discussion group deals with use of computers by lawyers.

6. **World Wide Web**—The Web is a part of the Internet that uses *hypertext* for point-and-click navigation among a variety of other types of Internet sites. Web access programs, or browsers, have been referred to as the "Swiss Army Knives" of the Internet because they can be used to perform many Internet functions that formerly required separate programs. An example is http://www.findlaw.com. This is the location of one of the best legal research sites.

APPENDIX C

Troubleshooting the Web

Because it is more user-friendly and downwardly compatible with older technologies like gopher and ftp, lawyers will use the World Wide Web most often for research purposes. Here are some potential solutions to commonly encountered problems on the Web.

Problem: You get error messages saying something like "Error Number 404, File Not Found," but you believe that the file you are seeking must be there.

Check the URL: Even a small typo, such as leaving a leading blank space or typing a letter in lowercase that should be uppercase, will prevent a connection.

Try truncating the URL: For example, say that you can't access the Supreme Court opinion that is supposed to be at the following Cornell University URL: http://supct.law.cornell.edu/supct/html/96-511.ZS.html. You could delete the file name, in this case 96-511.ZS.html, and try again. In this particular example, you would then see a list of all the files stored in that directory. (There are so many that this will take a few minutes.) You might be able to figure out which file you want from this list, since Cornell's Legal Information Institute uses a logical file naming system.

If deleting the file name doesn't work, you could delete the subdirectory (html/). If that doesn't work, delete the directory (supct/). If you were able to get into the site after any of these deletions, you could then look around for a way to get the file you need or an explanation of why it is unavailable. The site you are trying to contact may have been reorganized. By entering at a higher point in the directory hierarchy, you may be able to navigate to the new location of the information you are seeking, or at least figure out what happened to it.

Problem: You think it's taking too long to download pages.

Turn off your browser's automatic graphics downloading feature: If you are using a modern browser and decide you want to see a particular picture, you can click on it with the right mouse button.

Slim your browser: Installing too many plug-ins (integrated viewer-helper programs) can cause perceived slowness. For example, if you don't visit sites that use Shockwave, RealAudio, or QuickTime, try uninstalling those plug-ins.

Empty your cache: Modern Web browsers store sites you have visited in caches on your hard disk and in RAM. If these become too crowded, they drain resources and slow your browser. In Netscape, you can empty the caches by going to the menu under Options-Network Preferences-Cache.

Avoid the crowds: Remember that popular sites are often crowded. You may not be able to get in, or data transfer could be too slow if you do. You can try the following:

◆ Contact the most popular sites during off hours. With popular sites, it's a lot like the freeway. It's no fun driving to the beach on a Friday afternoon in August. You can make much better time if you drive the same route on Friday morning, and even better if you try it in January. Many people find that they get the fastest Internet connections on weekends, especially Sunday mornings.

◆ Remember that this is a national and also a global system—take time zones into account if you are contacting a popular site. For example, it seems like the traffic on the Internet is heavier after noon on weekdays. By then, the people in California are at work.

Get software help: Try an off-line browser, which is a computer program that you can set up to visit user-specified Internet sites during off hours and to download specified sites to your hard drive. You can check the sites that have been downloaded at your convenience. The loading time will be much faster than if you were downloading them "live" from the Internet.

Browser accelerators are another type of available software. While you are looking at one page, behind the scenes the browser accelerator automatically downloads other links on that page and stores them in easily accessible cache memory. If the browser accelerator has cached the next link that you select, it will appear very rapidly.

Bring out the heavy artillery: Upgrade to a faster modem, a better level of Internet connection (e.g., ISDN instead of regular phone line), a better ISP, or a faster computer. Adding more RAM (to a minimum of 8MB with Windows 3.1 and 16MB with Windows 95) can make a noticeable difference in the perceived speed of Internet use.

Problem: A page has been downloaded, but the colors look strange or there is some other problem with the visual appearance.

Click on your browser's Reload button.

Check your software and hardware's capacity: If it is a color graphics problem, make sure that your computer equipment (videocard and monitor) is capable of handling at least 256 colors and that your software is set to handle at least that many colors. Many older machines have the software default set to handle only 16 colors, even if the hardware is capable of higher performance.

Problem: You have connected to a site and the light signaling data transmission remains on, but little or no information appears on your screen after a few seconds or even minutes.

Select the button that causes data transmission to stop: If you are lucky, the text for the page will instantly appear. Web page designers sometimes don't include height and width information for the images in the HTML markup. When even a small part of an image is delayed in transmission (which happens fairly often because image files tend to be large), some browsers then delay showing the text because they don't know how much space to reserve for the missing image. When you tell the browser to stop downloading, it goes ahead and shows you what it has—which often includes the text of the page you want.

Problem: You can't get into a site.

Possible causes and solutions:

1. If you get an error message that says something like "socket disconnected," try again immediately. This is usually just a transient problem.
2. Your service provider may be having trouble with its Internet connection. There's not much individual users can do about this, except change service providers if the problem occurs frequently.
3. The site you are trying to connect to may be in the process of upgrading or may have a technical problem. Again, there's not much you can do in this situation.
4. You may have been accidentally disconnected from your ISP without noticing it. Check to see if you can still send Internet e-mail. If not, try to redial your ISP.

Problem: You repeatedly get error messages saying that your requested destination "failed DNS lookup," or something similar, but you know that the site exists.

A short-term fix: If you know, or can find out, the IP number of the destination computer you are trying to reach, substitute the number for the domain name. For example, if you are trying to reach the ISP Netrail, instead of the domain name netrail.net, try the IP number, 204.117.114.249. This technique uses direct routing, bypassing the DNS system. Don't know the IP number of your destination? Try the InterNIC DNS lookup database: http://www.internic.net.

A long-term fix: Talk to your ISP, and if you don't get a satisfactory answer, consider changing ISPs. Local ISPs are supposed to maintain at least one, and preferably two, computers (a main computer and a backup) designated as Domain Name Servers to accommodate their customers. These computers take the domain name that a customer types in and use a database to find the corresponding IP number for that site. IP numbers are vaguely like telephone numbers. They are needed to route information between computers on the Internet.

If this local DNS server does not work, your request is supposed to go to one of eleven "root servers" in the world that act as backups. Owing to the rapid growth of the Internet, and the fact that many ISPs who have just gotten into the business either don't know how to maintain a DNS server or neglect to do so, the root servers have become overloaded and unreliable. If you patronize this type of service provider, you are only aggravating the problem. Select a service provider that provides a high quality of service, including a reliable DNS server and a backup.

For More Troubleshooting Tips

The Netscape Unofficial FAQ is at http://www.ufaq.org. It includes a good trouble-shooting chart.

Go to http://www.vitalsigns.com, where you can download a limited trial version of Net.Medic, a program to diagnose Internet connection problems.

APPENDIX D

Internet Connection Pointers

This appendix deals primarily with individual dial-up Internet connections, the kind that are suitable for one person at a time. This type of connection is mostly used by small firms and solo practitioners. If you are hooking up a LAN to the Internet through a dedicated line, or establishing a server yourself, some of the information herein will be helpful to you, but you will also need other references, such as those listed at the end of this appendix.

Because the overwhelming majority of law firms use Intel chip systems (running DOS or Windows), I concentrate on that platform, but just about anything that can be done on these systems can also be done other platforms.

When deciding what level of connection you want, remember that the cheapest setup can be the most expensive in the long run. If your connection is too slow, unreliable, or difficult to use, you may not get much practical benefit from the Internet. Speed, reliability, and ease of use can greatly increase your productivity.

Hardware Pointers

For an ordinary dial-up connection, you need:

- A personal computer
- A modem
- An ordinary phone line (which need not be a dedicated line)

The Computer

If your office already has personal computers, you probably don't need to buy new ones just because you want to go on the Internet. More powerful computers will make Internet access faster and more productive, just like they will make word processing or bookkeeping more productive, but you don't need them to access the Internet.

The bare minimum necessary for e-mail access is an 8086 or 8088 IBM-compatible computer (i.e., a thirteen-year-old PC XT). You can use the Internet with such ancient hardware, but you won't be able to use the graphics features and modern easy-to-use software. If you have this type of base-level setup, your best approach is probably going through one of the older commercial online services like CompuServe, which can accommodate text-only operation. An Internet dial-up terminal, or shell, account is another possibility. Systems like Prodigy and America Online use only proprietary software that require more powerful equipment.

Although the entry-level requirements for Internet e-mail access are low, nearly all the best new easy-to-use communications software is being written for graphical operating systems such as Windows 3.1, Windows 95 and 98, and IBM's OS/2. (The latter operating systems include built-in Internet access capability.) These graphical operating systems require more powerful computers. If you can manage it, this is the best way to go.

If you have a high tolerance for slow screen redraws, you might be able to get by with a 386 model computer and 4 megabytes of RAM. For practical day-to-day business use, use at least a 486 computer with 8MB of RAM. If you are using Windows 95 or 98 or OS/2, a Pentium with at least 16MB of RAM is recommended. You will be happier with 32MB or even 64MB, and prices have fallen so much, these levels are no longer only for the most luxurious setups.

Again, you probably don't need to buy new computers to access the Internet. If, however, you decide to upgrade computers for some other reason, keep these recommendations in mind.

The Modem

A modem (modulator-demodulator) is a device that allows a computer to send and receive information over ordinary telephone lines. Until recently, the standard entry-level modem had a speed of either 28,800 or 33,600 bits per second (bps), often referred to as 28.8K and 33.6K. It's probably a good idea to stay away from the very cheapest models because they are frequently less reliable in making and maintaining a connection. If you have a 28.8K modem, it may not be worth investing the time to upgrade to 33.6K. You probably won't notice the difference, even if your phone line is good enough for you to connect consistently at higher speed.

56K modems use technical tricks that can provide effective data transmission speeds that were widely believed impossible on conventional phone lines just a couple of years ago. Look for V.90 compatibility, but be aware that there are still some catches:

- 56K modems are asymmetrical. Transmissions from users to their ISPs are limited to 33.6K.
- Many phone lines and corporate phone-switching equipment won't support 56K at all.

Even if your phone lines support 56K, don't expect to get that speed. FCC power restrictions limit the top maximum speed from the ISP to users to 53K. Moreover, other factors, including the quality of the phone lines between you and your ISP, prevent most users from reaching even 53K. Users in rural areas (where there is more likely to be a lengthy distance between switching stations where the signal will be amplified) are less likely to see large speed boosts from 56K modems.

Any time you buy a modem, look for one that has *flash ROM*. This lets you upgrade to new standards by downloading software, instead of having to insert new chips yourself or send the modem back to the factory for upgrades.

Virtually all modems sold today can send and receive messages to and from regular fax machines, a no-extra-cost fringe benefit that some people appreciate. Among other benefits, a fax sent directly from a file in your computer will look better upon receipt than one sent from a fax machine—you are skipping the image degradation induced by the sending fax's scanner. You can also get modems with simultaneous voice and data capacity that work with voice mail systems. A number of computer companies are heavily pushing what they call "digital telephony," which promises to integrate telephones with your computers.

People often wonder whether an internal or an external modem is best. Both have advantages and disadvantages. External models are more expensive and clutter up your desktop, but they don't increase the level of heat inside your computer's case, a factor to consider if your CPU is cheap or poorly designed. Many people like the feedback on modem status that they get from the lights on the front of an external modem. The internal versus external issue is mainly a matter of personal preference.

Modem performance is difficult to evaluate, even for experts. If you look at computer magazine modem ratings, it's not unusual to see a model that was given the highest rating by one reviewer be roundly condemned by another reviewer. Here's one simple tip that can be useful, though: If you know you will be calling one particular place (such as your ISP) most of the time, find out what model of equipment that party recommends. Some modems perform more reliably when connecting to an identical model, or at least one from the same manufacturer.

Technical modem issues: An Internet connection is radically different from a conventional telephone-line data transmission. There are many places along the transmission chain that can serve as bottlenecks, including the following:

- The computer that is sending you the data (i.e., the server)
- The Internet route along which the data is being transmitted
- Your ISP, whose equipment and lines the data must pass through

Most users seldom need to spend much time thinking about these issues, but modem and phone line issues can be amazingly complicated. When you hear top experts talk about the subject, you realize that this is much more an art than a science. If you want to get into these issues seriously, and fine-tune your modem for absolutely top performance, a good place to go for expert advice is the USENET newsgroup at comp.dcom.modems. The 56K modem site, http://www.56K.com, is a wonderful resource.

The Phone Line

Your modem can share a voice telephone line with no problem. Callers to that number will receive a busy signal only when you are actively using the modem, which for most people won't be for more than a short time each day.

Regular modems work with ordinary phone lines (the plain old telephone system, also known as POTS), which are analog. If your office is using a newer system, such as ISDN (for Integrated Digital Service Network) lines, there is good news and bad news. The good news is that ISDN lines can transmit data at up to 128,000 bps.

The bad news is that a regular modem won't work on ISDN lines. In this case, you have two options: (1) procure and install the more sophisticated and expensive equipment necessary to work with an ISDN line, or (2) have a regular analog phone line installed. The ISDN equivalent of a modem is called a *terminal* or *terminal adapter.* (Technically, there is no such thing as an ISDN modem, since digital signals don't have to be modulated and demodulated.)

ISDN lines can support small LANs. This saves the cost of dedicated analog modems and phone lines, as well as providing a higher quality of service. To perform this function, you will need a router instead of a modem. Router prices have dropped significantly, and some newer models are *relatively* easy for nonexperts to install.

Other Modem Issues

If you are using an older computer, you may need to install a high-speed serial port to get reliable transmission of data at speeds higher than 9600, especially if you are using Windows. These ports contain a device called a 16550 UART (for universal asynchronous receiver-transmitter). These are standard on newer computers. The Microsoft Diagnostics Program included with the more recent versions of MS DOS and Windows can be used to see what type of serial port your machine has. To invoke the Microsoft Diagnostics Program, enter the letters "msd" at a DOS prompt.

All good *internal* high-speed modems have a 16550 UART or compatible built in. (Check the box the modem came in to be sure.) External modems do not have one. If you have a high-speed external modem and you are not getting the speeds you expect or find mysterious problems transmitting data at high speeds, try installing a high-speed serial port card that contains a 16550 UART (about thirty dollars) inside of your computer. Some 56K modems need even faster serial ports that use 16650 UART chips.

With modern modems, you can often get better performance by setting the baud rate (more accurately, the bps rate) higher than the modem's rated speed. This lets the modem take maximum advantage of sophisticated error correction and data compression algorithms. For example, try running a 14,400 bps modem at 57,600 and a 28,800 bps modem at 115,200. Don't expect your modem's real-world performance to approach these theoretical maximums very often, though, since phone line quality is frequently a problem. Static that is inaudible to the ear can slow data transmission.

Most of the larger files transmitted (such as ZIP, GIF, or JPG files) are already compressed, so the modem's compression ability adds nothing.

Using more than one analog connection simultaneously is called *bonding*. You can do this with two modems using special software, or you can buy a unit that has two modems built in. Two phone lines are needed. Not all ISPs support this technology, and you should expect to pay more for the service where it is available.

Higher Bandwidth Alternatives

A dial-up connection is better than no connection, but better alternatives are available. The advantages of higher downloading speed are obvious, but a more subtle advantage may be even more important—the speed of establishing a connection.

Unless you have a dedicated dial-up connection (which tends to be expensive), dialing and establishing an Internet link typically takes about thirty seconds or so. By contrast, most of the technologies below start up much faster, maybe five seconds or less. This may not seem like a giant difference, until you have experienced it.

Having the Internet available to you almost instantly any time your computer is on can radically change attitudes and be a big productivity booster. All of a sudden, it can be more efficient to use an Internet dictionary instead of searching through your paper library. Logging onto the *New York Times* Web site to check a story from last week becomes much faster and more efficient than searching for a back issue of the paper.

The availability and cost of high-speed Internet access varies widely across the country. The following sections give a brief overview of some leading alternatives. I have avoided mentioning prices because they will be volatile as this market shakes out.

ISDN

ISDN connections are a popular alternative to analog dial-up accounts using modems. ISDN has been around for years but never reached the peaks of popularity predicted for it. The raps against it were expense and difficult installation. However, if it is available in your area at reasonable prices (set by local telephone companies), it can be an excellent alternative. ISDN availability, price, and ease of set up vary widely across the country.

All-digital terminal adapters connect reliably at up to 128Kbps and transfer data. This is much slower than the bandwidth levels promised by ADSL, cable, or satellite transmission, but even a 56K ISDN line is significantly better in actual performance than a 56K modem.

ISDN terminal adapters have dropped drastically in price, and many telephone companies seem to have gotten behind them more enthusiastically.

As previously explained, whether to buy an internal or external conventional modem is mainly a question of personal preference. It's a different story with ISDN terminals. Internal ISDN adapters are generally easier to install, and they may perform better. For example, if your PC's serial port is too slow, you will have to install a high-speed serial interface board for an external adapter. Internal adapters give fast performance more easily by connecting directly to your PC's ISA or PCI bus.

Some ISDN connections give the option of using two 64Kbps *bearer* (B) channels, either independently for voice, data, and fax calls or linked together into one wide 128Kbps digital connection, for the top ISDN connection rate of 128Kbps. Each B channel has its own analog phone number, so you can use two devices at the same time, like a phone and a fax machine. If both channels are in use for a data connection, the adapter can take a B channel from the data connection. This lets you keep the data line open at 64Kbps while you answer a voice call or send a fax. One ISDN line can replace two conventional phone lines.

It may not be wise to use both of your adapter's two B channels. If your ISDN provider charges separately for each B channel used, a 128Kbps connection could get expensive. Anyway, one B channel is usually fine for basic Internet activities like Web surfing. Even streaming video and audio may not work noticeably better at speeds over 64Kbps.

David Angell's *ISDN for Dummies,* Second Edition (IDG Books, 1996), is a good introduction to ISDN.

Leased Lines

Phone companies lease high-capacity fiber optic phone lines to those needing high-quality Internet access. These are dedicated, full-time connections that are always "on."

T3 lines, which make up the Internet's backbone, and might be leased by very large organizations, have a 45Mbps capacity. T1 lines, which can provide a high level of service to large to medium-size organizations, have a capacity of 1.5Mbps. If these are beyond your needs, you can also lease *fractional* dedicated lines.

Cable Modems

Cable modems can be an excellent option if available in your area. While download speeds (possibly in the 4 to 10Mbps range) are much higher than ISDN, uploads are usually significantly slower, since the cable system was originally designed with one-way transmission in mind.

Because the bandwidth is pooled, cable modem performance deteriorates as more users are added to a cable system. Further, the shared access makes them less secure than some other types of connections.

Satellite Dish

In the United States, you need a 21-inch satellite dish with a clear line of sight to the south. Download speeds can be 400Kbps or higher. Because the satellite dish cannot send any signal, the satellite downlink is supplemented by a dial-in channel to send information from the user to the Internet. While downloads are fast, the need to use a dial-in channel results in some "latency," which means that the system may react a little slower to your typed-in commands than some alternatives. On the other hand, downloading large files is fast. Satellite dishes may be the only practical high-speed alternative in some rural areas.

Digital Subscriber Line

Digital subscriber lines are dedicated regular copper phone lines that require special equipment. Much higher speeds than ISDN are available. The most common flavor is asynchronous digital subscriber lines, or ADSL. These operate over existing copper telephone wires. Expect to get about 1.5Mbps for downloads and 64Kbps for uploads.

Other Choices

The potential of the Internet access market has attracted other contenders, some of which may eventually become mainstream alternatives. For example, some electric companies have installed fiber optic cables beside power lines, for diagnostic purposes, and may try to enter the ISP business and sell unused bandwidth to anyone who wants it. Wireless transmission, similar to cellular phones, could develop into another alternative.

Software Pointers

It's worth taking some time to make sure that you get easy-to-use software because the alternative can cause you some headaches. As Caroline M. Halliday noted in her excellent book, *Hayes Modem Communications Companion* (IDG Books, 1994):

> The typical stumbling block for most new modem users is establishing the first connection and transferring the first file. The ease of doing so is directly related to the communications software. Before you give up telecommunications as a very technical and overwhelming topic, try and judge whether your frustration is due to communications software that is unnecessarily difficult to use.

The two major types of dial-up accounts are shell accounts and SLIP/PPP accounts. If you are accessing the Internet through a dial-up shell account, the only software you need is a terminal program of some sort. The free Terminal program included with Microsoft Windows or Hyperterminal included with Windows 95 and 98 will be adequate for many users.

With a shell account, you are not really connected to the Internet. You merely have an account on a computer that is connected to the Internet, usually one using the UNIX operating system. Part of this computer's hard disk space and processor power are available for your use. The software you use is typically already installed on the larger computer. Pine is the name of an easy-to-use UNIX e-mail program, for example, and TRN is a newsreader. There is even a Web browser, Lynx, but it does not let you see graphics. You move around the page using the tab and cursor keys. To invoke these programs, you just enter the commands pine, trn, or lynx at the UNIX prompt.

These programs are UNIX software, but don't let this intimidate you. Most of the common UNIX application programs have on-screen menus to help you. A few DOS commands, like dir, cd, and md (list directory, change directory, and make directory) will work; go ahead and experiment. The screens are text only. There are none of the graphics you are used to seeing with Windows or Macintosh computers, and your mouse will not work. These programs are like working in DOS, circa 1986.

Most lawyers using the Internet are better off with a graphical user interface. GUIs are programs like Windows and the Macintosh operating system that use graphics and a pointing device (typically a mouse) to make them easy to learn and use.

True command line fans sneer at GUIs as being computer resources hogs, as well as slow and generally wimpy. Testing shows, however, that when training time and error correction time are taken into account, GUIs are more efficient overall. GUIs are particularly appealing for those who aren't good typists or who don't want to memorize a lot of arcane keystroke commands.

The development of software that lets people access the Internet with GUIs is a major reason Internet use has grown so explosively over the past year or so. The learning curve is much lower and your typing ability is not as important.

The most common GUIs are for OS/2, the Macintosh operating system, the Motif graphical add-in for UNIX, and the three major flavors of MS Windows, Windows 3.x, Windows 95 and 98, and Windows NT.

The most important programs that a lawyer would need to do any work after getting on the Internet are an e-mail program and a Web browser. A newsreader and ftp program would be handy, but probably not essential for most lawyers. Good browser programs today can read newsgroups and transfer files one way (from a distant computer to yours), although they are not as efficient as stand-alone programs dedicated to those functions.

Don't let the acronyms and terminology intimidate you. At one time setting up Internet access software was complicated. If you had to go around and pick up a dialer program here, an e-mail program there, and so on, and then sit down to install them all one at a time, it could still be complicated.

Now there is a *better way* to do it. It's very easy to find software suites that will configure your Internet account with relatively little effort on your part. It has become common for operating systems to include basic Internet access software. You can be on the Internet in fifteen minutes, even if you don't know much about computers. Because this market is so volatile, I'll refrain from recommending particular packages. Go to your local software store and do some reconnaissance. If you have a LAN, you may need LAN versions of your Internet access software.

Software Distribution Mechanisms

Some of the best Internet access software is not distributed through conventional commercial channels. Since many lawyers are not familiar with the alternative distribution mechanisms, some explanation is appropriate here. There are four major categories of software:

1. Regular commercial
2. Shareware
3. Freeware
4. Public domain

Most lawyers have no problem with the concept of regular commercial software or of public domain software. You normally have to pay for regular commercial software. You aren't legally required to pay anyone for the right to use public domain software, although you might choose to buy a copy from someone if it is the most convenient way for you to get a copy. Once you obtain a copy of public domain software, you can do anything you want with it.

Shareware confuses many people. It is commercial software, but it is not distributed in the regular way. It has been called distribution "on the honor system." You can easily get free copies of shareware on disk or by downloading the program, but you are expected to pay and register with the author if you continue using it after an initial trial period. Some shareware vendors provide special upgraded versions or other benefits like printed manuals to registered users. Other shareware vendors (like the authors of the excellent Hot Dog program for designing World Wide Web sites) design their software so that it stops working after a certain period unless you register and pay for it. *Crippleware* is shareware that is distributed with some features disabled, except to users who register and pay for the full version.

Freeware is different. It is given away, but the author retains some intellectual property rights in the program—you can't modify it or sell it yourself. Freeware authors maintain the copyright to their programs but readily allow public use under certain circumstances. For example, some are free for personal use, but require buisnesses to register and pay.

There are also variations and combinations of these approaches.

In many cases, especially the area of computer telecommunications, shareware and freeware products are considered among the best available in their fields. Some examples are PKZip, the compression utility; Eudora Lite, an e-mail handling program; and Winzip, a compression utility for Windows. Free Agent is a popular shareware newsreader. Before using any such software, read the licensing information that accompanies it. Unless it clearly states that the program is public domain or freeware, you are probably supposed to pay for it.

Lawyers should be particularly careful to follow the rules in this area. At least one lawyer used to include in his signature block a PGP public key that had been generated by version 2.6.2 of the PGP encryption program. This could cause some to question not just his sophistication about security (since an e-mail signature block is not the most secure method of distributing a public key) but also his level of care when it came to respecting others' intellectual property rights. Versions of PGP below version 2.7 were noncommercial. Version 2.6.2 is still available, and it is free for noncommercial personal use. The only versions that are licensed for commercial use (which includes, as far as I know, use by a law firm) are versions 2.7 and higher. The net effect of this lawyer's action was that with every message he sent, he was distributing evidence that he was violating the software licensing terms—not the image he hoped to project, I'm sure.

There's nothing wrong with using freeware or shareware. In fact, they are often superior to their regular commercial equivalents. However, *make sure that you read and comply with the licensing terms* before using such software in your legal practice.

You can download copies of many of the other programs mentioned here and ones that became available after this book was printed through hypertext links at: http://www.netlawtools.com/download.html.

Internet Service Provider Pointers

The Internet access market is highly competitive and changes rapidly. The overall trend, however, is clear—lower prices and higher levels of service. It's a good idea to make sure that you are going to be satisfied with a particular service provider before widely distributing your new e-mail address or URL. It's easy to drop one service and start another if you are dissatisfied. However, unlike postal mail, e-mail is not normally forwarded when an address changes. Unless you have your own domain name, telling all your electronic correspondents your new e-mail address and URL and changing all your mailing list subscriptions is a major hassle. If you think that your firm will be using the Internet seriously, do careful research before selecting an ISP. It can save you major headaches later.

Mass Market Commercial Online Services

If you don't know much about computers, a commercial online service like America Online, CompuServe, or the Microsoft Network is an option. Unlike ISPs, discussed later, commercial online services offer their own proprietary areas that are usually inaccessible from "the Internet." Nearly all offer free software and a period of free trial access time.

Mass market commercial online services like America Online are often recommended for beginners because they are said to be easy to use. Even if ease of use is your top selection criteria, however, an online service could be a mistake.

In general, commercial online services do make it fairly easy to take the first few steps into the online world. Yet when it comes to sophisticated uses, online services are often more difficult than regular ISPs. With some online services you can use *only* their proprietary graphic software. This default software frequently lacks time-saving features that are common with good Internet access software, like signature blocks, filters, sophisticated filing of e-mail, powerful e-mail address books, and so on. These features can save you many hours and increase the amount of work you can accomplish on the Internet. Also, for technical reasons (including layering of protocols), Internet access from commercial online services is frequently much slower than a direct Internet connection.

Commercial online services may be a suitable choice for a few lawyers, but don't let the "easy to use" mantra cause you to make a selection you may come to regret. Ask yourself which is more important to you:

1. Making it easy to take the first few baby steps?
2. Making it easy to do significant work?

If you are more concerned about the latter, try a real ISP from the beginning. Even if you decide to start out with a mass market online service provider, you may want to do so with the objective of moving to a real ISP as soon as you have learned the basics of going online, or at least start using regular, powerful Internet software with your online service, if the service allows you to use anything except the default software provided.

If you want a higher level of Internet service at lower cost, you will have to move beyond the mass market commercial online service providers. There are a number of options.

E-mail Only Commercial Services

There are companies that provide *only* Internet e-mail. These can be a good route if e-mail is all you need. Some organizations prefer this type of account because they are afraid that their employees will waste time surfing the Net if they have full Internet access.

Full-Service Internet Access Accounts

If you are in the market for a powerful Internet connection, you will probably need to go through an ISP business. ISPs typically have no extensive closed proprietary areas like AOL, CompuServe, and like services. Instead, they merely provide access to the Internet.

An ISP typically has a high-capacity leased line connection to the Internet and a large computer with a number of modems. For a fee, they will let you piggyback onto their Internet connection. This is usually a dial-up account over a regular telephone line. A high-volume user might prefer a full-time dedicated connection, perhaps through an ISDN or T1 leased high-capacity telephone line.

ISPs can be local or national. Surprisingly, the ISP market is still more local and regional than national. This is partly for technical reasons: all other things being equal, you are more likely to get fast transmission of Internet data if getting onto the Net is only a local call for you. At last count, there were a few thousand such businesses in the country, and most of them operated in a few area codes only. I would consider about ten of them to be national in scope, and even in that group, coverage is spotty. Netcom, one of the largest, has POPs, or local access telephone numbers, in hundreds of the larger U.S. cities.

This is a relatively new type of business, and pricing structures for a dial-up account vary from one region to the next and from one provider to the next, and maybe from one month to the next.

Shop around. A reasonable ballpark figure for a high-quality single-user account would range from ten to thirty dollars a month. This could include unlimited use, or it could have a monthly ceiling of forty hours or so (which is much more than the ordinary user will need). This is a ballpark estimate. The area of the country where you live can make a difference.

Price is far from being the only factor to consider. ISPs vary in their ability and inclination to answer questions and help users with problems. Some say that they are providing the connection only, and it is up to you to configure the account and handle any problems that are not directly caused by a failure of the service provider's equipment. Others will help you and even provide free, high-quality software that is preconfigured for your system.

Boardwatch Magazine publishes an excellent guide to ISPs every few months. If you already have some Internet access, you can get more information at the magazine's Web site: http://www.boardwatch.com/isp. "The List" Web site has a searchable catalog of ISPs on the World Wide Web: http://thelist.com. There is a list of consumer ratings of various ISPs at:
http://www.mindspring.com/~mcgatney/isprate.html.

Bandwidth: Another significant issue is bandwidth, or information carrying capacity. One aspect of bandwidth is the ratio of the available modems to the number of customers. No ISP that I know of has a modem for each of its customers. They don't need to, because statistically only a few customers will be calling at any particular time. However, if you get busy signals consistently, it's time to think about moving to another service provider.

The other aspect of bandwidth, and the one that is more commonly the problem, deals with the system's data carrying capacity. This is commonly measured by leased phone line capacity. The most common sizes for serious ISPs are

T1 lines, and the largest in common use, T3 lines. These names refer to the amount of information that can pass through the phone line at any given time. If the bandwidth is too low, the practical effect is that you are sitting in front of your computer monitor staring at your screen too long while you are waiting for some data you want to be transferred to your computer. This can be a real productivity killer.

It's extremely difficult to determine which ISP will have the best effective bandwidth by listening to sales pitches and reading specification sheets. There are just too many complicated factors involved that can interact in too many different ways. The size of the *pipe* (T1 versus T3) is important, but there are many other factors involved, including the number of other customers and their demographics. Does your ISP have mostly business customers who are all trying to use the Internet at the same time you are? If so, you might be better off with an ISP whose customers are mostly home users. They will most likely be using the Internet at night, thus making it easier on you to get through during the business day. Other factors affecting bandwidth include how close the ISP is to an Internet backbone (one of the few ultra-high capacity lines that link key Internet connecting points) and redundancy. Does the ISP have more than one independent connection to the Internet?

Fortunately, there is a simple way to get a good grip on the bandwidth issue. Test and compare the service providers that you are considering, using your equipment, at the times of day you plan to call for business uses, doing the types of things you plan to do on the job. Most ISPs will give you a test period. Take advantage of it.

Types of Dial-Up Accounts

There are two basic types of dial-up accounts: dial-up terminal (shell) accounts and dial-up direct (SLIP, CSLIP, or PPP, in casual speech often generically lumped together as SLIP) accounts. Some providers will supply either type upon request. The dial-up terminal accounts are usually a little cheaper. While the shell accounts are easier to set up (no TCP/IP configuration hassles), the dial-up direct accounts are much easier to use once set up. With dial-up direct accounts you don't need to learn UNIX commands and you have access to a wide selection of easy to use Windows point-and-click interface software.

With a shell account you are not directly connected to the Internet. You are connected to the service provider's large computer, which is connected to the Internet. In essence, your PC becomes a terminal attached to your service provider's system. This can involve some minor inconveniences. For example, downloading a file becomes a two-step process. You must first manipulate the software to transfer the file from the distant computer to the one on which you have a shell account and *then* transfer it onto your PC. You can't download it directly to your machine. You are also limited in the choice of software you can use.

Dial-up direct connections using the techniques SLIP (Serial Line Internet Protocol) and PPP (Point to Point Protocol) are the alternatives to a shell account. A CSLIP (Compressed Serial Line Internet Protocol) account is a slightly improved variant of SLIP. A PPP account is considered slightly preferable technically to either of the others, so ask for that if you have a choice. These are all direct connections to the Internet. They are more powerful than shell accounts and will allow full World Wide Web access. You are not limited to using the software from your service provider and instead can choose from a wide variety of powerful but easy-to-use new interface software.

Most of this software comes preconfigured to make it very easy to set up with one or more designated ISPs. This is good, but there is a potential trap: The "default" ISPs are usually much more expensive than companies with equally good or better service that you can find locally. Check it out. You will probably be much better off not taking the easiest route here. Be prepared to do a little manual configuration work to set up your account with somebody local, if they are the better choice (as is usually the case).

Sometimes the ISP you have chosen will not use exactly the same terminology as the software you are trying to install. There is a simple trick that can make it easier. Copy the fill-in-the-blanks instructions from the software manual. Fax them to the ISP and have *the ISP* fill in the blanks. It is much easier for providers to translate their favorite terminology into that used by your software package than it is for you to do so.

Resources

The Lawyer's Quick Guide to Netscape Navigator, by G. Burgess Allison (American Bar Association: Law Practice Management Section, 1997), contains a section titled "Getting Connected" that is the best short guide I've seen to selecting an ISP.

Managing Internet Information Services, by Liu, Peek, Jones, Buus, and Nye (O'Reilly & Associates, 1994), has guidance on connecting a LAN to the Internet.

Connecting to the Internet, by Susan Estrada (O'Reilly & Associates, 1993), is dated but still has useful explanations.

APPENDIX **E**

Web Site Design: Selected Technical Issues

This appendix is not a complete guide to the nuts-and-bolts of Web site design. Ken Johnson's book *The Lawyer's Guide to Designing Web Pages* (American Bar Association: Law Practice Management Section, 1997) is a good place to go for more detailed information. This appendix is only intended to provide guidance on a few areas that seem to cause trouble, especially for lawyers who design their own Web sites.

Graphics

Don't overdo Web site graphics. What you experience while designing a page or during a typical Web demonstration will not be typical of the average user's experience in trying to access your actual Web page. When you are loading the draft Web page to test it during the design process, the page is read directly off your computer's hard drive. This is much faster than the typical access time over the Internet.

In real life, taking into consideration packet overhead and other factors, you can expect someone using a 14,400 bps modem to download your information at a rate of 1,000 bytes (1K) of information per second. The theoretical maximum is higher, but most people seldom get the maximum in actual practice. This means that if you have an 80K graphic on your opening page, you are asking a significant percentage of the people who visit your site to sit and stare at their computer monitors for eighty seconds just for the privilege of looking at that picture. This is not a way to generate goodwill, to put it mildly.

Studies have shown that many would-be Web site visitors will stop trying to connect to a site if it takes more than thirty seconds to load. Many businesses, not just law firms, do not grasp this. Some of them even boast that they deliberately design their pages with large graphics that will only appeal to visitors with high-speed Internet connections.

Even if we give these firms the benefit of the doubt and assume that their target markets consist *only* of high-tech businesses that *all* have very high-speed Internet connections like an ISDN line or better in their offices, such a strategy is questionable.

No lawyer is so clairvoyant that he or she can be certain that the CEOs or general counsels of targeted prospective clients will not be trying to access the law firm's site while on the road using a beat-up laptop with only a 9600 bps modem. Yes, modems of that speed are still out there, and people still use them. Many people don't like to tamper with their hardware once they have everything working satisfactorily.

Furthermore, many corporate executives don't work nine-to-five hours at the office any more. It's probable that some of them will try to contact a law firm's Web site from their homes, where the connection is more likely to be a 14.4K or 28.8K modem, instead of the high-speed connection at the office.

Even if you assume that a prospective client is using the high-speed connection in the corporate office, the client will still be annoyed by excessive graphics if he or she tries to connect at 3:00 p.m. on a Friday afternoon when network traffic congestion has slowed all Internet downloads to the speed of molasses in January.

Lastly, even if all your prospective clients have top-of-the-line equipment and connections, connect only during off hours, and always download your firm's page with great speed, your site won't help you market to the more sophisticated clients who understand the Internet if they see your graphics and question your judgment: "What's wrong with this law firm? Don't they know how long these giant graphics would take to download over the most common connection speeds? Why don't they have more concern for their clients?"

Why do so many law firms go overboard with graphics displays? One possibility is that Web site designers are taking advantage of most lawyers' lack of technical sophistication to sell them a bill of goods. While many of the older lawyers who are the decision makers in law firms don't have a great grasp of how the Internet works, they can appreciate flashy artwork. It can make them more willing to pay the $50,000 and up fees that some Web site design firms charge. Therefore, many Web site designers emphasize elaborate, slow-downloading graphics, including image maps, even though they are actually harmful to their customers' best interests. "Don't sell the customer what he needs. Give him what he wants."

Some Web site designers employ a deceptive tactic that hides the negative effect of giant graphics until it is too late. It is very easy to set up a browser so that it seems to be accessing sites over the Internet but is merely reading files that have been cached on its hard disk. This results in the law firm buying a site that looks wonderful during a demo but is nearly useless in the real world.

The size of the image on the computer monitor is not the problem. Rather, it is the amount of computer memory it takes to store the image. The more storage size needed, the slower the image display. Generally, plain text downloads rapidly, while graphic images are slower, especially if they are large or complex. File size is measured in kilobytes, abbreviated as "K."

A picture that displays rapidly while you are designing or viewing a demo of your page will appear with agonizing slowness to the average user who is downloading it over the Internet. While others are more liberal, my recommended rule of thumb is to avoid graphic images that are larger than about 20K, unless they are particularly valuable to viewers.

Skilled designers can make graphics that look good but don't take up much space. These will usually be simpler than the slower graphics and often more aesthetically pleasing.

If there are big images you want to include, consider whether it is better to just give your users the option of seeing them, by including *thumbnails* on your main page that are hotlinked to the full images elsewhere. This gives the visitor the option.

Make certain to include width and height information for all your images, even the small ones. Modern browser programs use this information to reserve a space on the page for the graphic, thus letting them display the text faster. This will greatly speed the perceived downloading time and reduce your readers' frustration. You can get the width and height information (in pixels) by loading the image into nearly any graphics program (like Paint Shop Pro). Modern HTML editing programs automatically measure the linked-to graphic and insert the image size information, but just in case you are using an older editor, here's what the markup looks like:

⟨IMG SRC="firmlogo.gif" WIDTH=400 HEIGHT=126⟩

For the sake of simplicity, in this example the ALT and ALIGN information that you would normally include are omitted. It's not the purpose of this book to teach HTML, but this example is included because so many law firm Web pages don't get this right.

Animated graphics are a distraction at an increasing number of law firm sites. You should be conservative with graphics in general, be ultraconservative with animated graphics, since they annoy many people. The main complaints against them are that they take longer to download, generally tend to look amateurish, and make it difficult to concentrate on the text of a page. The latter problem can be reduced by adjusting the animation to cycle a certain number of times and then stop. In general, be careful about using any animated graphics, and if you do indulge, don't use more than one image per page.

It is possible to have classy animated graphics. The best example I have seen is the main logo at Peter Krakaur's invaluable legal ethics Web site, http:///www.legalethics.com. It illustrates the limited-repetition technique.

Ken Johnson's tips for your Web site graphics (drafted specially for this book) are included in the accompanying sidebar.

▼ ▼ ▼ ▼ ▼

Tip Sheet for Doing Your Own Web Site Graphics
By Kenneth E. Johnson

Limit colors. A smaller number of colors means smaller file size and quicker download. You can do much with the sixteen-color palette of Windows Paintbrush. Professional Web graphic designers rarely use more than thirty-five different colors.

Keep 'em small. In general, graphics should be under 30K in size so that they transfer quickly. A few larger graphics are okay, but use them sparingly.

Use transparency for irregularly shaped images. Transparency is a graphics option that makes a certain color not display but instead show through the background. With an irregular graphic, this prevents the white "rectangle" shape from displaying around it.

Always use ALTernate text. If visitors to your site have graphics turned off in their browser, the Alternate text is what displays—without it, they see only a generic placeholder. This is especially true for graphics used as links, since the Alternate text displays as a regular hypertext link.

Use the same graphic on multiple pages. In addition to consistency, the graphic only has to be downloaded once to the browser's memory cache. After that, if another page uses that graphic, it can be quickly retrieved from the cache.

Backgrounds should contribute to, not hinder readability. Text and graphics should show clearly on the background graphic and be readable. For example, black text on a gray marble background might be your printed logo, but it is very hard to read on a screen.

Beware of BORDER = /0 on graphic links. This Netscape option turns off a graphic border, but if the graphic is used as a link, it also removes the color "link" border. Viewers may easily overlook the fact that the graphic is actually a link.

Consider a Text-only alternative. If your Web site heavily uses graphics, provide alternate pages that contain the same information but without the graphics, and with text navigation links.

Mr. Johnson is the author of The Lawyer's Guide to Creating Web Pages *and* The Lawyer's Quick Guide to E-mail, *both published by the ABA Law Practice Management Section.*

Universal Accessibility

Remember that not everyone looking at your Web page will see the graphics. Surveys show that about 5 percent of Web hits come from nongraphic Web browsers like Lynx. Many people who do have graphical browsers habitually turn off the graphics features to speed access or because they find the graphics distracting. One way to accommodate these users is to take advantage of the ALT feature, which lets you display text that will appear if a graphic image at your site is not used.

Nonstandard HTML tags introduced by Netscape, and now used by the Microsoft Explorer Web browser, are another problem. In theory, browsers should ignore nonstandard HTML markup that they don't know how to format. In practice, however, many pages "enhanced" to look better in one browser look horrible in others.

A few Web designers arrogantly proclaim that they do not care how their pages look in any browser except their favorite. Others, with equal ideological fervor, disdain the use of any browser-specific features. Some law firms go so far as to design multiple versions of their site for various browsers. These firms deserve commendation for their consideration for differing visitor needs, but such an extreme solution is unnecessary.

For practical law firm site design, the solution is pragmatic. There is nothing wrong with the judicious use of a few proprietary tags if they give a significantly improved appearance in your favorite browser, but be sure to test your pages in a wide variety of browsers, and make sure they look acceptable in all.

In this context, remember that while many handicapped readers can use Web pages composed completely of text, through speech synthesizers and other tools, pages that are heavy on graphics can cause problems. This issue may be of special interest to law firms because of the Americans with Disabilities Act. Lynx is a text-only browser that you can use for testing purposes. You can see what a page looks like through Lynx by going to the Lynx Viewer at: http://www.delorie.com/web/lynxview.html.

Color

It's not a good idea to have too many different colors on any given page of your Web site. Many computers with color monitors can't display more than 256 colors at a time, and many people whose machines can display more colors don't have their machines configured to do so. The 256-color limit is per screen, not per image. The Windows operating system reserves 20 colors for its own use. If you add graphics that take the total colors on a page over 256, bizarre color distortion may result.

The situation is further complicated by the fact that the JPG file format, used for most Web photo images because of its superior photo compression features, does not retain colors consistently when an image is modified. Therefore, even if you are careful to limit the total colors on a page to under 256, your efforts may go for naught if you include a photo on the page. (GIF images do not suffer from this problem, and further, GIFs do better at compressing most non-photographic images, like cartoons.)

More generally, remember that computers don't display colors identically. The monitor, video card, video driver, and software all affect the way the colors you design will be viewed by others. Furthermore, as monitors age, the way they display colors changes. None of these factors are under your control as a designer. Be conservative. What looks acceptable on your equipment may be unreadable to someone else.

Background images are another problem. Exercise great care in using them. Very few that I have seen are preferable to a plain background for readability. If you do use a background image that is not a texture type—a large logo, for example, or a stripe down the left side of the page—make sure that you avoid the common wrapping problem. Most people use a screen size that is either 640 pixels wide and 480 pixels high or 800 pixels wide by 600 pixels high. However, remember that other people, particularly those using 17-inch and larger monitors, select higher resolutions. A background image that looks fine on a small monitor can "wrap" (i.e., display more times than the designer intended) on a large one, causing it to look lousy, or even make large sections of text unreadable. This amateurish defect is common, even on pages from professional designers. Again, fight to avoid the trap of unconsciously assuming that all visitors to your site will be using a system like yours.

More Design Tips

Many people find it hard to read information from a computer monitor. Long blocks of unbroken text worsen the problem. Make your pages easy to read by using the following:

- Short paragraphs
- Bulleted and numbered lists
- Block-quoted text
- Centered text (where appropriate)
- Charts
- Strategically placed graphics

Don't let any particular page at your site get too large, since gargantuan pages are daunting. Spin off some elements into their own pages. Try to keep the essential elements on the basic pages, however, because analysis of page hit counts shows that readership for subpages can decline drastically, to as little as 10 to 1 percent of the readership of the main page in some circumstances.

Make it easy for users of your page to get in touch with you. You should include your hotlinked e-mail address, street address, and telephone and fax numbers at a minimum. I know this advice sounds obvious, but more than one law firm Web page has neglected to include any of that information. Some law firms include driving directions, or links to interactive map databases, like those available through Yahoo's map feature, at http://www.yahoo.com.

It's a good idea to include the date that each page was last updated. Including the page's URL will make it easier for people who print out a copy of the page to find their way back to it on the Web.

There are a number of proprietary formats that can be used to publish information on the World Wide Web. Adobe Portable Document Format (PDF) is the one most likely to be useful to law firms that want to post material on the Internet. It lets you easily preserve a document's desktop publishing features, including font, layout, color, and graphics, when you convert it into Internet format. You include a link to the PDF document from inside a standard Internet HTML document. When the viewer selects that link, a PDF viewer is started (if the user has one) and the document is loaded for viewing. Many government agencies are using PDF to distribute information, partly because it is a labor-saving method of doing so.

Some law firms use PDF to provide copies of government forms, as a service to clients and to give potential clients a reason to visit the site. Siskind, Susser & Haas was one of the first to take this approach at its site, http://www.visalaw.com/docs.

For law firms publishing their own information, one advantage of PDF is that it makes it a little more difficult for someone else to modify your information or to pass it off as their own work. For example, on every page of your FAQ or other document, you can have your firm name, logo, or watermark appear. These can't be removed without some effort. In addition, if someone prints out a hard copy of a PDF document, it will look almost exactly like the original. This is a plus if you are hoping that others will redistribute it. Adobe sells a variety of PDF creation programs, with varying levels of sophistication. The cheapest has a street price of about two hundred dollars.

A disadvantage of PDF is that users who don't already have a viewer program will have to get and install one. They are free, but this is still a barrier to part of your potential audience. If you use the PDF format, make sure that you include a hypertext link to the Adobe site where users can download the free viewer program: http://www.adobe.com.

Where to Locate Your Site

Should your files be located on a Web server operated by your law firm or on a commercial account? For most firms, the advantages of renting space on someone else's server are pretty persuasive.

Capital investment, technical expertise, and time are required to maintain a Web server. Do you think that you can duplicate this in house for less than thirty dollars a month? This is what Lew Rose pays for his Advertising Law site, one of the best known and most successful in the country. You can probably do comparably well if you shop around. Even if you are in a rural area where there is little competition, remember that your Web site can easily be located in a distant city where prices are lower.

While the Internet as a whole is not a notably secure environment, Web sites are particularly notorious hacker access targets. In widely publicized episodes, vandals successfully attacked Web sites run by the Department of Justice and the Central Intelligence Agency and substituted embarrassing material for the official content.

For these reasons, it makes sense to let someone else take on the hassles and risks of running your Web server, particularly since commercial accounts are so inexpensive.

Resources

Internet Tools for Attorneys: http://www.netlawtools.com

Web Developer's Virtual Library: http://www.stars.com

Center for Applied Special Technology, http://www.cast.org. Explains how to ensure web sites comply with the Americans with Disabilities Act.

APPENDIX F

Sample Internet Use Policy

Allowing law firm employees to use the Internet can result in big productivity improvements. It can also expose the law firm to embarrassment and litigation. A well-crafted Internet use policy can reduce the danger.

The policy in this appendix is a sample, not a model. It does not purport to be the best of all possible policies. Even if there were such a thing as "the best possible policy," it would probably have to be modified to meet the needs of your organization. For example, consider whether your firm should distinguish between partners and associates or between lawyers and non-lawyer personnel. Some firms place limits on the ability of associates or non-lawyers to send e-mail without prior approval.

Such policies can be reinforced by using software that screens incoming and outgoing Internet traffic or blocks access to particular Internet sites. Some such software can be programmed to screen for specified terms such as trade secret information. Do not let this software give you a false sense of security. It is far from being foolproof.

Each employee should be required to acknowledge receipt and understanding of your policy before being granted Internet access. An easy way to do this is to retain a copy of the policy signed by the employee.

The security and encryption policies referred to in the last two items are best handled in separate documents that can be easily updated as needed.

To facilitate customization of this policy, a version in word processing format is available at the Web site associated with this book: http://www.abanet.org/lpm/netbook.

Barrister, Attorney & Barrister Internet Use Policy

The following rules apply to all employees, including partners and associates, of Barrister, Attorney & Barrister (hereinafter BAB) using Internet connections supplied by BAB, whether or not during normal working hours and whether from BAB premises or elsewhere.

1. *No Privacy in System:* BAB's computer facilities are provided to further the business interests of BAB and its clients. BAB has the right, but not the duty, to monitor any and all employee communications passing through its computer facilities, at the sole discretion of BAB. Employees should never place information they intend to be personal or private on any BAB computer system.

2. *Improper Activities:* Employees will not disseminate or knowingly receive harassing, sexually explicit, threatening, or illegal information using any BAB computer, network, or Internet connection. This could include jokes or cartoons. Employees will not use BAB facilities for personal or commercial advertisements, solicitations, or promotions. Any employee who learns of such activities will report them to the System Administrator immediately.

3. *Nature of E-mail:* Because e-mail is more like paper communications than telephone conversations in its permanence and level of susceptibility to discovery by opposing parties and proof in the courtroom, all employees must exercise appropriate discretion in any e-mail comments. If you would not want your mother to read about it on the front page of the *Washington Post,* do not put it in an e-mail message.

4. *Avoiding Controversial Comments:* Employees will not use BAB computer facilities to send messages outside BAB expressing controversial, potentially offensive, or defamatory comments on politics, religion, social policies, individuals, etc., or comments that could result in embarrassment to BAB.

5. *Intellectual Property of Others:* Employees will not download or use material from the Internet or other sources in violation of software licenses, copyright, and trademark laws.

6. *Disclaimer Required:* All e-mail, newsgroup, and similar communications addressed to anyone outside BAB must contain a signature block with the following disclaimer: "The author of this message speaks only for [himself or herself], and is not authorized to speak on behalf of the law firm of Barrister, Attorney & Barrister." The computer support staff will demonstrate how to create signature blocks upon request.

7. *Network Security:* All employees will comply with instructions for virus protection, password selection and security, and other security matters issued under separate cover and periodically updated by the System Administrator. This will include, but not be limited to, using BAB-approved virus scanning software to check all files from outside the firm being placed on any BAB computer, whether they came from the Internet or elsewhere.

8. *Encryption:* Employees will not send e-mail messages containing sensitive information over the Internet without using an encryption method approved by the System Administrator, and ensuring that the System Administrator has a copy of the password and/or private key needed to decrypt the material.

Acknowledgment

I, ___*[Insert Name]*___ have read, understand, and agree to comply with the Barrister, Attorney, & Barrister Internet Use Policy, as set forth above. I understand that failure to comply with the policy may result in disciplinary action, including termination, as well as legal action against me seeking damages or indemnification.

_____   _____

Name   Date

APPENDIX **G**

Cyber Issues: Overview of the Substantive Law of the Internet

The substantive law of the Internet partially overlaps with, but is not the same as, what we have come to call "computer law." While a few law firms have already established reputations for excellence in this area, there is still plenty of opportunity for now-unknown firms to help develop the law of the Internet—and to profit in the course of doing so.

Discussions of some of the issues, like Internet use policies and contracts for Web site design, have been incorporated into other parts of this book. This appendix provides an overview of a few other Internet legal and law-related policy issues. It is intended only to assist in identifying a few of the key issues and to provide some starting points for further research. Remember that the law in this area is changing rapidly.

Robert C. Cumbow of Perkins Coie in Seattle suggested many of the topics covered in the following sections, and deepened my understanding of others. The Perkins Coie Internet Case Digest, a section of his firm's Web site, is an outstanding resource:

http://www.perkinscoie.com

Intellectual Property Protection in General

Anyone can be a "publisher" on the Internet. Infringing on intellectual property rights is easy—and tempting. The violators include both scofflaws and the ignorant.

There is a school of thought to the effect that conventional intellectual property laws should not apply to the Internet because information "wants to be free." Esther Dyson, who serves on a key subcommittee of the National Information Infrastructure Advisory Council, does not advocate the piracy of intellectual property, but she argues convincingly in *Release 2.0* (Broadway 1997) that even without legal protection for their intellectual property, content owners will want to make valuable material available on the Internet to build customer relations, strengthen brand recognition, and create add-on sales.

Until such time as they are abolished by Congress, intellectual property laws will apply on the Internet, just as they do elsewhere. Owing to the unique nature of this new medium, however, intellectual property owners are well-advised to exercise caution in exposing their material, and greater aggressiveness in protecting it may be necessary. Here are a few examples:

- Although copyright notices are no longer required (by virtue of the Berne Convention), placing a copyright notice on each page of a Web site can prevent confusion and show prospective infringers that you are serious about protecting your property.
- Similarly, registration with the Copyright Office is no longer required, but it can allow you to collect statutory damages (between $500 and $20,000 for each work infringed, and up to $100,000 if the infringement was willful) and lawyer's fees. See 17 U.S.C. § 504(c).
- Trade secrets should not appear on a Web site, even if protected by a "clickware" license.
- To avoid claims that a trademark has been abandoned, you should pursue infringers, perhaps affirmatively looking for them, using Internet search tools.

Web sites should include a legal notice reciting terms and conditions for use of the site. Bob Cumbow suggests that the basic elements of such a notice include the following:

- **Copyright notice** (e.g., "All copyrightable text, graphics, design, selection, and arrangement of information © 1998 My Firm LLP").
- **Trademark notice** (e.g., "MY FIRM and the My Firm design logo are service marks of My Firm LLP. WINDOWS is a registered trademark of the Microsoft Corporation, which is not affiliated with and does not sponsor or endorse the products or services of My Firm LLP. The WINDOWS mark is used by permission").
- **License** (e.g., "The materials on this site are provided as a public information resource only. Permission is granted to download a single electronic copy and to print a single hard copy for the user's information only. No other copying, distribution, modification, republication, or other use of

the materials on this Web site is permitted without the express written permission of My Firm LLP").

- **Liability disclaimer** (e.g., "My Firm LLP makes every effort to ensure that the information on this Web site is accurate and up to date, but accepts no liability for any alleged losses or damages incurred in reliance on the information contained in these pages. Further, My Firm LLP has no responsibility for, or control over, and therefore accepts no liability for, the contents, accuracy, or currency of sites we link to from this site or of sites that provide links to our site").

While technology can create problems, it can also solve them. Technological fixes to some intellectual property problems on the Net are possible. One approach is *secure container* technology. IBM calls its model the "cryptolope," and InterTrust calls its the "digibox." Both are digital equivalents of boxes and locks. Some believe that they will be more practical when simple, secure mechanisms for transferring payments of small amounts of money over the Internet like Digi-Cash and CyberCash become more popular.

Some firms placing valuable intellectual property on the Internet have considered including viruses or "rogue code" that would be harmless if used for its intended purpose but that would cause problems if the property were illegally copied or used. Could such "self-help" rise to the digital equivalent of "excessive force," giving rise to a cause of action against the firm that was trying to protect itself? The warning provided by the property owner and the extent of the damage done by the rogue code would seem to be among the relevant factors.

Before using a photograph on a Web site, or allowing a consultant to include one in your site, make sure that the permission of the owner of the copyright in the photo (usually the original photographer) as well as of any person depicted is obtained.

To the best of my knowledge, there is still no case law on use of personal information gathered from Web sites, like user names, addresses, locations, Internet Protocol (IP) numbers, purchasing habits, and Web browsing habits. If, however, a site collects any information about visitors, either through visible online questionnaires or the use of so-called "cookies," which may not be apparent to casual visitors, it may be advisable to include a privacy policy. There is increasing public concern over this issue in the United States, and European privacy directives are placing strong limits on uses of personal information gathered through Web sites. While some businesses require that consumers affirmatively consent to the use of information they provide, the "opt out" approach of Amazon.com is probably more typical of the approach favored by U.S. businesses:

We do not now sell or rent information about our customers. If you would like to make sure we never sell or rent information about you to third parties, just send a blank e-mail message to **never@amazon.com**.

Related Resources

- Atlanta attorney Jeff Kuester's award-winning site, with material on many aspects of intellectual property law and the Internet:
  http://www.kuesterlaw.com
- Oppedahl & Larsen LLP provides practical advice for protecting intellectual property on the Internet: http://www.patents.com/weblaw.sht
- Law Journal Extra Intellectual Property Overview:
  http://www.ljx.com/practice/intellectualproperty
- The Internet Sleuth Web site has convenient links to search engines at many intellectual property sites: http://www.isleuth.com/lega-ip.html
- CNET provides a simple overview of copyright, trademark, and libel law apparently intended primarily for Web page designers:
  http://www.cnet.com/Content/Features/Dlife/Law

Domain Names

As online legal pioneer Lance Rose has noted, brand names create geography on the Internet. Domain names are the part of an e-mail address that normally signifies an organization, and they are often used to reinforce a brand. Here are examples of three terms that commonly confuse lawyers new to the Internet:

This is a domain name: myfirm.com
This is an e-mail address: throckmorton@myfirm.com
This is a URL: http://www.myfirm.com/news/law.html

Originally, domain names were distributed solely on a first-come, first-served basis. *MTV Networks v. Curry,* 867 F. Supp. 202, 203-04, n.2 (S.D.N.Y. 1994). As the commercial potential of the Internet became apparent, the foresighted began to register potentially valuable domain names. For example, the Princeton Review tutoring service registered the name kaplan.com before its arch competitor Stanley Kaplan. A former MTV "video jockey" registered mtv.com before his former employer, MTV Networks. An author registered mcdonalds.com before the fast-food chain thought of it. In all these cases, the late would-be registrant succeeded in getting the rights to the domain name through negotiation or litigation.

Partly to avoid becoming embroiled in litigation, the company that assigns domain names—Network Solutions, Inc. (NSI), acting on behalf of InterNIC, the Internet Network Information Center—adopted new policies in 1995, available at http://www.internic.net. These policies require prospective registrants to make various representations before being assigned a domain name. Further, if a domain name is challenged by someone who has registered a federal or foreign trademark in that domain name, NSI may temporarily deactivate the domain name until the dispute is resolved by litigation or arbitration, with the domain name holder being required to post a bond to indemnify NSI for any damages it may suffer.

A domain name will be placed on hold *only* if the second-level domain name was registered and the domain name owner has no trademark registration of its own to support its entitlement to use the second-level domain. Further, the deactivated status merely means that the domain name cannot be used by either party, or anyone else, until the dispute is settled through negotiation or litigation.

The domain name system's technical underpinnings cause it to track poorly with conventional intellectual property law and NSI's attempt to piggyback on that body of law. For example, mere use of a trademark in commerce is enough to create an enforceable interest within the United States. Registration is not required, but NSI's policy disregards this.

On the other hand, mere use of a domain name as an Internet address (i.e., e-mail address or URL) is not necessarily a "trademark use" or a "use in commerce" such as should entitle a challenger to relief for trademark infringement or dilution. See, for example, *Patmont Motor Works, Inc. v. Gateway Marine Inc.*, 1997 U.S. Dist. LEXIS 20877 (N.D. Cal. 12/18/97), finding that a trademark used not in the domain name portion of a URL but as a file designation deep within the URL was not a trademark violation. Moreover, because NSI will apply its policy only against a domain name whose second-level domain is identical to the challenger's registered trademark, its sweep captures identical domain names that may not in fact be either infringements or dilution of the trademark in question, and it *misses* nonidentical but confusingly similar domain names that might well be infringements.

Despite a few possible incongruities between present problems and laws drafted before the Internet became a major commercial force, courts are trying to apply conventional principles like infringement and dilution to domain name disputes. The outcomes of such cases in domain name disputes may be different than they would be in analogous cases where the Internet is not involved.

Because the Internet is a global system, international law issues can easily arise. For example, a U.S. company has registered the domain name prince.com. The British equivalent of .com is co.uk. What will happen if the sporting goods company registers prince.co.uk? British law could prevent the U.S. company from challenging the latter domain name.

As I write, a proposal to add seven new top-level domain names (firm, shop, web, arts, rec, info, and nom), as proposed by the Internet Ad Hoc Coalition, is on hold, pending the cooperation of the Internet Assigned Numbers Authority (IANA).

Related Resources

- Sally M. Abel, "Trademark Issues in Cyberspace: The Brave New Frontier":
  http://www.fenwick.com/pub/cyber.html

Liability for Linking?

While most Web site owners welcome links built to their sites by others, occasionally site owners object to links that they consider improper. For example, one woman posted a memorial photo of her deceased daughter on her Web page. She was understandably offended to discover that the "Babes on the Web" site had linked to it.

Such disputes have typically been resolved by requesting the deletion of the offending link. Internet practice has been that, while it is polite to ask for permission before building a hypertext link to another site, there is no right to prevent someone from building a link. It was commonly stated that establishing a publicly accessible Web site constituted an implied consent for others to link to it.

The commercialization of the Internet has led to arguments for legal regulation of some forms of linking.

In *Washington Post v. TotalNews, Inc.*, frames were at issue. Frames allow one Web site to display a page from another site in a window on the screen. In the *TotalNews* case, the defendant provided links to the Web sites of many news organizations, but as a result of the use of frames, these links, when clicked on, did not cause the user's browser to disconnect from the TotalNews site and reconnect with the linked site, as normally occurs in linking. Instead, the link, when clicked, caused the browser to capture the content of the linked site and display it in a frame on the user's screen while keeping the user connected to the Total-News site. This made it difficult for visitors to leave the TotalNews site and could give unsophisticated visitors the impression that the information at the linked-to sites was created by TotalNews. Further, the frames could effectively obscure advertisements at the framed sites. The case was settled, with the defendant agreeing to restrict the "framing" of plaintiffs' material. A copy of the settlement agreement in the case is at: http://www.ljx.com/internet/totalse.html.

"Deep linking" was another technique at issue in a lawsuit brought by Ticketmaster relating to links to its sites from Microsoft's Sidewalk city guide series. Ticketmaster complained because Microsoft did not build links only to its home page, the section of the site that Ticketmaster preferred that visitors see first, but to particular sections deep inside the Ticketmaster site that Microsoft thought would be of more interest to its Sidewalk city guide series. See http://www.ljx.com/LJXfiles/ticketmaster/.

Many Web site owners welcome, and some even encourage, such deep linking on the theory that anything that leads more visitors to the site is a benefit. Other Web site owners, like Ticketmaster, object to deep linking. Among other things, it can reduce the value of advertising on the linked-to site's preferred main entry point.

While not necessarily dispositive of the legal claims involved, it is worth remembering that in many cases, the aggrieved party can protect itself by technological means. For example, Ticketmaster could have configured its Web server to block access by links from Microsoft's Sidewalk sites, or to permit visitors to enter its site only via the home page.

Related Resources

- Richard Raysmom and Peter Brown, "Dangerous Liaisons: The Legal Risks of Linking Web Sites": http://www.ljx.com/internet/0408lias.html
- Stefan Bechtold's "The Link Controversy Page": http://www.jura.uni-tuebingen.de/~s-beg1/lcp.html

---

Defamation

The Wild West culture of the Internet tempts many into overlooking the concept of libel. The America Online version of the "Drudge Report" boasted that its creator, Matt Drudge, "believes that 'gossip' is news that just hasn't been confirmed yet."

The lesser number of traditional intermediaries and gatekeepers, such as editors and publishing companies, complicates the problem. Most conventional publications with readerships in the tens or hundreds of thousands have access to professional legal advice to help them minimize liability exposure. Many Internet "publishers" with comparable numbers of readers lack such protections.

There is a school of thought that argues that there should be only limited liability for defamation occurring on the Internet. Language from *Gertz v. Robert Welch, Inc.*, 418 U.S. 323, 345 (1974), is cited in support of this theory:

> The first remedy of any victim of defamation is self-help—using available opportunities to contradict the lie or correct the error and thereby to minimize its adverse impact on reputation. Public officials and public figures usually enjoy significantly greater access to the channels of effective communication and hence have a more realistic opportunity to counteract false statements than private individuals normally enjoy.

This line of argument asserts that the new ease of communicating via the Internet gives many more people the ability to reply effectively to false statements. As Internet use becomes ubiquitous, this line of argument may become more attractive.

On the other hand, it has been argued that retractions should count for less in Internet communications because, owing to the unique nature of the Internet, it will be more difficult for the retractions to catch up with the "publications" of the original false statement. Internet mailing lists, for example, are frequently archived. A search through the archives may bring up the misstatement but not the retraction. In addition, the defamation may remain, and be circulated, on the Internet for many years after it has been retracted or corrected, continually renewing the harm to the defamed party. This is a special problem because, at least potentially, Internet communications reach a much wider distribution than do traditional newspaper or magazine publications or even television broadcasts.

The new medium gives rise to novel questions. Are online service providers like AOL common carriers, like phone companies, that are not responsible for the content of the information they transmit? Are they more like bookstores or newsstands, which also have a lesser standard of liability for what they sell? Or are they more like publishers, who have traditionally incurred greater liability because they have editorial control over the content of the publication?

Hosting a Forum or Moderating

Interesting legal questions can arise when some entity provides a forum or serves as a moderator on the Internet, such as via a chat room, mailing list, or interactive discussion group (which can be hosted through a Web page). To what extent is the forum provider or moderator liable for comments expressed by others in its forum? Is it more like a publisher or like a bookstore or library?

The leading case in this area is *Zeran v. America Online,* 129 F.3d 327 (4th Cir. 1997), *affirming* 958 F. Supp. 1124 (E.D. Va., 1997), *cert. denied* (6/22/98). The basic thrust of the decision is that the safe harbor provisions of the Communications Decency Act (which were *not* invalidated by the Supreme Court in *ACLU v. Reno*) immunize on-line services and Internet service providers against state-law claims for vicarious liability for defamation. This limitation of liability is an encouraging sign for those who seek to build "virtual communities" on the Internet that include discussion areas.

- ◆ Robert C. Cumbow and Gregory Wrenn, "Reputation On (the) Line: Defamation and the Internet",
  http://www.perkins.coie.com/resource/ecomm/cumb026b.htm

Point-and-Click Agreements

Shrink-wrap licenses have been used for years by software vendors. These rely on a notice to the buyer that by opening the box, or proceeding past a certain point of the installation, the buyer is agreeing to the terms of the vendor's license. *ProCD, Inc. v. Zeidenberg,* 86 F.3d 1447 (7th Cir. 1996), is a leading case upholding shrink-wrap licenses.

"Point-and-click" agreements are an Internet version, used for sales and licensing. In the case of *Hotmail Corp. v. Van Money Pie Inc.,* C98-20064 (N.D. Cal., 4/20/98), such an agreement prohibiting an ISP's customers from using the ISP's servers to send unsolicited commercial e-mail, or spam, was upheld. Although some case law supports the viability of this method of contracting and licensing, attacks are possible, including:

- ◆ Adhesion and unconscionable terms. Are the terms visible to offerees *before* they must indicate assent? Are the terms written in a readily understandable manner? Are the terms overreaching or unreasonable?

- The Statute of Frauds. Nothing is "signed" in a conventional manner in a point-and-click agreement.

Related Resources
- David L. Hayes, "The Enforceability of Shrinkwrap License Agreements On-line and Off-line": http://www.fenwick.com/pub/shrnkwrp.html

Anonymity

While many Internet communications leave the electronic equivalent of a paper trail, anonymity is possible. Some discussion groups or on-line services allow the use of pseudonyms. For a higher level of privacy, e-mail messages can be sent via anonymous remailers that strip the identity of a sender from a message and forward it. "Chaining" several remailers and combining their use with strong cryptography can make it difficult or impossible to trace a message to its sender.

Anonymity has social benefits, such as encouraging whistleblowers to speak out without fear of retaliation and making it easier for victims of sexual abuse to seek assistance without fear of public disclosure. Some corporations that allow anonymous e-mail on their internal systems find that it facilitates more constructive debate and honest suggestions from the workforce.

On the other hand, anonymous e-mail is a source of abuse. It can be used for sexual or racial harassment or to disseminate libelous statements. Anonymity can be used in furtherance of criminal schemes, including tax evasion, insider trading, or extortion.

In *McIntyre v. Ohio Elections Commission,* 131 L.Ed.2d. 426 (1995), the U.S. Supreme Court ruled that anonymous distribution of political pamphlets was protected by the First Amendment, but noted that such protection would not apply to "fraudulent, false, or libelous statements."

The "safe harbor" provisions of the Communications Decency Act contain some language protecting user anonymity.

Related Resources
- A. Michael Froomkin, "Anonymity and Its Enmities," *Journal of Online Law* (1995), http://www.law.cornell.edu/jol/froomkin.htm

Jurisdiction

Does using the Internet to communicate leave you vulnerable to suit in every jurisdiction where the Internet is accessible?

In deciding whether a defendant can be sued in a particular forum, the U.S. Supreme Court places heavy weight on whether a defendant has "purposely directed" his or her activities at the residents of the forum. See *World-wide Volkswagen v. Woodson,* 444 U.S. 286 (1980). Physical contacts by the defendant in the forum are not required. See *Burger King Corp. v. Rudzewicz,* 471 U.S. 462 (1985).

These general principles will probably be applied to the Internet on a case-by-case, fact-specific basis. Contrast *Pres-Kap, Inc. v. System One, Direct Access,* 636 So.2d 1351 (Fla. App. 1994) (jurisdiction based solely on accessing computer database in another state is not allowed; it would be "wildly beyond the reasonable expectations of such computer-information users") with *Hall v. Laronde,* Case No. B107423 (Cal. Ct. App., 2d App. Dist., Ventura County, Aug. 7, 1997) (telephone and e-mail contacts with the California plaintiff were enough to give California court jurisdiction over the New York defendant). It's likely that close factual analysis will be necessary to predict how the general jurisdiction principles outlined here will be applied in specific cases.

These factors were discussed in *State of Minnesota v. Granite Gate Resorts* 568 N.W. 2d 715 (Minn. App. 1997), in which the court found that Minnesota had jurisdiction over a Nevada business accused of deceptive marketing practices in connection with an on-line gambling Web site. Factors mentioned by the court included the following:

◆ The number of Minnesota residents that had visited the defendant's Web site (at least 248 computers located somewhere in Minnesota had done so)
◆ The fact that the defendant had a toll-free phone number
◆ The fact that Minnesotans had gotten on the defendant's mailing list.

These are other leading cases on jurisdiction:

◆ *Cybersell v. Cybersell,* 130 F.3d 414 (9th Cir. 1997)
◆ *Bensusan Restaurant Corp. v. Richard B. King,* 126 F.3d 25 (2d Cir. 1997), *affirming Bensusan Restaurant Corp. v. Richard B. King,* 937 F. Supp. 295 (S.D.N.Y. 1996)
◆ *Panavision International L.P. v. Dennis Toeppen,* 938 F. Supp. 616 (C.D. Cal. 1996), *affirmed,* 46 U.S.P.Q.2d (BNA) 1511 (9th Cir. 1998)

Zippo Manufacturing Co. v. Zippo Dot Com, Inc., 952 F. Supp. 1119 (W.D. Pa. 1997), did not go to the Circuit Court of Appeals, but the completeness of the court's analysis is likely to make it persuasive to other courts.

Choice-of-forum clauses may provide security in some cases, especially if they are part of a "click wrap" choice (i.e., the Web site operator limits access unless users affirmatively agree that jurisdiction and venue will lie only in a certain place).

Note that some choice-of-forum clauses can be used against the drafters. For example, in the *State of Minnesota v. Granite Gate Resorts* case, the defendant's Web site stated, "We can either sue you in your State or Belize." The court observed that Minnesota would be much more convenient for both parties than Belize, and it referred to this argument as the "coup de grace" in ruling against the defendant.

Some other ways of trying to decrease the likelihood of remote jurisdiction being based on a Web site are as follows:

- Limiting interactive features
- Declining business from remote locations
- Restricting access (such as programming a server not to send any pages to domains ending in the extension for Germany, .de, if that is the jurisdiction you are worried about)

U.S. companies that have foreign affiliates may be confronted by different twists on the jurisdiction question.

Can they be subjected to criminal prosecution in the U.S. for a Web site operated abroad that is legal in its home country but violates U.S. criminal law? This could include securities law violations, illegal advertisements (such as for drugs not approved by the FDA), or obscenity.

The *Restatement (Third) of Foreign Relations of the United States* prohibits the exercise of such extraterritorial jurisdiction if it is "unreasonable." Applying the factors listed in the *Restatement* requires analyzing the intrinsic nature of the Internet. Is a Web site like a television broadcast? Is it like a shortwave radio transmission? Is it more like mailing a physical newsletter? Or more like a telephone call?

Even if the foreign site is determined to be beyond the reach of U.S. jurisdiction, a U.S. company that is a licensor or close affiliate might be prosecuted under a conspiracy or aiding and abetting theory.

Related Resources

- John Marshall Law School's Cyberspace Law Jurisdiction Page:
  http://www.jmls.edu/cyber/index/juris.html

Pornography

Many are highly upset by the thought that pornographic material is available over the Internet. It's not isolated in some distant urban "combat zone" but available in their own homes, or their children's schools, at the click of a mouse.

In *ACLU v. Reno,* the Supreme Court ruled that a Congressional attempt to control "indecent" material on the Internet violated the First Amendment. The government failed to show that less restrictive means to shield children from indecent material were unworkable.

Distribution of "obscene" materials, as defined by *Miller v. California,* 413 U.S. 15 (1973), can be prosecuted. Under the *Miller* test, "community standards" control whether something is obscene. Defining the relevant "community" poses interesting questions where the Internet is concerned.

In the well-known "Amateur Action" bulletin board system case, *U.S. v. Thomas,* Nos. 94-6648, 94-6649 (6th Cir. 1996), a married California couple operated a bulletin board system with adult-oriented materials not considered obscene under the law of their home town. Bulletin board systems are an older technology that use the regular telephone system instead of the Internet, but are otherwise analogous to World Wide Web sites. After an undercover postal inspector in Memphis, Tennessee, ordered some of their material, both Californians were tried in Memphis and convicted of transmitting obscene computer files in interstate commerce. The Sixth Circuit Court of Appeals upheld the convictions, stating that the defendants could be prosecuted in any state through which they sent obscene material.

The court of appeals pointed out that the defendants in the *Thomas* case operated on a "members only" basis and had kept records showing where their customers lived. The rule in that case may not apply to Web sites that can't or don't track such information.

The federal child pornography statute, 18 U.S.C. § 2251, is vigorously enforced. A picture of a child that is merely suggestive can cause problems, even if it doesn't show any explicit activity.

Lawyers should advise their clients to take extraordinary measures to avoid anything that looks even vaguely like child pornography. Even pornography that merely purports to depict children when it actually does not (either because it really uses legal adults or because it uses computer morphing to create lifelike images of non-real children) may be prosecuted as child pornography in some states.

Related Resources

- The Communications Decency Act case, *ACLU v. Reno*:
  http://supct.law.cornell.edu/supct/html/96-511.ZS.html
- *United States v. Maxwell,* 45 M.J. 406 (C.A.A.F. 1996). An Air Force court held that the federal obscenity statute was applicable to online communications, but the defendant had a reasonable expectation of privacy in his America Online e-mail such that a warrant was needed to search it.

Criminal Law and Procedure

Criminal cases involving the Internet often include complex evidentiary and venue issues. A defendant may be prosecuted for the content of a file that is not merely on a computer he or she doesn't own but is located on a server in another country. Chain of custody and authentication issues can be daunting in such cases.

A number of cases referenced in the following resources section deal with the search and seizure of computer equipment by government agents. A recurring issue is whether the government can seize an entire computer system as a means of obtaining evidence that may reside in only a single file.

Related Resources

Following are a few of the major federal criminal statutes that could readily be violated by Internet use. Remember that nearly every state has adopted computer crime laws as well:

- Electronic Communications Privacy Act of 1986, 18 U.S.C. §§ 1367, 2232, 2510 *et seq.*, 3117, 3121 *et seq.* Limits unauthorized interception and disclosure of electronic messages.
- Computer Fraud and Abuse Act, 18 U.S.C. § 1030. Primarily protects federal government as well as financial and medical institution computers. Used to prosecute the 1988 Robert Morris "Internet Worm" case, among others.
- Wire Fraud, 18 U.S.C. § 1343. Has been applied to cases using computers, and may also apply to the Internet, since most Internet data transmissions occur via "wire" at some point. Wire fraud can be a predicate act for RICO prosecutions, 18 U.S.C. § 1961 *et seq.*
- Criminal Copyright Violations, 17 U.S.C. § 506.

The following treatises deal with computer crimes generally, but much of each is relevant to Internet crime.

- *Federal Guidelines for Searching and Seizing Computers,* from the Department of Justice. The original 1994 document and the 1997 update are both at: http://www.usdoj.gov/criminal/cybercrime/searching.htm
- *High-Technology Crime: Investigating Cases Involving Computers,* by Kenneth S. Rosenblatt (KSK Publications, 1995). An excellent treatise by an experienced prosecutor located in the heart of Silicon Valley.
- Kevin Manson, a former prosecutor, operates the Cybercop site: http://www.cybercop.org

General Internet Law References

Online

Perkins Coie Internet Law Web Site: http://www.perkinscoie.com

In Paper

Netlaw: Your Rights in the Online World, by Lance Rose (Osborne McGraw-Hill, 1995, 372 pages). Lawyers with little background in the area will find this paperback an excellent overview. It is also suitable for businesspeople and laypersons who are interested in this field of law. Rose was active in this field long before it became trendy.

Cyberlaw: The Law of the Internet, by Jonathan Rosenoer (Springer, 1997, 362 pages). A collection of previously published essays on Internet-related legal issues. There is a related Web site at http://www.cyberlaw.com.

Online Law: The SPA's Legal Guide to Doing Business on the Internet, Thomas J. Smedinghoff, Editor (Addison Wesley Developers Press, 1996, 544 pages). This paperback anthology was written by members of a Chicago law firm. Like *Netlaw,* it aims to be accessible to non-lawyers as well as lawyers, but it is closer to *Internet and Online Law* in its technical depth and overall approach.

Internet and Online Law, Kent D. Stuckey, Editor (Law Journal Seminars-Press, 1996, appx. 300 pages). A welcome addition to the publisher's commercial law series, this book includes chapters on contracting in the electronic environment (e.g., the effect of digital signatures) and defamation and intellectual property issues as they affect the Internet.

Cyberspace Lawyer, from Glasser Legalworks: http://www.legalwks.com. A monthly publication.

Internet Glossary

ActiveX   Umbrella name used to describe a set of techniques used by Microsoft to make interactive World Wide Web site features. Designed to compete with Java, it too has theoretical security drawbacks.

agent   A program that can use artificial intelligence to perform specialized tasks as designated by a user. For example, in theory, you could instruct an agent program to search the Internet for the best price on something you wanted to buy. An advanced agent could even negotiate the price and finalize a deal, within parameters you specified.

alias   A substituted name. For example, you could set up info@lawfirm.com as an alias to route e-mail requests for information to a person you designated to handle such inquiries, such as smith@lawfirm.com. Another example: If you have a law partner who does not know how to turn on his or her computer, you can make the partner's e-mail address into an alias for the e-mail address of a Net-savvy paralegal or junior lawyer who will print it out on paper for the partner every day.

alt   Prefix for Usenet newsgroups that are "alternative." Because they don't require compliance with the usual complicated creation requirements, many of them deal with frivolous or controversial subjects. Most of the sexually oriented newsgroups are in the alt hierarchy.

anonymous ftp   A system that allows users to transfer files between computers that are connected to the Internet, even if they do not have an account on the source machine. Some organizations set up computers to give files to anyone who logs in as "anonymous" and enters an e-mail address as the password.

ANSI terminal emulation   A method whereby someone using one computer can have it imitate a certain standard that will let it communicate with another computer. You usually set this through a menu choice in your software. The other common emulation standard is called VT-100.

AOL   America Online, presently the most popular commercial on-line system, with many millions of users.

applets   Small computer programs written to perform specialized tasks. The term has gained in popularity with the introduction of the new Java computer programming language.

Archie   A search system that helps you locate files on the Internet that you can transfer (download) to your computer by ftp.

ARPAnet The Department of Defense's Advanced Research Projects Agency. This computer network was the forerunner of the Internet.

ASCII The American Standard Code for Information Interchange, a standard way for computers to use bits and bytes to represent characters. An ASCII file is the computer version of "plain vanilla." It contains simple text without any special formatting codes, roughly equivalent to the characters you could produce with a typewriter keyboard. Because so many computer programs can import and export ASCII files, this format is often used as a common denominator to exchange data. Also known as "text" files because they contain no binary characters.

autoresponder A computer that has been programmed to respond in a particular way to e-mail messages fitting a certain pattern. For example, with an autoresponder you can distribute a free program or memorandum that will interest a certain category of potential customer. The customer merely has to send a message to an address like freeoffer@yourbusinessname.com. The customer gets the satisfaction of a nearly instantaneous response, and you get the satisfaction of obtaining a list of potential client e-mail addresses, with no labor costs involved in gathering and compiling them. Setting up an autoresponder is inexpensive.

backbone A high-capacity link between key Internet connections.

bandwidth A key Internet term referring to information carrying or processing capacity. High bandwidth is desirable. ("You can never be too rich, too thin, or have too much bandwidth.") Measured in bits per second (bps). A 14.4K bandwidth (14,400 bps) is low—downloading graphics-heavy World Wide Web pages will be slow, Internet phone will work poorly, if at all, and you shouldn't even think about Internet video. A T-1 line is very high bandwidth, transporting 1.5 million bytes per second. It can comfortably accommodate even full-motion video, if there are not too many other users sharing the same line.

baud rate A measurement of how quickly a modem transfers data. It's often confused with bps.

BBS See *bulletin board system.*

beta Early version of a program put out for public testing and comment.

binary file A file that is in computer language format, as opposed to a text file that a human can read without decoding software of some sort. For example, pictures are stored on computers as binary files. You need a special viewer program to see them.

Binhex Binary to Hexidecimal, a way of formatting computer programs, pictures, or other binary files so that they can be transmitted by e-mail (which was originally designed for text files only). Binhex is used primarily by Macintosh computers. MIME and UUENCODING are methods of doing the same thing that are incompatible with Binhex. If you are sending someone a file via e-mail, make sure you use an encoding system that the recipient can decode.

BITNET The "Because It's Time" network. One of the largest of the networks that make up the Internet, BITNET links primarily educational institutions. It's notable for the large number of Internet mailing lists that originated there.

bits and **bytes** Units of computer storage. A bit is the smallest unit, symbolizing 1 or 0. Bytes are the more commonly used unit of storage. A byte is made up of 8 bits. A standard 3.5-inch floppy disk can hold 1,440,000 bytes of data (usually referred to as 1.44 MB).

bits per second   A measure of data transmission speed. It refers to the number of bits of data that are transmitted each second. For example, 33.6K bps is a common modem speed.

bounce   What normally happens to an undeliverable e-mail message, meaning that it is sent back to the sender, with a computer-generated explanation.

bookmark   Browser feature that lets you store the location of a Web site so that you can return to it easily.

bozo filter   Filter set up in an e-mail program or newsgroup reader to block messages from someone whose comments you don't care to read. Same as *twit filter.*

bps   Bits per second.

browser   A client program that lets you access World Wide Web servers. (See G. Burgess Allison's excellent books *The Lawyer's Quick Guide to Netscape Navigator,* and *The Lawyer's Quick Guide to Microsoft Internet Explorer.*

BTW   The hip way to say "by the way" in an e-mail message.

bulletin board system   A computer system set up to allow other computers to connect so their users can read and leave messages or retrieve and leave files. Sometimes run by businesses, and often by hobbyists out of their homes, they are losing ground to the Internet, which is more universal and allows long-distance communication without long-distance telephone charges.

case sensitive   A computer routine that responds differently according to whether input is capitalized or not. The World Wide Web is one example: a file named Jones.html is not the same as one named jones.html.

chat   System that allows two or more computer users to "talk" with each other by typing in messages that are seen immediately by other parties to the "conversation." The Internet's version is called IRC, Internet Relay Chat. While this has the potential for practical benefits, it is now notorious for being a major time waster, with few serious communications taking place.

CIX   The Commercial Internet Exchange, an organization of commercial Internet service providers.

C++   A popular computer programming language. It features "objects," or reusable segments of code that facilitate recycling of work product.

client   Refers to a program or computer that is "serviced" by another program or computer (the server). For instance, a Web browser is a client program requests information from a Web server program.

client/server computing   A key buzz term in modern computing, describing a common way of distributing workload among networked computers. It's analogous to a bank teller (the server) who responds to request from the bank's customers (the clients). When you use the Internet, you and the programs on your local computer frequently function as clients of servers on the Internet. For example, when you send an e-mail message, it typically goes from your computer (the client) to another computer (the server) that sends it to the appropriate destination. The World Wide Web is a global client/server system.

collaborative filtering   Use of sophisticated software to build a database of user preferences that can be used to extrapolate probable preferences of new user, based on limited data about new user. Used to personalize Internet services.

commercial online services Businesses like America Online, CompuServe, and MSN that offer proprietary information and services. Some also offer Internet access, usually in a slower or otherwise watered-down version.

compressed files Computer files that have been reduced in size by a compression program to save time in transmission or reduce the disk storage space they need. PKZIP is presently the most common compression/decompression program in the DOS/Windows environment. Zipped files (one type of compressed files) usually have the three-letter file name extension .zip.

CompuServe The largest online service before it was surpassed in users by the newer America Online, which then purchased CompuServe.

cookie A text file that some Web servers send to your hard drive through your Web browser. In theory, cookies are used to customize the Web site to your tastes, for example, by making it easy for you to return to personalized settings at the Web site. Some people object to them because they are often used to store marketing information. Many browsers can be configured to reject cookies automatically.

cracker Someone who tries to break into or abuse computer systems.

crypto Term used to refer to software to encode communications intended as private. "Strong crypto" refers to programs like PGP that are difficult for even knowledgeable attackers to crack.

CSLIP Compressed SLIP. See *SLIP*.

CU-See-Me A type of video telephone that can be used over the Internet to transmit live video signals. It is still not very smooth, and will work better when higher bandwidth is generally

available, but it works surprisingly well even today.

cyberspace A theoretical concept used to describe a "virtual" universe that is made up of the world's connected computers. The phrase originated in a science fiction novel by William Gibson titled *Neuromancer*. It is now popular among people who fancy themselves computer visionaries, or who just want to sound trendy.

Cypherpunks A term adopted by a group of activists to describe themselves that encourages the use of strong encryption programs to maintain privacy.

daemon A program that runs "in the background" on multiuser operating systems like UNIX and activates when needed to perform specified tasks. For example, you might have a daemon run on your system to monitor suspicious activity that might mean an intruder was trying to access your system. Analogous to a TSR (Terminate and Stay Resident) program in a DOS system.

DARPANET The Defense Advanced Research Projects Agency network. This was another forerunner of the Internet, created by combining ARPANET and MILNET.

dedicated line A leased telephone line that is used for one purpose only. Dedicated lines are usually used to connect larger organizations to service providers' computers. While these can be regular telephone lines, they are usually higher capacity, such as ISDN, T1, or T3.

dial-in service A networking service that is used by dialing into a computer through a telephone line.

dial-in terminal connection An Internet connection that is accessed by dialing into a computer through a telephone line. Once connected, your computer acts as if it were a terminal connected to the service provider's computer. Usually referred to as a shell account.

digital cash   The electronic equivalent of paper money. There are a number of systems in use, most of which use some type of complex encryption scheme for validation.

digital signature   A number generated by a complex mathematical formula that can be used, in combination with specialized software, to authenticate the sender of a message and that the contents have not been altered in transit. The ABA has proposed standards for digital signatures, several states have adopted legislation recognizing them, and digital signature legislation is pending in many other states.

DNS   See *Domain Name System.*

domain name   A name given to a host destination on the Internet. For example, abanet.org is the American Bar Association domain name. (The American Banking Association has aba.org). The suffix .org is the "top level" domain. The rest of the domain name is selected by the organization using it. A domain name serves as part of an Internet address, or URL.

domain name server   A computer that is used to match up domain names with IP numbers. ISPs are supposed to supply and properly configure domain name servers for their customers, but many fail to do so, thus creating a strain on the limited number of "root servers" worldwide that serve as back-ups. If you receive a "failed DNS lookup" error message this is a likely cause. ISPs should have two domain name servers, so the system will work well even if one goes down.

Domain Name System   The system by which one Internet "host" finds an-

other so it can communicate. It pairs an IP number that humans don't usually see, like 192.21.8.1, with a more recognizable name, like harvard.edu or lawfirm.com, that the human enters to access a particular destination.

download   The process of transferring information from another computer to yours. Opposite of *upload.*

EDI   Electronic data interchange. Term used to describe systems set up by businesses, often financial institutions, that need to exchange large volumes of information electronically.

electronic discovery   Term used to describe discovery of potential evidence on computers or computer networks. Though potentially time-consuming and expensive, it is an essential avenue of pursuit in major cases, particularly as an increasing percentage of information created is never printed out on paper. E-mail is a particularly promising target for discovery, since many people will say things in e-mail they would never put into a paper memo.

Elm   A UNIX e-mail program like Pine. It's a little harder for novices but more powerful.

e-mail or **email**   Short for electronic mail, this is a system that lets people send and receive messages with their computers. The system might be over a company's own intraoffice network or over an external network such as Internet.

emoticon   The techie name for a keyboard-generated symbol used to convey emotion in e-mail, such as the ubiquitous smiley face: :-)

enclosure   A file sent with an e-mail message. For example, if you wanted to send a draft brief in a word processor file format by e-mail, it would have to be as an enclosure.

encryption   The process of scrambling information so that it can't be understood by unauthorized persons.

Ethernet   A very high-speed method of connecting two computers. Commonly used on local area networks.

Eudora   The name of a popular Internet e-mail program. It comes in Lite and more powerful Pro versions. The Lite version is free.

extranet   An intranet-type system that is used to share information with members of more than just one organization.

eye candy   Overly elaborate Web site graphics.

FAQ   A list of frequently asked questions, with their corresponding answers. These are used to acquaint people who are new to a particular topic with the fundamental points that they need to know.

file transfer protocol   See *ftp*.

finger   A UNIX program used to find information about a user who has an account on a host computer.

firewall   A system that puts a computer with special filtering software between your computer or computers and the Internet. It is a security measure intended to keep unauthorized users from accessing your system.

flame   A rude newsgroup or mailing list message. The absence of face-to-face contact in e-mail causes such messages to be more common than they should be.

frame relay   A technique for using special phone lines to provide relatively high-bandwidth 56Kbps to 1.5Mbps connections to the Internet.

frames   A way to divide a World Wide Web screen into multiple sections. A major annoyance to many Web users, especially those who don't have large

monitors. Framing raises legal issues when used to display a Web site created by someone else as if it were part of your own.

freenet   A community computer network that provides free or low-cost Internet access to citizens. Freenets are often affiliated with libraries. Their services are usually more limited than those from commercial ISPs. For example, all the ones I know about provide shell accounts only—you can't use graphic software like Windows.

freeware   Software that the author retains a copyright on, but allows free public use of, sometimes with restrictions. Contrast with *public domain software*, which anyone can use at any time for any purpose. Contrast also with *shareware*, which is commercial software, although it is not distributed through ordinary retail channels.

FTF   Face to face. Phrase sometimes used by computer users to refer to in-person meetings, as opposed to those over a computer network.

ftp   File transfer protocol. A protocol for transferring files from one computer to another.

fuzzy logic   A cutting-edge computer technology, intended to get computers away from their precise, ever-literal way of "thinking" and get them to think in the looser way that human beings do, which is a big advantage in solving some types of problems. For example, a regular database search program will give you precisely what you ask for, exactly as you described it. A fuzzy logic system would be more sophisticated. Using advanced artificial intelligence tecniques, it might figure out what you meant to ask for, not what you actually typed in. Fuzzy logic concepts are already being successfully used in some computer applications (such as automation of subway train operation) and may become more common in the future.

gateway   A system that allows two otherwise incompatible computer networks to share information. An example: America Online has gateways to allow its users to access parts of the Internet.

gearhead   Derogatory term for a technically oriented person. A *wirehead* is the Internet equivalent.

GEnie   A computer information service owned by General Electric. This used to be a major player in the industry, but since the advent of AOL, and the Microsoft Network, it has been reduced to primarily a games-playing network. (Of course, the pace of change being what it is in this industry, by the time you read this, it could have regained its former stature. Or then again, it could be bankrupt.)

GIF   Graphic Interchange Format. A format for compressing graphic files so they don't take up so much space and can be transmitted faster. It is not as good as JPEG for photographs, but it is much better for line drawings and other graphics that contain broad areas of the same color.

gopher   A system for using text-based hierarchical menus to navigate easily from one computer to another on the Internet to find information. This was the rage through the early 1990s, but its popularity has declined greatly since the advent of the more powerful and flexible World Wide Web.

gopherspace   A trendy term like cyberspace, this means any information you can access using gopher.

graphical user interface   See *GUI.*

Green Card Lawyers   A small Arizona law firm named Canter and Seigel that in 1992 used unacceptably invasive techniques to advertise on the Internet their availability to assist clients in entering the INS "Green Card Lottery." Specifically, they "spammed" thousands of Usenet newsgroups that had nothing to do with immigration or law. Their crude misbehavior prejudiced many Internet users against the idea of any lawyers on the Internet.

GUI   graphical user interface. Pronounced "gooey," a GUI makes it easier to learn to use a computer by allowing the user to select various screen symbols using a pointing device (usually a mouse) instead of typing in commands. While people who are good touch typists, or who have become comfortable with older style computer operating systems such as UNIX or DOS, often resist GUIs, studies show that when user training time is taken into account, GUIs are much more efficient than text-based operating systems for most users.

hacker   Originally a complimentary term used to describe someone whose knowledge, skill, persistence, or intuition enable them to improvise solutions to computer problems. It has acquired a negative connotation in the public mind, as referring to someone who uses such skills for abusive purposes.

helper   A program that is used in conjunction with a World Wide Web browser to allow the user to access certain file types. For example, to hear Real Audio files, you need a helper program. Sometimes called viewer programs. Plug-ins are helper programs that are seamlessly integrated with a browser program.

hit   1. An item found by a search engine in response to a request. 2. An access of (i.e., a viewing of) a World Wide Web page by a visitor. Often defined rather loosely by those who wish to give the impression that a given site is popular.

home page   Commonly used to refer to the default entry point into the World Wide Web site of an organization or individual, although there is no precise definition of this term. For a large Web site, this page normally contains an index to the contents of the rest of the site. This file is often named index.html, in fact.

host   A computer that is "on," i.e., connected directly to, the Internet. It will have a unique IP number.

hotlink   phrase sometimes used instead of hyperlink.

HTML   Hypertext Markup Language. This is the language used to format ASCII text documents so that they can be transmitted via the World Wide Web. For example, inserting the letters *<h1>Jones</h1>* into a document will cause the word Jones to appear as a top-level heading ("heading level one") when the document is viewed with a Web browser.

HTTP   Hypertext Transfer Protocol. the system used for transferring information via the World Wide Web.

hyperlink   The section of a hypertext document that links to another document or part of a document.

hypertext   A system in which documents contain highlighted words, phrases, or images that are selectable links that can move users easily between areas of the same document, other documents on the same computer, or, if the computer is on the Internet, a document on a file located on a computer thousands of miles away. This allows the organization and presentation of information in unique, easy-to-use ways that cannot be duplicated in print media. The World Wide Web is the Internet's major hypertext area. The Microsoft Windows Help sys-

tem is another example of a hypertext system. Courts are beginning to grapple with the issue of whether to allow hypertext briefs instead of paper briefs.

HYTELNET   A directory of Internet sites that allow access via telnet. (You can access it via the World Wide Web: http://www.einet.net/hytelnet/ HYTELNET.html.)

ICQ   A popular Internet "chat" program. (Name is to sound like "I Seek You.").

IMO and **IMHO**   Abbreviations for "in my opinion" and "in my humble opinion." Useful in e-mail messages, where you might otherwise worry about sounding arrogant, or even triggering a dreaded "flame war."

internet   The term internet spelled with a small *i* refers to networks connected to one another. "The Internet" is not the only internet.

Internet   Term used to describe the system made up of all the computers on the world's largest network that use the TCP/IP protocol to communicate with each other.

Internet Explorer   Microsoft's flagship Web browser, competitor to Netscape Navigator.

Internet Protocol   The standard protocol used by systems communicating across the Internet. Other protocols are used, but the Internet Protocol is the most important one.

Internet service provider   See *service provider*.

Internet Society   The organization that "runs" the Internet as much as anyone does. It selects the Internet Architecture Board, which sets technical standards for Internet protocols.

InterNIC   The Internet Network Information Center. It is responsible for assigning domain names (although it has contracted with a private firm to do the actual work).

intranet A system that uses Internet-style technology for distributing information privately, as opposed to publicly. It is becoming very popular. At last count, more Internet Web server software was being sold for the purpose of establishing intranets than to set up open Web servers on the Internet. One of the hottest concepts in networked computing today.

IP See *Internet Protocol.*

IPX Protocol used by Novell networks.

ISDN Integrated Services Digital Network, a form of high-capacity digital phone line that can carry information at speeds of up to 128Kbps, much faster than conventional analog lines.

ISOC See *Internet Society.*

ISP See *service provider.*

Java New computer programming language (related to C++) whose strengths are (a) It is cross-platform, i.e., it can be used to write small programs called applets that can run on multiple types of computer systems without being rewritten; and (b) The applets can be small enough to be downloaded over a network to perform tasks on users' computers on an as-needed basis.

JPEG/JPG Abbreviation for a method of graphics compression developed by the Joint Photographic Experts Group. As the name implies, it is particularly effective with photographs. It is a "lossy" method of compression, as some data is lost.

K56Flex A method of getting high-speed modem transfers developed by a group of modem manufacturers. Superceded by V.90 standard.

kill file List of names or topics to be screened so that a user does not have to read them. Compare *bozo filter.*

knowbot A program that can search the Internet for information such as e-mail addresses. Compare *agent.*

LAN Local area network, an organization's internal computer network that covers users in a relatively small geographic area. A LAN can be connected to the Internet.

leaky reply Term used to describe a reply to an e-mail message that is accidentally sent to unintended recipients as a result of using the e-mail program's Reply feature. Potentially very embarrassing.

leased line See *dedicated line.*

Linux A form of the UNIX operating system that can be used on personal computers. Owing to its ability to handle multiple operations simultaneously, it is often used by smaller Internet service providers to operate their computers. It runs on 386, 486, and Pentium computers.

Listproc A program that is used to automate Internet mailing lists.

listserv Term commonly used to describe an Internet mailing list that lets people with common interests share information easily. Technically, this term is only the name of one particular program for running such lists, but it has taken on a broader meaning and is commonly used to refer to any such list, whether or not it uses the Listserv™ software.

log A record of computer network activity. Some possible uses would be to analyze visitor patterns to a Web site or, if you were a network administrator, to look for suspicious patterns that could be a sign of hacker activity on your system. Such a log is a potential source of very useful evidence in discovery.

logging on Initiating an interactive session with an online system. With a shell account or in a telnet session, this usually involves simply typing in a user name (also known as an account name or user ID) and a password. This procedure is intended to prevent unauthorized people from accessing the account. Also known as logging in.

logging off Stopping an interactive session with an online system. You usually just type a word like *exit, off,* or *bye.* If you are working from a command line, it's better to do this instead of just hanging up the phone line via your modem, because if you don't log off properly, the system may think you are still attached, thus tying up system resources that someone else could use. You might even incur further charges if your system charges based on the time you are logged on.

login The procedure of "signing into" a computer system to initiate an interactive session.

lurking Reading newsgroup or mailing list messages without responding to them. This term does not have the sinister connotations on the Internet that it does in real life. In fact, it's recommended to lurk for a while before participating actively in a newsgroup or mailing list, so you can become familiar with the group's mores.

Lynx A nongraphic (i.e., text only) World Wide Web browser program, developed at the University of Kansas. Often used with UNIX shell accounts. There is also a DOS version.

Majordomo A program like Listserv that is used to automate Internet mailing lists.

mail reflector Sometimes referred to more colorfully as a "mail exploder." This is software that accepts e-mail messages and then remails them on to a predefined list of other e-mail addresses. Such systems are used to facilitate the exchange of information among groups of people sharing special common interests. Thousands of such "mailing lists" exist on various topics. Listserv, Majordomo, and Listproc are three of the most common programs that perform this function.

MB Abbreviation for megabyte.

megabyte Literally, a million bytes. A measure of the quantity of computerized data. A high-capacity 3.5-inch floppy disk holds 1.44 megabytes.

MIME Multipurpose Internet Mail Extensions, a system that lets you send computer files as e-mail. Compare *Binhex* and *UUENCODE,* two systems with a similar function that are incompatible with MIME and each other.

modem A device that converts digital signals from your computer into analog signals for transmission through a phone line (modulation) and converts the phone line's analog signals into digital signals that your computer can use (demodulation).

Mosaic The first graphical Web browser program (used to access the World Wide Web).

Netcom A major national Internet service provider.

netiquette Peter Kent's definition: "Internet etiquette, the correct form of behavior to be used while working on the Internet and Usenet. Can be summed up as 'Don't waste computer resources, and don't be rude.'" "Don't waste computer resources" is often phrased as "Don't waste bandwidth." One example: If you can download a file from a computer close to you or one in Europe, choose the computer close to you. There are only a finite number of trans-Atlantic Internet links, and if you are using the bandwidth unnecessarily, this may hurt someone who has a more pressing need to get information from Europe.

Netscape The name of a computer company, this is also popularly used as a shorthand way to refer to its most popular product, which is actually Netscape Navigator, not Netscape.

newsgroup A collection of e-mail-type messages on a particular specialized topic. At last count, there were more than 15,000 newsgroups on Usenet, a network that is connected to and accessible through the Internet. The Internet equivalent of a BBS or discussion group (or CompuServe forum) in which people leave messages for others to read. See *Usenet.*

newsreader A program to help you obtain information from a newsgroup efficiently.

news server A computer that collects newsgroup information from Usenet and makes it available to local users. Note that news is passed from news server to news server around the world, but most users get their news server access from a local machine provided for this purpose by their ISP. ISPs can decide not to carry particular newsgroups (or even not to carry any at all) and many choose not to carry those known to carry sexually oriented material.

online or **on line** A word and phrase used in a variety of contexts to invoke the idea of using a computer network.

Opera A browser program, widely praised for being slimmer and faster than its more bloated competitors, Microsoft Internet Explorer and Netscape Navigator.

packet A small unit of information being transmitted over the Internet. Large Internet data transmissions are broken down into packets, transmitted (sometimes over different routes), then reassembled at their destination. This process is known as **packet switching.**

PDF Portable Document Format, a technique developed by Adobe Corporation that allows files on the Internet to be stored in a format that preserves the original appearance of a paper document, including fonts, colors, and layout. This is the technique used by the IRS to make tax forms available at its Web site.

PGP "Pretty Good Privacy," a public key encryption program used to encode data. This is the most popular strong encryption program.

PNG Portable Network Graphic. Nonproprietary format for compressing graphics. Designed specifically for Internet use. A major impetus for the development of PNG was demands by the developer of the GIF format that it be paid royalties by developers who included GIF creation features in their software.

Pine A UNIX e-mail program that's easy to use and popular on UNIX shell Internet accounts.

PKZIP A program that is commonly used on DOS and Windows systems to compress computer files so they will take up less space on a disk, or can be transmitted faster over a network. Also used to decompress the same files. This compression program was designed by Phil Katz.

plug-in A viewer or helper program that is seamlessly integrated into a browser. Adobe's newest viewer for PDF files is an example.

point of presence   Often called a **POP,** this means a local telephone number that you can call to access an Internet service provider without incurring a long-distance phone call charge.

Point to Point Protocol (PPP)   A way to connect computers to the Internet via telephone lines, similar to SLIP. PPP contains extra error-checking routines, but experts differ as to whether it is really better than SLIP. Windows 95/98 defaults to using PPP.

polymorphic virus   A computer virus that can change its "signature," or identifying characteristics, to make it more difficult to detect.

POP   1. Post Office Protocol. Standard used to receive Internet e-mail. You typically configure your e-mail program with the name of a POP server. 2. See *point of presence.*

port   1. The part of your computer hardware through which computer data is transmitted, such as the serial and parallel plugs on the back of your PC. 2. On the Internet, this word has a special meaning. It is an access point (not necessarily a piece of physical hardware) that lets a "client" contact a "server." There is a number to go along with all such ports, but the average user very seldom needs to know what it is, because most good software is set up to automatically route a particular type of message to the correct port. You may notice the port number included automatically by your software, but you don't usually need to know it or type it in unless for some reason the destination is not using the default port number for your application.

Portable Document Format   See *PDF.*

POTS   "Plain Old Telephone System." What people who want to sound cool call regular phone company lines.

postmaster   The person designated to handle problems with e-mail in a particular organization. You can usually reach them by sending e-mail to postmaster@hostname.

PPP   See *Point to Point Protocol.*

private key   Part of a "dual password," or public key encryption system. See *public key.*

PRODIGY   A major Internet Service Provider. It began as an online service provider like AOL, Now it provides only Internet access.

protocol   A set of rules that defines how computers transmit information to each other, allowing different types of computers and software to communicate with each other. For example, TCP/IP is the basic protocol used to transmit Internet information.

public domain software   Software that is not owned by anyone. You can freely use and distribute such software. See also *freeware* and *shareware.*

public key   Part of a "dual password" encryption system, used in connection with public key encryption systems. You use someone's public key to send that person a message. That person uses his or her private key to decode it. This system differs from, and in many ways is superior to, conventional encryption, in which the same password must be used to encode and decode a message.

reflector   Term sometimes used to describe an Internet mailing list. Messages sent to a mail reflector's address are sent on automatically to a list of other addresses.

rot 13   Rotation 13, a method used to encode potentially offensive material, such as certain jokes, to avoid offending people who do not like the topics.

It's a very simple substitution cipher. Most good e-mail packages and news-readers have decoders built in, but you have to make a conscious decision to invoke them. This way you can't complain that offensive material was thrust on you without your having expressed a desire to see it. For example, you might see a newsgroup message subject line that said *Joke about Blondes (Rot 13)*. If you want to read a tasteless joke about blondes, decode it. If not, skip it.

router   A device used to distribute information between two or more computer systems or networks. For instance, a company with a permanent connection to the Internet will need a router to connect its computer to a leased line. At the other end of the leased line, a router is used to connect it to the service provider's network.

search engine   Computer program used to find desired information from a database.

Serial Line Internet Protocol (SLIP)   A method for connecting a computer to the Internet using a telephone line and modem. Once connected, the user has access to services similar to those available to the user of a permanent connection. Compare *Point to Point Protocol*.

server   A program or computer that "services" another program or computer (the client). For instance, a World Wide Web server delivers information to browser (client) programs.

service provider   A company that provides a connection to the Internet.

shareware   Software that is freely distributed but for which the author expects payment from people who decide to keep and use it. See also *freeware* and *public domain software*.

shell   1. In UNIX, a program that accepts commands that you type and "translates" them for the operating system so it will do what you want. 2. In DOS, a program that similarly "insulates" you from the command line, often providing a menu for the benefit of novice users.

shell account   An Internet account that lets a user contact the Internet indirectly though a large computer using the UNIX operating system. Usually limits the user to text screens and UNIX-based software only. Shell accounts are often used in universities and on freenets to provide inexpensive Internet access by holding down costs.

signature   A short piece of text included at the bottom of an e-mail or newsgroup message. It serves a function similar to letterhead in paper mail, identifying the sender and/or the sender's organization, and sometimes giving a hint of their personality. All good e-mail software should allow you to attach a signature block of your design automatically to any of your outgoing messages, with little work on your part. Not the same as a *digital signature*.

SLIP   See *Serial Line Internet Protocol*.

smiley   A symbol created by typing various keyboard characters, used in e-mail and newsgroup messages to convey emotion, or simply for amusement. For instance, :-(means sadness.

SMTP   Simple Mail Transfer Protocol. Protocol used to send mail over the Internet. When you set up your e-mail software, you frequently must enter the name or IP number of an SMTP server computer.

snail mail   The type of mail your postman brings you. Derogatory term used by those who have come to prefer e-mail.

spam Using e-mail or newsgroups to send information (such as commercial promotions) to people who have not asked for it and probably are not interested in it. Used as both a noun (to describe the information sent) and a verb (to describe the process of sending it). It is a sure way to make yourself very unpopular.

Surf Term used to describe accessing the Internet in a nonstructured manner, often for recreation.

T1 A high-capacity leased telephone line, commonly used by larger organizations to connect to the Internet directly, instead of using a dial-up connection.

T3 The highest-capacity leased telephone line in use as of this writing. This would be adequate to provide an Internet connection for a large organization such as a major university.

tar files Files compressed using the UNIX Tape ARchiver program. Such files usually have file names ending in .tar. If you download one of these files, you will have to run a decompression program on it before you can use it. The most recent version of a program called Winzip will decompress tar files.

TCP/IP Transmission Control Protocol/Internet Protocol. The "lingua franca" of the Internet, these are the key rules that control how data is transferred between computers on the Internet.

telnet An Internet protocol that lets you log into a remote computer on the Internet and use it as if you had a terminal directly attached to the remote computer.

terminal The ISDN equivalent of a modem. Used to interface between your computer and an ISDN (high-capacity digital) phone line.

tilde A squiggly symbol, found in the upper left-hand sections of most keyboards. It looks like this: ~ . Often confusing to new Internet users. By convention, the tilde is used on many UNIX-based Web servers to symbolize a directory devoted to a particular user. For example, the URL http://www.enormousstateu.edu/students/~jsmith probably refers to a directory assigned to an Enormous State University student known as J. Smith.

time out Excessive delay in some computer interaction. If one computer goes too long without receiving any communication from another, it may be programmed to break their connection, or take some other action, such as sending an error message. This is known as "timing out."

TRN The name of a popular newsreader program commonly used on UNIX shell accounts.

upload The process of transferring information from your computer to another. Opposite of *download*.

USENET A large network connected to the Internet, best known for its Newsgroup feature.

URL Uniform Resource Locator, which is an Internet address. Often mistakenly spelled out as Universal Resource Locator.

UNIX A multiple-user computer operating system that is used on most of the larger computers attached to the Internet.

UUCP UNIX to UNIX copy program, a way to transfer files between UNIX computers. Often used to transmit e-mail on the Internet.

UUDECODE To translate a UUENCODED message back into its original binary format.

UUENCODE UNIX to UNIX encoding. A system used to convert a binary computer file into an ASCII file so that it can be transmitted via e-mail as a text message. Compare *Binhex* and *MIME*.

UUNET A large Internet service provider. Microsoft's partner on the Microsoft Network.

Veronica Very Easy Rodent-Oriented Net-wide Index to Computerized Archives, a search program for use with gopher. Searches titles of gopher menus worldwide.

viewer See *helper*.

virus A program that can "reproduce" and spread from computer to computer without the computer owner's knowledge. Some can do malicious damage; most are relatively harmless.

VRML Virtual Reality Markup Language. A system for using the World Wide Web to transfer computer files containing three-dimensional and other complex effects. It has little apparent value for law firms at this time.

VT 100 The product name of a particular brand of computer terminal that is widely imitated. For compatibility with a particular computer system, it may ask you to have yours "emulate" (act like) a VT 100. You usually do this by a menu choice somewhere. The other most common type of terminal emulation is ANSI.

WAIS See *Wide Area Information Service*.

WAN Wide area network, an organization's internal network, linking users that are widely dispersed geographically.

Web browser See *browser*.

Web page A particular group of one or more related files on the World Wide Web, usually displayed as one document.

Web site A collection of Web pages operated by some person or organization. Some prefer the term **Web page set.**

Webmaster The person responsible for operating a World Wide Web server or World Wide Web site.

whois A UNIX program used for searching for information about Internet users.

Wide Area Information Service A sophisticated system used to search Internet databases.

World Wide Web A hypertext system that allows users to "travel through" linked documents, following any chosen route. World Wide Web documents contain topics that, when selected, lead to other documents.

X2 Term used for U.S. Robotics proprietary 56K modem technology. Superceded by V.90 standard.

zip To compress a file using special software to make the file smaller.

Index

Selected Books From . . .
THE LAW PRACTICE MANAGEMENT SECTION

ABA Guide to Lawyer Trust Accounts. This book deals with how lawyers should manage trust accounts to comply with ethical & statutory requirements.

ABA Guide to Professional Managers in the Law Office. This book shows how professional management can and does work. It shows lawyers how to practice more efficiently by delegating management tasks to professional managers.

Billing Innovations. This book examines how innovative fee arrangements and your approach toward billing can deeply affect the attorney-client relationship. It also explains how billing and pricing are absolutely intertwined with strategic planning, maintaining quality of services, marketing, instituting a compensation system, and firm governance.

Changing Jobs, 2nd Ed. A handbook designed to help lawyers make changes in their professional careers. Includes career planning advice from nearly 50 experts.

Compensation Plans for Law Firms, 2nd Ed. This second edition discusses the basics for a fair and simple compensation system for partners, of counsel, associates, paralegals, and staff.

Computer-Assisted Legal Research: A Guide to Successful Online Searching. Covers the fundamentals of LEXIS®-NEXIS® and WESTLAW®, including practical information such as: logging on and off; formulating your search; reviewing results; modifying a query; using special features; downloading documents.

Connecting with Your Client. Written by a psychologist, therapist, and legal consultant, this book presents communications techniques that will help ensure client cooperation and satisfaction.

Do-It-Yourself Public Relations. A hands-on guide for lawyers. with public relations ideas, sample letters and forms. The book includes a diskette that includes model letters to the press that have paid off in news stories and media attention.

Finding the Right Lawyer. This guide answers the questions people should ask when searching for legal counsel. It includes a glossary of legal specialties and the ten questions you should ask a lawyer before hiring.

Flying Solo: A Survival Guide for the Solo Lawyer, 2nd ed. An updated and expanded guide to the problems and issues unique to the solo practitioner.

How to Draft Bills Clients Rush to Pay. A collection of techniques for drafting bills that project honesty, competence, fairness and value.

How to Start and Build a Law Practice, 3rd ed. Jay Foonberg's classic guide has been updated and expanded. Included are more than 10 new chapters on marketing, financing, automation, practicing from home, ethics and professional responsibility.

Visit our Web site:
http//www.abanet.org/lpm/catalog

To order: Call Toll-Free 1-800-285-2221

Law Office Policy and Procedures Manual, 3rd Ed. Provides a model for law office policies and procedures. It covers law office organization, management, personnel policies, financial management, technology, and communications systems. Includes diskette.

The Lawyer's Guide to Creating Web Pages. A practical guide that clearly explains HTML, covers how to design a Web site, and introduces Web-authoring tools.

The Lawyer's Guide to the Internet. A guide to what the Internet is (and isn't), how it applies to the legal profession, and the different ways it can -- and should -- be used.

The Lawyer's Guide to Marketing on the Internet. This book talks about the pluses and minuses of marketing on the Internet, as well as how to develop an Internet marketing plan.

The Lawyer's Quick Guide to Microsoft® Internet Explorer; The Lawyer's Quick Guide to Netscape® Navigator. These two guides offer special introductory instructions on the most popular Internet browsers. Four quick and easy lessons including: Basic Navigation, Setting a Bookmark, Browsing with a Purpose, Keeping What You Find.

The Lawyer's Quick Guide to WordPerfect® 7.0/8.0 for Windows®. This easy-to-use guide offers lessons on multitasking, entering and editing text, formatting letters, creating briefs, and more. Perfect for training, this book includes a diskette with practice exercises and word templates.

Leaders' Digest: A Review of the Best Books on Leadership. This book will help you find the best books on leadership to help you achieve extraordinary and exceptional leadership skills.

Living with the Law: Strategies to Avoid Burnout and Create Balance. This multi-author book is intended to help lawyers manage stress, make the practice of law more satisfying, and improve client service.

Practicing Law Without Clients: Making a Living as a Freelance Lawyer. This book describes the freelance legal researching, writing, and consulting opportunities that are available to lawyers.

Running a Law Practice on a Shoestring. Targeted to the solo or small firm lawyer, this book offers a crash course in successful entrepreneurship. Features money-saving tips on office space, computer equipment, travel, furniture, staffing, and more.

Survival Guide for Road Warriors. A guide to using a notebook computer and combinations of equipment and technology so lawyers can be effective in their office, on the road, in the courtroom or at home.

Through the Client's Eyes. Includes an overview of client relations and sample letters, surveys, and self-assessment questions to gauge your client relations acumen.

Women Rainmakers' 101+ Best Marketing Tips. A collection of over 130 marketing tips suggested by women rainmakers throughout the country. Includes tips on image, networking, public relations, and advertising.

Order Form

Qty	Title	LPM Price	Regular Price	Total
_____	ABA Guide to Lawyer Trust Accounts (5110374)	$ 69.95	$ 79.95	$_____
_____	ABA Guide to Prof. Managers in the Law Office (5110373)	69.95	79.95	$_____
_____	Billing Innovations (5110366)	124.95	144.95	$_____
_____	Changing Jobs, 2nd Ed. (5110334)	49.95	59.95	$_____
_____	Compensation Plans for Lawyers, 2nd Ed. (5110353)	69.95	79.95	$_____
_____	Computer-Assisted Legal Research (5110388)	69.95	79.95	$_____
_____	Connecting with Your Client (5110378)	54.95	64.95	$_____
_____	Do-It-Yourself Public Relations (5110352)	69.95	79.95	$_____
_____	Finding the Right Lawyer (5110339)	19.95	19.95	$_____
_____	Flying Solo, 2nd Ed. (5110328)	59.95	69.95	$_____
_____	How to Draft Bills Clients Rush to Pay (5110344)	39.95	49.95	$_____
_____	How to Start & Build a Law Practice, 3rd Ed. (5110293)	32.95	39.95	$_____
_____	Law Office Policy & Procedures Manual (5110375)	99.95	109.95	$_____
_____	Lawyer's Guide to Creating Web Pages (5110383)	54.95	64.95	$_____
_____	Lawyer's Guide to the Internet (5110343)	24.95	29.95	$_____
_____	Lawyer's Guide to Marketing on the Internet (5110371)	54.95	64.95	$_____
_____	Lawyer's Quick Guide to Microsoft Internet® Explorer (5110392)	24.95	29.95	$_____
_____	Lawyer's Quick Guide to Netscape® Navigator (5110384)	24.95	29.95	$_____
_____	Lawyer's Quick Guide to WordPerfect® 7.0/8.0 (5110395)	34.95	39.95	$_____
_____	Leaders' Digest (5110356)	49.95	59.95	$_____
_____	Living with the Law (5110379)	59.95	69.95	$_____
_____	Practicing Law Without Clients (5110376)	49.95	59.95	$_____
_____	Running a Law Practice on a Shoestring (5110387)	39.95	49.95	$_____
_____	Survival Guide for Road Warriors (5110362)	24.95	29.95	$_____
_____	Through the Client's Eyes (5110337)	69.95	79.95	$_____
_____	Women Rainmakers' 101+ Best Marketing Tips (5110336)	14.95	19.95	$_____

*HANDLING	**TAX		
$10.00-$24.99 ... $3.95	DC residents add 5.75%	SUBTOTAL:	$_____
$25.00-$49.99 ... $4.95	IL residents add 8.75%	*HANDLING:	$_____
$50.00+ $5.95	MD residents add 5%	**TAX:	$_____
		TOTAL:	$_____

PAYMENT

☐ Check enclosed (to the ABA)   ☐ Bill Me

☐ Visa ☐ MasterCard ☐ American Express   Account Number:_____

Exp. Date:_____ Signature_____

Name_____

Firm_____

Address_____

City_____ State_____ ZIP_____

Phone number_____

Mail to: ABA Publication Orders   **Phone:** (800) 285-2221   **Fax:** (312) 988-5568
P.O. Box 10892
Chicago, IL 60610-0892   **World Wide Web:** http//www.abanet.org/lpm/catalog
Email: abasvcctr@abanet.org

 THE SECTION OF
LAW PRACTICE
MANAGEMENT

CUSTOMER COMMENT FORM

Title of Book:_____

We've tried to make this publication as useful, accurate, and readable as possible. Please take 5 minutes to tell us if we succeeded. Your comments and suggestions will help us improve our publications. Thank you!

1. How did you acquire this publication:

☐ by mail order   ☐ at a meeting/convention   ☐ as a gift

☐ by phone order   ☐ at a bookstore   ☐ don't know

☐ other: (describe) _____

_____

Please rate this publication as follows:

	Excellent	Good	Fair	Poor	Not Applicable
Readability: Was the book easy to read and understand?	☐	☐	☐	☐	☐
Examples/Cases: Were they helpful, practical? Were there enough?	☐	☐	☐	☐	☐
Content: Did the book meet your expectations? Did it cover the subject adequately?	☐	☐	☐	☐	☐
Organization and clarity: Was the sequence of text logical? Was it easy to find what you wanted to know?	☐	☐	☐	☐	☐
Illustrations/forms/checklists: Were they clear and useful? Were there enough?	☐	☐	☐	☐	☐
Physical attractiveness: What did you think of the appearance of the publication (typesetting, printing, etc.)?	☐	☐	☐	☐	☐

Would you recommend this book to another attorney/administrator? ☐ Yes ☐ No

How could this publication be improved? What else would you like to see in it?

_____

_____

_____

Do you have other comments or suggestions? _____

_____

_____

Name _____

Firm/Company _____

Address _____

City/State/Zip _____

Phone _____

Firm Size: _____ Area of specialization: _____

We appreciate your time and help.

Fold

BUSINESS REPLY MAIL

FIRST CLASS   PERMIT NO. 16471   CHICAGO, ILLINOIS

POSTAGE WILL BE PAID BY ADDRESSEE

AMERICAN BAR ASSOCIATION
PPM, 8th FLOOR
750 N. LAKE SHORE DRIVE
CHICAGO, ILLINOIS 60611–9851

Fold

AMERICAN BAR ASSOCIATION

Membership Application

ABA Law Practice Management Section

Access to all these information resources and discounts – for just $3.33 a month!

Membership dues are just $40 a year – just $3.33 a month.
You probably spend more on your general business magazines and newspapers.
But they can't help you succeed in building and managing your practice
like a membership in the ABA Law Practice Management Section.
Make a small investment in success. Join today!

☑ **Yes!** **I want to join the ABA Section of Law Practice Management Section** and gain access to information helping me add more clients, retain and expand business with current clients, and run my law practice more efficiently and competitively!

Check the dues that apply to you:

❏ $40 for ABA members   ❏ $5 for ABA Law Student Division members

Choose your method of payment:

❏ Check enclosed (make payable to American Bar Association)
❏ Bill me
❏ Charge to my: ❏ VISA®   ❏ MASTERCARD®   ❏ AMEX®

Card No.: _____   Exp. Date: _____

Signature: _____   Date: _____

ABA I.D.*: _____
(* *Please note: Membership in ABA is a prerequisite to enroll in ABA Sections.*)

Name: _____

Firm/Organization: _____

Address: _____

City/State/ZIP: _____

Telephone No.: _____   Fax No.: _____

Primary Email Address: _____

Get Ahead. 🏃

ABA Law Practice Management Section

Save time by Faxing or Phoning!

▶ Fax your application to: (312) 988-5820
▶ Join by phone if using a credit card: (800) 285-2221 (ABA1)
▶ Email us for more information at: lpm@abanet.org
▶ Check us out on the Internet: http://www.abanet.org/lpm

750 N. LAKE SHORE DRIVE
CHICAGO, IL 60611
PHONE: (312) 988-5619
FAX: (312) 988-5820
Email: lpm@abanet.org

I understand that Section dues include a $24 basic subscription to Law Practice Management; *this subscription charge is not deductible from the dues and additional subscriptions are not available at this rate. Membership dues in the American Bar Association are not deductible as charitable contributions for income tax purposes. However, such dues may be deductible as a business expense.*